From Urban Village to East Village

From Urban Village to East Village

The Battle for New York's Lower East Side

Janet L. Abu-Lughod and others

Oxford UK & Cambridge USA

First published 1994

Blackwell Publishers
238 Main Street
Cambridge, Massachusetts 02142
USA

108 Cowley Road
Oxford OX4 1JF
UK

Library of Congress Cataloging-in-Publication Data

From Urban Village to East Village: the Battle for New York's Lower East Side / Janet L. Abu-Lughod and others.
p. cm.
Includes bibliographical references and index.

(ISBN 1–55786–523–X (hbk.) (alk-paper). — ISBN 1–55786–525–6 (pbk.)

1. New York (NY) — Social conditions. 2. East Village (New York, NY) — Social conditions. 3. Neighborhoods — New York (NY) 4. Gentrification — New York (NY) 5. Pluralism (Social sciences) — New York (NY) Abu-Lughod, Janet L.
HN80. N5F76 1994 93–31977
307.3′362′097471—dc20 CIP

British Library Cataloguing in Publication Data

A CIP catalogue record for this book is available from the British Library.

Typeset in 10 on 12.5 points Baskerville by Pure Tech Corporation, Pondicherry, India.

Printed in Great Britain by Hartnolls Ltd, Bodmin

This book is printed on acid-free paper

Contents

List of Plates

List of Illustrations

List of Tables

Acknowledgments

From Urban Village to East Village is the collective product of scholars initially drawn together in an *ad hoc* monthly seminar coordinated by REALM, a center for *RE*search *A*bout *L*ower *M*anhattan I directed at the New School for Social Research. REALM was established in 1988 under a grant from the Alfred P. Sloan Foundation whose invaluable assistance is gratefully acknowledged. I am also deeply indebted to Ira Katznelson, then Dean of the Graduate Faculty of the New School, for his enthusiastic intellectual support and advice, and to members of an advisory committee of New School faculty and administrators with special urban interests who helped guide our work. Thanks are also due to Christopher Mele and Dorine Greshof who served as able administrative assistants to REALM for several years.

The Lower Manhattan Seminar met somewhat irregularly during the academic years of 1987–90 to share knowledge about and reactions to the dramatic events then occurring on the Lower East Side and, more specifically, those subportions of it referred to as the East Village, or the even smaller zone called Alphabet City. The meetings drew advanced graduate students and professors from a half dozen universities in the New York area, as well as some residents of and activists in the neighborhood. Although we began with a nucleus of some ten interested participants, several years later REALM was sending session invitations to a snowball mailing list of some 150 persons. Attendance at the seminars once reached as high as 70, although the number was usually about 25 persons, drawn from a revolving pool. Papers were presented and critiqued, issues were explored and debated, and information was exchanged within the network.

By the end of the second year of the informal seminar, it had become evident that no single scholar would ever be able to grasp the full complexity of this fascinating and contentious Manhattan neighborhood, nor could all of its aspects be explored in a single volume. A smaller nucleus from the seminar met to plan a collective book, deciding to focus on spatial contestations, outlining the chapters that were needed, and tentatively accepting responsibility for them. Some of the chapters in this book were presented in preliminary form at the third academic year's seminar and were immeasurably strengthened by the comments, additions and corrections made by seminar attendees. A common framework began to emerge, although the authors were not all in agreement in their analyses. We have tried to retain some of these disagreements, acknowledging that interpretations can, and, perhaps inevitably, must vary when it is definitions of reality that are also being contested.

The volume is remarkable for the diversity of its contributors. Professors and graduate students appear in successive chapters and a reader would be hard pressed to make distinctions among their works. Sociologists, political scientists, geographers, planners, and historians are all represented, since the task of studying an urban neighborhood requires a variety of disciplines. The cross-fertilization that occurred from this interdisciplinary exchange deepened our understanding and has made this book more comprehensive than would otherwise have been possible.

Many others contributed to the preparation of this book. For several years I taught urban sociology to a cohort of talented graduate students of the New School. The Lower East Side was singled out as a possible field laboratory site and a number of students chose to study it. Among those whose studies and term papers, in or out of the classroom, expanded and deepened our knowledge of the area, even though they did not contribute to this book, were: Marie Herb, Umberto Blumati, Abby Scher, Hai-Shan Liu, and Marianne Cocchini. The editor wishes especially to single out Abby Scher, who helped edit the contributions, not only to make them read more smoothly but to identify discrepancies, eliminate repetitions, and to assist me in building a coherent whole out of what were originally discrete contributions. Her skills as a journalist and editor and her intelligent and synthetic judgments were invaluable. Nina Aebi, a graduate student in Political Science and Historical Studies at the New School, rendered enormous help in the final burst of work required to prepare the manuscript for publication; her cheerful reactions to labor exploitation and her computer skills transformed a highly edited text into a clear final document.

Janet Lippman Abu-Lughod
New York

A Note about the Contributors

JANET L. ABU-LUGHOD is professor of sociology at the Graduate Faculty of the New School for Social Research and director of REALM, a research center focusing on lower Manhattan. Among her books are *Housing Choices and Constraints*; *Third World Urbanization*; urban histories of *Cairo* and *Rabat*; *Before European Hegemony*; and *Changing Cities*.

JOHN DALE was a graduate student in sociology at the New School for Social Research when he conducted his fieldwork among New York's homeless population.

DIANA R. GORDON is associate professor of political science at the City College of New York. Her most recent book is *The Return of the Dangerous Classes: Drug Prohibition and Policy Politics.*

BETSY DUNCAN, a graduate student in geograpy at Columbia University, is writing a thesis examining art and gentrification in the East Village.

DORINE GRESHOF, a graduate student in sociology at the New School for Social Research, is currently a research associate at the University of Amsterdam, studying homelessness in that city.

JEANNE HOUCK, who teaches American history at Eugene Lang College, collaborated with Marci Reaven in converting her museum exhibit text to a chapter for this book.

JAN CHIEN LIN is currently an assistant professor of sociology at the University of Houston. He was a graduate student at the New School for Social Research at the time his chapter was written. His 1992 dissertation is entitled 'Capital and Community in Urban Change: Chinatown, New York City.'

MARIO MAFFI teaches American culture at the University of Milan, Italy. He is the author of a forthcoming book on the Lower East Side, *Gateway to the Promised Land: Ethnicity and Culture in New York's Lower East Side.*

CHRISTOPHER MELE teaches sociology at the University of North Carolina, Wilmington. He was a graduate student at the New School for Social Research when his chapters were written, based on research for his 1993 doctoral dissertation at the New School.

MARLIS MOMBER, a former high-fashion photographer, has spent the past ten years in the East Village photo-documenting changes in the Lower East Side. She is currently completing work in urban studies at Empire State University.

RICHARD PLUNZ is professor of architecture at Columbia University and an authority on New York housing. His latest book is *A History of Housing in New York: Dwelling Type and Social Change in the American Metropolis.*

LAURA REID was a student of Neil Smith's at the time their article was written.

MARCI REAVEN, a museum planner with the American History Workshop, prepared an exhibit on the history of Tompkins Square Park which was widely shown in the New York area.

WILLIAM SITES teaches sociology at Queens College. His chapter draws upon his 1993 doctoral dissertation in sociology at the City University of New York and his experience as a tenant organizer on the Lower East Side.

NEIL SMITH is professor of geography at Rutgers University. He has done extensive theoretical and empirical research on gentrification and the broader processes of uneven geographical development. He is, *inter alia*, author of *Uneven Development: Nature, Capital and the Production of Urban Space*, and co-editor of *Gentrification of the City.*

ANDREW VAN KLEUNEN is a graduate student in sociology at the New School for Social Research. He worked for several years as a community organizer in the Bronx and is currently researching recent shifts in neighborhood activism and community development in New York City.

SUZANNE WASSERMAN is assistant professor of history at Iona College. Her chapter summarizes material from her 1990 doctoral dissertation in history at New York University, which deals with the Lower East Side in the Depression years.

Introduction

Janet Abu-Lughod

In 1983, several thousand residents of Manhattan's Lower East Side massed on the steps of New York's City Hall, chanting 'This Land is Ours.'[1] They were staking claim to hundreds of the neighborhood's vacant lots and apartment buildings (many of them abandoned) owned by the city. These *in rem* properties had come into municipal ownership in the wake of New York City's fiscal crisis of 1975, when landlords in several of the city's more insalubrious slums walked away from their buildings in a rash of tax defaults. Now that the economy had begun to boom and demand for housing grew stronger, residents were worried. Their fears were well justified. 'Gentrifiers,' 'developers,' and 'yuppies' were invading their turf, threatening their homes and ways of life, and seeking to create, in this last low point of land values and rents in Lower Manhattan, a new 'urban frontier' to be reclaimed by strangers. Only the city-owned properties stood between them and massive change. The roots of this current crisis lay in the 1970s.

By the mid-1970s the economy of the city lay in shambles, triggered in 1973 by two international changes. That year followed the demise of the Bretton Woods Agreement which, since the end of World War II, had pegged international trade to the dollar and thus supported American dominance of the international economy. It also marked the start of a rapid escalation in oil prices, precipitated by reactions to the 1973 Arab–Israeli war. The American economy was considerably weakened by these two international events. The term 'restructuring' is the euphemism used to refer to the changes which, among other things, witnessed a recession and then a reduction in the proportion of well remunerated and unionized manufacturing jobs in the United States, particularly in the northeast and midcentral regions of the country.

Within New York City, what had up to then been a gradual decline in manufacturing began a precipitous descent. Unemployment soared, expanding the need for subsidized city services and assistance. There was a temporary collapse in the real estate market and a significant number of property owners postponed paying their taxes. This reduced city revenues just as demands on them were increasing. The combination of the two trends created a severe budgetary shortfall, but when the city appealed to Washington for relief, its cry for help was peremptorily rejected.[2]

Rescued from imminent fiscal collapse by the issuance of special bonds, New York sought new ways to raise revenue and cut expenditures. To compensate for the declining revenues caused by real estate tax delinquencies and hoping to raise funds in a hurry, in the late 1970s the city changed its procedures for foreclosing on real property in tax arrears. Instead of the three-year grace period property owners had previously enjoyed before the city could take their properties for failure to pay taxes, owners were given only one year (albeit with possible extensions). The ploy backfired. Instead of raising instant windfall cash as anticipated, the legal change helped to precipitate a rash of tax delinquencies. What ensued was a stepped-up pace of arson and the abandonment of a substantial portion of the city's housing stock in poor people's neighborhoods such as the South Bronx and the Lower East Side. Landlords had their buildings torched for insurance money or simply 'walked away' from their already-amortized investments through tax default. This is how the city became the proud possessor of some 500 properties on the Lower East Side.

But by the late 1970s the city had absorbed some of the effects of the economic restructuring. While manufacturing continued its decline, two sources of a new boom appeared.[3] On the one hand, there was a rapid expansion of well paid jobs in the sectors of finance, law, insurance, information, and administration, as headquarters of major firms continued to centralize their control functions in the New York region, even though they moved their plants to other regions of the US or even abroad. This fed a revived center-city real estate market which, as these new jobs were filled by maturing baby-boomers with a strong preference for city living, led to escalating housing prices, even for older properties – if they could be renovated to accommodate a 'higher' class. To some extent, the Lower East Side felt the impact of this. On the other hand, the largest expansion in jobs during the recovery was either in the unskilled service sector, where wages were so low that only low-rent apartments could be afforded, or in a burgeoning return to 'sweatshop' production, into which many new immigrants were shunted. The housing available to these groups was concentrated, among other places, on the Lower East Side.

This put the demands of upgraders and seekers of affordable housing on a collision course. It is this conflict of interests that frames the process to be treated in this book: gentrification. The demonstration that took place on the steps of City Hall expressed support for one wide set of interests, namely, that of lower-income renters in the area. In this early confrontation, their will prevailed. The demonstration helped residents gain a temporary reprieve from what they most feared, namely, a massive transformation of their neighborhood via the sale to developers of the city-owned properties. Although gentrifiers could still purchase privately owned tenements on the Lower East Side, empty them out, warehouse the vacant units, and eventually convert them into coops and condominia for new and wealthier residents,[4] a moratorium was declared on the sale of properties already in municipal ownership. The city reluctantly agreed to this, even though it had hoped to sell such properties to private developers at a good profit during the period of economic recovery.

Eventually, negotiations between neighborhood groups and the city government led to an agreement reached in September 1987 to 'share' the city's housing and land stock via a so-called 'cross-subsidy' plan. According to this agreement, the city would sell its vacant land to private developers wishing to build market-rate housing on the sites. In return for 'permitting' this, non-profit neighborhood groups would be given the city-owned tenements[5] and the funds needed to rehabilitate them for low- and moderate-income tenants.[6] Ironically, this agreement was finally reached at another turning point in the city's wildly fluctuating economic history. The collapse of the stock market in October 1987 issued New York into the next downturn of its development, a phase intensified in 1990–1 by another national recession, associated with another Middle East war. In the first shock, housing demand collapsed at the top end of the market as investment firms and banks cut back on staff; prices of prime apartments stabilized and then declined. In the second shock of a national recession, the city again entered a fiscal crisis that necessitated cutbacks in municipal employees and services. Unemployment and reductions in production dislodged even more poor people – from low-quality housing into no housing at all.

All of these events precipitated changes in the Lower East Side, changes whose effects are still being revealed. One effect was an increase in the number of homeless in the neighborhood.[7] A second was a decline in interest on the part of developers in either bidding on the vacant land the city was now free to sell or in continuing to create high-rent apartments for 'yuppies' out of the old housing stock. The modest changes currently visible in the neighborhood are confined to an intense rehabilitation of a fraction of the old tenements, undertaken by the mutual housing associations that had been newly established to participate in the cross-subsidy program.

The events of the early 1990s certainly do not constitute the last chapter in the history of the Lower East Side. An area that since the second half of the nineteenth century has played such an important role in immigrant absorption in the city, that occupies a special place in the imagination and lore of New York and indeed of America, and that continues to occupy so strategic a location in the spatial ecology of the city cannot have a last chapter. But given the temporary hiatus that has occurred in its dizzying pace of change, this does seem a propitious moment to evaluate the recent past.

The battle for the Lower East Side of Manhattan in recent decades is the primary focus of this book, but the book is not just about one neighborhood nor just about the recent past. The experiences with abandonment, arson and disinvestment, with the processes of reinvestment and 'gentrification,' and with community battles over who shall occupy and control given center-city neighborhoods are not unique to the Lower East Side of Manhattan. The same processes, albeit different in their details and perhaps not so extreme in their manifestations, were also operating in many other inner slums in major cities of the northeast and midcentral regions of the United States during the same time period. A study of one such neighborhood may help to illuminate the 'tug-of-war' that has been taking place in many American cities between poor (and often minority[8]) residents and what some urbanists have characterized as the 'growth machine' that drives urban change in contemporary America.[9] It may help us trace the deeper causes of such changes, causes that are equally operative in places where their manifestations may not have been as visible nor as violent as in New York.[10]

There is a second reason why the Lower East Side merits special attention. Because it has such a long history of change, it is possible to place the developments that have taken place over the past decades within a deeper time frame. The causes of neighborhood change are to be found not only in recent international, national and local events, but in the more distant past. How local areas were built up and with what types of housing, how they were populated, and how different groups of occupants succeeded one another when their functions changed, even past experiences with local mobilizations, political action, and ways of exerting local will, all influence how change will be played out in unique ways in unique neighborhoods. While such patterns cannot be generalized nor assumed to apply automatically to areas with different histories, the model we follow in our analysis can be replicated in studies of different areas elsewhere.

This volume represents an effort to produce a new type of community study. Older ethnographic methods for studying urban subcommunities no longer seem able to capture the economic and social complexities found in our newest forms of inner-city neighborhoods, zones that have lost their common culture and consensus and have become, instead, the contested turf of diverse groups which intermingle in physical space but which pursue disparate lifestyles and, often, conflicting goals.[11] Increasingly, neighborhoods in the central zones of our largest cities no longer fit the old model of 'ethnic enclaves' or 'urban villages.' Many no longer constitute – if indeed they ever did – natural communities where residents share a common culture and pursue a relatively unified set of interests *vis à vis* 'outsiders.'[12] Rather, in addition to the major black ghettos and barrios of the largest cities, which almost constitute cities in themselves, there are now numerous multi-ethnic, highly diversified districts containing subgroups with varying lifestyles, class interests, goals and ideologies. Such areas do not form unified or 'natural' communities, but are indeed the arenas within which subgroups struggle, not only with 'outside' interests such as developers or city governments, but with one another.

The Lower East Side is now that kind of area. The way that it engages in struggles over turf and over its future may help illuminate processes that are likely to become more and more common elsewhere.

The Organization of This Book

Chapter I introduces the Lower East Side today, focusing especially on the northern portion of the district which has alternatively been called 'The East Village'[13] or 'Alphabet City.'[14] This area has recently attracted national press coverage and gained a certain amount of notoriety because of a series of dramatic events centering on Tompkins Square Park. It was there in August of 1988 that hundreds of undisciplined police battled hundreds of residents and bystanders over the issue of a park curfew. In that round, the police lost and the city rescinded its decision to close the park at night. It was there between 1987 and 1991 that a growing population of (mostly) men without homes formed a settlement which, with the addition of tents and self-constructed shanties, increasingly preempted sections of the heavily used public park. It was there in July and again in December of 1989 that the city's Parks Department made abortive attempts to dislodge them. And it was there at the beginning of June 1991 that a large and well organized force of police, supported by helicopters, command and communications vehicles and armed with unlimited movable barricades and tall chain-linked fencing materials, finally evicted the homeless from their camp, destroyed their shelters, and proceeded to close off the park for more than a year, despite strong community opposition. While the details of these events are reserved to later parts of this book, chapter 1 helps to set the scene.

Although today's residents of the East Village/Alphabet City are a diverse lot, they coexist in a zone with a long history whose nineteenth-century ethos still pervades memory and associations, and whose similarly old spatial pattern and poor housing stock continue to structure daily life. And although today's controversies over replanning and gentrifying the zone may appear to be new, they too hark back to the past. In part I of the book, therefore, we turn back the clock to trace the sources of today's economic problems, spatial patterns, housing stock, the park itself, and the precedents for redeveloping the area.

The economic base of manufacturing that once supported the Lower East Side's immigrant working-class population, admittedly at the most marginal levels of subsistence, has long since vanished. Chapter 2 by Jan Lin traces the economic history of the Lower East Side, showing that the final collapse of the industrial job market in the 1970s was preceded by a long-term erosion in the economic base of the area. The Lower East Side had, from the beginning, been a place of employment, especially for dock workers, manual laborers in small machine shops, and workers in the garment trade, whether employed in centralized sweatshop lofts or as piece-work sweated labor in their overcrowded tenements. Gradually, however, one after the other of the local trades disappeared, leaving the zone without an economic base. Only recently has the economy of the Lower East Side been reinfused, but that revival has taken place largely in a rapidly expanding Chinatown which now stretches northward toward Houston Street and, more recently, has entered the East Village itself.

While jobs are mostly gone from the area, many of the tenement houses that were originally thrown up to accommodate the streams of poor immigrant workers who found their first haven in the city on the Lower East Side, are still there. Outside the newer 'projects' and some newer 'old' apartment houses, the tenements constitute the basic housing stock of the area. These overcrowded warrens with no light and little air were documented at the turn of the century by, among others, photo-journalist and muckraker Jacob Riis, in his *How the Other Half Lives.*[15] While such structures were not confined to the Lower East Side – indeed they were to be found throughout the city – they have remained there long after being cleared and replaced elsewhere. They leave an intractable residue that greatly complicates the task of rehabilitation. Chapter 3 by Richard Plunz and Janet Abu-Lughod examines early tenement reform attempts and presents information on the Lower East Side from the first tenement house surveys.[16]

Even predating the massive construction of tenement houses was the 'heart' of the neighborhood, Tompkins Square Park. In chapter 4 Marci Reaven and Jeanne Houck recount the history of the park itself over its more than 150 years of existence and change. They demonstrate that conflicts over the park's functions are permanent features of that history, and that the park is a site where larger political and economic controversies often rose to violent expression. Battles between residents and police and controversies over redesigning park spaces have, indeed, been recurrent themes in the area's history. That such battles erupted in the 1960s when the park became the preferred open space for 'hippies' and Vietnam War protesters, or again in the 1980s when 'cleaning up the park' became central to the city's and developers' strategy of 'cleaning up the neighborhood,' should come as no surprise to anyone who knows the park's history.

Chapter 5 by Suzanne Wasserman concludes part I. Persons familiar with the current controversies over the future of the area will be struck with a strong sense of *déjà vu* when they read that very similar debates took place in the 1920s and 1930s. Plans to renovate the 'slums' of the Lower East Side peaked, quite predictably, during the booming 1920s when real estate investment was one of the most attractive speculative ventures available.[17] Even then, the 'camps' were divided between those who envisaged the future of the Lower East Side as an upper-class 'town-in-town' whose apartments would be demanded by flapper 'yuppies' working on Wall Street and in the business headquarters of Lower Manhattan, and those who sought to improve affordable housing for its immigrant working class. Even then, the lines were drawn between those reformers who wanted to tear down all the old tenements and build anew and those who argued for their renovation and redesign. But none of these future visions worked out exactly as their advocates had hoped, and for reasons not unlike those that now partially immobilize change. The Great Depression struck, the gentrifiers withdrew their claims, and the reformers from the settlement houses worried more about providing food and clothes to a desperate population than about improving housing. It was in the 1930s, however, that the first public housing project was undertaken by the city,[18] even before federal funds were available. Later, massive projects drastically transformed the fringes of the zone in ways none of the parties had foreseen.

In part II we turn to the more recent changes that have been occurring in the area. But even here, such transformations cannot be understood except in historical perspective. One of the most striking facts about the Lower East Side and the East Village in particular has been the radical depopulation that occurred in the 1970s and 1980s when certain subareas lost as much as half of their populations. One might be tempted to see this 'collapse' as the result of only the most recent phase of restructuring of the American economy and as a function of only the most recent cycle of disinvestment and reinvestment in New York's real estate history. Such a conclusion would be wrong.

The population of the Lower East Side had been declining even before the 1920s. Its earlier declines were in many ways welcomed improvements over the past, when large numbers had been accommodated only through extreme overcrowding. The decline in immigration to the United States, which culminated in the 1921–4 legislation that virtually cut off the supply of newcomers, had a dramatic impact on the Lower East Side which had for so long served as a first 'port of entry' for foreigners. As immigrants assimilated and gained a firmer foothold in their new city, they tended to disperse to more attractive areas of second settlement in Brooklyn and the Bronx. Their places on the Lower East Side, however, were taken by newcomers. Once the cut-off in immigration occurred, however, the area's population ceased to be replenished. The Lower East Side began to thin out from its incredibly overcrowded former state when it was reputed to have been the most densely settled urban area in the world.

And yet, the area did not undergo complete decimation because one new group of migrants did finally begin to replace the missing Europeans, namely, the Puerto Ricans who came to New York in increasing numbers in the 1950s. Christopher Mele traces this later stage of ethnic succession in chapter 6. He attributes the deteriorating situation of the Puerto Rican community to basic changes in the economy of New York, which deprived them of the jobs they had formerly held as factory operatives and semi-skilled workers. Their declining market position set the stage for the cycle of disinvestment that followed. It was only after the Puerto Rican immigrants proved to be 'the end of the line' that the demographic and housing cycles of the East Village simultaneously collapsed.

But collapse is not the operative term. Rather, in a situation some investigators have called 'neighborhood blow-out,' the intentional devaluing of real property is causally connected to gentrification. Chapter 7, by Neil Smith, Betsy Duncan, and Laura Reid, traces why and how values 'collapsed,' arguing that disinvestment in real property (devalorization) is not merely the result of declining demand, but, rather, is often a necessary prelude to new profit making (revalorization). They argue that disinvestment and reinvestment are rational processes that can be observed and measured by tracing tax-delinquency decisions of property owners. They apply their innovative methods to the East Village, mapping the waves of disinvestment–reinvestment that swept through the neighborhood from northwest to southeast between 1975 and 1985.

Christopher Mele explores this process in greater detail in chapter 8. Disinvestment opened up 'economic space' for a variety of investors who played different and often symbiotic roles in the complex choreography of neighborhood change. Mele examines real estate transactions in the 1980s, developing a powerful model of how gentrification worked through a sequence of steps involving quite different investors playing quite different games.

Hints that housing investment decisions are based on more than the operation of simple market forces are presented throughout the preceding chapters. These hints are made more explicit by William Sites in chapter 9. The policies of local government shape the environment within which such decisions are made and, in the fate of cities and their subareas today, have become one of the most important variables in the equation. This was particularly true in New York City during the crucial post-1975 period. Sites focuses his discussion directly on the pro-growth/development policies of the Koch administration, tracing the intimate relationship between city incentives and developer responses.

When such radical changes occur in urban areas, the affected populations do not remain passive. They react – often with a remarkable grasp of the forces that are at work and often with increasing virulence and even violence, especially when they perceive that they may be driven out or that the neighborhood will change so drastically that it will cease to be their familiar home.

Part III focuses on these reactions. It begins with the reminiscences of a long-term resident of the East Village, political scientist Diana Gordon, who has been an observer, part-time participant, and thoughtful analyst of local political controversies. Her observations, recorded in chapter 10, set the scene for the next chapter which describes the recently escalating violence in the area. In chapter 11, Janet Abu-Lughod recapitulates the 'police riot' of August 1988 that brought neighborhood emotions to a boil but also brought neighbors to a peak moment of unified purpose when their opposition to a park curfew and to further gentrification seemed destined to succeed. This chapter also analyzes the subsequent fragmentation of this united front over two issues of mounting debate: who was to control the provision of 'affordable housing' through the cross-subsidy program, and what was to be done about the growing number of homeless persons who had made the park their home. Skirmishes over control of specific buildings put local squatters and housing reformers increasingly at loggerheads, while disagreements about the 'homeless' generated other conflicts and cleavages within the community. Groups that had formerly constituted a united defensive front against gentrification began to fragment and fight one another.

One issue that drove a serious wedge between factions that had previously maintained a defensive coalition against the city was the existence of an encampment of several hundred homeless persons in the small 10-acre park. What to do about this 'problem' engaged the attention and occasionally inflamed the emotions of most neighborhood residents. John Dale and Dorine Greshof both did 'fieldwork' for several years among the homeless and carefully followed the escalating neighborhood controversy over their situation. In chapter 12 they describe the life cycle of the park community, showing how it came into being, how it carved out a symbiotic niche in the neighborhood's ecology, how social life was organized within it, and what happened after it was destroyed.

Among the most vocal and active supporters of the right of the homeless to live in the park was a loosely organized set of squatters (some but not all of whom define themselves ideologically as anarchists) who currently occupy a number of the abandoned buildings in municipal ownership. Andy Van Kleunen conducted lengthy interviews with one of the most vocal leaders of the squatters' movement in the East Village and with others who have, in one way or another, been participants in the movement. In chapter 13 he gives us extracts from these interviews, as well as his interpretation of the range of their views.

In recent years, the squatters came into conflict not only with the police over the rights of the homeless to live in the park and with the city over their own right to occupy city buildings without official authorization, but with the largest faction of organized housing reformers who, since about 1985, have been the major force in Community Board 3, the appointed body of 50 residents with advisory powers over land use decisions in the Lower East Side. The reformers gathered a variety of smaller neighborhood organizations under their umbrella organization, the Joint Planning Council, and succeeded in using their collective strength to attain positions of leadership and legitimacy in dealing with the city government. It was they who, through the housing committee of Community Board 3, negotiated on behalf of the neighborhood to reach the Memorandum of Understanding with then mayor Koch, which set the cross-subsidy program on its way. It is they who negotiated with the city's Department of Finance and Real Property and the Department of Housing Preservation and Development for the actual assignment of properties to mutual housing associations. And it is they who got the city to commit an estimated five million dollars to pay for the first phase of the cross-subsidy plan. Their goal was to minimize gentrification by outsiders while maximizing the number of rehabilitated units of affordable housing in the area. Since many of the units promised to them in this agreement were already occupied by squatters, one could predict an eventual clash with the squatters!

Based on observations of community meetings, relevant documents, and interviews with a number of community leaders, Janet Abu-Lughod, in chapter 14, tries to capture the viewpoint of these proponents of the cross-subsidy plan.[19] They define their position as proactively 'realistic,' believing on the basis of their long work on housing reform in the Lower East Side that it is the best 'deal' the neighborhood could have obtained. As can easily be seen, the views of the squatters and the housing reform activists – both committed to preserving the neighborhood for its current residents – defy reconciliation. Thus far, the squatters have interacted mostly with the police while the housing reformers have been the ones who have interacted with the city officials. Clearly, both are deeply affected by what the city government is and is not willing to do.

Between the riot of August 1988 and the closing of the park in June 1991, the city administration, while remaining Democratic, changed leadership. Mayor Koch was defeated in his third-term bid by the former president of the Borough of Manhattan, David Dinkins. In part because Dinkins had taken more charitable stands toward the poor when he was borough president, and perhaps because he is an African-American, many residents of the neighborhood hoped that he would prove more supportive of the goals they could agree upon. They expected him to be less complicit with the interests of the real estate developers than former mayor Edward Koch had been. They expected him to be a staunch supporter of 'affordable housing' and the social services that were required to keep poor people employed and housed. In short, they expected him, perhaps naively, to live up to the campaign promises that had enticed the area's voters to give him an overwhelming plurality.[20]

In his early days in office that seemed likely. The cross-subsidy agreement was not stalled or subverted, as some had feared it might have been under Koch. The infamous SROs (single room occupancy) were to be closed down and smaller shelters and even apartments were to be made available to persons without homes and to those illegally doubled up in the public housing projects. There was talk about a crackdown on drugs, expanded police protection, and more neighborhood foot patrolmen in place of infrequent squad cars. Social services were to be expanded and teachers and municipal workers were to be better paid. And the shortages of jobs and affordable housing were to be addressed.

Perhaps that was only rhetoric, but even if sincere, reality soon set in. Larger deficits than the previous administration had confessed (or shown in its books) were discovered to have been inherited. The generous labor settlement reached with the teachers could not be extended to other municipal workers, no matter how hard they protested. At first, the announced plan to enlarge the police force was rescinded,[21] and additional personnel cuts were planned in fire, police, garbage pick-up and the like. And by summer of 1990, the national and local economies entered recession as the Gulf War tensions undermined consumer and investor confidence. By spring of 1991, the city seemed to be replaying the fiscal crisis that had precipitated collapse in 1975. The question was: would the rest of history be repeated?

We conclude the book not with a crystal ball focused on that ultimately unanswerable question, but on an analysis of the main reasons why the Lower East Side is what it is today and how our understanding of it might offer some broader insights into what is now happening in other American cities. At the minimum, we offer our case study as one that can be compared with other neighborhoods elsewhere, but even more, we hope that the processes of neighborhood change we cover in detail and the methods we developed to study them can serve as a model for a different type of community study – one able to capture not the encapsulated 'urban villages' that have become less common, but the diverse zones that are now more characteristic of our inner cities and even suburbs. Our ultimate hope is that this project will initiate a revival of the 'community study' tradition in urban sociology.

NOTES

1 See, for example, the account in *Village Voice* on 6 September 1988, p. 10. But see also chapter 14 for a fuller description of the massive campaign mounted in the early 1980s to stop the auctioning of city-owned properties.

2 On this fateful day, the headline in a New York newspaper read: 'President Ford to New York: "Drop Dead".' The federal government had begun its process of disinvesting in America's cities.

3 A number of scholars have discussed this bifurcated expansion which was occurring in many other major cities, not only in the US but abroad as well. John Friedmann and Goetz Wolff, in their pathbreaking article, 'World City Formation: An Agenda for Research and Action,' *International Journal of Urban and Regional Research* 6 (1982), pp. 309–43, were among the first to link the appearance of 'citadels' and 'ghettos' in central cities to the restructuring of the international economy. Saskia Sassen has traced some of the causes for their common appearance in London, Toyko, and New York. See her *The Global City: New York, London, Tokyo* (Princeton: Princeton University Press, 1991).

4 New York still maintains a complicated system of rent controls and rent stabilization regulations that create numerous anomalies in its housing market. Apartments that have been continuously occupied by the same renters who held them when rent controls were imposed during World War II are entitled to remain in them at artificially low rents (below what they would bring on the open market). In addition, apartments formerly under rent control but which have experienced changes in occupants come under rent stabilization laws that permit modest annual increases. When these units are upgraded, other one-time increases are permitted. Only vacant units and those in buildings added to the housing stock after World War II can command rents set by what the 'market will bear.' Owners of older buildings seek to escape

from rent controls and rent stabilization regulations by emptying enough apartments to permit them to convert their buildings to cooperatives or condominia. The term used to refer to this strategy is 'warehousing,' i.e. keeping vacant units empty until a sufficient number are accumulated to make conversion possible. This suggests that New York may be an extreme case of what has occurred elsewhere. However, it should be pointed out that even in cities without rent regulations of any kind, the processes of arson, abandonment, and gentrification have been occurring. At least some scholars, e.g. Richard Appelbaum and John Gilderbloom, argue that the explanation must therefore be broader than rent control alone. See their *Private Interferences and Public Intervention in the Rental Housing Market* (Santa Barbara, CA: Foundation for National Progress, 1984).

5 Clearly, only unoccupied tenement buildings in city ownership would be eligible for such conversion, since tenants in city-owned buildings are protected from eviction by the same rent control laws that govern private owners.

6 Some have attributed the rise in homelessness in cities throughout the nation to this decrease in the stock of affordable housing, although this explains only part of the situation.

7 The clearing in June 1991 of the shantytown of homeless persons that had formed in Tompkins Square Park, one of the few public open spaces in the tenement house district, did not solve this problem but merely displaced it, at first to empty lots in the vicinity and eventually to sites farther afield.

8 Unlike many such areas elsewhere, the Lower East Side of Manhattan is not a black ghetto. It contains a racially and ethnically diversified population. Its relatively small black population is concentrated in public housing projects along the East River. Its larger Latino population is distributed between the housing projects and the older tenements in a zone that was once so specialized that Puerto Ricans called it, in Nuyorican (New York Puerto Rican) Spanish, 'Loisaida' (Lower East Side). Remnants of earlier Italian and eastern European/Jewish waves of immigrants are concentrated on the western edges or in islands of middle-income cooperatives. Its growing Asian population is infiltrating from an expanding Chinatown, while sprinklings of white students, artists, ex-hippies and middle-class professionals liberally dot the zone. Because of this, one cannot attribute all of its problems to racism.

9 See Harvey Molotch, 'The City as a Growth Machine,' *American Journal of Sociology* 82 (1976), pp. 309–30; as well as John Logan and Harvey Molotch, *Urban Fortunes: The Political Economy of Place* (Berkeley: University of California Press, 1987).

10 If Max Weber's advice to deal with 'ideal types' is at all valid, there may be merit in studying a case as extreme as the Lower East Side. Extreme cases demonstrate in heightened profile phenomena which are also present in other cases.

11 See Janet Abu-Lughod, *Changing Cities* (New York: HarperCollins, 1991) for a fuller discussion of these concepts. A few recent studies have emphasized such diversity. See, for example, Elijah Anderson's study of two West Philadelphia neighborhoods, *Streetwise: Race, Class, and Change in an Urban Community* (Chicago: University of Chicago Press, 1990).

12 The 'Chicago School' of urban sociology, which grew up in the 1920s at a time and place when ethnic enclaves had created a mosaic of such neighborhoods, assumed that such neighborhoods were 'natural areas' where shared physical and moral space gave rise to community coherence. Herbert Gans, in his classic study of an Italian neighborhood in Boston, coined the term *The Urban Villagers* (originally Free Press of Glencoe, 1962; reissued New York: Macmillan, 1983) to refer to such urban areas. However, Gerald Suttles, in his *The Social Construction of Communities* (Chicago: University of Chicago Press, 1972), cautioned that community coherence was just as likely to be generated by a desire to defend a place against outsiders as to come from shared ethnicity or culture.

13 An attempt, some say by real estate agencies, to capture some of the cachet and prestige already bestowed on Greenwich Village, which lies due west of the zone. The border between the two 'villages' is Fourth Avenue.

14 Fourteenth Street is the northern border and Houston Street is the southern edge of both the East Village and its subsection, Alphabet City. However, there are three fairly distinct subdivisions from west to east: between Fourth Avenue and First Avenue; Avenue A to Avenue D; and east of Avenue D to the East River Drive. The nomenclature 'East Village' includes the two most westerly zones. The nomenclature 'Alphabet City' is applied only to the subdistrict where the north-south avenues carry letter rather than number names. Interestingly enough, the easternmost zone occupied by the public housing projects is not considered part of either the East Village or Alphabet City, even in cases where a project lies west of Avenue D. The terms, therefore, represent 'social' or 'cognitive' maps as much as they do maps of geographical space. Certain social groups in the area never use either of these terms. Since the term 'East Village' is associated in the minds of progressives and radicals with their arch enemies, the developers and gentrifiers, they prefer to say they live in the Lower East Side. Puerto Ricans also eschew the term East Village, preferring their own pronunciation of Lower East Side (Loisaida). Since the zone between Fourth and First Avenues has undergone progressive gentrification in recent years, the term Alphabet City has taken on a useful function, since it allows a speaker to differentiate between that part of the East Village that has already been 'lost' and that part – Alphabet City – whose future is not yet fully determined.

15 Jacob Riis, *How the Other Half Lives* (New York: Scribners, 1890).

16 Some of this information in fuller detail appears in Richard Plunz's *The History of Housing in New York City* (New York; Columbia University Press, 1990), especially pp. 1–49. Parts of chapter 3 have been drawn from this important source, although the detailed information on conditions in the Lower East Side has been added by Janet Abu-Lughod.

17 Recall that it was in the 1920s that land around American cities was enthusiastically subdivided and sold on the prospect of speculative gain; when the Depression hit in the 1930s this land remained undeveloped, until the post World War II boom not only reclaimed this earlier subdivided land but spread far beyond it.

18 The very first project, on Third Street between First Avenue and Avenue A, aptly entitled 'First Houses,' was a unification and renovation of a long stretch of party-wall tenements. The renovation was so drastic and expensive that some critics claimed that the city would have been better off tearing them down and constructing anew. However, this 'project' remains the most attractive and livable of all the subsidized housing ever proferred on the Lower East Side. Its interior garden and play area offer a still relevant model for today's more piecemeal attempts at renovation. For details, see Plunz, *The History of Housing in New York City*, pp. 209–10.

19 It is important to point out here that the 'leaders' and organizations singled out for this exposition are not the only important 'actors' in the community. We could string together here a series of acronyms for the many smaller organizations that have been active on the Lower East Side, only some of which are officially affiliated with the Joint Planning Council; even those connected to the umbrella organization itself often dissent from the positions of the so-called 'leaders.'

20 In one of the more poignant scenes I can recall, a homeless man from Tompkins Square Park confronted the mayor's representative who, the very day the park was closed and the homeless evicted, was trying to explain and defend the action before a public meeting of the Parks Committee of Community Board 3. (Such meetings usually attracted no more than a handful of attendees, not counting board members and researchers! On this particular occasion, however, there were more than 150 angry residents crowded into a hot unventilated meeting hall.) The homeless man was furious. He said that the first time he ever voted in his life was for Mayor Dinkins, a fellow black. He told how he had fought for the rights of the homeless to register and how he had 'busted ass' to rally the homeless in various parts of the city to register and to vote. He ended his presentation on a discouraged note: he would never vote again!

21 Once more firmly entrenched, the mayor was able to enlarge the police force substantially through the 'Safe Streets, Safe Cities' Omnibus Crime Bill of 1991, funded by an additional city tax.

Plate 1.1 Aerial photograph of Manhattan Island showing density profile

1

Welcome to the Neighborhood

Janet Abu-Lughod

'Come for a walk in one of the most fascinating of New York's many interesting mini-cities,' I often suggest to visitors – partly as an excuse to check on what is new in this rapidly changing area, partly because their responses will help me see the area with fresh eyes and also because, in my attempts to 'explain' it, I will have to struggle once again to define and grasp its essence. Ever since I moved to New York in 1987 and, without conscious plan, walked eastward from Greenwich Village on yet another 'exploratory mission' in the new (to me) city,[1] I have been trying to understand how, in one of the oldest quarters of an American city, a new form of urban community seemed to be emerging, and I have been trying to visualize the future in the tenements of the past.[2] I invite the reader to do the same.

But first examine an aerial photo of Manhattan. It is hard to explain how a district so close to the financial, governmental, and corporate centers of one of the world's greatest cities has persisted for some 150 years as a zone housing people of very modest, even marginal, means, apparently insulated from the tremendous forces of change which washed around it. The Lower East Side (the area south of Fourteenth Street and east of Fourth Avenue/Bowery) is a decayed residential zone that occupies prime centrally located space in Lower Manhattan. As such, it is a conspicuous anomaly in the ecology of New York City. The low profile of the area's mostly four- to six-story buildings stands in marked contrast to the skyscrapers both north and southwest of them, and their low values and rents reflect the zone's anomalous position. The wide spread between current returns on investments in the zone and the potential profits that might be reaped, if its proximity to high-rent zones nearby could be more fully exploited, has made the area a tempting target for planned 'improvements' of various kinds. Particularly anomalous is the zone just around Tompkins Square Park, since lots abutting open spaces have been ever prized and privileged in the competitive land market of the city.

Several historic factors account for the creation and persistence of this anomaly. First, the eastern margins of the zone originally lay in swampland and were therefore bypassed in the first march of the city northward. Second, the land mass that bulges eastward toward the East River from First Avenue, so-called 'Alphabet City,' was left out when the subway system was designed to favor the larger avenues; indeed, the original elevated lines that had most closely serviced the district were later torn down and never replaced by underground lines.[3] Third, much of the area's housing stock did not filter down from 'better' uses, but rather was built initially during the late nineteenth century to accommodate a poor immigrant population. It therefore consists primarily of very densely-spaced tenements which had from the outset been designed as rental units for very poor families. Such structures were cheap to build and, given the almost limitless demand for them and the high densities at which they were occupied, were very profitable to the persons who built them on speculation or who bought them for their rental returns. In more recent times the existing structures, once they ceased yielding such high profits, became less attractive to landlords while they remained inherently unattractive to renovators. Only the pockets of better townhouses near Astor Place, occupied before the mid-nineteenth century by a mercantile elite which later moved 'uptown,' could have attracted rehabbers. From time to time, plans were put forth recommending large-scale clearance of the housing stock[4] and, from the late 1930s onward, some clearance was done to make room for massive housing projects. But most of the area remained 'set in amber,' long after comparable buildings were replaced in other parts of Manhattan.

DIVERSITY IN PHYSICAL SPACE

With this background in mind, we are now ready to start our tour of Community District 3, since 1976 under the jurisdiction of Community Board 3, a quasi-political organization intended to represent neighborhood interests).[5] (See figures 1.1 and 1.2.) This zone lies south of Fourteenth Street and stretches eastward from Fourth–Third Avenues to the East River. (In Manhattan, streets run east and west whereas avenues run north and south.) We begin at the southeast corner of Fourteenth Street and Fourth Avenue, near the entrance to a distinctly un-exotic Apple Bank.

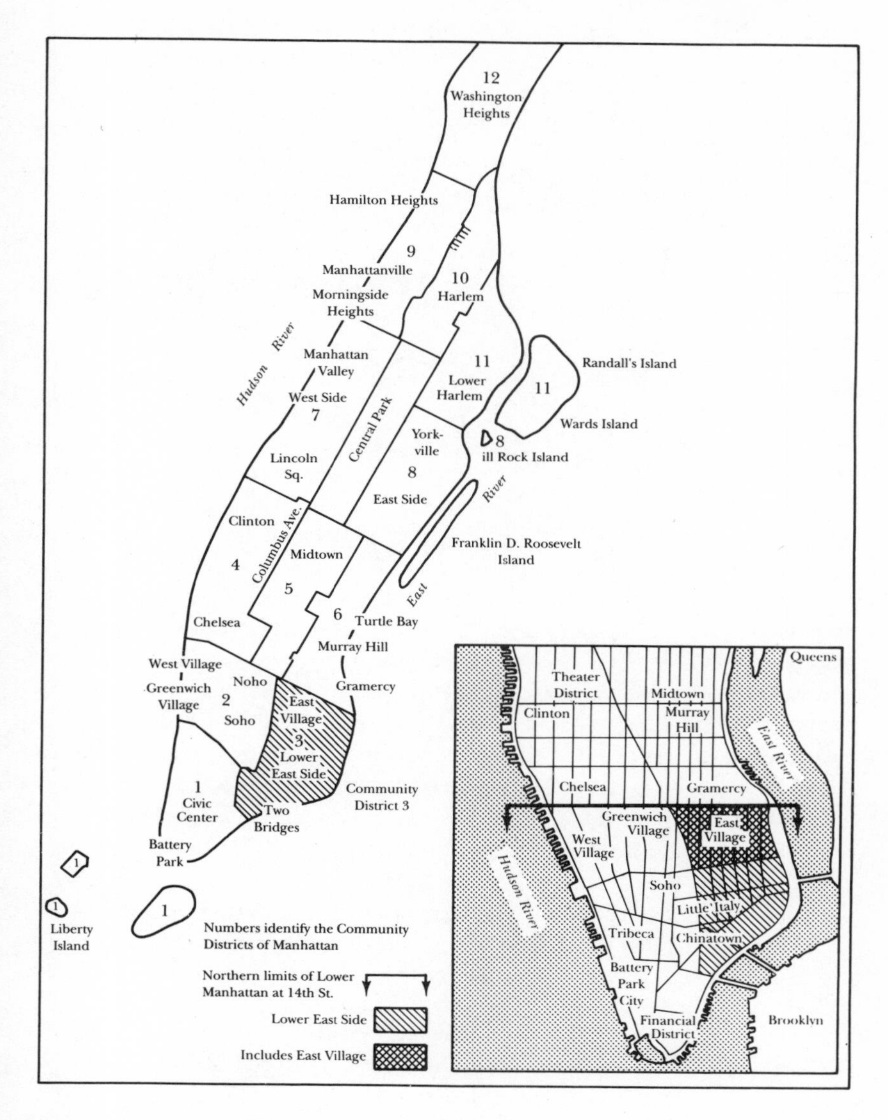

Figure 1.1 Map of Lower Manhattan Island, showing the boundaries of Community District 3 (called the Lower East Side) and of the study area (called the East Village)

Fourteenth Street is a clear marker between the Lower East Side to its south and the somewhat better areas to its north – as it always has been. This now degraded commercial thoroughfare, with its still-frequented Palladium dance hall, its boarded up buildings, its flop houses, its cheap shops and cut-rate vegetable markets, was once socially 'uncrossable,' as

Figure 1.2 The streets of the East Village, showing locations of major buildings

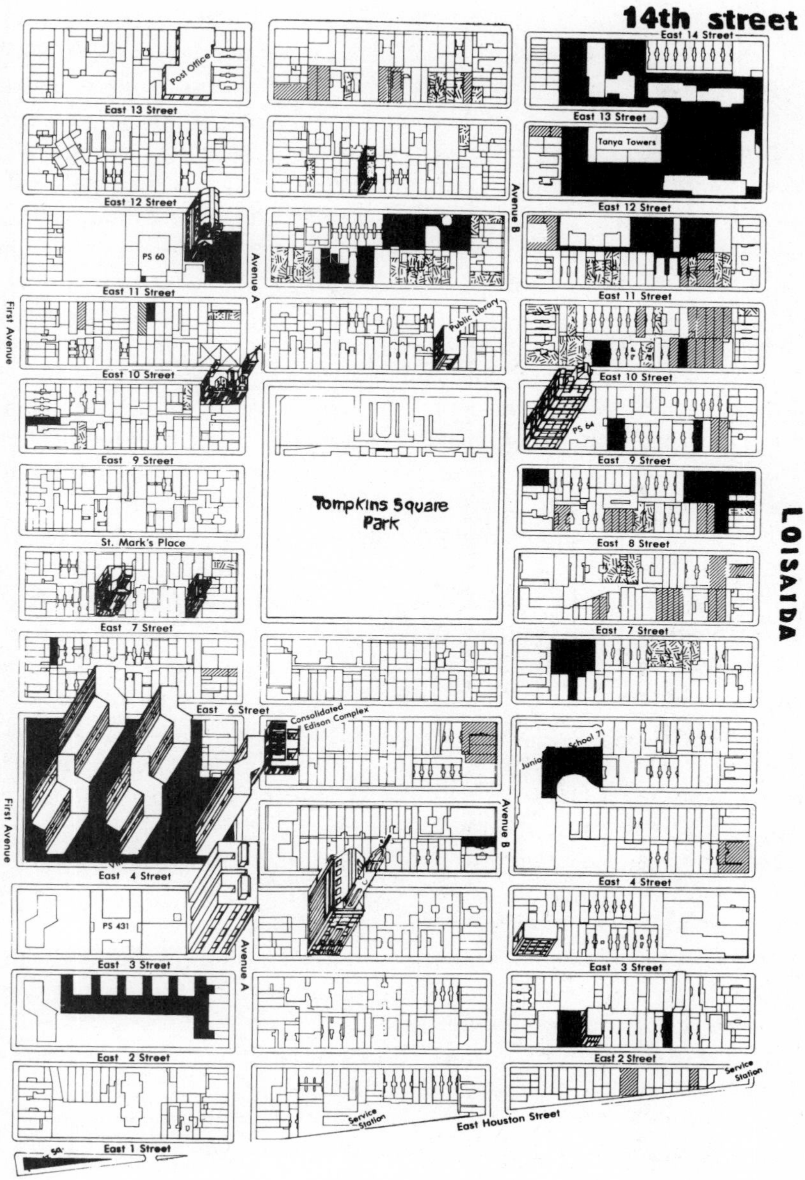

14th street

LOISAIDA

East 14 Street
Post Office
East 13 Street
East 13 Street
Tanya Towers
East 12 Street
East 12 Street
Avenue B
PS 60
Avenue A
East 11 Street
East 11 Street
First Avenue
Public Library
East 10 Street
East 10 Street
PS 64
East 9 Street
East 9 Street
Tompkins Square Park
St. Mark's Place
East 8 Street
East 7 Street
East 7 Street
East 6 Street
Consolidated Edison Complex
School 71
First Avenue
Avenue B
East 4 Street
East 4 Street
PS 431
Avenue A
East 3 Street
East 3 Street
East 2 Street
East 2 Street
Service Station
Service Station
East Houston Street
East 1 Street

Jerome Weidman's autobiographical novel about growing up in the Lower East Side in the early twentieth century recounts dramatically,[6] a social fact also confirmed by old-time residents.[7]

Fourth Avenue is also a clear marker, a dead-space wedged between the bustle of Lower Broadway, which marks the eastern edge of Greenwich Village, and the Lower East Side 'proper.' Commercial along its length, Fourth Avenue is flanked by cheap and nondescript eateries, interspersed with neighborhood service establishments (dry cleaners, groceries, hardware stores), wholesale antique shops, and large apartment buildings. It merges with Third Avenue just below the Medici-like Florentine palazzo that is Cooper Union. In the triangular space remaining is a sometimes flea market (mostly evenings and week-ends) so marginal that one wonders where the rags, old shoes and 78 records spread on old blankets on the pavement have come from, and who might want to buy them. Where the two avenues converge, the name changes to the Bowery, celebrated in American vaudeville as a den of iniquity ('I won't go there anymore,' as the song put it) and later defamed as a notorious skid row for alcoholic men (as in 'a bum on the Bowery'). The street dates back to the seventeenth-century settlement of New Amsterdam. At that time it was spelled 'bouwerij' and referred literally to a bowered plantation there; today it is devoid of trees and any vegetation.

'Grungy' might be the best descriptive term for this southern stretch of low buildings that gradually gives way to car repair shops and then restaurant supply stores. To a trained urbanist's eye it is clear that some past demand has dried up here (although an old mission survives from skid row days and a garish music hot spot with a reputed drug parlor attached recalls past 'iniquities') and is patiently awaiting rebirth. The land is being held fallow by speculators until a new and better use for this potentially high-value location can be found. Hints that such a use has already been found are the sprinklings of Chinese language signs that have been appearing south of Houston Street, interspersed among older references to kosher foods. This encroachment from Chinatown is confirmed when one examines real estate transactions on the Bowery within the past few years and learns that most recent buyers have Chinese surnames. Chinatown, whose northern border was once Canal Street, has lately been bursting at the seams. It has gravitated northward to Houston and has sent out feelers even farther north.[8]

Well below Houston Street (a wide divided thoroughfare insulating the social neighborhoods north and south of it) begins an increasingly elaborate specialized commercial zone for lamps and lighting fixtures – a concentration of shops whose ceilings sprout densely arranged fixture displays and whose floors are equally congested. This single strand of glitter, however, is mere facade for the crowded and poor housing of

Chinatown that lies behind. At Canal Street, Community District 3 jogs to the west to encompass the eastern edge of Chinatown, before it ends almost at the tip of the island where Pearl Street meets the Brooklyn Bridge. The southern and eastern boundaries of the district follow the shoreline of the East River.

Community District 3 is divided into four horizontal strata: the 'Two Bridges' area at the southern extremity, so called because it stretches between the approaches to the Brooklyn and Manhattan Bridges; Chinatown 'proper' to its west; the 'lower' Lower East Side, that is, the eastern zone between Two Bridges and Houston on the north; and what is now called the 'East Village,' the northernmost section between Houston and Fourteenth Street. Since the latter is the zone on which this book concentrates, to conserve space (and energy, if indeed this were a real walk!) we shall confine our walking tour to this district.

Retracing our steps, then, let us follow Third Avenue northward to Fourteenth Street. After crossing St Mark's Place (at Eighth Street, a singular east–west street that constitutes the commercial 'heart' of what was New York's 'Haight-Ashbury' in the 1960s), Third Avenue presents an anomaly whose transformation has occurred primarily in the past few years. When the Third Avenue elevated mass transit line darkened this commercial avenue, only small shops with noisy, and therefore cheap, apartments above graced this street; even after the elevated line was torn down in the 1950s, the zone remained distinctly unattractive and neglected. Now, however, it has been transformed into what is informally referred to as 'Dormitory Row,' since its new highrise structures house students from nearby universities. The students have attracted a rash of new businesses and entertainment spots. In place of the seedy x-rated porno houses of a few years ago are new movie palaces showing first-run films. And in place of greasy-spoon luncheonettes are more upscale but often fast-food shiny replacements. Only a single mission shelter, just south of Fourteenth Street, reminds us of the street's past status.

From the corner of Third Avenue and Fourteenth Street we walk eastward to Second Avenue and then south on this commercial thoroughfare which, during the heyday of Yiddish theater at the turn of the century, was the Lower East Side's ethnic 'Great White Way.' Few remnants of that era remain. The theaters mostly stand derelict and closed, although just recently an extravagant 'moorish palace' was restored and reopened as a multiplex cinema. The Hebrew letters on the marquee and the stained-glass windows of the famous and still-busy Second Avenue Deli are virtually the only semiotics to this vanished past. More visible are the signs of residual Ukrainian and Polish settlement: some restaurants, organizational headquarters, and churches. But few pedestrians who throng this street are of Ukrainian origin. In fact, when the annual

Ukrainian street fair is held in front of the local Eastern Orthodox Cathedral, it is clear that the churchgoers and stall operators have almost all driven in from other parts of New York, while the browsers and samplers of pirogies and sausages are young Americans from the neighborhood, unstained by the stigmata of visible 'ethnicity.'

Moving southward along Second Avenue, we truncate our walk at Houston Street which is the southern boundary of our study area, even though the borders of Community District 3 extend southward to encompass the formerly Italian, now mini-barrio of Latino residence, with its thus far stable housing stock and its bodegas, coffee shops and botanicas, before merging with Chinatown.[9] Walking eastward along the broad traffic thoroughfare of Houston Street, we see in both directions unmistakable signs of a street in transition, partly old, partly derelict or cleared, partly redeveloped, all in the process of change (plate 1.2).

Plate 1.2 'Red Square' on Houston Street, the southern boundary of the study area
Source: Courtesy of Marlis Momber

Turning north on First Avenue, these transitions become even more abruptly discontinuous, suggesting that changes have been speeding up at this 'divider' between an already 'gentrified' strip demarcated by Third–Fourth Avenues and Second Avenue on the west, and a more recently 'gentrifying' strip between First Avenue and Avenue A to its east. Block by block and even building by building, the scene changes. The first block is straight 'barrio,' but some buildings have already been emptied for renovation. The vegetables offered for sale along First Avenue, which are displayed outside the shops in bins and on wooden shelves that sprawl onto the sidewalks as is typical throughout this area, are cheaper and of markedly lower quality than those on Second Avenue. But a block or two northward, newer facades and fancier uses appear.

The large open blocks of an apartment complex called Village View Houses can be seen on the east side, while on the west side of the street begin the numerous Indian restaurants that in recent years seem to have mushroomed overnight to invade the cross streets to their west. To an uninitiated observer, this proliferation of restaurants, interspersed with small groceries selling Indian spices, condiments and other ethnic goods, might signal the existence of an Indian enclave worthy of the name 'Little Calcutta,' but that would be a misreading of 'street signs.' In actual fact, virtually no East Indians live in the neighborhood and the restaurants are almost exclusively patronized by non-Indians seeking exotic meals at relatively low cost. Fictitious Little Calcutta vanishes almost as abruptly as it began, giving way to a virtual United Nations of establishments, mostly gustative. Side by side are intermixed an entire archaeology of successive ethnicities: restaurants advertising Polish, Mexican, Italian, Arab, and other cuisines. A storefront mosque is next to a butcher shop selling halal (Muslim-slaughtered) meats and Arabic specialties, which is adjacent to a bodega. Sprinkled along the street are Italian bakeries (with elaborate white confections in the window and highly palatable breads and rich pastries inside) and coffee shops, where authentic espresso and cappuccino are available. But all are somewhat downscale from similar facilities on Second Avenue, and their customers are drawn from a more local catchment area.

Large medical facilities dominate the northern end of First Avenue as it approaches Fourteenth Street. Just north of that barrier can be seen the southwesternmost corner of Stuyvesant Town, a massive fortress-like complex of middle-income rental housing that in the 1950s displaced the notorious tenements of the Gas-House district documented by Jacob Riis.[10] Turning east again on Fourteenth Street one is made sharply aware that the boundary into another mini-zone of use has been crossed. This is confirmed when we walk south on Avenue A. For the most part, the avenue at its northern end is still Hispanic, but as one approaches the northern edge of Tompkins Square Park at Tenth Street, the signs of gentrification can be seen in small boutiques, an art gallery, and some fancier cafes, although older bodegas and unpretentious eastern European restaurants persist opposite the park.

Signs of gentrification decrease rapidly thereafter. On Avenue A south of the park are two 'no-longer-so-in music scenes,' both unaccountably named for Egyptian themes (one, now defunct, called King Tut's Wah-

Wah Hut, the other, the Pyramid Club), a new video rental store in a recently refaçaded apartment house, and then the rear of Village View Houses. Beyond this, the older slum surfaces. By the time we begin to approach Houston Street, we are back in the barrio, although signs of gutted or partially refurbished apartment buildings hint that it may soon be gone.

Doubling northward along Avenue B we find a quite different scene. Few signs of renovation are visible and the commercial establishments are almost all pre-yuppie. Along the eastern edge of Tompkins Square Park between Seventh and Tenth Streets are a string of religious institutions, a few abandoned. The most imposing of these structures is St Brigid's Church, whose priest, Father Kuhn, has played an important role in community life;[11] the church not only has extended its services to the homeless but has made its facilities available for organizing neighborhood protests. Just north of St Brigid's Church is the Christodora House, symbol of hope or object of hate, depending on whether one is for or against gentrification. This 1920s art deco structure towers above its surroundings, and its glistening polished brass fittings and its beautifully restored lobby seem oddly out of place, as do its well dressed and often furtive residents. While they can now buy their produce and groceries from a new upscale Korean deli a block north, beyond that, Avenue B takes a sharp downward plunge. Burned-out shells of large apartment houses and a gutted row of tenements line the block directly north of Tenth Street, and Avenue B continues to Fourteenth Street in unrelieved depression.

Nor does the situation improve east of Avenue B. Walking eastward on Fourteenth Street to Avenue C one senses that one is entering yet another social terrain. At the northern end of Avenue C is a middle-income housing project, but below it begin the scattered rubble-covered vacant lots that testify to the arson and disinvestment that since the late 1960s literally destroyed this subarea of the neighborhood. Avenue C was once the vital commercial artery of the Latino/Puerto Rican neighborhood known as Loisaida. Although its vitality is now gone, as are many of the buildings, the ghost remains on the green street signs that still designate Avenue C as 'Loisaida.' Between Avenues B and C, on most of the cross streets, the zone is pockmarked with open spaces. However, if one primarily notices the *few empty lots between buildings* in the strip between Avenues B and C, one mostly notices the *few remaining buildings scattered among the vacant lots* between Avenues C and D (plate 1.3).

From our description thus far it should be evident that the wide north–south avenues contain the business uses of the district and divide it into a series of vertical strata that gradually become increasingly proletarianized as one moves eastward. The sharp downward gradient of quality and price is palpable from Third Avenue to Avenue D, where

Plate 1.3 The few remaining buildings scattered among the vacant lots between Avenues C and D
Source: Courtesy of Marlis Momber

the shops finally peter out on the west side. On the east side of Avenue D, in a solid phalanx of red brick towers interspersed by green open space, are 'the projects' (constructed in 1949–50 and named to honor two housing reformers, Jacob Riis and Lillian Wald) that extend to the limited-access East River (FDR) Drive. From the upper floors, residents can view the river and the adjacent strip of park on landfill, but from the ground level neither of these amenities is really accessible. Only a few overpasses allow users to cross the barrier of fast-moving traffic to reach the neglected park and the bicycle path that skirts the river.

In contrast to the wide avenues, all the cross streets are narrow and predominantly residential. Deciduous trees, conspicuously absent from the avenues, still give welcome green and shade to the streets. The buildings are usually three- to six-story-high walk-ups on narrow lots, and most are adorned by that legally prescribed and distinctive feature of Lower Manhattan architecture – the fire escapes, zig-zagging up the exterior, that have clearly been appended later. While the fire escapes often obscure the remarkably beautiful decorations on the stone facades, they serve to lead the eye up toward the flat rooflines, encrusted with outcroppings of wonderfully ornate cornices sharply delimited from the sky. These are the tenements!

To an observer who has a template for tenements engraved in his mind, the structures come as a remarkable surprise. They are beautiful: diverse and interesting in ways that the tall glass cubes and towers along the canyons of midtown will never be. And they are historically important, being among the last remnants of this architectural form in a city where they once stretched all the way up the east side of Manhattan from the Brooklyn Bridge to the Harlem River at 129th Street. According to Lawrence Veiller, writing in 1903, 'the tenement houses in the Borough of Manhattan are, to a very large extent, located in distinctively tenement house districts, with more definite boundaries than can be found in other cities.'[12] From the beginning, the Lower East Side was one such district; today, one of the city's largest concentrations of still-extant tenements can be found between Houston and Fourteenth Streets, east of Third Avenue.

To a certain extent, the east–west cross streets of the East Village are more like one another than are the distinctive north–south avenues. But along each one of them one notes a similar declining gradient of condition. In general, the western blocks are in better condition than the eastern ones, although there are so many exceptions that the generalization is not very useful. Rather, the intersections of avenues and streets create distinct micro-zones that can change block by block in unpredictable fashion. Figure 1.3 (opposite) shows one attempt to capture the complex micro-ecology of the East Village.

Diversity in Social Space

Just as physical space is fragmented – block by block, building by building, even apartment by apartment[13] – into subunits which, while they recur throughout the fabric of the neighborhood, are not necessarily contiguous, so the social space of the East Village is fragmented, subgroup by subgroup, differentiated by age, ethnicity, income, values, and lifestyles. These differences create interwoven networks of association, identity, and loyalty that criss-cross through physical space and that yield a new type of neighborhood in which mutual tolerance and careful attention to social, physical, and temporal boundaries are required if harmony is to prevail. Such a neighborhood does not have an automatic set of consensual goals. What unanimity and organization are achieved must be hammered out in a complex process of conflict and negotiation. It is this, more than any other fact, that makes the East Village the site of 'contested turf.'

The Lower East Side of course is not one neighborhood but many, a fact that might easily be predicted from its large size. The total population

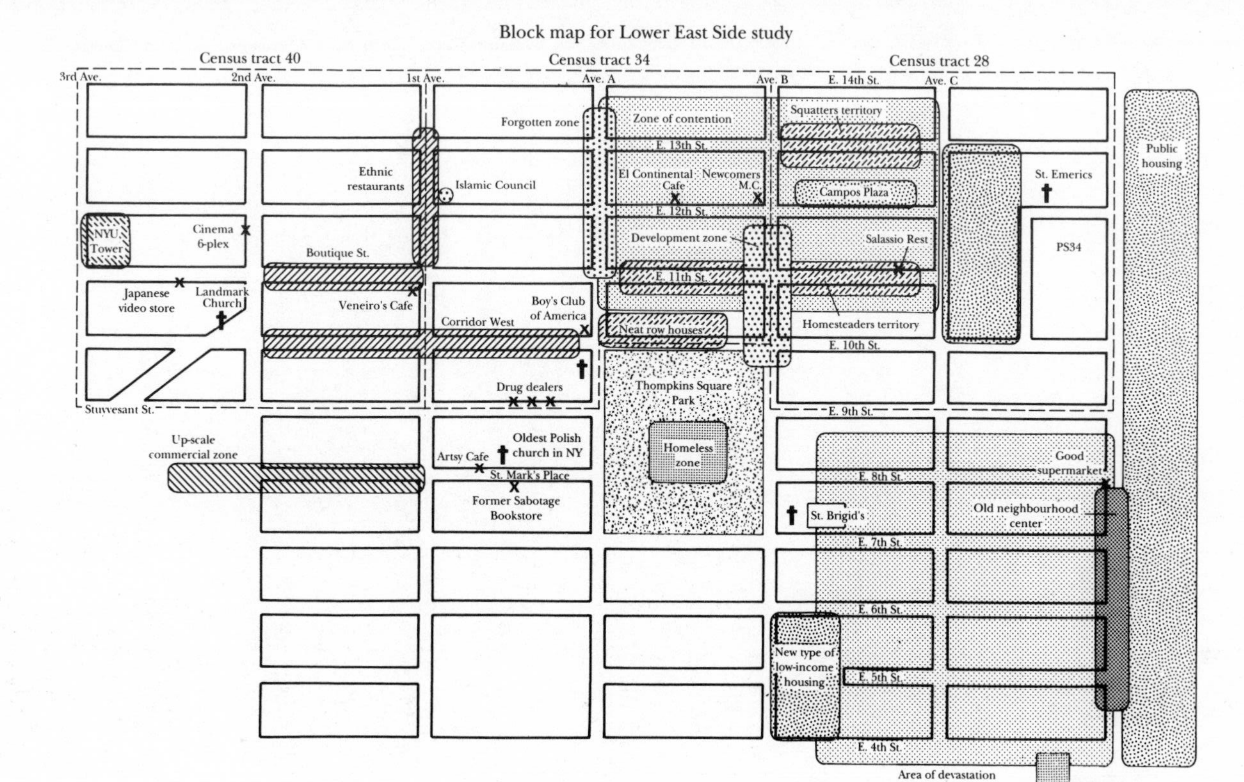

Figure 1.3 Impressionistic sketch of blocks around Tompkins Square Park
Source: Courtesy of Hugh Bareiss

living in Community District 3 in 1980 was equivalent to that of a relatively large American 'city': some 154,848 persons residing in 66,780 dwelling units. This represented a slight decline from the preceding census year, thus continuing a trend of 'deconcentration' that had been noted for the area ever since the 1920s but which was dramatically intensified by the widescale destruction of the housing stock through abandonment in the late 1960s and the disinvestment years of the 1970s.

Between 1980 and 1990, however, that long-term trend was modestly reversed. By 1990, the total population of the zone had risen by 4.3 percent to 161,617. In contrast to the 66,780 dwelling units in the district in 1980, there were 68,849 dwelling units by 1990.[14] Such growth, however, was largely confined to Chinatown and its expansion. It did not take place within the smaller area of the East Village, bounded by Fourteenth and Houston Streets and by Fourth Avenue–Bowery and the East River.

The total population of the East Village in 1990 was 64,000 persons, only slightly more than the approximately 63,000 who had lived there ten years earlier. If indeed the neighborhood was being 'rebuilt,' there was little evidence of repopulation, since the gain was less than 2 percent during the ten year interval. Population seems to have stabilized at this new level, substantially below what it had been during the heyday of foreign immigration. If the zone no longer teems with 'the masses' associated with the late nineteenth century, there are good reasons. At the turn of the century, the Lower East Side contained the densest concentration of humans in the world. According to an exhaustive survey of tenement houses made in New York in 1902–3, Wards 11 and 17 (which, combined, included almost exactly the same area we now call the East Village) housed a remarkable 204,000 persons, which was up 60 percent from the 128,020 persons who had lived there forty years earlier.[15] Only a small amount of the decline to the present can be attributed to the obvious destruction of the area's housing stock, most evident in the 'demilitarized bombed-out zone' between Avenues C and D. Most was due to a gradual dispersion and thinning out of the immigrants from this, their prime 'port of entry' into the country and the city.

Today's 64,000 residents, however, are far from constituting a homogeneous social group. As we have seen in our physical description, the East Village is divided into quite distinctive zones, the most specialized and isolated of which are the public housing projects at the eastern edge. Figure 1.4 shows the boundaries and identifying numbers of the 13 census tracts (and their constitutive census blocks) north of Houston that made up the East Village in 1990.[16] This map should be read in conjunction with Figure 1.5, which shows the locations of subsidized housing.

The two census tracts at the extreme east (numbers 20 and 24) contain large public housing projects. Both apparently lost population between

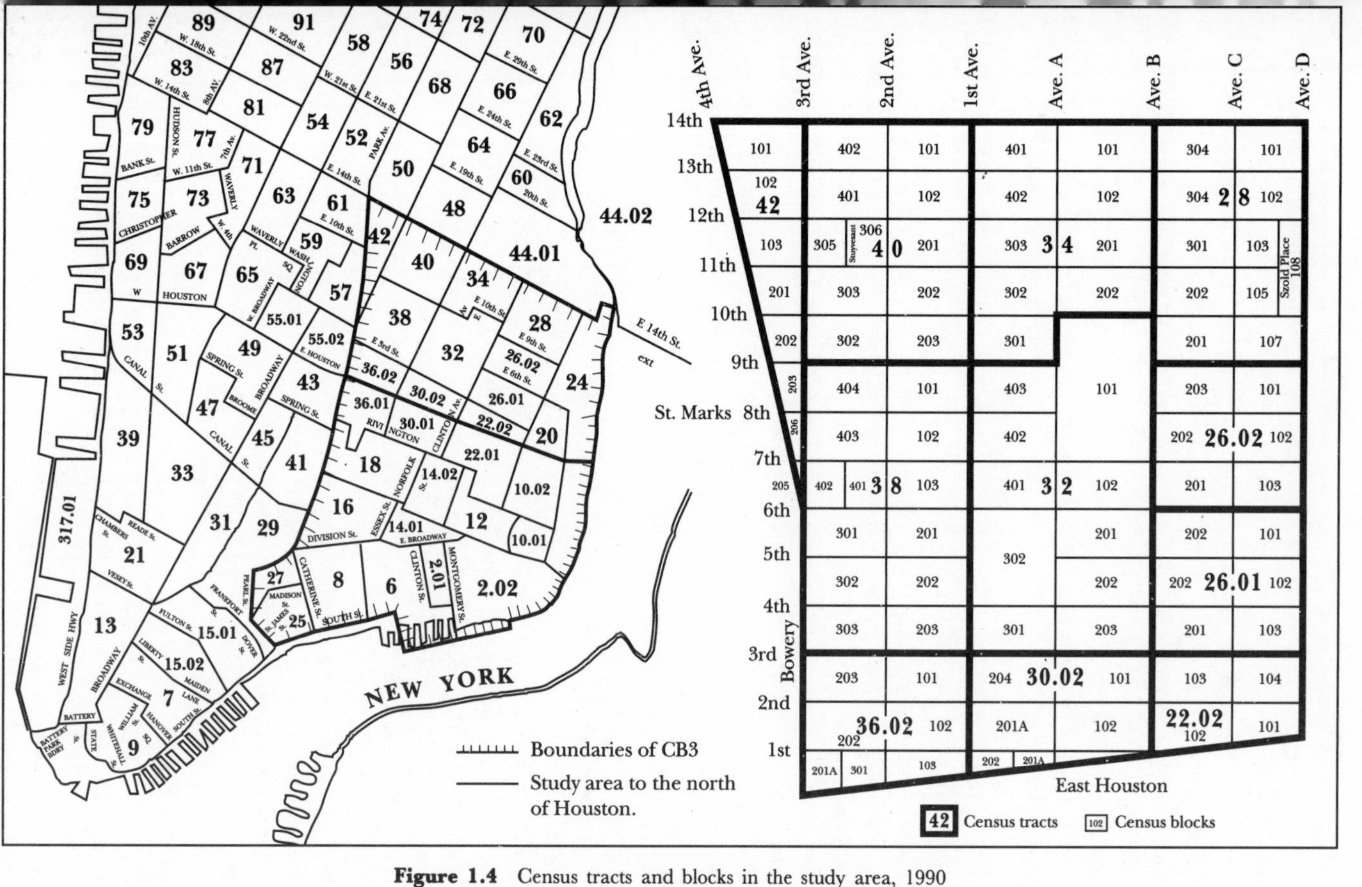

Figure 1.4 Census tracts and blocks in the study area, 1990

Numbers refer to tract identities in the US censuses of 1980 and 1990. These correspond to data in tables 1.1, 1.2, and 1.3.

Source: Computer-generated map from the US Census of 1990

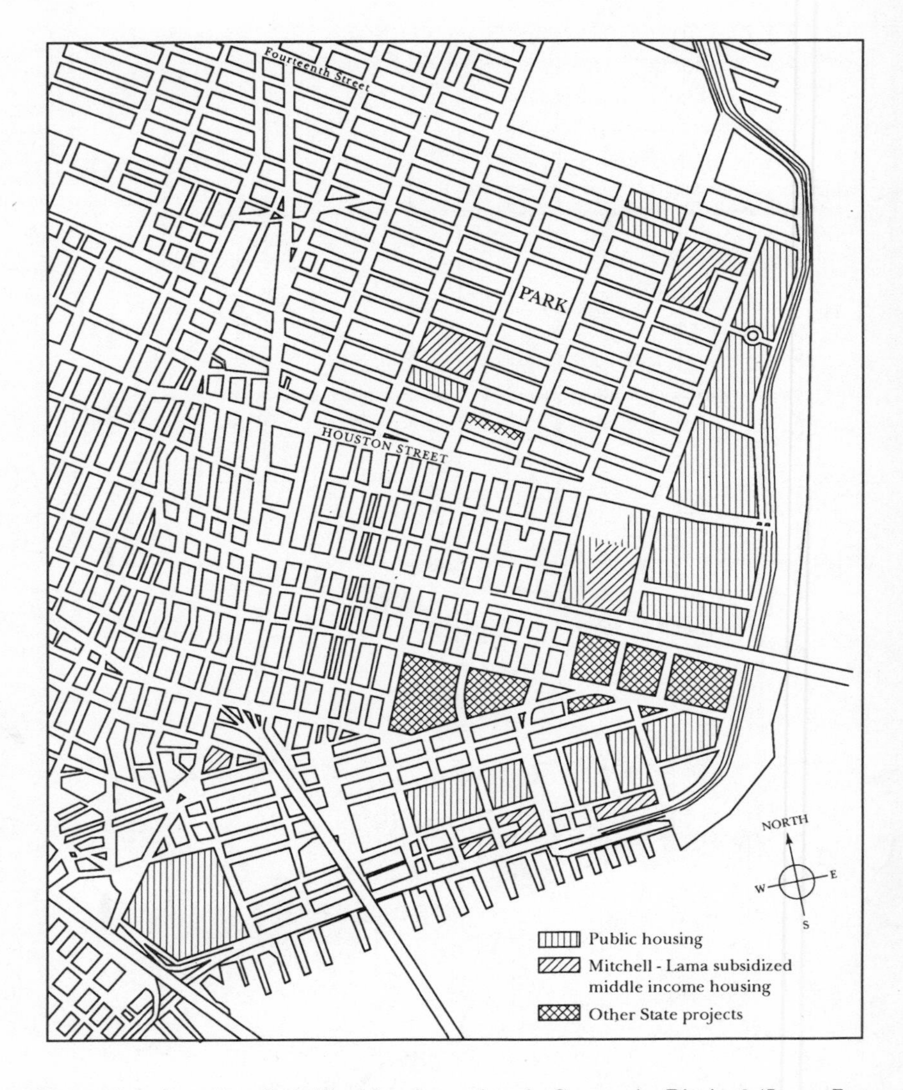

Figure 1.5 Location of subsidized housing projects in Community District 3 (Lower East Side) by type of subsidy: low-income public housing; middle-income Mitchell-Lama; and subsidized state projects

1980 and 1990, their combined totals decreasing from 12,810 to 11,706 residents in the decade. Such a decline is suspect, however, since it is widely acknowledged that in the economic retrenchment period of the late 1980s, New York City housing projects actually received a substantial number of 'illegal' residents, mostly unauthorized family members doubling up with legal residents. Since such long-term guests are not permitted and their presence, if known, could constitute grounds for eviction, it is extremely unlikely that they would have been reported in the census of 1990. In any case, since our study focused chiefly on the non-project population of the East Village, such discrepancies need not concern us.

Excluding the project population, we find that the population in the remaining census tracts rose slightly, from 50,232 in 1980 to 52,300 in 1990, an increase of about 4 percent in the decade.[17] This increase, however, was not distributed evenly throughout the various parts of the non- project East Village, as can be seen from table 1.1. In fact, the gentrifying westernmost stratum reported very little net change in the decade; the middle stratum, now beginning a more intense phase of gentrification, actually lost population in the period; in contrast, the most destroyed eastern stratum, which between 1970 and 1980 had lost over half of its housing stock and population, actually began to regain population, albeit on a very low base.

Table 1.1 Population change, 1980–1990, in the East Village, by strata (west to east, excluding projects)

Western stratum		*Middle stratum*		*Eastern stratum*	
1980 Population		1980 Population		1980 Population	
Tract 38	8,665	Tract 34	6,588	Tract 28	5,402
Tract 40	7,144	Tract 32	8,369	Tract 26.02	1,876
Tract 36.02	3,437	Tract 30.02	2,602	Tract 26.01	2,721
Tract 42	2,144			Tract 22.02	1,284
Total	21,390	*Total*	17,559	*Total*	11,284
1990 Population		1990 Population		1990 Population	
Tract 38	8,395	Tract 34	6,312	Tract 28	6,827
Tract 40	8,450	Tract 32	7,832	Tract 26.02	2,725
Tract 36.02	2,458	Tract 30.02	2,781	Tract 26.01	2,786
Tract 42	2,510			Tract 22.02	1,224
Total	21,813	*Total*	16,925	*Total*	13,562
% change	+ 0.2	% change	– 3.6	% change	+ 20%

Source: US Census by blocks and tracts. Our reorganization and computations

More important than the change in absolute numbers, however, was the change in population composition. Among the more noteworthy changes since 1980 have been: a decline, outside the projects, of minorities (blacks and Latinos);[18] a slight increase in the 'white' and Asian populations; a not-unrelated decline in families with children; and a compensatory increase in the proportion of young adults. The shift away from

Table 1.2 Percentage of residents in East Village census tracts who were listed as white in 1980 and 1990, by strata (west to east, including projects)

	Western stratum		*Middle stratum*		*Eastern stratum*		*Public housing*	
	1980	*1990*	*1980*	*1990*	*1980*	*1990*	*1980*	*1990*
Tract 38	76	70[a]						
Tract 40	73	71						
Tract 36.02	51	56						
Tract 42	84	86						
Total	*72*	*76*						
Tract 30.02			63	57				
Tract 32			81	74				
Tract 34			63	56				
Total			*72*	*75*				
Tract 28					45	28		
Tract 26.02					56	47		
Tract 26.01					40	17		
Tract 22.02					39	35		
Total					*45*	*45*		
Public Housing								
Tract 20							30	24
Tract 24							35	24
Total							*32*	*24*

[a] Difference is made up by increase in Asian population.

Source: US Censuses. Data for 1990 are as of February 1991; the city requested a 'correction' for undercount but that request was rejected

families can be seen in the marked drop in the number of residents who were under 18 years of age – from 37,682 in 1980 to 32,252 in 1990.

In all of Community District 3, the non-Hispanic white population remained virtually constant, decreasing by only 279 persons between 1980 and 1990. In both years, non-Hispanic whites constituted less than 30 percent of the total population. In contrast, black non-Hispanics and the population of Hispanic origin both declined significantly during the decade, dropping by 9.63 and 7.89 percent respectively. As might be expected from the earlier descriptions of the area, their loss was more than made up for by a growth in the Asian population of the portion of burgeoning Chinatown that falls within District 3. Between 1980 and 1990, the population classified as non-Hispanic Asian and Pacific Islander increased from about 35,000 to close to 48,000, or by 37 percent. In the East Village, the changes were in the same directions, but far less dramatic in magnitude.

Table 1.3 Percentage of Hispanic[a] residents in East Village census tracts in 1980 and 1990, by strata (west to east, including projects)

	Western stratum		*Middle stratum*		*Eastern stratum*		*Public housing*	
	1980	*1990*	*1980*	*1990*	*1980*	*1990*	*1980*	*1990*[b]
Tract 38	13	12						
Tract 40	22	12						
Tract 36.02	21	20						
Tract 42	8	6						
Total	*13*	*12*						
Tract 30.02			29	26				
Tract 32			16	12				
Tract 34			45	29				
Total			*28*	*21*				
Tract 28					47	47		
Tract 26.02					58	35		
Tract 26.01					73	60		
Tract 22.02					72	45		
Total					*58*	*47*		
Tract 20							77	81
Tract 24							78	79
Total							*78*	*80*

[a] While the definitions changed between the two census dates and therefore these figures are not entirely comparable, they can be used for comparative purposes when looking at individual census tracts. Note that the declines are consistent with what we know to have been an overall reduction in the Latino population of the East Village in the past decade. The decline is also consistent with the overall decline of Hispanics in Community District 3 between 1980 and 1990.

[b] Because Hispanics can be either black or white, this figure underestimates the extent to which the projects are exclusively 'minority,' just as the figures in table 1.2 overestimate the number of non-minority residents. In actual fact, by 1990, there were only 86 non-Hispanic whites in tract 20 and only 79 in tract 24. Therefore, out of a combined resident population in the projects of some 11,700 in 1990, only 1 percent could be classified as 'non-minority' white. Most persons identified as Hispanics in the East Village are of Puerto Rican origin.

Source: Our computations from US census data

But such gross figures conceal more than they reveal, since the neighborhood is riven by more than age, race, and ethnicity. Census data cannot tell us much about these other sources of diversity, since whether one wears one's hair in a duck tail, a pony tail, in yellow and green spikes, or has shaved it off entirely is not a matter of census interest. And whether one has purchased a gentrified co-op apartment, lives rent free in a squat or on a park bench, or has made some other imaginative housing arrangement is not clear from census data.[19]

The East Village contains one of the most diversely constituted populations in the city, in part because newer groups have entered the zone without ever completely displacing those who came before them. To the earlier somewhat proletarian mix of older white ethnics (chiefly eastern European and Italian) and newer and younger African-Americans and Latinos (the former concentrated on the west side of Tompkins Square Park, the latter two largely concentrated on the east and southeast fringes) had been added, in the 1960s, members of the so-called counter-culture, some of whom have remained on, albeit now a quarter of a century older. In the 1970s, they were joined by 'pioneering' artists and cost-cutting adventurous students, driven by rising rents from the nearby 'Bohemian' districts of Greenwich Village and then even from SoHo. Old age, departures, and mounting mortality gradually reduced the size of the white ethnic population on the west (largely but not exclusively Italian and Ukrainian), while shifts in the patterns of net migration from Puerto Rico, combined with the effects of abandonment and arson, have been decimating the formerly vital Latino community of Loisaida. Pockets of Puerto Ricans, now joined by other Spanish speakers of diverse origin, remain on side streets that have not yet felt the gentrifier's hand, but their days seem numbered. A newer group of professional and semi-professional residents, able to pay much higher prices for their housing, began to gravitate to the area during the 1980s, attracted by the limited gentrification that was occurring. These newcomers reinforced the middle-class population that, up to then, had been pretty much confined to elite town houses and solid apartment buildings on a few of the side streets north and west of the park.

But such conventional sociological categories cannot capture the true level of diversity in the neighborhood, a diversity that often makes next-door neighbors of Hell's Angels (easily found by their massed motorbikes outside); Rastafarians, punks, and Krishnas (recognizable by their distinctive hair styles, *inter alia*); worker priests and nuns (both presentday and former) and drug dealers and users; runaway teenagers in rebellion and thrown-away homeless unemployed men camping in the park and on empty lots; ideological squatters fighting the capitalist cash nexus and undocumented aliens hiding from the INS; and the largely unsung but numerous 'ordinary' people who find affordable housing to rent or to homestead in, and who just like the 'feel' of the neighborhood.

All of this should yield a classic case of the anomie and social disorganization that standard urban sociological theories predict. And yet, this incredible diversity of population and array of lifestyles – which generate truly divergent interests and often conflicting goals for the neighborhood – has not prevented residents from forming a common identification with and even a special loyalty to the area. That loyalty, however, is never bland or apathetic. Throughout history, it has led to a vigorous engagement in struggles over the area's future. At the present time, the struggle concentrates on the issue of gentrification (how much, by whom and for whose benefit), but contained within that simple economic term are attitudes and values that are far from exclusively monetary, as we shall see.

If the test of an interesting city is that it juxaposes in somewhat unpredictable fashion enough different mini-cities and micro-neighborhoods to make any walk interesting and surprising, then New York must be the most interesting city in the nation, if not the world. And applying that same test to Lower Manhattan and especially its east side, then that area is near the top of any list of New York's quintessentially 'urban' neighborhoods, even though it lacks the skyscrapers and glitz that most visitors associate with the city.

But is this district a 'neighborhood' in the way we traditionally define it, namely, a distinctive physical space set off from adjacent spaces and containing a group of residents who have enough in common to identify with the place and one another and who share enough vision of their interests and the future to reach a common voice and work for common goals? Here our answer must be more equivocal. Despite a nomenclature that employs the term 'village,' this is no 'urban village,' as that term has come to be used in urban sociology. Its residents are not bound together by preexistent 'primordial' ties that our theories of community suggest must exist, if a neighborhood is to constitute a socially coherent community seeking collective ends. They are bound together neither by dominant shared identities of race, class, or ethnicity (as a 'traditional' community is defined) nor even by affinities and identities of choice that might yield a more 'modern' type of community or neighborhood based upon common lifestyles.

Instead, this is a neighborhood whose unity has been forged in contest. In one of his most prescient works, the nineteenth-century German philosopher-cum-sociologist Georg Simmel explored the paradoxical effects of conflict, arguing that it bound its participants together as strongly as more positive interactions; its true antithesis was not lack of conflict but indifference.[20] Whatever East Villagers are, they are not indifferent either to one another or to the fate of their neighborhood. Georg Simmel would have found a prime example of his thesis in the East Village. In part I we turn to the historical background of the Lower East Side, the East Village, and its 'heart,' Tompkins Square Park, demonstrating that the bonds, loyalties, and conflicts of today have deep roots. They have always characterized this unique area.

NOTES

1 Even though I had stumbled on this area so accidentally and early, I had absolutely no question in my mind that this would be the field site for the ethnographic study I intended to undertake in New York – both for its own sake and as a way of training graduate students at the New School in urban research methods. In 1988, the Sloan Foundation provided a grant that helped establish REALM, an urban research center focusing on Lower Manhattan. Graduate students in a number of my courses became involved in this research, and some began doctoral dissertations on specific aspects of the neighborhood. Our collaboration over the years has greatly enriched and invigorated our work.

2 See Janet Abu-Lughod, 'The East Village of Manhattan: New Methods to Study Diversified Urban Neighborhoods,' presented to the American Sociological Association's Community Section, August 1990.

3 The much discussed Second Avenue line, if and when it is ever replaced, will have the dramatic effect of reintegrating this area into the rapid-transit network of the city. The opening of such a line may possibly seal the fate of the Lower East Side as a low-rent district.

4 The most recent of these was promulgated in the late 1960s. See Harry Schwartz, assisted by Peter Abeles, *Planning for the Lower East Side* (New York: Praeger, 1973). This is a reissue of *Forging a Future for the Lower East Side*, a plan prepared by Abeles, Schwartz and Associates for the City of New York, dated December 1970.

5 Community boards were institutionalized throughout the five boroughs by the Charter Reform of 1976, replacing community planning boards. They are intended to represent various interests within the neighborhood. Each consists of 50 members, half appointed by the mayor and half appointed by the area's elected representative on the City Council. Boards are encouraged to review all proposals for land use changes but have only advisory power. Many boards are quite active. They elect their own officers, hold frequent public meetings to hear residents' views, and divide themselves into working committees that focus on particular issues. Each community board is served by an administrator paid by the city. Working together with the council member, the board is assumed to 'speak for' the neighborhood and to represent its views to various city agencies. The community board of District 3 has been particularly active in recent years.

6 Jerome Weidman, *Fourth Street East* (New York: Pinnacle Books, 1970). He describes the panic that both he *and his teacher* experienced when they 'crossed' the barrier, going to Washington Irving High School at Seventeenth Street where he was to participate in a debating contest.

7 For example, my interview with L., an Italian man in his late sixties who always lived in the area and has been associated with the local Boys' Club for half a century.

8 See unpublished paper by Abby Scher, 1988, for information on location and prices of buildings purchased by persons with Chinese surnames. See also Jan

Lin, 'Capital and Community in Urban Change: Chinatown, New York City,' doctoral dissertation, New School for Social Research, 1992.

9 How long this stable area can resist the incursions of gentrification from the north and Chinatown's expansion from the south is a moot question.

10 The Gas-House district was so named because it abutted the plant which provided gas for the lights of Lower Manhattan. That plant is gone, superseded by the gigantic electric generating station of Con Edison, which occupies both sides of the roadway between Stuyvesant Town and the East River Drive.

11 After the unannounced eviction of the homeless population from Tompkins Square Park on 3 June 1991, and the closing of the park for renovations, Father Kuhn et al. brought a class-action suit against the city for its failure to study the environmental impact of its arbitrary action on the neighborhood. This author filed an *amicus curiae* deposition in connection with this suit.

12 Lawrence Veiller, 'Tenement House Reform in New York City,' in Robert DeForest and Lawrence Veiller, eds., *The Tenement House Problem* (originally issued in 1903 by the Macmillan Company; reprinted New York: Arno Press and the New York Times, 1970), Vol. 1, p. 194.

13 Because of the uneven way that rent control and rent stabilization laws work in New York City, it is not uncommon to find that the rents on identical apartments within the same building may range quite widely. The lowest rents are paid by residents who occupied their apartments when rent control was first introduced during World War II. Somewhat higher rents are paid by occupants of apartments where the turnover has been minimal and therefore, where rent stabilization laws have permitted only modest and gradual increases. Higher rents are paid when turnover has been frequent, since upward adjustments are permitted when new tenants move in. The highest rents are paid for apartments that have been held empty (warehoused) and then partially 'upgraded,' since this removes them from control. (See table 8.6.)

14 1990 census PL94–171, reported February 1991 and distributed by the Population Division of the New York Department of City Planning.

15 See Lawrence Veiller, 'A Statistical Study of New York's Tenement Houses,' pp. 191–240 in DeForest and Veiller, eds. *The Tenement House Problem* (1903), data taken from Vol. 1, pp. 202–3, 206.

16 Data from the census are collated by city blocks, not the best unit of homogeneity (block faces would be more realistic), and adjacent blocks are grouped into census tracts. The map of the census tracts in 1990 is presented as figure 1.4.

17 It is very likely that the population of the East Village has been undercounted in the 1990 census, since squatters, undocumented aliens, the homeless, persons illiterate in English, runaway youths, and persons ideologically opposed to government (the self-styled anarchists), all of whom are found in the East Village, are very unlikely to have been counted. It is hard to tell, however, whether the undercount was greater in 1990 than in 1980; we have therefore not attempted to adjust the figures in either year.

18 It is not possible, because of the way the census dealt with Hispanics and race in 1980 and its shift to a more reasonable method of reporting in 1990, to directly compare data on Hispanics for the two censuses.

19 At the time this was written, the census department had not yet released housing tenure information by census block and tract. But even if these data had been available, they could not have provided all the information needed.

20 Georg Simmel, 'Conflict,' in *Conflict and the Web of Group Affiliations*, ed. and trans. by Kurt Wolff and Reinhard Bendix (Glencoe, IL: Free Press, 1955).

Part I

The Past Is Still There

2

The Changing Economy of the Lower East Side

Jan Chien Lin

The classic images that spring to mind when we consider the economic history of Manhattan's Lower East Side are dense rookeries of sweatshops, streets congested with noisy hawkers, pushcart peddlers, and entrepreneurial shop owners, eking out meager existences. Another picture is of a militant immigrant proletariat, agitating for humane wages and working conditions. Still another less popularized picture is of a secretive underground economy of contraband and gang activity, prostitution, and associated 'cheap amusements.' The one image of the Lower East Side one does not have is unemployment, little economic activity, or a population only tenuously linked to the city's economy. And yet, all of these are more or less persistent characteristics of the area. This is all the more remarkable, given the revolutionary changes in the area's functions – from the mercantile period to the industrial age to the present 'postindustrial' period. This chapter traces these changes.

The Mercantile Period: The Rise of New York Port and the East Side Shipyards

New York City's earliest functions were categorically mercantile. After its cession to the English in the latter part of seventeenth century, the fur-trade interests of the initial Dutch colonists of Nieuw Amsterdam gradually gave way to a more diverse network of commodity exchanges linked with the British Empire's 'triangular' Atlantic trade. The entrepôt shipped flour, biscuit, bread, barreled meats, and timber to the Atlantic and Caribbean Islands (Bermuda and the Bahamas), in return for sugar, dyewood, slaves, Spanish coin, and English bills of exchange. New York shippers then traded these goods, as well as agricultural produce from the mid-Atlantic colonies, in New England harbors, bringing back fish, dairy products, rum, and English and European imports which were, in turn, sold locally or re-exported to southern colonies and the mid-Atlantic islands.

Although the trans-Atlantic trade had primarily been handled through Boston throughout the 1700s,[1] by the early 1800s New York City had become the premier port on the eastern seaboard. Port facilities were initially located on the East River side of Manhattan, which was better sheltered from winter gales, tides, and floating ice than the Hudson River shore; the earliest docks were built around present-day South Street. The South Street docks employed an itinerant population of sailors, longshoremen, carters, porters, and casual laborers. Artisans were engaged in more skilled trades such as ship carpentry, caulking, rigging, ropemaking, and sailmaking, while merchants, importers, and dry goods dealers employed many clerks.[2] In 1810, the city's major proto-industries were sugar refining, tanning and leather processing, and tobacco milling. Some of the earliest innovations in steam power were made by mechanics of the sugar plants.[3] Most goods, however, were made by craftsmen or through household production. Shipbuilding was just beginning to emerge as the major industry of the mercantile era. The first shipyard was established in 1701 on Dover Street and by 1740 there were two more in the vicinity. When the city expanded northwards, the shipyard district was relocated to Corlears Hook by 1805, especially where the intertidal flats were filled in around an island located in the vicinity of Houston and Fourth Streets, east of Avenue D. The first steamboat, the *Clermont*, was built there in 1805 by Robert Fulton.[4] By 1824, 64 ships were launched by 14 shipyards on the mile of East River shoreline extending north from South Street.[5]

Also in 1824 was the chartering to shipbuilders Steers and Thomas and the newly created Eleventh Ward Bank (later the Dry-Dock Bank), of a dry dock at the foot of Tenth Street and the river. The country's first ship-railway was completed there in 1826, first powered by horses and later by a steam engine.[6] The shipyards relied initially on the demand for trans-Atlantic trade and passenger vessels. The opening of Chinese ports and the gold discoveries in Australia and California in the 1840s brought orders for rapid deep-ocean clippers for the Pacific Ocean. The Smith and Dimon Shipyard at Fourth Street was famed for its clipper engineering, including the *Rainbow* (a China clipper) and the *Sea Witch* (which broke many speed records).[7] The real heyday of New York City shipbuilding was 1849 to 1855 as hundreds of orders for ships and barks, brigs, schooners, steamboats, and warships came in.

A number of industries linked to shipbuilding agglomerated nearby, including iron works and machine shops, coppersmiths and brassfounders, sawmills, boat builders, and ship suppliers. The iron works were the largest employers in the city. The Novelty Works and the Morgan Works each employed over 900 workers, producing steamship engines, bed plates, locomotives, mill presses, and gearing boilers. Other major industries included sugar refining, brewing and distilling, cabinetmaking, metalsmithing, and such labor-intensive activities as leathermaking and clothing production, mainly located in the southern wards near City Hall. Employees in the more capital-intensive industries such as shipbuilding, sugar refining, and brewing were predominantly men, whereas the leather and clothing industries employed men and women in more equal proportions.[8]

As the city's economy expanded, formerly residential areas near the City Hall and Wall Street area were converted to commercial uses. Merchants, attorneys, and bankers began to move uptown to newly established fashionable areas at Washington, Union, and Stuyvesant Squares, leaving the former 'silk stocking' district of East Broadway and Chatham Square to newer migrants. Their abandoned mansions were converted into multi-unit dwellings and any empty lots were in-filled with tenement buildings.[9] The 'Collect,' a fresh water pond at Foley Square, which had become polluted by industry and refuse, was drained in 1805 via a 40-foot-wide canal which emptied into the Hudson River; the canal was filled and paved in 1820, resulting in the present-day Canal Street.[10]

As land became more valuable in the expanding city, some owners neglected their residential properties on the assumption that they would be torn down and replaced by more profitable commercial buildings. These dilapidated structures served the poorest migrants, and the area around the filled-in Collect Pond and Five Points became the main area of Irish settlement by mid-century.[11] Settling farther north in the Rivington-Canal-Elizabeth Street area, German immigrants had established a *Kleindeutschland* as early as the 1830s. In the 1840s and 1850s, employment opportunities in the growing shipyards drew them even farther north to the area currently known as the 'East Village.'[12] Highly skilled working-class immigrants occupied this area, where 1,200 'new-style' so called 'Old-Law' tenement buildings were rapidly erected between 1846 and 1850, replacing the ramshackle wooden shacks in the blocks just west of the shipyards.[13] (See chapter 3.)

The skilled German mechanics and carpenters brought their socialist ideals and trade unionism with them. Their organizing efforts resulted in reducing the 15-hour day to 10. A Mechanics Bell, erected in 1831 in the vicinity of Rivington and Stanton Streets, rang the hours of the more humane 10-hour day.[14] Occupational solidarities born at the workplace were reinforced in the neighborhood when workers met in the after-work saloons. These saloons were 'switchboards' of news in times of industrial and political dispute and also defensive 'resources for class survival' against the 'middle-class moral interventions' of temperance.[15]

In addition to the specialized artisans, the shipyards and docks also employed a shifting army of semi-skilled craftsmen and laborers. In the loading docks south of Corlears Hook and around South Street, stevedores and longshoremen (many of them Irish) staged a successful strike for higher wages in 1836. A more dramatic episode in 1852 pitted 'turnouts' against non-strikers and municipal police in a mêlée in which stevedores used their cotton hooks as defensive weaponry.[16] There were actions in other industries; in 1850, some 900 tailors struck for higher wages and regulatory price-setting, with the support of German trade unions.[17]

The waterfront also provided opportunities for piracy by 'wharf rats,' night-time thieves who operated from rowboats in gangs of three or four, plundering cargo boats and steamships on both the East and Hudson Rivers. The 'Daybreak Boys' were renowned on the East River docks in the 1850s and 1860s.[18] Stolen goods were sold to 'fences' and pawnshops around Chatham Square and along the Bowery, with jewelry, silverware, and fine cloth being the most sought-after items.[19]

Lower East Side gang activity originated in the early 1800s in the Chatham Square vicinity, which was formerly called 'Five Points' (being at the intersection of five streets). An immense brewery there was converted to a lodging house in 1837, and came to be populated by up to 1,000 prostitutes, vagrants, and criminals in a maze of rooms and cellars. The area was branded a 'den of thieves,' a 'rabbit warren' of cheap amusement and crime.[20] Five Points gangs such as the Roach Guards, Chichesters, Plug Uglies, Shirt Tails, and Dead Rabbits fought with an assortment of gangs from the Bowery (usually lumped together as the 'Bowery Boys'). The activities of these gangs stemmed more from protection of neighborhood turf (they usually congregated around a local greengrocer) than from any economic motives. Tammany Hall politicians eventually made use of them, giving them meeting and hiding places in exchange for assistance in vote currying.[21]

By the early 1800s, the Bowery, especially in its lower reaches near Canal Street, had become a lower-class entertainment thoroughfare, peppered with an assortment of pawnshops, cheap hotels, dance houses, concert saloons, and bawdy theaters. The clientele was mainly Irish and German, but a range of Spanish, Portuguese, French, Italian, Chinese, and Mexican visitors joined in the revelry. As described by McCabe: 'They are all "of the people." There is no aristocracy in the Bowery. The Latin Quarter is not more free of restraint.'[22] Streetwalkers operated nearby, in the quieter blocks surrounding lower Broadway and lower Fifth Avenue.[23] Casual prostitution was sometimes required for survival for single women, since the female labor market provided inadequate wages.[24] Houses of prostitution could also be found in the waterfront area.

The early 1850s had been a time of great economic prosperity; the shipbuilding industry was thriving and street life on the Bowery had great energy. A downturn in the economy started in 1854, however, compounded by a harsh winter.[25] The gold rush ended in that same year, resulting in a precipitous drop in orders for clippers. In any case, iron-hulled vessels (a specialty of British shipbuilders) were becoming the standard for deep ocean shipping. The East River wood-hull shipyards revived slightly on repair work during the Civil War, but the demand for new wooden-hulled ships never recovered.[26] The East River was also declining as a docking area. The opening of the Erie Canal in 1825 and the growing use of larger-hulled ships and steamboats by the 1840s favored relocation to the larger Hudson River wharves. Furthermore, continental rail lines generally terminated on the Jersey shore, where freight was transshipped by tug and barge to western piers. The only line to run into Manhattan, the Hudson River Railroad, established a terminus on the west side in 1846. The East River docks were reduced to serving as a landing point only for smaller sailing ships and grain barges.

THE INDUSTRIAL ERA: GARMENT PRODUCTION AND IMMIGRANT LABOR

New York City's role as a seaport and commercial emporium persisted past the Civil War, but the decline of shipping and shipbuilding on the Lower East Side was symptomatic of wider changes in the metropolitan economy as US cities changed from mercantile to industrial functions. Indeed, by 1900 New York's metropolitan area held 11 percent of the nation's manufacturing workers while the 16 largest cities in the US employed one-third.[27] Between 1860 and 1900 employment in manufacturing grew by 325 percent in Manhattan, while population rose only by 127 percent.[28] The rise of manufacturing was linked with the growing supply of immigrant labor, particularly in the garment trade.

Garments, iron working, printing and publishing were Manhattan's major industries in the 1860 to 1900 period (see table 2.1). Printing and publishing establishments were concentrated primarily south of City Hall, well outside the boundaries of the Lower East Side, but many Lower East Side immigrants set type and ran the presses of the newspapers, journals, and publishers, as well as labored in the workshops of lithographers, engravers, and bookbinders. Iron manufacturers clustered north of City

Table 2.1 Growth of the three principal manufacturers in Manhattan, 1860–1900

	1860	*1880*	*1900*
Clothing			
No. of establishments	582	1,380	7,757
Labor force employed	29,443	70,411	107,757
Value of total product	$27,203,898	$82,259,756	$292,985,229
Iron manufacture			
No. of establishments	539	1,627	3,814
Labor force employed	10,591	25,058	40,836
Value of total product	$14,721,099	$43,950,217	$94,204,259
Printing and publishing			
No. of establishments	306	782	1,893
Labor force employed	7,454	15,720	34,283
Value of total product	$12,587,369	$31,856,385	$95,312,380

Source: Patricia E. Malon. 'The Growth of Manufacturing in Manhattan, 1860–1900: An Analysis of Factoral Changes and Urban Structure' (New York: Columbia University, doctoral dissertation, 1981), p. 394.

Hall along both shorelines, especially at the East River edge near the shipyards. Initially stimulated by the shipyards, the iron works industry diversified beyond shipping. Whereas ship engine and boiler manufacture and repair had been their mainstays during the mercantile era, the iron foundries and machine shops shifted production to a range of equipment for other industries (including construction and household products). Heavy items included architectural and ornamental ironwork such as stairs, railings, structural bars, fire-escapes and cast-iron fronts for loft buildings, conveyances, printing presses, sugar molds, and stoves.[29] Lightweight products included sewing machines, hardware, tools and instruments, gas meters, plumbing fixtures, and household appliances.[30]

During the industrial era, however, garment production became the economic locomotive of the Lower East Side. Much more labor intensive than publishing or iron working, the garment industry's growth stemmed from the Lower East Side's status as a portal and residential enclave for immigrant labor. In reciprocal fashion, the growth of the industry encouraged more immigration into the district. Labor comprises nearly 30 percent of production costs in garment manufacture, as compared with 10 percent in manufacturing as a whole.[31] Any tendencies towards technological innovation and fixed capital expenditures are counteracted by the availability of low-wage labor, since sewing machines remain the chief equipment of production. Fluctuations in demand discourage mass production technology and product standardization, particularly in the women's and children's apparel segments, which are generally riskier because product success is more dependent on the vagaries of seasonal fashion changes. A segmentary structure in the industry is traditional to hedge against the risks of changing demand.

In garment production the typical process is broken down by a division of labor into 'jobbers' who do design, marketing, and textile purchase and cutting, and 'contractors,' typically immigrant firms who do the actual work of assembling garments. The costs of providing a production space, sewing machines and other equipment, and of hiring and paying the workforce are thus borne by the contractor. Start-up costs for such concerns are not high, and competition among contractors for 'bundles' from jobbers can be quite fierce. Jobbers may split piece-clothing work into section-work. They can open up the bidding process to more contractors by the creation of such detail processes. Greater competition for work among contractors exercises a downward pressure on the wages they can pay employees. Workers effectively 'sweat out' the differential between one bid and another. Contractors also cut corners on working conditions, so that sweatshop workers endure poor lighting, fire and safety hazards, poor job security and pay. Since sweatshop owners rely on ethnic ties and kin networks to recruit workers, their profit levels depend on their 'self-exploitation' of other members of their ethnic community.

Garment workers are mainly women, some argue because they have nimble fingers, patience, and an eye to detail. More significantly, however, women's subordinate position in the labor force means they must accept low-wage jobs rejected by men.[32] They can also be the target of the employers' strategy of extending the labor process to the home as a way to increase total working hours. Homework may be a necessity for the women themselves since they bear the brunt of child-rearing and housekeeping obligations, responsibilities which are reproduced by patriarchal ideology and wage discrimination in the labor market. Immigrant women are especially prone to engage in homework if they lack the English-language skills required for factory work.

Household production and custom-made tailoring satisfied most clothing demand in early New York City. Demand for men's work clothing, particularly for seamen and southern slaves in the early nineteenth century, created the initial market conditions for a ready-made garment industry. On the supply-side, a range of cotton, woolen, and silk fiber textile dealers agglomerated in lower Manhattan with the dumping of British 'dry goods' after the War of 1812. The attics and backrooms of the textile merchants were the original locales of ready-made clothing workshops. Brooks Brothers opened such a shop on Catherine Street in 1818.[33] By 1828, there were nearly 20,000 garment industry workers in the four largest east coast cities.[34] The invention of the sewing machine by Elias Howe in 1846 accelerated expansion of the industry. Newly arrived Irish and German immigrants entered the trade. The Civil War buoyed contracts for military uniforms. By 1860, New York City, especially the Lower East Side, had become the center of national production. Sewing machine manufacturers, textile companies (engaged in printing, dyeing, and bleaching cloth), and button, tape and binding, trimming, and embroidery makers clustered in direct proximity.[35]

Retailing took place along Broadway near City Hall. Nearby hotels housed visiting out-of-town buyers and merchants. The southern and western states, as well as Latin America, were the principal export destinations. German Jews were commonly the contractors, employing Irish and German immigrant workers. The tenement district around Mulberry, Mott and Baxter Streets became known at this time for its home sweatshops.[36] Russian and Polish Jewish immigrants settled, beginning in 1870. An informal labor exchange on the corner of Hester and Essex Streets became known as the 'pig market.'[37] In the late 1870s, loft manufacturing space increasingly began to be built north of Canal Street (the cast-iron frame structures of five to ten stories in the area presently known as 'SoHo') by apparel and fur merchants who could not find space downtown. By 1900 this area had become the heart of warehousing and manufacturing in Manhattan.[38] (See figure 2.1 for shifting locations.)

The increasing entrance of middle-class women into employment in offices and retail trade in the late nineteenth century fueled a growing demand for ready-made women's clothing. In response, the sweatshop and homework system was widely institutionalized in the Russian and Polish Jewish concentrations south of Houston Street and east of the Bowery.[39] Sixty percent of the Lower East Side's workers were employed in the garment industry, according to the 1890 census. Italians also entered the industry, constituting 15 percent of women's apparel employment by 1900.[40] By that year, New York City was producing over two-thirds of the total US product value of $159 million in women's clothing.[41] Working and living conditions were appalling. One writer of the time observed:

> Take the Second Avenue Elevated and ride up half a mile through the sweater's district. Every open window of the big tenements, that stand like a continuous brick wall on both sides of the way, gives you a glimpse of one of these shops as the train speeds by. Men and women bending over their machines or ironing clothes at the window, half naked . . . The road is like a big gangway through an endless workroom where vast multitudes are forever laboring. Morning, noon, or night, it makes no difference; the scene is always the same.[42]

Documents such as Jacob Riis' *How the Other Half Lives* graphically brought the situation to the attention of a middle-class public. The resulting outcry

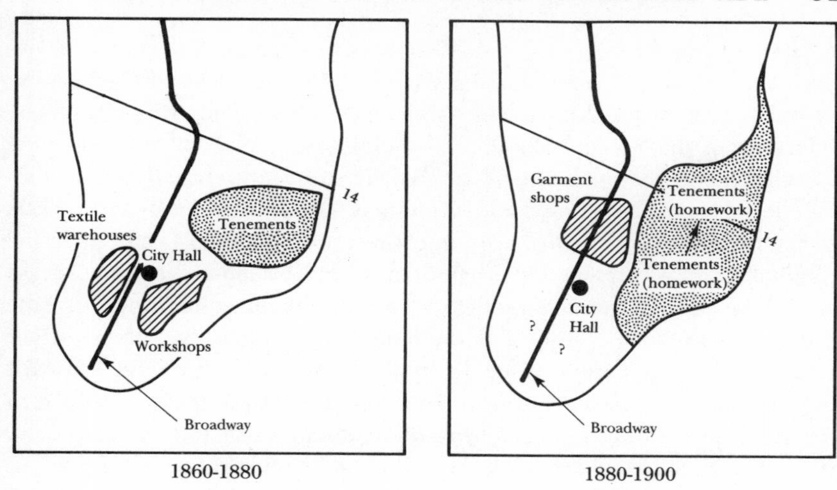

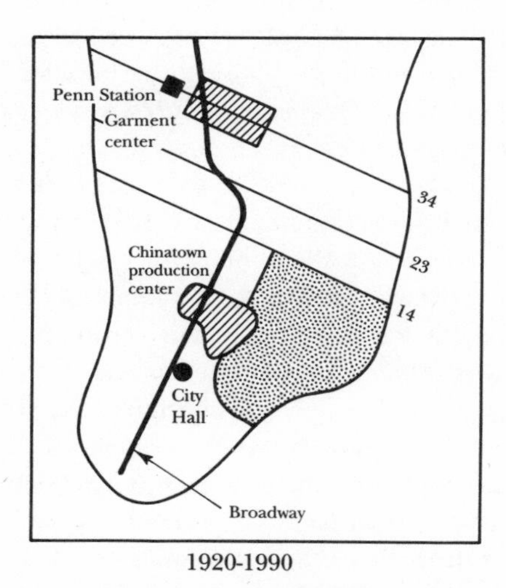

Figure 2.1 Changing relationship of garment production centers to the Lower East Side tenement district, 1860–1990
Source: Sketch map by Jan Lin

over the living and working conditions of the sweatshop workers stemmed partly from fear of the potential health hazards of buying clothes made in the tenement district. The New York Tenement House Act of 1892 limited the number of employees allowed in each work space and forbade homework without a license. Another law was passed to restrict homework by families. It was amended in 1899 to include non-relatives. These laws were mostly ineffectual. In 1911, there were still 13,000 tenements licensed for homework in the city.[43]

Workers began organizing for better working conditions at the turn of the century. Cloakmakers formed the core of the International Ladies'

Garment Workers' Union (ILGWU), which met for the first time in 1900. The Cap Makers' Union was formed in 1901, the Fur Workers' Union in 1904, and the Amalgamated Clothing Workers' Union in 1914. The 'Uprising of the Twenty Thousand,' a bitter strike in 1909 led largely by women shirtwaist workers (first sparked by teenage firebrand Clara Lemlich at an Astor Place rally), and the 'Great Revolt' of 60,000 cloakmakers throughout 1910, brought many into the ranks of the ILGWU after ten difficult years of organizing. Richly chronicled by labor historians, these two strikes remain heroic episodes in labor and feminist literature.[44] Many settlement workers, clergy, and the concerned middle classes gave their support to these actions. The Triangle Shirtwaist Factory fire of 1911 brought more public attention to the conditions of the trade. Trapped in the burning building by locked fire-doors, almost 150 women jumped to their deaths or were burned with the building. Government investigations led to the Factory Laws of 1912, which established safety and health standards and regulated the length of the work week.

Lower East Side women were political activists for a number of other causes in this period. In 1902 Jewish housewives organized a boycott of kosher meat dealers to protest rising prices; two years later women led several hundred residents in actions to protest rising rents. With the support of affiliated trades' organizations, they formed a New York Rent Protective Association. In 1908 a more dramatic round of rent strikes erupted, this time coordinated with the help of the Eighth Assembly District of the Socialist Party. Several thousand tenants in the Lower East Side, Brooklyn, and Harlem participated.[45]

While sweatshops and homework continued to thrive on the Lower East Side, garment industry retailers, 'inside shops,' and the contractors were gradually moving their operations uptown along Broadway. Concentrated just south of Washington Square in 1900, the Garment Center moved to Twenty-third Street and Broadway and then to Thirty-fourth Street and Broadway, near the Pennsylvania Railroad terminal which had been established in 1910 at Seventh Avenue (see figure 2.2). The blocks around this regional transportation hub became a magnet for garment industry showrooms. The Garment Center consolidated in this district over the next fifteen years; style-setting women's clothing firms moved first, followed by 'copyists' and 'knock-off houses.'[46] Proximity to Penn (Pennsylvania) Station also spurred the development of the Times Square theater, entertainment, and hotel district in the blocks between it and Forty-second Street.[47] These establishments continue to service the flood of garment industry buyers that seasonally converge on the Garment Center.[48]

Even as the establishment of the Garment Center around Penn Station consolidated New York City's position as the design and retailing center

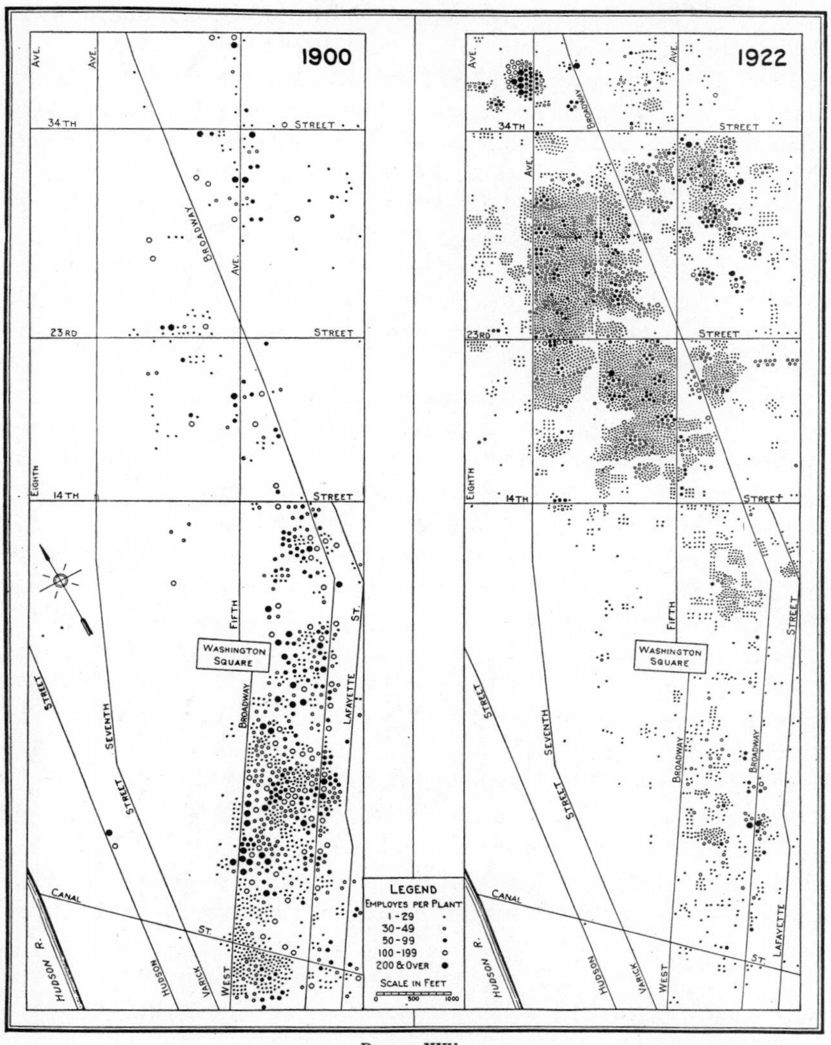

DIAGRAM XXV
Location of plants in women's garment industry in the area of greatest concentration in Manhattan in 1900 and 1922
86

Figure 2.2 Location of plants in women's garment industry in the areas of greatest concentration in Manhattan in 1900 and 1922

Source: R. M. Haig, *Major Economic Factors in Metropolitan Growth and Arrangement*, a volume of the Regional Plan of New York and its Environs, 1927. Reproduced from p. 86

of the US apparel industry, there were portents of its future decline as a production center. One major factor was labor. The Immigrant Restriction laws of 1917 and 1921 effectively cut off southern and eastern Europeans as an incoming supply of low-wage labor. Another variable was declining demand. The Depression led consumers to seek cheaper and less specialized apparel, and mass production and standardization in the industry were encouraged by this turn toward simpler clothing. Transportation was also a factor. As highways were constructed in the 1920s and 1930s, trucking emerged as an alternative means of transporting goods. Production increasingly moved to lower-cost labor regions in rural New England, northwestern Pennsylvania, and southern New Jersey.

The 1920s marked the apex of New York City's role as a manufacturing center. The growing use of automated, continuous-material-flow production processes made the vertically oriented urban loft manufacturing building obsolete. Factories that could spread horizontally were preferred, and these would be built in the suburbs where land costs and taxes were lower.[49] This marked the beginning of a long period of gradual decline in the city's industrial-era infrastructure. Obsolescence was marked by increasing vacancy rates in the loft space inventory. Along with these economic and technological factors went a simple but potent political reality: employers were also avoiding the labor conflict that rocked the Lower East Side and center-city labor enclaves in other turn-of-the-century manufacturing cities.[50]

The construction of bridges and tunnels and improvements in mass transit facilities also encouraged the dispersal of Lower East Side residents to the outer boroughs. Total population in the district declined from

Table 2.2 Population of the Lower East Side by region of birth, 1855–1930

	Year				
	1855	*1905*	*1910*	*1920*	*1930*
Born in the US	91,999	194,292	171,186	173,734	117,892
Northwest Europe[a]	105,318	27,178	14,324	8,608	5,893
South and Eastern Europe[b]	722	295,760	354,206	231,258	120,513
All others born abroad	1,885	1.068	1,541	2,191	3,125
Non-white	–	–	204	317	2,332
Total	199,924	518,298	542,061	416,108	249,755
Persons per acre	200.1	518.8	542.6	416.5	249.8

[a] Chiefly Irish and German

[b] Chiefly Italian and Russian

Source: Homer Hoyt and L. Durward Badgley, *The Housing Demand of Workers in Manhattan* (New York: Corlears Hook Group, 1939), p. 20

542,061 in 1910 to 249,755 in 1930. During the same period, population density per acre decreased from 542.6 to 248 (see table 2.2). This population decline was only partially moderated in the 1940s and 1950s by an inflow of Puerto Ricans and southern blacks. Economic activity also continued to decline with the further dispersal of garment industry production to low-wage zones in the southern and western states. The 1960s saw many garment center jobbers looking to 'offshore' production zones in East Asia, Latin America and the Caribbean, for garment assembly.

Information on the grey economy in the industrial period is rather sketchy. The Times Square/Hell's Kitchen area was emerging as the new entertainment and cheap amusement center, and the Bowery began a gradual decline into a 'skid row' of lodging houses and soup kitchens. Some organized crime activity in gambling and prostitution occurred in Chinatown in the decades preceding the Depression. Little Italy was also a control center for local and metropolitan-wide racketeering and contraband activity.

THE POSTINDUSTRIAL ECONOMY: NEW SWEATSHOPS, TOURISM, AND REDEVELOPMENT

The economic landscape of the postindustrial Lower East Side eludes facile characterization. The shipyards and wharves have long gone, replaced by a waterfront expressway and park and by an almost uninterrupted wall of public and subsidized medium-to-high-rise housing blocks stretching from Fourteenth Street to the Brooklyn Bridge. A patchwork of ethnic 'urban villages' in varying stages of retrenchment or expansion (including Latino Loisaida, Little Italy, the Jewish quarter, and Chinatown) occupies the bulk of the tenement zone. This space is shared, particularly in the East Village and Alphabet City north of Houston Street, with a shifting and eclectic assortment of students, artists, and people of alternative lifestyle, who possess a 'high threshold' of tolerance for cramped and deteriorated tenement apartments (see Mele, chapter 8).

No driving production industry can be identified. Instead, there is a motley configuration of new garment sweatshops and immigrant petty entrepreneurial operations that mainly satisfy local demands for discount ethnic goods and services. Some of these retail enterprises, however, cater to consumers, especially tourists, from *outside* the 'urban village' economy. The tourist orientation intersects with investment and redevelopment interests that seek to *restructure* the local economy towards the consumption demands of more affluent classes (the new urban 'gentry') as well as financial/services functions. This functional tension between center-city financial and upmarket consumption demands and the traditional demands of the proletarian residents is central to political conflicts over urban planning policies in the postindustrial Lower East Side.

There are some specialized commercial agglomerations not linked with distinct urban villages. A wide assortment of eating and drinking establishments, retail shops, and arts and entertainment operations catering to the consumption demands of a post-1950s 'youth culture' permeates the East Village and spreads eastward into Loisaida. The concentration of Indian restaurants serves tourists in the East Village. A discount lighting district is moored to the Lower Bowery, and a wholesale clothing area to Rivington Street. East European and Jewish eateries, groceries, and wholesalers are scattered throughout the East Village. These establishments are a much diminished vestige of the once vast pushcart peddler market that flourished during the turn-of-the-century industrial period. The elderly remnants of the Jewish presence are currently anchored in middle-income cooperative housing on Grand Street.[51] Similarly, Little Italy has shrunk to just several square blocks north of Canal Street, mainly containing tourist-oriented restaurants, jewelry shops and groceries.

Loisaida and Chinatown are the new urban villages of the postindustrial period. They are the product of liberalized immigration laws that brought a new wave of Latin American, Caribbean, and East Asian immigrants to match the earlier massive flows of east European Jews and Italians at the turn of the century. Chinatown, in particular, has grown explosively, tripling in population from 1960 to 1980. The immigrant inflow has led to a revival of the sweatshop system, as garment center jobbers have once again found local labor as exploitable as that in 'offshore' low-wage regions. The Chinese involvement is the most dramatic and visible; the 'Chinatown production center' of about 500 contractors employs some 20,000 Chinese women workers. Occupational, gender, and ethnic solidarities among these Chinese garment workers have spurred labor action on a scale that begins to match that of the 1910s. Two demonstrations of 15,000 and 10,000 in the summer of 1982 successfully averted an attempt by their Chinese contractor employers to withdraw from the guidelines of union-enforced contract regulations.

The dramatic growth of Chinatown's population has been accompanied by an expansion of enclave-specific petty entrepreneurial activities that serve a co-ethnic demand for ethnic food, clothing, and services. The density of street-level hawking activities, coupled with the sweatshop problem, invites comparison with the high point of Jewish immigration at the-turn-of-the-century.[52] What is different, however, is the extent to which postindustrial ethnic urban villages serve the consumption demands of non-enclave clientele and tourists.

Chinatown has become a popular weekend stop for out-of-town tourists who converge to gawk and shop, along with outer-borough Chinese, on thoroughfares packed with sidewalk peddlers, discount import-export dealers, fishmongers, greengrocers, meat markets, and curio shops. Their gastronomic desires are satisfied by nearly 200 restaurants and tea houses offering a diversity of regional Chinese cuisines. The workers at nearby municipal and federal government buildings in the City Hall area also assure a steady stream of restaurant patrons. Ethnic festivals (the Chinese New Year and the Italian patron saint festivals) attract the largest throngs. Even more dependent on tourism than on co-ethnic demand are the restaurants, bistros, and groceries of Little Italy, which is steadily shrinking as residents move to the outer boroughs and the second generation assimilates. Enterprising local boosters and city planners preserve an 'old world flavor' through public policy and commodify the historic ethnic vernacular of the district into an upmarket *quartier* for the consumption of the affluent classes, like nearby SoHo or Tribeca.[53]

In contrast, the continuing flow of poor rural immigrants into Chinatown perpetuates a human din and third world grittiness that mitigates against a similar gentrification. Strong currents of investment capital also flow into Chinatown, however, most notably from overseas (mainly Hong Kong and Taiwan). The result is a polarization of the local economy into 'lower' and 'upper' circuits, replicating the structure found in third world cities.[54] Since the late 1970s the district has become a 'mini-finance' center with some 30 domestic and overseas bank branches reporting FDIC deposits totaling $3 billion as of 1988.[55] Recognizing the fiscal advantages of stimulating this development capital, in 1981 the City of New York established a 'Special Manhattan Bridge District' (SMBD) which would have allowed the construction of spectacular luxury high-rise condominium projects in what is primarily a built environment of tenements. Two proposed projects were legally overturned by activist community organizations which favored maintaining the district's character as a locale suited to the needs of the existing low-income population. At another site, plans for a 'Chinatown Trade Center' (later switched to plans for a massive new city prison) brought out 12,000 irate residents in opposition.

Garment industry representatives and planners have warned that rising rents on industrial space and conversion of manufacturing lofts into upmarket residential condominia greatly threaten the continued viability of garment contractors in the Chinatown production center. Speculative land market activity by overseas investors, some in secretive dealings, has also inflated commercial rents, endangering the livelihood of many petty street-level enterprises. Exorbitant 'key money' payments are required supplements to most leases. Low-income tenants are plagued by poor building services and some are harassed by landlords eager to displace them in favor of new tenants who must pay higher decontrolled rents. There are signs that redevelopment and economic restructuring in Chinatown, even if temporarily slowed, are moving inexorably forward. Dozens of medium-scale condominium projects have been built. Large-scale redevelopment essentially shifted to the office and commercial building market in response to the legal reversals in the SMBD. The 15-story pink limestone 'Glory China Tower,' financed by the Ka Wah Bank of Hong Kong, towers over the fishmongers and greengrocers at Chatham Square. The Hong Kong-based Bank of East Asia is building a seven-story North American headquarters on Canal Street. There are proposals for at least three luxury hotels.

At the periphery of these central economic configurations and political conflicts are revived sublegal economic activities. Drug smuggling on a secretive but large scale pervades Chinatown, involving internationally active Chinese tongs deriving local economic strength through their operation of gambling parlors and protection rackets.[56] Tong operations and 'turf' are defended by tightly trained corps of teenage and young adult 'warriors' with names such as 'Flying Dragons,' 'Ghost Shadows,' and 'Born to Kill.' Violent clashes between these gangs in restaurants and vacant lots in the Chinatown area have been occurring since the early 1970s. A smaller-scale drug trade flourishes in Loisaida on night-time street corners, and from the basements and backrooms of Latino bodegas.

These underground activities promote an atmosphere of danger and terror which, to some extent, inhibits an inflow of affluent residents to Loisaida and Chinatown. The new urban gentry is also deterred by the general deteriorated look of the tenement district and by the efforts of community-level 'anti-gentrification' protesters and activists. Social polarization and community conflict over redevelopment are observed in the East Village and Alphabet City, where the invading 'gentrification frontier' is capitalized by institutional investors (such as real estate companies, non-local commercial banks, and multiple-property owning speculator 'slum landlords') from *outside* the 'community.' These are displacing not only residents but the existing configuration of 'mom and pop' shop and property owners (see Smith et al., chapter 7 and Mele, chapter 8). Tenacious disputes have erupted over the use of public space and the disposition of tax delinquent city-owned property.[57] Community organizations, squatters, and homeless are pitted against the local state, police, and developer interests in a tumultuous snarl of acrimonious debate, protest, and violent confrontation. Some of the actors are new and some of the issues differ, but there are certain parallels between this thumbnail sketch of the economic history of this proletarian tenement enclave and today's struggle for turf on the Lower East Side.

NOTES

1 Eric E. Lampard, 'The New York Metropolis in Transformation: History and Prospect. A Study in Historical Particularity,' in Hans-Jurgen Ewers, John P. Goddard and Horst Matzerath, eds. *The Future of the Metropolis* (Berlin: Walter de Gruyter & Co., 1986), pp. 29–35.

2 Robert Ernst, *Immigrant Life in New York City, 1825–1863* (Port Washington, NY: Ira J. Friedman, Inc., 1949), p. 38.

3 Allan R. Pred, *The Spatial Dynamics of U.S. Urban-Industrial Growth, 1800–1914* (Cambridge, MA: MIT Press, 1966), p. 168.

4 John H. Morrison, *History of New York Shipyards* (Port Washington, NY: Kennikat Press, 1970), pp. 9–23; Kenneth Dunshee, *As You Pass By* (New York: Hastings House, 1952), p. 168.

5 Susan Lyman, *The Story of New York* (New York: Crown Publishing, Inc.), p. 121.

6 Dunshee, *As You Pass By*, p. 169; Morrison, *History of New York Shipyards*, p. 51.

7 Dunshee, *As You Pass By*, p. 168.

8 Lampard, 'The New York Metropolis,' pp. 58–9.

9 Abeles, Schwartz and Associates, *Forging a Future for the Lower East Side: A Plan for Action* (New York: New York City Planning Commission, 1970), p. 1; Joan Turner, 'Building Boundaries: The Politics of Urban Renewal in Manhattan's Lower East Side,' doctoral dissertation, City University of New York, 1984.

10 Gerald R. Wolfe, *New York: A Guide to the Metropolis* (New York: McGraw Hill Book Co., 1988), p. 133.

11 Some of the poorest German and Irish immigrants, however, squatted vacant land on the northern periphery of the expanding city. There they built rudimentary shanties and trekked downtown daily to work on the docks, to clean houses, sell goat milk, or pick rags.

12 Ernst, *Immigrant Life*, pp. 39–42.

13 Edward K. Spann, *The New Metropolis: New York City, 1840–1857* (New York: Columbia University Press, 1981), p. 154.

14 The bell was moved to Fifth Street in 1845 with the movement of the shipyards upriver. It is now housed in a museum. Mechanics Alley just south of the Manhattan Bridge is another present-day vestige of the shipbuilding industry. See Morrison, *History of New York Shipyards*, pp. 85–9.

15 Iver Bernstein, *The New York City Draft Riots* (New York: Oxford University Press, 1990), pp. 105–6.

16 Richard C. McKay, *South Street* (New York: G. P. Putnam's Sons, 1934), pp. 207–8.

17 Bernstein, *The New York City Draft Riots*, pp. 80–1.

18 Herbert Asbury, *The Gangs of New York* (New York: Dorset Press, reprint of 1927 edition), pp. 66–70.

19 James R. McCabe Jr., *Lights and Shadows of New York Life* (New York: Farrar, Straus and Giroux, 1970), p. 540. Originally published in 1872.

20 Wolfe, *New York*, pp. 84–5.

21 Asbury, *The Gangs of New York*, pp. 66–70.

22 McCabe, *Lights and Shadows*, p. 192.

23 McCabe, *Lights and Shadows*, pp. 589–94.
24 Christine Stansell, *City of Women: Sex and Class in New York, 1789–1860* (New York: Alfred A. Knopf, 1986), p. 176.
25 Spann, *The New Metropolis*, p. 309.
26 Morrison, *History of New York Shipyards*, p. 156.
27 Lampard, 'The New York Metropolis,' p. 61.
28 Emanuel Tobier, 'Manhattan's Business District in the Industrial Age,' in John M. Mollenkopf, ed., *Power, Culture and Place* (New York: Russell Sage Foundation, 1988).
29 The Eccentric Mill Works on Centre and Duane Streets was the pioneer in constructing a cast-iron front building in 1848, a style subsequently widely reproduced elsewhere in lower Manhattan. See Patricia Malon, 'The Growth of Manufacturing in Manhattan, 1860–1900,' doctoral dissertation, Columbia University, 1981, p. 121.
30 Ibid., p. 81.
31 Saskia Sassen-Koob, 'Changing Composition and Labor Market Location of Hispanic Immigrants in New York City, 1960–1980,' in George Borjas and Marta Tienda, eds., *Hispanics in the U.S. Economy* (New York: Academic Press, 1985), p. 312.
32 Helen I. Safa, 'Runaway Shops and Female Employment: The Search for Cheap Labor,' *Signs* 7 (winter 1981), pp. 418–33.
33 Malon, 'The Growth of Manufacturing,' p. 83; Roy Helfgott, 'Women's and Children's Apparel,' in Max Hall, ed., *Made in New York* (Cambridge, MA: Harvard University Press, 1959), p. 47.
34 See Isaac A. Hourwich, *Immigration and Labor* (New York: G. P. Putnam's Sons, 1912).
35 Malon, 'The Growth of Manufacturing,' pp. 109–12.
36 Robert D. Parmet, *Labor and Immigration in Industrial America* (Boston: Twayne Publishers, 1981), pp. 90–1.
37 Malon, 'The Growth of Manufacturing,' p. 212.
38 Chester Rapkin, *The South of Houston Industrial Area* (New York: New York City Planning Commission, 1963), pp. 10–11.
39 Malon, 'The Growth of Manufacturing,' p. 219.
40 Parmet, *Labor and Immigration*, p. 93.
41 Irving Howe, *World of Our Fathers* (New York: Harcourt Brace Jovanovich, 1976), pp. 154–5.
42 Louis Levine, *The Women's Garment Workers* (New York: B. W. Huebsch, 1924), p. 19.
43 Howe, *World of Our Fathers*, p. 156; Malon, 'The Growth of Manufacturing,' pp. 310–12.
44 Ann Schofield, 'The Uprising of the 20,000: The Making of a Labor Legend,' in Joan M. Jensen and Sue Davidson, eds., *A Needle, A Bobbin, A Strike* (Philadelphia: Temple University Press, 1984), p. 180.
45 Jenna Weissman Joselit, 'The Landlord as Czar,' in Ronald Lawson and Mark Naison, eds., *The Tenant Movement in New York City, 1904–1984* (New Brunswick: Rutgers University Press, 1986), pp. 43–7.

46 The 'march uptown' was reflected also in employment patterns. Eighty-two percent of women's apparel employees worked below Fourteenth Street in 1900, compared with 4 percent in 1935; in the men's apparel segment, the drop was from 80 percent to 37 percent over the same period. See Homer Hoyt and L. Durward Badgley, *The Housing Demand of Workers in Manhattan* (New York: Corlears Hook Group, 1939), p. 20.
47 Originally centered on Lower Broadway south of Canal Street, the entertainment district similarly experienced a 'march uptown,' along the Bowery, to Fourteenth Street and finally to Times Square. See Hoyt and Badgley, *The Housing Demand*, p. 20.
48 Edgar M. Hoover and Raymond Vernon, *Anatomy of a Metropolis* (Cambridge: Harvard University Press, 1959).
49 Ibid., p. 27.
50 David Gordon, 'Capitalist Development and the History of American Cities,' in William K. Tabb and Larry Sawers, eds., *Marxism and the Metropolis* (New York: Oxford University Press, 1978), pp. 49–50.
51 Jonathan Boyarin, 'Waiting for a Jew: Marginal Redemption at Eighth Street Shul,' in Jack Kugelmass, ed., *Between Two Worlds: Ethnographic Essays on American Jews* (Ithaca: Cornell University Press, 1988), p. 64.
52 The 'informal,' unregulated character of these small-scale operations also suggests comparison with the economies of third world cities.
53 The 'special preservation district' designation was recommended by the Department of City Planning and the Little Italy Restoration Association (LIRA) in a 1976 report. The trend towards gentrification is perhaps best symbolized by the restoration of the giant Beaux-Arts architectural-style former police building to luxury condominia, rather than to the community space previously planned.
54 Jan Lin, 'Polarized Development in the "World City": The Chinese Enclave of New York City,' presented at the International Housing Research Conference, Paris, 3–6 June 1990.
55 Jan Lin, 'Capital and Community in Urban Change: Chinatown, New York City,' doctoral dissertation, New School for Social Research, 1992.
56 One of the new Chinatown banks, the United Orient Bank, has been linked with organized crime. One of the bank's offices is located on the ground floor of the An Leung tong's headquarters building on Mott Street. One of the leaders of the tong, Eddie Chan, was appointed vice chairman. When federal prosecutors began legal proceedings against Chan in 1984, United Orient Bank depositors staged a run which resulted in the withdrawal of $6 million before the bank announced Chan's resignation. See Peter Kwong, *The New Chinatown* (New York: Noonday Press, 1987), pp. 116–28.
57 The battle around tax delinquent properties, or the 'cross-subsidy' issue, is over whether these properties should be converted to market-rate housing, rehabilitated for low-income residents, or made available to squatters and the homeless.

Plate 3.1 The 'last' Ukrainian: a tenement home
Source: Courtesy of Marlis Momber

3

The Tenement as a Built Form

Richard Plunz and Janet Abu-Lughod

The Lower East Side is almost synonymous with the term 'tenement,' even though tenements are to be found throughout the older portions of Manhattan, Brooklyn, and even the Bronx. The term itself conjures up in the American imagination a vision not so much of a building as of a way of life: teeming masses, foreign tongues, noisy streets cluttered with push-carts, tired men in frayed undershirts and husky women in loose cotton housedresses, panting on fire escapes to gain a breath of air on fetid summer nights, children playing and weaving between horse-drawn carts that rumble through the streets. That image has been engraved in our minds by novels that describe proletarian life in New York at the time of the 'Great Migrations' of the late nineteenth and early twentieth centuries. We also carry in our mind's eye the negatives of old sepia photographs that draw us into that world, even as we congratulate ourselves that those 'bad old days' are gone forever. Nostalgia and curiosity linger, however, as demonstrated graphically by the solid crowds that line up daily for the boat trip to visit the new immigrant museum on Ellis Island.

But the term 'tenement' was not invented in nineteenth-century New York. Deriving from the same root as our words 'tenure' and 'tenant,' a tenement is literally a *portion* of a building rented by its occupant. In late medieval times the word tenement simply meant a dwelling place, but by the sixteenth and seventeenth centuries in England and Scotland, it had come to refer more specifically to a building subdivided into rooms and apartments rented by separate families or individuals.[1]

In the United States, however, the association of tenements with immigrants and with New York in particular was not a capricious one. Although American households during colonial times were hardly 'nuclear' (since they often contained subfamilies, servants, apprentices, and even boarders), rental apartments, especially those expressly built for multi-family occupancy, were not a common form of housing. Throughout the first half of the nineteenth century, the predominant forms of housing for the poor in New York were either reconstructed space that had previously served other uses, or self-built squatter shacks. New housing was only for the affluent, and it consisted almost entirely of single-family houses. Former single-family row houses in older areas, however, were frequently divided into substandard cubicles for poor people.

There is some evidence of scattered tenement construction in the early 1800s. James Allaire has been credited with investing in the first new substandard building expressly designed for poor families, a four-story house on Water Street intended for many tenants. Other sources cite a tenement on Cherry Street built in 1838, and there is some evidence of an earlier example dating from the 1820s, a seven-story tenement at 65 Mott Street.[2] The earliest fully documented new project for the poor was Gotham Court, built in 1850 by Silas Wood on Cherry Street.[3] But it was only in the latter half of the nineteenth century that this building form came to dominate New York's construction industry. Its appearance coincided temporally with, and was designed to meet the demands of, the massive migrations of that period. Between 1820 and 1860 the population of the city grew from 123,706 to 813,699 persons, at least half of the gain coming from immigrants.

It was then that the dominant characteristics of the city's housing began to emerge: New York became a city not of 'houses' but of 'housing.' A growing proportion of its inhabitants lived in collective accommodations that were unique in the nation. This condition crossed class lines, from the tenements of the poor to the increasingly dense row housing of the upper middle class. In 1847 a famous observer of the New York scene, Philip Hone, remarked that New York was appropriating certain characteristics of metropolitan Europe: 'Our good city of New York has arrived at the state of society found in the large cities of Europe; overburdened with population, and where the two extremes of costly luxury in living . . . are presented in daily and hourly contrast with squalid misery and destitution.'[4]

Dr John H. Griscom, who served as city inspector in 1842 and became one of New York's first crusaders for housing reform, presented the first comprehensive analysis of slum formation.[5] Writing in 1842 about the difficulties of enforcing housing standards for the poor, Griscom identified landlords as the only actors who had the resources to improve housing conditions. However, because he could find no sound economic reasons within the capitalist system for landlords to pursue such improvements beyond the minimums set by law, he was forced to call upon their good will.

Griscom placed his faith in the capacity of the private landlord to improve housing conditions but was worried that the growing preponderance of absentee owners making large investments would undermine any attempts to raise standards. Instead of owning single buildings and living alongside their tenants, by then landlords were investing in scores of buildings and were increasingly removed from their tenantry. The new scale of housing enterprises was creating a system of absentee landlordism, rather than large-scale philanthropy. Furthermore, owners were managing their structures through a system of sublandlords who collected the rents and then turned them over to the owners.

> The *system of tenantage* to which large numbers of the poor are subject . . . must be regarded as one of the principal causes of the helpless and noisome manner in which they live. The basis of these evils is the subjection of the tenantry to the merciless inflictions and extortions of the *sub-landlord* . . . The *owner* is thus relieved of the great trouble incident to the changes of tenants, and the collection of rents. His income is from one individual, and obtained without annoyance or oppression on his part.[6]

Griscom's worries were fully borne out by the experience of Gotham Court. That project, consisting of two rows of six tenements back-to-back and six stories in height, was a lucrative investment. Designed for 140 families, by 1879 it was alleged to contain 240. Overcrowding, filth, crime, and disease made it a notorious slum. It became a favorite target for reformers who succeeded in securing its demolition in 1895, under new provisions added to the Tenement House Law in that year. Insalubrious as such tenements were, they continued to attract investments because the returns on them were so lucrative.[7]

By 1865, when the city's population was approaching one million, a total of 15,309 tenements existed in New York City.[8] By then the word 'tenement' was a well established term in the technical vocabulary of housing for the urban poor. As a housing type, the tenement was generated by the desire to maximize densities within the constraint of the 25-by-100-foot building lot system which the New York gridiron plan of 1811 had made the most feasible dimension. The 25-foot width of the tenement was also dictated by practical structural constraints, such as the maximum spans of wooden floor joists, and by the prevalent practice of building only in single-lot increments. The length of the tenement was often more than 90 percent of the 100-foot depth dimension with a height of five or six stories. The long tenements were commonly called 'railroad flats' because the rooms were organized like cars on a train. Frequently, older structures were converted to tenements by adding more floors on top and by filling in the rear-yard areas with additional housing. Figure 3.1 shows six steps in the evolution of the New York City tenement from an original single-family row house to a typical railroad flat covering 90 percent of a 25-by-100-foot lot. In many railroad flats, the rear yard was eliminated entirely or might consist of only a few inches.[9] In these tenements, only the rooms facing the street received light. Back buildings were common in every area of Manhattan where high densities prevailed. By 1865 hundreds of Manhattan blocks had been overbuilt as converted tenement housing, with no standards for minimum space, light, or ventilation.

Political pressures were building for a legal intervention in the tenement house problem. In 1856 the first legislative commission was set up to study the housing problem; its work described in detail the condition of the tenements, but no legislation was advanced.[10] Instead, the deteriorating condition of the poor was further aggravated by disasters. The national economic difficulties of 1857 were so severe that the Common Council was forced to provide jobs for the unemployed and to distribute food to the poor. By 1858 there were 25,000 unemployed who, with their families, represented approximately 100,000 people in dire need. Conditions in the city were also taking their toll in terms of the general social order. Major riots in 1849 and 1857 pointed toward the increasingly agitated state of the tenement population. The locations at which the 'draft riots' (ostensibly protests against military conscription) erupted in July 1863 indicated a connection between poverty, the housing problem, and threats of civil disturbance.

Immediately following the draft riots, a group of influential citizens formed the Citizens' Association of New York to advocate improvements in the sanitary conditions of the city. The Citizens' Association appointed a subcommittee to undertake a comprehensive survey. Their monumental report, published in 1865, remains a unique document for its scope and thoroughness, and it had the desired impact. In 1866 and 1867 the pressure for serious government legislation yielded the first initiatives toward change. In 1866 the state legislature approved a comprehensive law defining standards for building construction in New York City.[11] The following year, the legislature passed its first comprehensive housing law, the Tenement House Act of 1867. The 'tenement' was at last legally defined:

> Any house, building, or portion thereof, which is rented, leased, let, or hired out to be occupied or is occupied, as the home or residence of more than three families living independently of one another and doing their

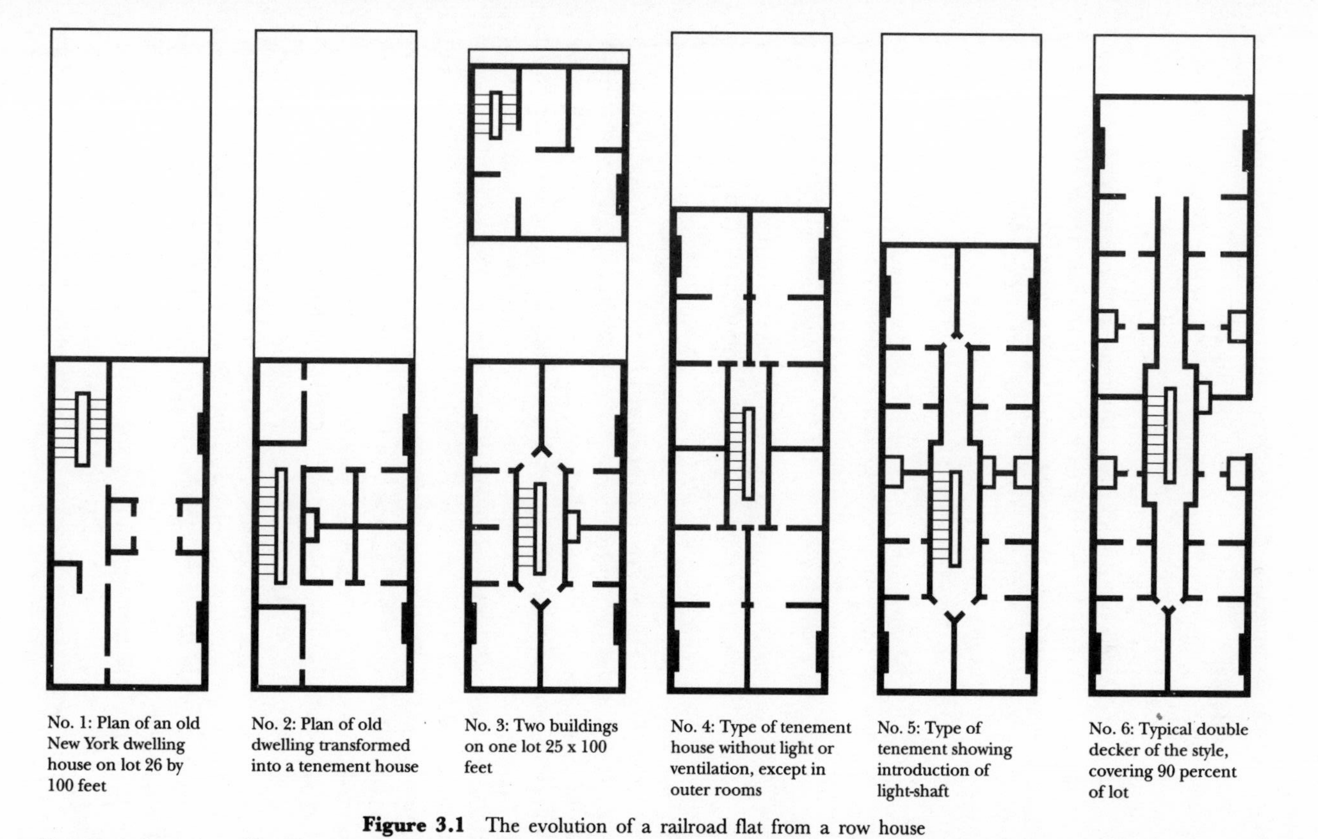

Figure 3.1 The evolution of a railroad flat from a row house

Source: New York State Assembly, Tenement House Committee, Report of 1885, as reprinted in Richard Plunz, *A History of Housing in New York City* (New York: Columbia University Press, 1990), p. 13

> own cooking on the premises, or by more than two families upon a floor, so living and cooking and having a common right in the halls, stairways, yards, water-closets, or privies, or some of them.[12]

Combined, these two laws were intended to cover both new and existing buildings.

One of the fundamental elements of these regulations was their insistence that fire escapes be provided to all tenements, a requirement which eventually gave to New York tenements their most distinctive architectural feature – the zig-zagging wrought iron appendages that constitute a remarkably decorative feature of the facades. But the mere existence of laws and of a housing bureaucracy did not guarantee compliance. One of the most blatant failures involved the provision of fire escapes. By 1900, out of a sample of 2,877 tenements, 98 had no fire escapes at all, and 653 had only rear fire escapes.

The emerging profession of architecture generally did not involve itself with the problems of tenement design. The economic constraints which firmly controlled the form of tenements put their planning totally within the province of building contractors. In any case, even the best architects failed when they tried to design livable apartment units within the narrow procrustean bed of 25-by-100-foot lots, which had been selected largely to permit maximum profits from land speculation. Architects did begin quite early, however, to look for mechanisms to modify lot sizes.

In 1878 Edward T. Potter, who was to become one of the most interesting nineteenth-century theorists for housing,[13] began publishing his research on how the gridiron pattern could be modified to improve light and ventilation in tenement housing. His analysis indicated that by building on multiple rather than single lots, the restrictions of the 25-foot module could be overcome. For example, a series of double lots would allow a system of back-to-back air slots. Light and ventilation would be vastly improved over the railroad flat. This principle proved to be an important one for future tenement house legislation.

The Tenement House Act of 1879 revised only sections 13 and 14 of the Tenement House Act of 1867, but the revisions were substantial.[14] The most radical provision was that no new tenement house could occupy more than 65 percent of a 25-by-100-foot lot, but this was not enforced. Another important provision prohibited the practice of tenement back buildings, unless adequate light and ventilation could be provided. The famous 'dumb-bell' tenement, also commonly called 'Old-Law Tenement,' which had actually been suggested by architects in a recent architecture competition, was enforced as a kind of compromise, permitting 80 percent coverage of a 25-by-100-foot lot. While the dumb-bell was an improvement over the railroad tenement, lot coverage remained very high, insuring continued maximum profitability.

The bureaucracy was content that it maintained some control over tenement building, but contentment was not universal. In a paper presented at the 1880 National Convention of the New York chapter of the American Institute of Architects, its secretary Alfred J. Bloor condemned the tenement house competition and the resultant dumb-bell design enforced by the Board of Health: 'The recent tenement house competition . . . resulted in the prizes being awarded for designs each of which included the dark middle room, which is the horror of physicians and visitors among the poor, which has been so strenuously inveighed against by the Board of Health.'[15] Bloor argued that the 25-by-100-foot lot could never produce satisfactory results. Many architects agreed with him, recommending that solutions could only be found by combining adjacent lots to free up the design constraints, but these proved very hard to achieve in practice.

Indeed, housing reformers noted that conditions were deteriorating rather than improving, making even the new-styled tenements of New York far worse than any abroad:

> The tall tenement house, accommodating as many as 100 to 150 persons in one building, extending up six or seven stories into the air, with dark, unventilated rooms, is unknown in London or in any other city of Great Britain. *It was first constructed in New York about the year 1879, and with slight modifications has been practically the sole type of building erected since, and is the type of the present day.* (italics added for emphasis)[16]

But agitators for reform continued to press for changes. During the decades of the 1880s and 1890s, populist reformers became the driving force that focused national attention on the tenements. New tools such as photo-journalism added an element of realism to the documentation of tenement housing conditions. Jacob Riis was the giant among these reformers, almost turning tenement reform into a political crusade. Riis, an immigrant who worked as a newspaper reporter, published his first crusading article, 'How the Other Half Lives,' in *Scribner's* magazine in 1889, followed by his first book of the same title in 1890.

The reform movement was reacting in part against the social disruptions caused by the massive presence of immigrants. By 1890, immigrants made up 42 percent of the city's population and occupied almost all of the tenements. By then, tenement buildings constituted a very high percentage of the city's housing stock; more than 80,000 tenements existed in greater New York City. These buildings housed 2.3 million people, out of a total population of 3.4 million. In February 1890 reformers and some architects were shocked into greater awareness by an exhibition on tenements, sponsored by the Charity Organization Society and organized by reformer Lawrence Veiller. One of the exhibition's architectural models depicted an existing tenement block on the Lower East Side. This 200-by-400-foot block was found to house 2,781 persons at the astounding density of 1,515 persons per acre. Of 1,588 rooms, 441 received no light or ventilation at all, while another 635 rooms faced air shafts. The exhibit had its intended shock effect.

Two major studies relating to tenements emerged by the mid-1890s, and both remain documents of major importance. The first was the report of the Tenement House Committee, established by the New York State legislature in 1894. The report traced in detail the evolution of tenement house reform and produced unprecedented documentation of conditions based on a survey of 8,441 houses, occupied by 255,033 persons. This documentation revealed an appalling fact. Whereas New York ranked sixth among world cities in population, it was found to rank first in density, with an average of 143.2 persons per acre. A portion of the Lower East Side, the most crowded district in the city, was found to have reached a density of 800.47 per acre, which even surpassed the highest known foreign agglomeration – a section of Bombay with 759.66 persons per acre.[17] The committee's report indicated that over one-half of New York's population lived in tenements. In 1895 the federal government tackled the housing problem for the first time, producing the second major tenement study of the decade. The large special report of the US Department of Labor, called *The Housing of the Working People*,[18] documented the various European techniques being employed to achieve better housing for workers, but aside from stimulating the imaginations of reformers already committed to philanthropic housing, this report had little immediate effect. The economic profitability of tenements provided through private enterprise was too strong a force in New York to be undermined.[19]

New York architects, still under the hegemonic influence of Beaux-Arts, were slow to respond. Yet, at least three names stand above the normal practice of the day: Grosvenor Atterbury, Ernest Flagg, and Isaac Newton Phelps Stokes. All were graduates of the Beaux-Arts, but had never joined the ranks of the sycophants. All had an intense interest in issues relating to the production of housing, to which each made invaluable contributions. Those of Ernest Flagg were the earliest and perhaps the most influential. In 1894 Flagg published his first proposals to improve tenement housing. The prototypes he recommended were a clever translation of the courtyard apartment house, so prolific in Paris, into terms that responded to the New York tenement dilemma. These prototypes combined four 25-by-100-foot lots into a single building incorporating an internal central courtyard entered directly through an opening from the street. This combination redistributed the identical amount of square footage typically contained in four dumb-bell tenements, but with vastly superior light and ventilation for each apartment. In 1896 he submitted a variation on this plan to the tenement house design competition sponsored by the Improved Housing Council of the Association for Improving the Condition of the Poor where it won first place. A more studied variant on the same strategy was submitted by I. N. Phelps Stokes.[20]

In 1900, in response to pressure from the Charity Organization Society, the New York State legislature appointed its fourth Tenement House Commission. Robert DeForest served as chairman and Lawrence Veiller as secretary. Their edited two-volume study, *The Tenement House Problem*, eventually published in 1903, was the end product of their detailed inquiries. For the first time, studies by architects on the design ramifications of alternative tenement controls were taken seriously. Various architects were invited to prepare plans to test the provisions of the proposed legislation.[21]

In 1901 the state legislature finally made a definitive legislative response to the agitation of the previous decades. The Tenement House Act of 1901, commonly called the 'New Law,' set a national standard for tenement legislation. Although it was subsequently modified extensively, its provisions are still the basis for the regulation of low-rise housing design in New York City. The law required that the dimensions for the dumb-bell air shaft be increased to courtyard proportions, which in effect eliminated the enclosed air shaft. The rear yard had to be at least 12 feet deep and no building could be higher than one and one-third times the width of the street it faced. Every apartment had to have running water and a water closet. Every room had to have an exterior window of specified minimum dimensions, and a series of construction and egress requirements were imposed to limit the likelihood of death by fire. The dimensional constraints of the New Law effectively eliminated single 25-foot lot development from the mass market. Small developers who built on a lot-by-lot basis could no longer participate in the production of higher-density tenements. Large capital began to monopolize the tenement market.

The change in the law had an immediate effect on the types of tenement houses that were subsequently built. Of the 579 tenements constructed in Manhattan during the first year and a half of the new law's operation, only 45 were built on single lots of 25 feet or less; the modal size of lot shifted upward to between 37.5 and 45 feet in width. Some 236 of Manhattan's new units were on combined lots this size, while the remaining 211 structures were built on lots of at least 50 feet.[22] Under the new law, economies of scale also dictated – in order for developers to achieve their goal of squeezing the highest returns out of the permitted structures – a fairly universal switch to the six-story building. Buildings above that height were required to include costly additional structural improvements. To avoid these expenses and to conform to the new ratio required between the height of the building and the width of the street, six stories became the economic maximum; and this maximum also became the minimum. Indeed, of the 579 New-Law tenements built in Manhattan during the 18-month period following the law's passage, 507 (or 88 percent) were exactly six stories high. Of the remainder, 53 went to five stories, and only 18 went higher.[23]

Figure 3.2 shows the locations of the New-Law tenement structures that were put up in Lower Manhattan during the 18-month study period. As can be seen, the heaviest concentrations of New-Law tenements were in 'Alphabet City,' where their appearance caused a buzz of excitement. They filled in all remaining spaces and even replaced some of the oldest and most disreputable buildings of the zone which, even then, had been defined as an abominable slum. It is perhaps ironic that this area of relatively 'new' housing is the very zone in which maximum abandonment and demolition of the housing stock have been concentrated in recent years.

Every study of tenement houses made during the nineteenth-century period of attempted reforms revealed the Lower East Side to be the most egregious example of why reform was needed. The very first sociological study ever made of tenement conditions was conducted in 1854, in the 11th Ward (between Rivington and Fourteenth Streets and from Avenue B to the East River), even before tenements had become the dominant housing form there. At that time, the area contained 53,282 residents in 2,218 buildings. Most buildings were still relatively small. Some 263 were single-family structures, 889 had between one and five families in them, 720 had between five and ten families, 309 had ten to twenty families, while 37 contained over twenty families each. The area was occupied almost exclusively by immigrants; three-fourths of all occupants had been born abroad, including 23,683 Germans, 13,411 Irish, and another 2,535 persons from diverse countries.[24]

Conditions deteriorated rather than improved in the next half century of true tenement-house construction on the Lower East Side. The remarkable survey made in 1900, in connection with reform efforts, had singled out the Lower East Side for special attention because of the great concentration of tenements there. As Lawrence Veiller pointed out in his chapter entitled 'A Statistical Study of New York's Tenement Houses':

> The tenement houses in the Borough of Manhattan are, to a very large extent, located in distinctively tenement house districts, with more definite boundaries than can be found in other cities, extending along the east and west sides of the city. *The district on the east side may be said to begin at the*

Figure 3.2 New-Law tenement houses erected in Lower Manhattan in 1902 and 1 January to 1 July, 1903 (● = 1902; ▲ = 1903)
Source: *First Report of the Tenement House Department of the City of New York, 1902–1903*, Vol. 1. Portion of larger insert map (New York: Martin B. Brown, n.d. but probably 1903 or 1904)

> *Brooklyn Bridge . . . The western boundary extends up Centre and Marion Streets to Houston; from there over to the Bowery, and up the Bowery to Fifth Street, where the Bowery merges with Third Avenue.* From there the western boundary of the tenement house district may be said to be Third Avenue as far up as the Harlem River at 129th Street. All east of this line, with one or two slight exceptions, are tenement house districts. (italics added for emphasis)[25]

The survey reported findings for each of the city's wards, which makes it possible to examine in detail conditions in the area that eventually came to be called the East Village, and to compare the situation in 1900 with what had prevailed in 1864, when a prior survey had been made. The boundaries of Ward 17 coincide almost exactly with those of the western half of the East Village, while those of Ward 11 similarly coincide with the East Village area east of Tompkins Square Park (see figure 3.3).[26]

The 11th Ward east of Tompkins Square, with an area of 213 acres, was in the worst state, and conditions had actually deteriorated between 1864 and 1900.

> It has been for many years a large tenement district, and contains at the present time [1900] 2,031 tenement houses, of which 182 are rear buildings . . . 20,303 families were found living in tenement houses, comprising a population of 89,361 persons . . . Comparing conditions to-day with conditions in 1864, we find that the total number of tenement houses has practically remained stationary, [while] the number of families living in tenements has increased from 13,433 to 20,303, or 51 percent . . . [The total population had] increased from 64,254 to 89,361 [or by 39 percent].[27]

Conditions in the 17th Ward, bounded on the south by Rivington, on the east by Avenue B and Clinton, on the north by Fourteenth Street and on the west by Bowery-Fourth, were changing even more drastically. By 1900 this zone contained some

> 2,877 tenement houses, of which 268 are rear buildings . . . There were found 28,035 families . . . comprising a population of 114,559, of which 13,519 were . . . under five . . . Comparing conditions . . . to-day with conditions 40 years ago, [namely] in 1864, we find that great changes have taken place. The number of tenement houses in the ward increased from 1,890 in 1864 to 2,877 in 1900, or [by] 52 per cent, while the . . . population . . . increased [even faster] from 63,766 to 114,559, or [by] 79 per cent.[28]

In the decades since 1900, tenements in many other parts of Manhattan were torn down, either to clear space for the rapid commercial development of midtown or, farther north on the now-exclusive Upper East Side, to make room for more elaborate housing for the middle and upper classes. This did not happen on the Lower East Side where tenements continued to be built up to about 1910. After that time, the area began to lose both population and housing stock. This decline has been well documented in Leo Grebler's exemplary study of housing in the Lower East Side. According to this source, the number of dwelling units in the area decreased by about 34 percent between 1909 and 1940 while the population dropped even more, declining by 62 percent between 1910

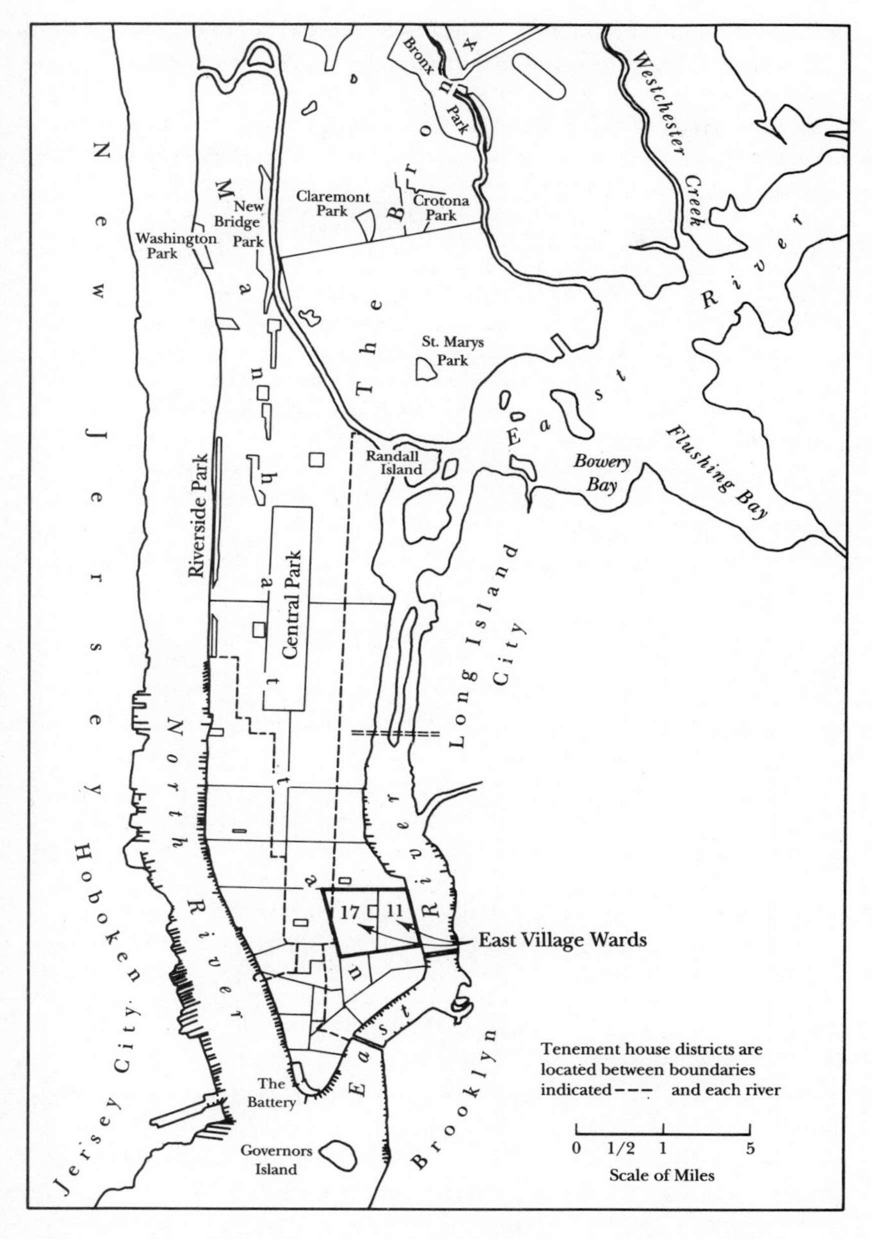

Figure 3.3 The wards of Manhattan in 1900. Wards 11 and 17 conform roughly to the boundaries of today's East Village

Source: Robert DeForest and Lawrence Veiller, eds., *The Tenement House Problem* (New York: Macmillan, 1903), Vol. 1

and 1940. Interestingly enough, the disappearance of the housing stock was not due to significant 'upscale' rebuilding at lower densities. Rather,

> about one-half of the demolitions occurred in conjunction with public improvements such as bridge approaches, street widenings, and housing projects, or are attributable to more vigorous law enforcement during the late thirties. The other half may be ascribed to the operation of market forces alone, that is, factors other than public land use or exercise of police power . . . [The existence of a] large number of vacant lots resulting from demolition illustrate[s] the anemia of the Lower East Side and the difficulties of redevelopment on a piece-meal, property-by-property basis. The removal of slums through the action of market forces alone appears to be related not so much to physical or economic depreciation as to alternative uses for the land . . . Alternatives for more profitable uses on the Lower East Side have been poor.[29]

This explanation, while valid, is insufficient. One must ask why Lower East Side demand became 'anemic.' To some extent, one must attribute the decline in the 1930s to the Depression, but this followed close on the heels of a temporary stabilization of the city's population. Once immigration was cut off, New York City itself grew more slowly, and the Lower East Side, which had been the major 'port of entry' for new immigrants, felt the brunt of the reduced demand. One can only hypothesize that it was doubly neglected because of its unattractive housing stock. And this brings us back to the question of whether it was not the tenements themselves that stood in the way of stabilization.

Certainly, the authors of a 1970 plan for the Lower East Side believed so. They found that:

> more than nine-tenths of the old law tenements are not fit to live in and should be replaced. They are five and six-story walk-ups with most of the rooms having no light or air. They destroy the possibility of decent living conditions for their inhabitants and the maintenance of a decent neighborhood for all who reside in the area.[30]

On the other hand, the planners thought that a good proportion of the New-Law tenements could be reconstructed to make them more habitable. Interestingly enough, their plans to restructure the tenements replicated solutions that had been proposed by the architect-reformers at the turn of the century – namely, to combine at least four lots to create courtyard structures, or even to replan entire blocks to create communal open space.

This chapter thus ends on a note of *déjà vu*. It is amazing how certain themes, dilemmas, and solutions surface over and over again in the history of the Lower East Side. Controversies over who shall use Tompkins Square, and for what purposes, have dogged the park since it was first built in the 1830s, as will be seen in chapter 4. Similarly, there have been recurring debates about what to do about the tenements. From time to time, housing reformers have thrown up their hands in despair and recommended their wholesale clearance, hopefully to be replaced by 'better' housing for 'better' types of occupants. Others, as we have seen in this chapter, sought ways to redesign and rehabilitate the tenements for their current occupants. Some of these debates are covered in chapter 5, which focuses primarily on the 1930s and 1940s. Today, some one hundred and fifty years after the 'invention' of the New York City tenement, housing reformers are still trying to find a solution to the problems they symbolized. The most recent attempts at solution are to be found in the work of today's housing reformers in the form of the cross-subsidy program, which will be covered more fully in part III.

But as these debates went on, the housing stock continued to be destroyed and the resident population continued to drop. Although the more Draconian proposals to clear the tenements and build from scratch were never carried out, except in the riverfront zone where they were replaced by public housing projects, the fact is that since the early 1970s there has been a very serious erosion of the housing stock of the East Village, with little replacement thus far. Whether planned or not, the tenements have been disappearing – the result of arson, abandonment, and demolition.

Here, we might simply point to a major difference between the two periods. The earlier declines in density and population on the Lower East Side were well warranted; they represented a great improvement over the rabbit-warren densities of the past. However, since the 1960s, and especially in the 1970s and 1980s, a different type of population reduction has been occurring, with different roots and with very negative effects. The causes and consequences of this most recent phase in the history of housing on the Lower East Side will be covered in part II of the book.

NOTES

This chapter has been adapted by Janet Abu-Lughod from materials contained in the three opening chapters of Richard Plunz, *The History of Housing in New York City* (New York: Columbia University Press, 1990). The exact wording of Plunz has been retained wherever possible, although the selections have been condensed and reassembled and editorial connections and interpretations have been added. The opening and final sections of this chapter were written by Janet Abu-Lughod.

1 *The Oxford Universal Dictionary on Historical Principles* (Oxford: Clarendon Press, 1933), p. 2149.

2 *Plumber and Sanitary Engineer*, 15 December 1879, p. 26; Tenement House Building Company, *The Tenement Houses of New York City* (New York: Albert B.

King Press, n.d.); and Charles H. Haswell, *Reminiscences of an Octogenarian of the City of New York: 1816–1860* (New York: Harper, 1896).

3 *Evening Post*, 20 August 1850. See also 'Gotham Court,' *Frank Leslie's Sunday Magazine*, June 1879, p. 655.

4 Philip Hone, *The Diary of Philip Hone, 1828–1851*, ed. Allan Nevins (New York: Dodd, Mead, 1927), p. 785.

5 John H. Griscom, *The Sanitary Condition of the Labouring Population of New York: Annual Report of 1842* (New York: James van Norden, 1843).

6 Ibid., p. 6.

7 It is not possible to reconstruct the finances of the earliest tenement buildings, but we do have detailed documentation on the remarkably high rate of return from tenement investments at the turn of the century. See Elgin Gould, 'Financial Aspects of Recent Tenement House Operations in New York,' in Robert DeForest and Lawrence Veiller, eds., *The Tenement House Problem*, Vol. 1, pp. 355–66, published originally by Macmillan in 1903.

8 Citizens' Association of New York, Council of Hygiene and Public Health, *Report Upon the Sanitary Condition of the City* (New York: D. Appleton, 1865), p. lxix.

9 DeForest and Veiller, eds., *The Tenement House Problem*, Vol. 1, pp. 293–300.

10 New York State Assembly, *Report of the Special Committee on Tenement Houses in New York and Brooklyn*, Assembly Document no. 199, 4 April 1856: *Report of the Select Committee on Tenement Houses in New York and Brooklyn*, Assembly Document no. 205, 9 March 1857.

11 New York State Legislature, *Laws* (1866), ch. 873, pp. 2009–47.

12 New York State Legislature, *Laws* (1867), ch. 980, sec. 17, pp. 2265–73.

13 A compendium of Potter's research, 'Concentrated Residence Studies,' dated April 1903, can be found in special collections at the Schaffer Memorial Library, Union College.

14 New York State Legislature, *Laws* (1879), ch. 504, pp. 554–6.

15 Alfred J. Bloor, 'Suggestions for a Better Method of Building Tenant-Houses in New York,' *American Architect and Building News*, 12 February 1881, pp. 75–6, quote from p. 75.

16 Quoted from DeForest and Veiller, eds., *The Tenement House Problem*, Vol. 1, p. 8.

17 New York State Assembly, *Report of the Tenement House Committee of 1894*, Legislative Document no. 37, 17 January 1895, pp. 11, 256.

18 Elgin R. L. Gould, *The Housing of the Working People: Eighth Special Report of the Commissioner of Labor* (Washington, DC: Government Printing Office, 1895).

19 This, indeed, was the problem, as Gould's 1903 analysis of profitability revealed so clearly. See Elgin R. L. Gould, 'Financial Aspects of Recent Tenement House Operations in New York,' in DeForest and Veiller, eds, *The Tenement House Problem*, Vol. 1, pp. 355–66. Net returns on mortgaged tenements on the Lower East Side ranged between 5 and 10 percent annually, with most properties yielding in the higher range. See unheaded table on p. 361.

20 Stokes is perhaps best remembered as the author of the greatest book on New York City's development that has ever been produced. Originally

published in six folio volumes and handsomely illustrated, his *The Iconography of Manhattan Island 1498–1909* is a rare book whose price ranges between $4,500 and $8,000! Even the edition reprinted in 1967 is beyond the reach of a scholar's purse.

21 Some of these plans are published in James Ford, *Slums and Housing*, in 2 volumes (Cambridge: Harvard University Press, 1936).

22 See the tables on pp. 146–7 of *First Report of the Tenement House Department of The City of New York, 1902–1903*, Vol. 1 (New York: Martin B. Brown Press, n.d. but probably 1903).

23 Ibid., pp. 148–9.

24 See Lawrence Veiller's chapter, entitled 'Tenement House Reform in New York City, 1834–1900,' pp. 69–118 in DeForest and Veiller, eds., *The Tenement House Problem*, Vol. 1, especially pp. 84–5 which present data from the 1854 study of tenement conditions.

25 Ibid, pp. 191–240.

26 The only boundary differences are on the southern edges of the two wards which included both sides of Houston Street down to the northern side of Rivington.

27 Data for Ward 11 are presented on pp. 202–3 of Veiller's article in DeForest and Veiller, eds., *The Tenement House Problem*, Vol. 1.

28 Ibid., p. 206.

29 See Leo Grebler, *Housing Market Behavior in a Declining Area* (New York: Columbia University Press, 1952), p. 15.

30 See *Forging a Future for the Lower East Side: A Plan for Action*, prepared for the City of New York Housing and Development Administration, City Planning Commission, by Abeles, Schwartz and Associates, and dated December 1970, p. 19.

4

A History of Tompkins Square Park

Marci Reaven and Jeanne Houck

About 5:30 the morning of Monday, 3 June 1991, some 300 members of the New York City Police Department, backed by command trucks stationed at all four corners of the site, surrounded Tompkins Square Park and summarily evicted the 150 residents who were still encamped there. They then closed the park for the foreseeable future. The official announcement by the Parks Department – that the closing was motivated by their desire to completely renovate and improve the facility for the good of the neighborhood's residents – was greeted with disbelief and, in many cases, by feelings of outraged betrayal, not only by ordinary citizens but by such elected officials as Ruth Messinger, Borough President of Manhattan, and Miriam Friedlander, then still the City Council representative of the district. Both officials claimed that the decision to close the park had been taken unilaterally by the Mayor's office, that they had been neither consulted nor informed, and both issued public letters of protest to Mayor Dinkins. Opposition to the closing was not unanimous, however. Other citizens applauded the city's decision to reinstitute its authority over the park, clamping down on the homeless encampment, but also on the all-night music and hanging-out.

The mayor's claim to determine the design and use of Tompkins Square is part of a long history of such contests enacted within the park's borders. Who can use the park and for what purposes, and who controls access to and design of the park are questions that have often fueled conflict on the Lower East Side. This chapter shows how the physical and human landscape of this important public space has been continually shaped and reshaped in the context of demographic and economic changes in the surrounding neighborhood. A study of the park's origins and transformation may help explain why, throughout its 150-year history, Tompkins Square Park has been a sensitive barometer of the city's tensions.[1]

The history of this 10-acre green and forested oasis set in the midst of acres of tenement buildings begins with its construction in the 1830s, when it was intended to spur the urban development of the surrounding area. During the subsequent hundred years, Tompkins Square remained the largest – and practically the only – open public space on the Lower East Side. It was not until the 1930s that, under the direction of Robert Moses, other parks were finally constructed on the Lower East Side. But even after these additions, Tompkins Square continued to attract crowds and remained the prime focus of controversy.

While the reputation of Tompkins Square has been fed by conflict, the park itself has served essential functions for its multiple users. From the start, it offered a welcomed respite from the noise and heat of city streets, a place to breathe fresh air after long hours spent in factories and tenement kitchens. It was also a place to enjoy festivals and music and to socialize with neighbors, and for children to run and play. And almost from its inception it was also a place to gather in public debate and protest. Open to all comers, it was a crucial centerpiece of neighborhood life.

Throughout its history, the park was recognized by locals, social reformers, and city planners as an important neighborhood resource. Many considered it so important that they played an active role in shaping it. The style of landscape design, the kinds of recreational facilities to be provided, and the range of social organizations encouraged or permitted within its space, have all been seen as critical influences on the character and beliefs of generations of users. Perhaps for these reasons, Tompkins Square has achieved a fairly high degree of visibility within the city, despite its small size and its working-class character. Throughout periods of contention and during times when physical deterioration threatened to overwhelm the park, neighborhood users have shown resolve and resourcefulness in continuing to make Tompkins Square work.

The idea for a public space on the site was first set forth in the 1811 city plan for New York. The Commissioners' Plan organized a street system for Manhattan which established the island's rectangular grid. Land was quickly subdivided into standard rectangular parcels which could be easily sold without requiring complex surveys. And for the first time in the city's history, some open spaces for parades, markets, small squares and the like were planned in advance. As Manhattan expanded northward in the 1820s and 1830s and new streets were constructed, six open squares were developed: Union, Madison, Gramercy (the only one in non-public ownership), Washington, Stuyvesant, and Tompkins.[2] The squares were intended to stimulate construction in residential neighborhoods and to enhance land values in their vicinities.

Tompkins Square was developed in 1834, when the city spent $93,000 to purchase the swampy site from its owners, to drain, fill and grade it, and to plant trees and other vegetation. Higher taxes imposed on properties abutting the park were expected to reimburse the public treasury for its investment. The priority given development was well expressed in a report to the Board of Aldermen which warned that if work should 'be delayed for an indefinite period, then indeed will this already most unfortunate part of the Island be doomed to utter despair.' The city and local land owners anticipated that the rather elegant districts that had been developing a few blocks to the west – along Second Avenue and Lafayette and Bond Streets – would expand eastward, drawn by the new amenity.[3]

Instead, the housing market collapsed as the economic panic of 1837 swept the city and the nation. No grand homes would grace Tompkins Square until the late 1840s, and then only along its northern border, Tenth Street. But by mid-century, demographic changes in antebellum New York City were altering the square's prospects. Between 1820 and 1860 Manhattan's population grew from 120,000 to over 800,000, primarily from immigration. In the latter year, half of New York's residents had been born abroad. Located in what became the immigrant East Side, Tompkins Square never achieved the elegance planned for it. The surrounding area soon housed the laboring classes.

The area around the square, known as the Dry-Dock neighborhood, was a center for New York's shipbuilding industry before the Civil War (see chapter 2). The Irish immigrant workers lived crowded into cellars and subdivided units in converted buildings. As the neighborhood grew, however, they also moved into the newly constructed tenements. Although lacking light, air, plumbing, sewerage, and clean water from the Croton Reservoir, these tenements were such an improvement over older housing that they attracted the families of skilled workers; a tenement directly on Tompkins Square could command a relatively high rent of $115 per year. The park, of course, offered an enhanced amenity. In 1847, the *New York Daily Tribune* advertised the opening of 'new and desirable tenements' along the square's southern border. The ad stipulated that 'none but families of respectability and quiet habits will be admitted.'[4]

Although the importance of the park as a neighborhood landmark was underscored by the construction along its eastern border of a Methodist church in 1843 (which later became Trinity Lutheran) and St Brigid's Catholic Church in 1849,[5] few amenities were added to the site until the 1850s, after local property owners petitioned for improvements. By 1860 the park had taken on a more attractive appearance. Trees had been planted around the edges and flagstone paths provided pleasant walkways that directed circulation around the square. The city planted shrubbery and flowers and built a central fountain. Iron fences were installed to protect the plantings from horses, pigs, goats, and small children. The Board of Aldermen reported that 'seats have been placed in good positions; large numbers of good, healthy, young, thriving trees [have been] planted; handsome designs [have been] made in the centre of grass-plots, ornamented with evergreens.'[6]

This landscaping corresponded to the then-prevalent ideal of park design. In a city whose aesthetic was largely constrained by the gridiron plan and closely spaced surrounding streets, parks were seen as offering an oasis of grass and flowers. During the 1850s, the parks movement of New York City gained widespread support as cultural leaders began to rethink the possibilities for restructuring an urban environment that was undergoing dramatic growth. Central and Prospect Parks were crowning examples of this in New York. But while park designers had rest and the contemplation of beauty as goals for their landscaping, nearby poor residents often had other pressing needs. They used parks as places of public assembly.

Tompkins Square's importance for this purpose was convincingly demonstrated during the business depression and ensuing economic panic of the winter of 1857. Thousands of working men and women found themselves jobless, homeless, and unable to afford even basic foodstuffs. The city promised relief in the form of public works projects. At the start of November the unemployed were gathering regularly in Tompkins Square to demand that this promise be kept; they formed a 'workingmen's committee' to meet with the mayor and, on 6 November, marched to the stock exchange. With still no relief in sight, the crowds at Tompkins Square grew. Benches and fences were carried off for firewood. The largest reported meeting was held on 10 November; the next day witnessed a 'bread riot.'[7]

The use of Tompkins Square as a forum for debates that occasionally erupted into passions was not unusual for the era. The class and ethnic divisions of the pre-Civil War era often extended into the public spaces of New York. Along with electoral politics and labor struggles, the streets were important arenas for social action. Sometimes these activities were semi-official, as when thousands wound through the streets in parades in which different social groups ceremoniously displayed themselves. At other times the public spaces of the city exploded with collective violence, revealing a complex web of animosities and cross-currents of cultural perceptions. One such instance occurred in May 1849 in nearby Astor Place, triggered by the seemingly insignificant issue of an English actor's performance in *Macbeth*, but actually reflecting class and ethnic tensions.[8] Perhaps the most well-known and violent civil disturbance in the nation's history was three days of anti-draft rioting in New York City in July 1863, in which predominantly Irish participants caused mayhem throughout the city, attacking civic institutions and officials, wealthy homes, and murdering African-Americans. Incidents such as these convinced both state and city officials that the public thoroughfares of New York needed more policing.

The history of public confrontations in the parks and streets of the city helped to create the context determining the future of Tompkins Square in the immediate post-Civil War era. The military's needs for the park often conflicted with those of local residents. Although Tompkins Square had been nicely renovated in the late 1850s, much of the park's landscaping had inevitably been destroyed by Civil War troops who briefly encamped on the site in 1863. Soon after the war, unhappily just after renovations had been completed in 1866, the state legislature ordered the city of New York to 'remove all trees and other obstructions' from Tompkins Square so that a military parade ground could be built for the Seventh Regiment of the New York National Guard![9] That summer the trees were removed and the ground regraded, and by fall the square was put to military use.

Military parade grounds were a well established tradition in nineteenth-century urban America. Indeed, Central Park and Washington Square had also been sites for military drills. But by the post-Civil War era, the more well-to-do residents in their vicinities had objected to the often rowdy military presence in their neighborhoods and had succeeded in banning them. Poorer people had less influence. The motivation for turning Tompkins Square into a drill ground was practical enough. As the city's largest public square, the 10-acre site seemed an ideal spot for regimental and brigade drills. And even if the neighbors objected, they wielded too little political power to defend their park.

During these years, the Dry-Dock neighborhood around the square gave way to a steadily growing 'Little Germany.' The shipyards left, together with many of their Irish workers, and small manufacturing shops run by Germans moved in. Factories, slaughter houses, cavernous beer gardens, and deteriorating tenements were packed in, side by side, in this densely populated neighborhood of the city.[10] Perhaps ever more than before, residents needed breathing space, so that even military drills did not deter them from using the square to fulfill their recreational needs.

Despite Tompkins Square's new identity as a parade ground, then, it was never abandoned by the neighborhood. Children watched as the Seventh Regiment drilled and the Fire Department tested its new engines. Barren though the park was, men and women flocked there after work and on week-ends for fresh air and companionship. In contrast to the city's growing variety of expensive leisure activities, the square offered free recreation. When not in military use, the square hosted musical, gymnastic, and literary events. Fraternal and political organizations continued to meet there.[11] In 1873 the recently established Department of Public Parks responded to this heavy use by replanting trees around the square's borders to 'relieve in some degree its forlorn appearance, and to make it of some little use for the recreation of the adjoining dense population.' The Department of Parks also sponsored 'promenade concerts' in the evening.[12]

In 1873 an illustrated article in *Harpers Weekly* described a seemingly typical night in Tompkins Square, voyeuristically capturing its excitement for readers who presumably would not have ventured to this 'grand plebeian plaza of New York city.'

> Through the long summer day its bare stretching distance of sand is a glaring Sahara: but when the sun has gone behind the high houses of Avenue A, the great square is the attractive centre of the whole neighborhood – a reservoir of cool air, calling laborers out of their tenement homes as soon as they have eaten supper . . . Tompkins Square this evening presents everyday life; not church or picnic, with better coat and brighter ribbon, but home turned out on exhibition, bareheaded and barefooted. Stout arms that have become sinewy through the toil of the machine-shop and the wash-tub are brawny, bare to the elbow. Human life is uncovered here, and takes its last draught of air before it retires to hired chambers, and throwing itself on welcome beds, too often in stifling inside bedrooms, tired nature closed the eyelids until another day.[13]

It was precisely this plebeian character that both fascinated and alarmed more well-to-do New Yorkers.

But hard times were descending on neighborhood, city, and nation. By the winter of 1873–4, a severe economic depression left many people unemployed and suffering. On 13 January, some 10,000 workers from all over the city assembled in Tompkins Square for a planned march on City Hall where they were to demand relief. Unbeknownst to the demonstrators, city officials late the night before had rescinded their permit to assemble at City Hall and changed the end point of their line of march to Union Square. Thus, among the various workingmen's groups that had gathered in the morning's bitter cold, there was confusion about what direction they should take. But before they were able to organize themselves, legions of police on horseback plowed into the crowd, swinging their nightsticks in indiscriminate fashion and pursuing shocked protesters through the streets.[14] This officially instigated violence was directed against political action outside the traditional boss and party framework. The city government wanted to curb 'freedom of the streets' which could undermine its efforts to maintain order in the face of a rapidly changing popular culture and an increasingly fragmented political geography.

During the last half of the nineteenth century and continuing into the twentieth, New York City came to contain a wide range of cultural activities. As definitions of high culture became more codified and less spontaneous, the ethnic immigrant and working-class groups in the city forged a more diversified and vibrant popular culture. Access to music, books, newspapers, art, and staged performances increased, and places of spectacle, such as Coney Island and music halls, served the masses. New modes of establishing order were required to cope with this diversity. A centralized police force, the partnership between government and commerce in mounting festivals and spectacles, the development of commercialized culture, and the physical remaking of the city – all contributed to curbing the freedom of the streets. Public squares such as Tompkins, therefore, took on a renewed significance as meeting places for the organized expression of non-mainstream politics at a time when the streets were becoming less accessible.

It was perhaps in this spirit that in August 1874, six months after the 'riot,' some 2–3,000 people gathered in Tompkins Square to affirm their right of free assembly; the crowd resolved that Tompkins Square should always remain 'open to the people for their free assembly.'[15] It would not be long before local residents would also seek to reclaim the square, demanding that a park be designed to replace the badly deteriorating parade ground. A turnover in leadership at the Department of Parks, and the philosophy of the parks movement, well established by the 1870s, created a climate more receptive to residents' demands.[16]

Park designer Frederick L. Olmsted described a rising chorus of voices between 1872 and 1875 urging sweeping improvement of the square. One voice took the form of a petition from mothers in the vicinity, pleading for their little children. In 1875, a bill to restore Tompkins Square as a public park was introduced in the state legislature.[17] The Department of Parks, arguing that Tompkins Square was ideally situated near the 'centre of Population' and that it was the only adequate space for military and fire drills, proposed a compromise. Half of the square would be turned into a park, leaving the other half as a parade ground.[18]

In 1875, Frederick Law Olmsted, renowned landscape architect of Central and Prospect Parks, designed the two tiny corner sites to be detached from the parade grounds. He planned a simple array of benches and flowers for the southwest corner, situated to view the parade ground. A more elaborate and visually isolated northwest corner was to include a fountain, hanging vines, and a goldfish pond, but this northwest arbor was never executed. There was a disagreement between the Board of

Aldermen and the Department of Parks over how laborers would be hired. In addition, Olmsted, in an angry letter to the mayor, accused the city of being reluctant to spend so much money landscaping a park in a working-class neighborhood.[19]

Several years of haphazard renovations ensued which left the park in a sorry state. Reports of the municipal squabbling over day versus contract labor regularly appeared in the newspapers, and neighborhood protests mounted. Taxpayers petitioned for relief from the 'disgraceful condition of Tompkins Square.'[20] On 3 June 1876, almost 5,000 citizens attended a mass meeting in the square. *The New York Times* described the night-time scene, as speaker after speaker addressed the crowd in English and German from a platform lit by Chinese lanterns. They demanded that the park be repaired. Infuriated not only by the condition of the park, which they called a 'chaotic wilderness,' but also by what they viewed as an abuse of power by public servants, those present at the meeting formally resolved to hold accountable all responsible officials and established an investigative committee for this purpose.[21]

Bowing to the community's unity and growing political strength, the Department of Public Parks issued a remarkable promise. *They stated that the city would adopt no plans for the improvement of the square until residents had been given an opportunity to express their views concerning them.*[22] And in 1878 the state legislature reinstated all 10 acres of Tompkins Square as a park. Soon after, local citizens formed the 'Tompkins Square Union' to track the improvements and 'see that the park is kept in good order [t]o render it an ornamental pleasure ground of the first order.'[23] Representatives of the community and the city presumably approved the new design by Julius Munckwitz, and the Seventh Regiment left the square for good.

When the renovation was completed in the summer of 1879, the *New York Daily Tribune* commented favorably on the improvement, contrasting its new fresh grass and shade trees with the 'barren, dusty and forsaken waste which it was less than a year ago.'[24] In September some 10,000 celebrants assembled in the reopened park. German singing societies and bands performed and dignitaries gave speeches. *The New York Times* had nothing but praise:

> Four hundred and fifty trees have been planted; two large and handsome spray fountains have been built; there are the grass plots, and in the center of the park is a pavilion for musicians in course of construction. At night the park is lighted by 160 gas lamps and two large candelabras having five lights each. At each corner of the park are drinking fountains.[25]

This event may have marked the high point for the park. The achievement was not unrelated to the fact that the surrounding neighborhood contained a large and stable enclave of German-Americans who had the resources and organization to force City Hall to do something about their park. The subsequent set of neighborhood residents reaped the benefits. Beginning in the 1880s, thousands of immigrants (Italians, Slavs, Hungarians, Poles, and Jews from eastern Europe) poured into the rapidly proliferating tenement houses of the district, taking the places of the somewhat more prosperous residents of 'Little Germany' who were now moving farther uptown.[26] Unable to speak English, often transient, and forced to concentrate on sheer subsistence, these newer immigrants did not take command of the park as the Germans had done.

By the 1890s, stewardship of the park shifted to social workers, upper- and middle-class Progressive Era reformers, many of whom sought direct engagement with underprivileged industrial workers. They moved into the Tompkins Square neighborhood to improve the environment and uplift the 'deserving poor.' As never before, the municipality, spurred on by the reformers, paid attention to the design and use of Tompkins Square. Previously, concern about the square had centered on two questions. Was the city committed to providing a park for the Lower East Side? And if a park was to be created, what public behavior was appropriate in it? These questions continued to be relevant, but now a new one was also being asked. How could the square serve as a vehicle to 'uplift' neighborhood residents, morally and culturally?

Those who asked this question were new kinds of neighbors, and their new agenda concentrated on the children of immigrants. For half a century Tompkins Square had been the only major New York park serving a working-class district; then, in 1894, it became one of the very first city parks to host a children's playground. Private citizens Lillian Wald and Charles Stover established the Outdoor Recreation League that built nine playgrounds in the city, staffing them with professional play leaders. The League argued that organized play would get the children off the dangerous streets, would protect them from crime and the ill effects of poverty, improve their health, and teach them to become good citizens. Tompkins Square was credited with influencing the character of the local population. One city report appreciated 'the change wrought by the beneficent agency of the park,' as contrasted with the days when Tompkins Square was 'where half the turbulent elements of the East side had their meeting place.'[27]

Tompkins Square Park was thus changed from a passive garden paradise to an active recreational mecca. The additions were clearly popular with neighborhood children. Movie footage shot in 1904 by Thomas Edison shows masses of children using the jungle gyms, race tracks, and enclosed gym pavilions.[28] During one summer month in 1912, the Parks Department counted 45,713 visits to the park by children.[29] One young neighbor also appreciated the park's natural beauty:

> When spring came to Tompkins Square, the large but rather barren park opposite which our house was situated, when the grass plots turned green and the small only recently planted trees put forth their buds, when the sparrows chirped merrily in those trees and the sun was warm on the walks and benches, I began to feel like any young animal at that season of the year . . . I wanted to play in Tompkins Square.[30]

The concern for children revealed itself not only in park play but in the other institutions being set up to advance the physical, moral and intellectual development of young people. In 1876 philanthropists founded the first Boys' Club on Tompkins Square, and by 1901 their permanent (still existing) facilities were constructed at the corner of Tenth Street and Avenue A. In 1886 the Children's Aid Society established a home for boys on Avenue B at the square. A public library was constructed in 1905 on the northern perimeter of the park, and its stacks were trod almost as heavily as the park's grounds. A unique institution, the Young Women's Settlement House, was opened in 1897; it was renamed Christodora House in 1905 when young men were admitted. In 1927 Christodora's wealthy sponsors erected a large art deco building at the corner of Avenue B and Ninth Street.[31] Its top floors provided subsidized apartments in exchange for time devoted to community service, and on the lower floors the settlement house offered a wide range of cultural and health services to neighborhood residents.[32] Other educational and political organizations were centered nearby.[33]

The park was heavily used in the 1920s and 1930s. For radical activists and labor organizers, Tompkins Square provided a forum for public discussion and a rallying point for feeder marches to Union Square.[34] For children, Tompkins Square continued to be a magnet. A 1927 Russell Sage Foundation study documented nearly 1,200 different visits to the park by children during an 11-hour period one summer day.[35] City maintenance efforts could not keep pace with the park's heavy usage. One contemporary observed: 'Tompkins Square . . . is a life saver for this part of the city. It is so violently used by the kids that every spear of grass has been scoured off.[36] The dilapidated conditions (and huge constituency) of the park made it a good candidate for reconstruction under the public works programs initiated during the Depression.

In 1934, Mayor Fiorello LaGuardia appointed Robert Moses sole commissioner of a unified Department of Parks for the City of New York. Using labor provided through New Deal relief funding, Moses embarked on a massive program of park reconstruction. Under his auspices, the total renovation of Tompkins Square Park began in 1936. Moses drastically changed the physical appearance of Tompkins Square, employing the standardized designs and construction techniques for which he became famous. In a drive for efficiency, similar design elements were replicated in a number of New York parks.[37]

This was a new era. Previous preoccupations with pastoral landscapes or structured play no longer seemed relevant. Play had become recreation, to serve an urban population with leisure time newly at its disposal. Rather than seeking to influence the inner lives of park users, Moses' designers were more interested in accommodating citizens' diverse recreational desires. One solution was to spatially segregate competing kinds of park uses. In 1936, a wide east–west road was built through the park at Ninth Street, sectioning off zones to be used actively from those for more passive uses. The northern part provided a wide strip of land for handball, basketball, shuffleboard, horseshoe pitching, and other active sports. The southern portion was reserved for quieter contemplation and offered abundant greenery, benches, and shaded paths. Work on the southern section was never fully implemented because of funding shortages, but minimal restoration was completed and the section reopened in January 1942, six years after work had begun and only one month after Pearl Harbor.[38] War needs took precedence over parks, and when peace came, new needs were evident.

Not only had the park suffered from official neglect, but now, demographic changes added new tensions. The postwar period witnessed major shifts in the occupancy of the neighborhood around Tompkins Square Park. The division between active and passive activities did not solve the problem of absorbing the new diverse groups of the postwar era. The square still served a crowded neighborhood, but with an influx of Hispanic and African-American residents, the area surrounding it became one of the most ethnically diversified districts of the city. Not only did these groups need to accommodate and respect each other's needs, but the old and young now found themselves competing for space within the park. In the Tompkins Square Park rebuilt by Robert Moses, chain linked fences separated the running, exercising, and ball-playing on the north from the families and elderly who congregated in the park's less active areas. But by the mid-1950s, neighborhood boys were defying the fences and playing hardball all over the park.

By 1957, angry residents were complaining to the Parks Department about the dangers to bystanders from flying balls. Residents also complained that teenagers reacted with hostility when asked to stop; older users no longer felt able to enforce discipline nor could they rely on Parks Department personnel to enforce the rules. In a now minimally supervised park, frustrated adult users looked to the police.[39] The Parks Department responded to these complaints by proposing to install a Little League baseball diamond in the middle part of the park, a plan that would have entailed cutting down trees. Despite a warning from one savvy department employee that 'there will be objections . . . when we attempt to further remove greenery,'[40] the Parks Department went forward with reconstruction plans and requests for funds. Mounting complaints from the public confirmed the prescient employee's remarks.

Everyone agreed that the park badly needed improvements but residents wanted a larger role in determining any redesign. However, they could not agree on neighborhood priorities. Should constructive activities to discourage 'juvenile delinquency' be emphasized? Or would designs for more recreational space compromise park aesthetics? When the baseball diamond was voted down in a community meeting, the *Village Voice* reported:

> Artists, housewives, the elderly and exiles from Greenwich Village won a victory over the forces supporting the institution of a Little League and its appurtenances . . . in Tompkins Square Park. The . . . square . . . has long been a favored sitting area for the neighborhood's Polish, Russian, and Jewish old people. The heated debate over . . . the Parks Department plan . . . took place at a meeting . . . last Thursday night . . . Proponents of the ballpark included most of the social agencies in the area and the Lower East Side Neighborhoods Association . . . The anti-ball-field contingent, which calls itself the Committee for the Preservation of Tompkins Square Park . . . [claimed] that taking away trees . . . to create an admittedly needed facility for teenagers was 'robbing Peter to pay Paul.'[41]

Although the plan for a ball field was eventually dropped, the controversy among neighborhood groups continued and even extended beyond the neighborhood's borders when some sought outside alliances with prominent architects and urban planners.[42] Participants in the debate raised basic issues. Could the many communities now represented in the area be equally served? Did the park have a historic tradition worth preserving?

These difficult issues were raised against the backdrop of a radically changing social situation. Juvenile crime was referred to most frequently. The Lower East Side was hit hard by gangs and an explosion of heroin use in the late 1950s. In a survey of New York City park users made in 1962, the predecessor of today's Parks Council found that crime, not design, was the number one concern. One respondent in Tompkins Square explained that the park had been where everybody went on summer evenings – no one stayed home. Now it was mostly deserted at night because people were afraid.[43] Controlling juvenile crime prompted the establishment of a 'teen canteen' in the park where supervised programs of dancing, table games, and other activities were offered once a week. Concern over crime also prompted some to support the ball field proposal because it might, by removing greenery, increase 'visibility' and therefore safety.

It is likely that underlying the open discussions about park plans were hidden anxieties on the part of some long-term residents about ethnic, racial, and cultural changes in neighborhood composition. The relatively homogeneous 'Little Germany' of the 1870s had been supplanted by ethnic divisions among the new southern and eastern European immigrants, which were translated into neighborhood enclaves. For youngsters, at least, these enclaves divided into areas of friendly and hostile turf. By the 1950s, massive urban renewal projects and high-rise public housing projects, along with the flight of middle-class whites and migrations from the American south and the Caribbean, had added new groups to this neighborhood ecology – African-Americans and Puerto Ricans. Tensions existed. As one current Hispanic resident recalled: 'When you went into Tompkins Square you were always cautious. Whatever you did – handball, softball, whatever – you'd be cautious because you weren't in an area where a majority of people around welcomed you. Not just whites, but it could be other gangs, other Hispanics, or blacks.'[44] The debate over park redesign was partially over these unspoken concerns.

Finally, after a year of debate within the community over the renovations, Parks Commissioner Newbold Morris announced acceptance of a plan that emerged from discussions with a committee representing community groups.[45] The new plan provided for improved and enlarged active recreation areas, and for additional benches, game tables, and greenery. Significantly, the plan did not eliminate trees nor did it include the controversial Little League ball field. Instead, it proposed an elevated stage and bandshell, in front of which a paved plaza for dancing or seating was to be built.

It took four more years to execute this plan which, in response to community pressures, was to be done in phases so that at least one section of the park would always be open.[46] Although the compromise plan for the reconstruction of Tompkins Square Park did not please everyone, it did demonstrate that local groups could discuss and eventually reach consensus on a unified statement of community intent and it did set a precedent for active community involvement over park replanning. The debate over the ball field had triggered this involvement. In 1961, after the community voted to reject the Little League field, one resident commented: 'Finally, an issue came up that made people so mad they had to become a community.'[47]

Tompkins Square Park, featuring a new bandshell completed in 1966, was reconstructed just in time for an era of sweeping changes. The surrounding neighborhood became the east coast version of 'Haight-Ashbury.' Rock musicians, poets, hippies, and political activists transformed downtown Manhattan into a center for counter-cultural activities and political protest. It was during the mid- to late-1960s that the area surrounding Tompkins Square Park came to be called 'The East Village.' The *East Village Other* described it this way:

> Today the new "East Village" (a term we have to accept because it draws the distinction between the old world immigrants and the more recent west side immigrants) is the expanding real estate market of sometimes squalid, often quaint and authentic old New York streets that made famous the west village of 25 or more years ago.[48]

In Tompkins Square, love-ins and smoke-ins, interracial relationships, and stepped-up community organizing began to counteract some of the fears and suspicions that troubled the neighborhood. Although not always successful, the members of the counter-culture tried to create a more tolerant atmosphere, even as they agitated for political change.

Tompkins Square had once before been the site of powerful expressions of joy and rebellion. A century earlier, German-Americans had transformed the square with their *volkefestes* and mass demonstrations. Their spirit and command of the space were being revived – only now in 1960s terms. Young people demonstrated at the bandshell against American involvement in Vietnam and in favor of women's and third world liberation movements. They gathered to hear bandshell concerts put on by the Fugs, the Grateful Dead, and Charles Mingus. They were certainly ignoring signs that cautioned 'keep off the grass.' Yet, beneath this swirl of activity, relations among the square's diverse racial, class and cultural groups – young and old, black, Puerto Rican and white, hip and straight – began to fray. The groups clashed, sometimes physically, over cheap apartments, music volume, lifestyles, and turf, foreshadowing conflicts that would resurface in the 1980s.

On Memorial Day, 1967, a resident's complaint about loud congas in the park brought the city's Tactical Police Squad to the square to confront a small group of people sitting on the grass. Furious at being greeted by defiant chants and linked arms, the police grabbed the guitars and shoved and clubbed the protesters. They arrested 38, charging them with disorderly conduct. A month later, on 30 June 1967, the judge dismissed all charges, saying: 'This court will not deny equal protection to the unwashed, unshod, unkempt, and uninhibited.'[49] Several days after the hippies had been arrested, other tensions surfaced in the square. There was a confrontation between hippies attending a concert at the bandshell and Latinos who demanded Latin instead of psychedelic music. The subsequent mêlée involved violence and property damage. The police, this time sensibly leaving their nightsticks behind, broke up the fight. To defuse the situation, Puerto Ricans and hippies, among them Linda Cusamano and Abbie Hoffman, proposed a concert of Latin music for the next night. The delegates from the two communities met with representatives of the Parks Department to plan the concert, which went off peacefully.[50]

A truce was thus established, but the underlying tensions remained and indeed became even more complicated in the ensuing years, as other groups and interests joined the contest for Tompkins Square Park. Significantly, the most recent controversy culminated some 24 years after the events noted here. They were triggered by another 'Memorial Day Riot' which took place in 1991 and which involved a similar altercation between police and concert goers. While the various players and the specific causes of the dissension have changed over the years, the striking fact is that many of the themes that characterized the earlier struggles for control over the park's design and usage have surfaced over and over again. To someone familiar with the history of Tompkins Square Park, current events evoke déjà vu.

NOTES

A version of this chapter was presented at an exhibit, 'Tompkins Square: Past and Present,' produced by Diane Mitchell and Marci Reaven and presented at the Tompkins Square branch of the New York Public Library and the Municipal Art Society during the winter of 1989–90. The National Endowment for the Arts, the New York State Council on the Arts, the New York Council for the Humanities, and the Vincent Astor Foundation provided the funding for the exhibit.

1 The details of this latest phase in the Tompkins Square Park controversy are reserved for chapter 11 which chronicles recent protests and riots. Chapter 12 discusses the formation and devolution of the community of homeless persons who lived in the park in the late 1980s.

2 Tompkins Square was named for Daniel D. Tompkins (1774–1825), former New York State governor from 1807 to 1816 and vice president of the United States from 1817 to 1825. Tompkins was known for his advocacy of the common man and for his anti-slavery stance.

3 Documents of the Board of Aldermen of the City of New York, Vol. 1, document no. 7 (9 June 1834), pp. 53–5, Municipal Archives of the City of New York.

4 Elizabeth Blackmar, *Manhattan For Rent, 1785–1850* (Ithaca: Cornell University Press, 1989), pp. 205–9; *New York Daily Tribune*, 1847.

5 St Brigid's Church has continued to play a very active role in the community during the crises of the past few years. Father Kuhn of this church was a community spokesperson and intermediary between 'rioters' and police in the August 1988 mêlée, and a defender of the homeless for whom the church opened a soup kitchen. When the homeless were evicted from the park, some resettled on the vacant lots just east of the church on which an eventual AIDS facility is to be built.

6 Proceedings of the Board of Aldermen of the City of New York, Vol. 33 (13 September 1847), p. 656. For more accounts of city repairs and improvements, see Proceedings of the Board of Aldermen, 1855–1864, New York City Municipal Archives.

7 For a brief description of Tompkins Square during the economic panic, see Iver Bernstein, *The New York City Draft Riots* (New York: Oxford University Press, 1990), pp. 138–41. Also see Documents of the Board of Aldermen, Vol. 24, no. 19 (9 November 1857), p. 4, Municipal Archives of the City of New York.

8 Peter Buckley, 'To the Opera House: Culture and Society in New York City, 1820–1860,' doctoral dissertation, State University of New York, 1984.

9 Documents of the Board of Aldermen, Vol. 30, no. 19 (30 September 1863), p. 63; Vol. 31, no. 17 (30 June 1864), p. 60; Vol. 33, no. 17 (30 June 1866), p. 57, Municipal Archives. Also see New York State Legislature, chapter 593 of the Laws of 1866.

10 Stanley Nadel, *Kleindeutschland: New York City's Germans, 1845–1880* (Urbana: University of Illinois Press, 1990); Robert Ernst, *Immigrant Life in New York City, 1825–1863* (Port Washington, NY: Ira J. Friedman, Inc., 1949).

11 *The Daily Graphic*, 4 October 1873, p. 668; *Harpers Weekly*, 13 September 1873, p. 802; Nadel, *Kleindeutschland.*

12 Department of Public Parks, *The Third General Report of the Board of Commissioners of the Department of Public Parks, May 1872–December 1873*, p. 21, Municipal Archives; Report from the Department of Public Parks to Mayor Havermeyer, 6 August 1873, box 80, Mayor Havermeyer's Papers, Municipal Archives.

13 *Harpers Weekly*, 13 September 1873, p. 802.

14 See the classic article by Herbert Gutman, 'The Tompkins Square "Riot" in New York City on January 13, 1874: A Reexamination of its Causes and its Aftermath,' *Labor History* 6 (winter 1965), pp. 45–70.

15 Ibid., p. 67.

16 Department of Public Parks, *The Third General Report of the Board of Commissioners of the Department of Public Parks, May 1872–December 1873*, p. 21, Municipal Archives. For a description of the poor condition of the park, see Park Commissioner Stebbins to Mayor Wickham, 27 January 1875, box 81, Mayor Wickham's Papers, Municipal Archives; Ethan Carr, *Three Hundred Years of Parks: A Timeline of New York City Park History* (New York: City of New York Parks and Recreation, 1988), p. 18.

17 Frederick Law Olmsted to the Honorable W. R. Martin (9 August 1875) reel 48, Olmsted Papers, Manuscript Division, Library of Congress, Washington, DC; *The New York Times*, 27 January 1875, p. 7; *New York Daily Tribune*, 1 June 1875, p. 5.

18 Stebbins to Wickham, 27 January 1875; *New York Daily Tribune*, 1 June 1875, p. 5.

19 Olmsted to Martin, 9 August 1875.

20 Proceedings of the Board of Aldermen, Vol. 141 (20 April, 4 May 1876), pp. 136–7. For debate regarding completion of Tompkins Square repairs, see Proceedings of the Board of Aldermen, Vol. 141 (February–November 1876). Also see *New York Daily Tribune*, 7 July 1876, p. 2; 28 July 1876, p. 8; 5 August 1876, p. 5; 24 November 1876, p. 8; *The New York Times*, 3 June 1876, p. 10.

21 *The New York Times*, 3 June 1876, p. 10.

22 Proceedings of the Board of Aldermen, Department of Public Parks to the Board of Aldermen, (16 July 1878), p. 98, Municipal Archives. Presumably, property holders would have more say than tenants. Nevertheless, official recognition of community interest was a significant gain.
23 New York State Legislature, Chapter 411 of the Laws of 1878; *The New York Times*, 20 May 1879, p. 10.
24 *New York Daily Tribune*, 29 August 1879, p. 3.
25 *The New York Times*, 5 September 1879, p. 2.
26 Richard Lieberman, 'Social Change and Political Behavior: The East Village of New York City,' doctoral dissertation, New York University, 1976.
27 Report of the Small Parks Advisory Committee to Mayor William L. Strong, 28 October 1897, box 90, Mayor Strong's Papers, Municipal Archives.
28 Thomas A. Edison, Inc., ca.1904. George Kleine Collection of Early Motion Pictures, no. FLA1872, Library of Congress, Washington, DC.
29 Report of the Bureau of Recreation, Department of Parks, *Park Playgrounds of the City of New York, 1911–1912*, pp. 31–9. Municipal Library.
30 Meta Lilienthal, *Dear Remembered World: Childhood Memories of an Old New Yorker* (New York: R. R. Smith, 1947).
31 Ironically this structure, renovated in the 1980s and subdivided into expensive co-op apartments, now symbolizes gentrification and is the object of much resentment, as shall be seen in later chapters.
32 As youngsters, the Gershwin brothers played at the Christodora House.
33 Cooper Union, with its Great Hall and educational programs, was only three blocks away. Emma Goldman lived at 212 East Thirteenth Street. Before World War I, the International Workers of the World had headquarters at 64 East Fourth Street, and during the 1920s, the American Communist Party was located at 80 East Eleventh Street.
34 Personal interview with Mrs Miriam Singer, April 1989.
35 'Regional Survey of New York and Its Environs,' *Public Recreation* 5, p. 154. Municipal Library.
36 F. Hulbert, *New York: City of Cities* (New York: J. B. Lippincott Co., 1937), pp. 123–4.
37 For an account of New Deal parks renovation and Moses' philosophy, see Robert A. Caro, *The Power Broker: Robert Moses and the Fall of New York* (New York: Vintage Books, 1974).
38 Design blueprints for Tompkins Square, Department of Parks and Recreation, Olmsted Center, Flushing Meadows–Corona Park, Queens, New York. Also see Department of Parks press release to Jack Galin, *PM* newspaper, 6 January 1942, box 102596, Department of Parks Records, Municipal Archives. For funding shortages, see R. Moses to *East Side News*, 28 June 1939, box 102451, Department of Parks Records, Municipal Archives. In addition, see Tompkins Square folders, correspondence from 1939 to January 1942, Department of Parks Records.
39 Correspondence and memos, April–August 1957, box 102984, Department of Parks Records, Municipal Archives.
40 G. Quigley to S. Constable, 10 June 1957; J. Mulcahy to S. Constable with 'Development Plan for Reconstruction,' 19 August 1957, box 102984, Department of Parks Records, Municipal Archives.

41 'East Side Wins Fight for Air, Green Space,' *Village Voice*, 5 October 1961, p. 1.
42 'Recommendations of the Rehabilitation of Tompkins Square,' report compiled by the Committee for the Preservation of Tompkins Square Park, 21 November 1961, Department of Parks Records, box 103125, Municipal Archives.
43 'Citizens View Their Parks,' Park Association of New York City, Inc. (later renamed the Parks Council), September 1962, p. 2.
44 Personal interview with Chino Garcia, April 1989.
45 Department of Parks press release, 24 June 1962, box 108719, Department of Parks Records, Municipal Archives.
46 Correspondence and petitions, April–August 1964, Department of Parks Records, Municipal Archives.
47 'East Side Wins Fight for Air,' p. 1.
48 'Does an East Village Exist?' *East Village Other* 1 (15 February to 1 March 1966), p. 2.
49 Jonathan Soffer, 'The Story of the Mass Arrests of Hippies in Tompkins Square Park, Memorial Day, 1967,' Masters thesis, Columbia University, 1986, p. 18.
50 Ibid., pp. 21–2. See Gordon, chapter 10, for more details.

5

Déjà Vu: Replanning the Lower East Side in the 1930s

Suzanne Wasserman

> *10th ST. E. VILLAGE COOP BLDG has prime apts avail for immed sale Great loc for students and Wall Streeters.*

Listings in the real estate section of New York City newspapers, such as the one above, had become common in the 1980s at the height of the housing market boom on the Lower East Side. They seemed finally to be realizing a powerful fantasy about a gentrified Lower East Side, one that had been dreamed almost sixty years earlier by a group of local merchants, city planners, architects, and developers who envisioned the renovation and renewal of the Lower East Side exclusively for upper-middle-class professionals, freed of any vestiges of immigrant life. Their vision, often contested by local residents, was interrupted by the Depression and after that by the LaGuardia administration, only to re-emerge in the 1980s. Many of the conflicts over housing and the future that characterize the present period were foreshadowed in that earlier cycle of aborted 'gentrification.'

The contest over housing in the 1920s and 1930s involved attempts to displace the traditional working-class poor who had populated the East Side for at least a century. Then, as now, the proponents of remaking the Lower East Side underestimated East Siders' fierce attachment to place, while developers and urban planners ran into trouble when they sought to override the wishes of existing residents. And then, as now, the 'space' opened up by displacement was seen as an opportunity for change.

As Grebler noted in his study of housing on the Lower East Side, the zone had been losing population since the 1920s. Deteriorating housing, coupled with upward mobility, had been a major contributor to the exodus. In 1927–8, the tenement vacancy rate on the Lower East Side was already averaging some 14 percent.[1] The Depression intensified this. By 1930 the Tenement House Commission found more than 13,000 vacant tenement apartments on the Lower East Side, representing a vacancy rate of 20 percent.[2] The vacant units were in very poor condition. A study in 1933 reported that more than half of the buildings on the East Side lacked central heat and private toilets. Three out of five apartments had only hall bathrooms, and two out of five had no baths at all. Two-thirds of all toilets were still in the backyard and 78 percent of tenements still had no steam heat.[3]

One of the worst problems was the persistence of rear dwellings. Rear houses were Old-Law tenements, built behind 'front houses;' they drew light exclusively from a tiny courtyard that separated the rear and front houses. Joseph Platzker of the *East Side Chamber News* reported that in 1930 over 10,000 inhabitants (some paying as little as $2 per room per month, as compared to the Lower East Side average of $6) lived in rear houses on the Lower East Side. Most occupants were illiterate and unskilled immigrants.[4]

The persistence of horrendous living conditions stimulated Lower East Side radicalism during the Depression. These same conditions put different notions into the heads of some developers, planners and local merchants. Deteriorating living conditions, coupled with the dramatic exodus that had occurred in the 1920s, created the illusion of an empty neighborhood, up for grabs. In reality, however, in 1930 the Lower East Side remained the most densely populated neighborhood in the city; five years later, it was second only to East Harlem.[5]

During the 1920s and even in the 1930s, local residents and outside developers and planners clashed over the fate of the Lower East Side and over who its future occupants would be.[6] Decrepit conditions, for example, convinced some members of the Lower East Side Chamber of Commerce that the time was ripe for an area renaissance. In fact, initial efforts in the mid-1920s to widen Allen, Chrystie, and Forsyth Streets gave these Lower East Side merchants hope that the city supported their renewal aspirations. The merchants initially believed that street widenings would stimulate improvements in other arenas. 'Our historic neighborhood is due for a great revival . . . 1930 should be crowded with public improvements,' Peter P. Cappel wrote in the *East Side Chamber News* on the very eve of the stock market crash.[7]

Convinced that improved housing conditions could lure newly middle-class ex-Lower East Siders back to their former neighborhood, local merchants supported housing reforms. 'A great many [former residents] want to be back with their friends and neighbors with whom they had spent so many years of their life in peace and contentment,' wrote one merchant in the pages of the *East Side Chamber News*.[8] Their return depended, however, on ridding the East Side of its immigrant vestiges. 'The "new" East Side is not lacking in gemutlichkeit' (a sense of homey warmth), wrote one businessman. The 'new' East Side, merchants hoped, would bring ex-East Siders back to live, but in a de-ethnicized and sanitary community.

In retrospect at least, their expectations were not ridiculous. In fact, just before 1930 several builders were investing in modern high-rise buildings on Second Avenue. Samuel Ageloff, for example, was 'prepared to stake his fortune in helping to rebuild the East Side.' In May 1928, construction of Ageloff Towers began at the cost of $2.5 million. With terracotta trim and an Italianate garden in the rear, this building on Avenue A and Third Street was intended to 'rival any structure in beauty on West End Avenue.'[9] Saul Birns, another developer, built the Stuyvesant Apartments at Tenth Street and Second Avenue, renting them for $50 per room per month.[10] One indication of how untimely these investments were is that when the stock market crashed, Samuel Ageloff committed suicide by jumping from the top of his completed Towers.

In 1929, several months before the crash, a number of articles were recommending that downtown neighborhoods could be revitalized to house white-collar workers of the financial district. For example, H. I. Phillips suggested that a 'back to the city' trend was in the making.[11] Although Lower East Side merchants felt that newly rich ex-East Siders were the most likely candidates to repopulate the 'new East Side,' they also hoped to appeal to workers on Wall Street. Edwin Lahm, vice-president of Citizens' Savings Bank, predicted that the Lower East Side would become the 'hub of lower civic and financial districts' whose tenants would be bankers and brokers. Why not re-create the walking city, he urged.[12] Members of the East Side Chamber themselves showed their faith in the renaissance by collecting $1,000 from 100 businessmen in order to build modern apartments for white-collar workers from the financial district. They hoped to rent these for $20 per room per month.[13]

The idea of housing white-collar workers close to their workplaces had already been successfully tested by developer Fred F. French. In the mid-1920s French had razed the eastern part of 42nd Street for his $100 million Tudor City which covered several acres and included lawns, trees, and an 18-hole miniature golf course, all within a five-minute walk of midtown.[14] French was also secretly amassing land on the Lower East Side for a similar venture. French coined the expression, 'Walk to Work,' in his Tudor City campaign; advocates of 'Walk to Work' soon directed this phrase to the Lower East Side.

In March 1931, the influential *Survey Graphic* magazine ran an article by Loula D. Lasker that advocated renovating the Lower East Side as a residential district. Manufacturing had peaked on the east side in 1917, just before the garment trade fled uptown to escape rising land values. Lasker reasoned that because land values were so high, the only hope for the east side to rejuvenate itself was to build for Wall Streeters. Her analysis made no mention of working-class and poor Lower East Siders; presumably they would simply move away.

> The East Side must look for its regeneration to an influx of a population much higher in the economic scale. It must no longer lose its people who prosper. It must put on a white collar. Land values [make] it practically impossible to erect new buildings within the means of the 'under $2000' income group.[15]

Members of the Regional Plan Association (RPA) heartily agreed. Funded by the Russell Sage Foundation beginning in 1922, the RPA unfolded its comprehensive urban planning scheme in 1929. The men who made up the RPA were drawn almost exclusively from the city's banking and business elites and included members of the First National Bank, the J. P. Morgan Trust, and the Rockefeller Institute.[16] Their intention was to 'map out a course for systematic and orderly growth' for New York City and the tri-state area.[17] The RPA published specific recommendations for the Lower East Side in an article that appeared in the *ESCN* in March 1930. George B. Ford, General Director of the RPA, suggested that the Lower East Side needed to be 'opened up, to let in more sunlight and air. The streets must be cleaned and made "orderly".'[18] On 1 July 1930, the RPA announced that the Lower East Side should be recreated 'as a commodious and inviting residential district.' The RPA's call for deconcentrating the Lower East Side amounted to displacement of local residents. The population had already dropped drastically; the question was what to do with those who remained. The RPA concluded that they should be 'decentralized' to cheaper land in the other boroughs and outlying areas, thus making room for more middle-class newcomers. Members of the RPA implicitly assumed that East Siders could be passively and easily dislodged from their roots and that those still there simply had no alternatives.

The Regional Plan Association made clear for whom this residential district was to be renovated: 'the Lower East Side has a strategic location because of its proximity to the business and industrial centers of the city, and it has the natural advantage of a marvelous waterfront along the East River.'[19] *The New York Times* quoted Thomas Adams, former Housing and Town Planning adviser to the Canadian government, who directed the RPA's survey of the East Side: 'This district may be converted into one of desirable and comfortable homes, including both high-class residences and those with moderate rentals, accommodating the varying requirements of those seeking quarters convenient to the business and industrial areas of southern Manhattan.' His plan was so elitist that he even suggested yacht basins be installed on the East River![20] On 20 April 1931, the RPA released an official information bulletin entitled 'The Lower East Side, Its Past and Present. What Should Be Its Future? Certain Projects and Proposals.' It reiterated the East Side's 'strategic merit as a residential district for the so-called white collar workers.'[21] The plan envisioned a 'four-block square with quarters for 7,000 people . . . in a light, airy community of towers and terraces, playgrounds and gardens.'[22]

Plans to construct an East River Drive and to rezone the Lower East Side entailed displacing existing residents. Although attempts to institute both began with the rest of the upscaling efforts in the late 1920s, ironically, these two efforts were only realized in the late 1930s when other attempts to create a middle-class white-collar Lower East Side had collapsed. In 1929, Manhattan Borough President Julius Miller introduced a plan for the East River Drive to the Board of Estimate. He explicitly saw this as a way to encourage luxury building.[23] Other reformers endorsed his idea, linking the roadway to middle-class renewal ambitions. Loula Lasker, for example, argued that the waterfront was the 'crux of the situation' when it came to revitalizing the Lower East Side. 'Probably no single undertaking is more vital than the construction of the East River Drive and the enlargement of Corlears Hook Park,' she wrote.[24]

The new roadway required rezoning the waterfront, however. Vacant stores, factories, stables, garages, and chemical plants lined the East River and these needed to be removed. Furthermore, future non-residential buildings had to be prohibited. The struggle by local merchants and developers to rezone the waterfront soon extended to the entire Lower East Side. While half of the area was zoned for business use and the rest was unrestricted, proponents of rezoning wanted to redesign the Lower East Side for exclusively residential use.[25] As early as 1928 the East Side Chamber of Commerce began to demand new zoning laws.[26] This had as much to do with renovating the Lower East Side as it had to do with regulating business. Although the area had lost almost half of its population and its industry had fled, the number of retail shops actually increased between 1920 and 1930. Zoning restrictions would rid the avenues of 'side-street competition' which was 'no credit to the community.'[27]

In 1930, a City Planning Bill passed in the Board of Estimate, despite opposition from four borough presidents.[28] John Sullivan, head of the City Planning Commission, agreed with the merchants and builders that rehabilitating the waterfront on the Lower East Side was pivotal. A year later, the Lower East Side Planning Association became the first district planning association in the city. Its goal was to work in conjunction with the City Planning Commission.[29] Its Board of Directors included five bank presidents, three vice-presidents, and several members of the New York Taxpayers' Association. The absence of any settlement house workers, community activists, or working people made perfectly clear in whose corner the Planning Association would be. The planning and creation of several housing developments on the Lower East Side during the first half of the 1930s made even plainer the upscale vision this group had mapped out for a 'new' Lower East Side.

New Housing for the Old Neighborhood

East Siders had fought for many years for better housing, but their goals focused on winning concessions from landlords, not having their homes renovated for others. The developers, on the other hand, just wanted the tenants gone. The creation of the Amalgamated Houses and of Knickerbocker Village illustrated attitudes toward current residents that ranged from paternalism to contempt. While these attitudes were not necessarily new, what was new was the belief that a depopulated Lower East Side was ripe for middle-class development and that displacement of the poor and working class was a necessary and acceptable part of it.

One editorial put the issue succinctly when it concluded that the present population would have to go; the land was too valuable for use as low-income housing.[30] Similarly, Harold Buttenheim asked a rhetorical question in his article in the *American City*: Should East Siders be rehoused in modern tenements on high-value land or, more appropriately from his perspective, should they be removed to 'cheaper land in outlying boroughs or in the suburbs' to allow the Lower East Side to be rebuilt for the middle and upper classes?[31] Housing and town planning expert Carol Aronovici went even farther, recommending that the Lower East Side be rebuilt exclusively for the wealthy. Even the white-collar class was to be excluded:

> Perhaps it would be best if the most expensive land be devoted to the creating of very high-grade apartment house property and let the rich come back to Manhattan and the lower east side where they once created the city and developed it . . . [W]e should quit trying to rehabilitate lower Manhattan for the poor and give it back to the well-to-do. The rich could live close to the financial district.[32]

Ironically, at least one project intended to house local workers in the garment trades ended up housing a middle-class population drawn mostly from other areas. The builders of Amalgamated Houses held it up as a shining example of what could be accomplished in housing reform for the Lower East Side. The reality, however, was something altogether different. In effect, Amalgamated Houses turned out to be a shining example of what could be accomplished for white-collar workers in a 'new' and upgraded Lower East Side, because its apartments were well beyond the price range of most working and poor Lower East Siders. The details are illuminating.

On 3 April 1929, the State Housing Board, formed under the leadership of Governor Al Smith to promote the building of New-Law tenements, announced plans for the development of a model housing project. Aaron Rabinowitz of the State Housing Board and Lt Governor Lehman bought at public auction for $550,000 two square blocks of land occupied by the R. Hoe Printing Company, in turn transferring the land to a limited-dividend corporation called the Amalgamated Dwelling Corporation, sponsored by the Amalgamated Clothing Workers' Union. Rabinowitz became treasurer of the corporation. The guidelines of the State Housing Law exempted this 'limited-dividend' project from local taxes for 20 years, limited investors to a 6 percent annual return, and prohibited rents from exceeding $12.50 per room per month. The project was to receive no direct government subsidy nor would it receive any private funds either.[33] Within five weeks of announcing these plans, the *ESCN* received 500 requests for applications.[34] By September 1929, another 500 requests had been received.[35] Lasker later waxed ecstatic over the Amalgamated building at 504-20 Grand Street:

> It was as if a fairy wand had been waved, for there in front of our eyes stood a modern six-story elevator apartment building right in the midst of one of the worst tenement districts. We entered a large central court which formed a charming garden. A fountain in the center and shrubs everywhere . . . This represents the East Side of Tomorrow.[36]

Some suggested that East Siders would have to alter their behavior if they hoped to be included in the 'East Side of Tomorrow.' For example, a 1930 article in *The New York Times* expressed concern that East Siders would not make appropriate residents for this modern building because at first 'old habits may manifest themselves.' The article worried about the persistence of 'slum' living attitudes:

> Grandmothers will probably want to air their bedding on window frames, boys will shout across the courtyard or try to play ball there, women will try to string clothes-lines on the roofs, children may throw banana peelings out onto the street or into the courtyard.[37]

But such worries were in fact unnecessary since few East Siders could afford an apartment there. Residents required an average salary of $2,000 per year, which then represented the salary of a fairly prosperous middle-class American urban dweller.[38] In addition, tenants had to become stockholders in the corporation. Apartments sold for $500 per room, with a credit union assisting tenants by a loan of up to $350. Even to be considered as potential tenants, then, families needed at least $450 in cash. A *New York Times* editorial called the project 'too ambitious,' saying that a workingman's family with an average income of $100 to $125 a month could not pay $12 per room:

> The model tenements, from the practical point of view, are too model. There ought to be some middle ground between the old dumbbell rookeries east of Allen Street . . . and Park Avenue standards. Garden courts, communal libraries, swimming pools, electric refrigeration are not essential. If costs can be reduced by building on 60 percent of the plot instead of only 50 percent, it is worth thinking about. Any economy that pushes acceptable sanitary housing a dollar a month a room downward to the average of $8 a month which the poor can afford deserves consideration.[39]

This editorial pinpointed the contradication inherent in the creation of Amalgamated Houses. Ostensibly built for Lower East Siders but emulating middle-class standards and aesthetics, by the time it was completed only business and professional tenants could afford to move in.[40]

By December 1930, 90 percent of the apartments had been sold, and when the project opened a month later, occupancy was complete. But significantly, almost one-third of the tenants came from outside, hailing from Brooklyn, the Bronx, Harlem, and even New Jersey.[41] Almost half of the renters were independent businessmen, 15 percent were professionals, and 8 percent were government employees. The others were skilled laborers and salesmen.[42]

The Amalgamated had professed to be for the working class, even though the opposite turned out to be the case. In contrast, Fred F. French's project, Knickerbocker Village, expected to attract only the rich. In April 1929 word leaked to the press that 100,000 people living in 19 blocks between the Manhattan and Brooklyn Bridges had received notice to vacate their homes within six months. Although the plan had still not been made public, an article in the *New York Herald Tribune* noted that 'reports persisted among real estate brokers and lawyers that the property was being bought to build a restricted apartment house section from which business men could walk to their work in the Wall Street district.'[43]

French had originally hoped his project would cover 40 acres and house some 30,000 persons at a cost of $150 million, but the Depression altered these plans considerably.[44] When French's plan solidified late in 1931, he announced a scaled-down $50 million 'White Collar City.' To avoid rampant speculation, between 1928 and 1931 French had secretly purchased 14.5 acres of land in some 250 to 300 separate parcels, buying up the properties through four dummy corporations. In the scaled-down version French still hoped to create large apartments (to be rented at about $20 per room) for executives, bankers, brokers, and office workers in the City Hall and Wall Street areas.[45]

Although the city had halted all municipal improvement projects in January 1932, French forged ahead. The Depression eventually caught up with him when, in the spring of 1932, he failed to get mortgage funds. Ultimately, the newly created US Reconstruction Finance Corporation bailed him out. In 1933, the State Housing Board awarded him a mortgage loan of $8,075,000, but stipulated that the development would be a limited-dividend project with rents not exceeding $12.50 per room per month. By July 1934, French had received more than 400 applications, including many from Queens, the West Village, New Jersey, and Connecticut.[46] Although 1,600 apartments in two 12-story towers were planned, by the fall of 1934 only one of the towers was complete. On 3 October 1934, six weeks behind schedule, the first residents moved in. *The New York Times* wrote on 3 October 1934 that Knickerbocker Village was a 'fine venture in slum clearance and an indication that the 'Walk to Work' slogan is not without its appeal.'[47]

Even though the Depression frustrated French's plans for a truly exclusive housing venture, Knickerbocker Village, like Amalgamated Houses, was still far beyond the reach of an average Lower East Sider. Neighborhood residents were chiefly laborers, dock workers, pushcart peddlers, shopkeepers, and shoemakers. Few could afford the rent of $12.50 per room. French had never pretended to care what happened to the former tenants of the area. In 1931, when his plans were more grandiose, he had predicted that 8,000 would be displaced. 'People who will be forced to leave the old district will find housing in other boroughs,' he announced nonchalantly.[48]

Ultimately, French's disregard for Lower East Siders extended even to those tenants of moderate means who actually moved into his complex. French and the management of Knickerbocker Village conflated their middle-income tenants with traditional 'slum dwellers,' treating them with contempt from the beginning. While the tenants were certainly not the prosperous customers he originally had in mind, they were middle-class clerks, secretaries, salesmen as well as artists, lawyers, nurses, doctors, and stenographers.[49] They certainly did not expect to be treated like slum dwellers of the Lower East Side. Nevertheless, they were. Knickerbocker Village management advised all 800 tenants to move in on the same day, even though construction had not been completed. Some apartments lacked finished floors, bathroom and kitchen fixtures, and painted walls.[50] The apartments were without promised amenities such as dryers, refrigerators, and central radio installations.[51] But what infuriated the new tenants most was the manner in which management treated them. One tenant told a *New York Herald Tribune* reporter that she had 'friends in other Fred French apartments and they do not receive such treatment as we do. I really am losing my self respect. I sort of feel that I am the object of charity.'[52]

In protest, four women in the building called a meeting in early October 1934 to which more than 600 of the 800 tenants came. Residents formed the Knickerbocker Village Tenants' Association and voted to go on rent strike. Three days later representatives met with French and the State Housing Board, asking that their October rent be applied to November. On 30 October they voted to withhold one month's rent entirely as a rebate.[53] By the middle of November, French had agreed to rebate individuals, but refused blanket concessions. Three weeks later, activists organized a permanent tenant association.[54] When French refused to renew 14 leases in the summer of 1935, the tenant association threatened to sue. Although the State Housing Board said it had no jurisdiction over leases, it urged French to renew the leases and stated that 'representative tenant organizations are desireable and necessary in large projects to foster and engage in community activities to be a mechanism by which a harmonious relationship between tenant and management may be established and maintained.'[55] Ultimately the 14 tenants lost their leases, but by March 1936 a City-Wide Tenants' Council had been organized, instigated in large part by the tenants of Knickerbocker Village's sympathetic rent strike in solidarity with a building service strike.[56] The rent war at Knickerbocker Village triggered a re-emergence of vigorous tenant organizing in the 1930s on the Lower East Side. Ironically, the organizing impetus in the mid-1930s came not from grassroots radicals and reformers, but from the very source of displacement itself – the tenants of Knickerbocker Village.

The broader history of Lower East Side tenant organizing is well told elsewhere, but French's plan, even in its greatly declassed execution, was undermined by those for whom he created it. Not only had French failed to alter a section of the Lower East Side, but the radicalism that emerged from his tenants reinserted Knickerbocker Village into the texture of traditional Lower East Side life. Despite the creation of Knickerbocker Village, a 'new' Lower East Side failed to emerge. The hopes of Fred F. French, Robert W. A. Rodgers of Rutgerstown, Thomas Adams, Carol Aronovici, and members of the East Side Chamber of Commerce for a 'new' East Side were but a pipe dream.

ATTACHMENT TO PLACE

Both renewed tenant activism and economic reversals contributed to the failure to alter the Lower East Side. In addition, and not to be underestimated, was the deep commitment and attachment Lower East Siders had to their neighborhood. While it could not prevent all development, it did strengthen resistance against displacement. Developers and planners had underestimated how attached residents were to their community. They had viewed the resident population as transient and passive, ignoring the power of tradition and the attachment to place felt by East Siders. This attachment to place energized their fight for better conditions and stimulated opposition to gentrification. In 1936, an editorial appeared in the *Henry Street Bulletin* which reflected this resentment: 'I haven't quite gotten over the shock of Knickerbocker Village which was built for the Wall Street businessmen while advertised as being being built for the people of the slum area.'[57] This anger was exacerbated by the fact that the cost of constructing even one of the 12-story towers of Knickerbocker Village equaled the aggregate investment in new housing on the Lower East Side over the previous ten years.[58]

Even more than resentment, though, was the reality that the area would be more difficult to transform than developers originally imagined. The displaced tenants just moved to other buildings on the Lower East Side. In 1933 the Lavanburg Foundation and Hamilton House Settlement carried out a study called 'What Happened to the 386 Families Who Were Compelled to Vacate Their Slum Dwellings to Make Way for a Large Housing Project.' The survey focused on the experiences of those forced to move to make way for Knickerbocker Village. It found that the vast majority were long-term residents who had found other housing in the immediate neighborhood. Only 6 percent had lived in the neighborhood less than five years. Some 83 percent of the displaced tenants moved to other Old-Law tenements in the neighborhood. More significantly, many families who had been on the same block or building for years insisted on staying together. Ultimately, despite difficulties resettling, only 14 percent left the area.[59] A 1938 survey found, not surprisingly, that of the 386 displaced families, only three had actually moved into Knickerbocker Village's 1,600 new apartments.[60]

Knickerbocker Village had mostly displaced Italian families, but another study carried out a year later by the Henry Street Settlement found that Jewish families had a similar fierce attachment to their community. The report, entitled 'What Some Slum Dwellers Want in Housing: Findings of A Study of One Square Block in the Lower East Side,' presented responses from 234 families, primarily Russian or Polish Jews, who were all living in Old-Law tenements.[61] Some 60 percent had lived on the East

Side for more than 20 years. The interviewers asked whether respondents would be willing to move to new garden apartments 'in outlying sections of the city provided transportation were available and rent was within the family means.' About three-fourths of those living on East Broadway stated that they did not want to leave the Lower East Side, although almost half said that they were unhappy with their living conditions. Of those on the other streets, 68 percent were unhappy with conditions, but almost 50 percent said they were unwilling to leave. This was so, despite the fact that some families paid up to 60 percent of their incomes to rent.[62] This attachment to place clearly impeded the creation of a 'new' East Side for the middle class and wealthy. In sum, many remaining Lower East Siders were firmly entrenched in the neighborhood and, most importantly, if given a choice, would remain.

Their reasons were well illustrated in Michael Gold's autobiography, *Jews Without Money*, which described his mother's motives for wanting to stay on the East Side, since she was comfortable with old friends, language and customs:

> The East Side was her village now, she saw no reason for leaving it even on Sunday. She still lives on the East Side, on the same street, in the same tenement, an unhurried peasant. She has never been out of New York City. There are millions of such peasants in New York.[63]

Many social workers were unable to fathom this attachment to place, perceiving it as sociopathic. For example, Harry Shulman was horrified to hear one of his respondents claim: 'I would die if I had to move where I did not know families – to another block – even with cheaper rent.'[64] Shulman, in his study of the fictionalized 'Tyler Street' on the Lower East Side between 1925 and 1932, found the slum a 'way of living and thinking.' He deplored the 'growth of a social class . . . content with inferior housing, inferior living standards and inferior ethical controls over the younger generation [who] constitute a menace to urban community life.' Shulman's conclusion, however, was completely contradicted by his own evidence, for rather than subject to instability and chaos, Lower East Siders were deeply rooted in their community. An unusually high percentage of families on 'Tyler Street' had lived on the same block for years; 40 percent had been there for more than 20 years.[65] They also demonstrated their fierce attachment to place by fighting for better housing. They were not simply passive residents wallowing in poverty, although social theorists such as Shulman portrayed them as such. Housing, in fact, was the one issue that always galvanized Lower East Siders into action.

Women of the area had always been active in the movement for better housing conditions. In the late 1920s, the Housing Committee of the

United Neighborhood Houses urged the League of Mothers' Clubs to study the housing problem and to canvas for improvements. Subsequently, members of Mothers' Clubs on the Lower East Side became active advocates for housing reform, attending meetings at City Hall and testifying before the legislature in Albany.[66] In 1934, the League of Mothers' Clubs sent a delegation to Albany to try to get legislators to enforce the 1929 Multiple Dwelling Law requiring toilets and fire retarding in every apartment.[67] Several years later, representatives rode the bus all night to Washington DC to testify before the Senate in support of the Wagner-Steagall Housing Bill which promoted the formation of the United States Housing Authority. They took with them a book of 600 photographs of Old-Law tenements, each snapshot signed as a protest. 'We made those senators cry before we got through,' recalled one mother.[68]

THE LAGUARDIA YEARS: RAZING THE SLUMS AT ALL COSTS

This attachment to place – compounded by economic considerations and renewed tenant activism – stifled developers' and planners' hopes for a transformed Lower East Side. The final nail in the coffin of the 'new' East Side came with the arrival of the LaGuardia administration and its unprecedented ability to pour federal funds into slum clearance. Although committed to creating livable conditions for poor and working-class people, LaGuardia went about attempting to clear the slums in the same strident manner in which he did everything. And although out of very different motives, LaGuardia's solutions for the East Side paralleled those of the developers and planners because, in his zeal, he both ignored and trod on Lower East Siders' attachments to their community.

Although defeated in Congress in 1932, LaGuardia launched a successful bid for mayor under the Fusion movement which melded together reformers and anti-Tammany Democrats. LaGuardia was idealistic and compassionate, but his responses to problems were also spontaneous, often bordering on rash.[69] LaGuardia was obsessed with issues of public health and housing, instituting a pace of change with the help of the federal government that was unparalleled. Housing became LaGuardia's personal crusade. He revelled in the excitement of dramatic change. On the Lower East Side he saw an opportunity to dramatize the issue of housing by rebuilding; such a mammoth accomplishment would win New York City a place in the national limelight.[70]

LaGuardia's determination to clear slums became a priority in part because of the New Deal's unprecedented commitment to helping troubled

American cities. The Civil Works Administration created work for four million unemployed Americans by funding federal improvements in localities. For the first time ever, the federal government offered money directly to cities. LaGuardia went not to Albany but to Washington where he found a sympathetic ear for his dreams and plans for New York City in the like-minded liberal pragmatist, Franklin Delano Roosevelt. New York City received $1.5 billion between 1933 and 1938. In return, Roosevelt saw a way to create jobs and to capture the immigrant urban vote.

LaGuardia's strategy, however, was often hardest on East Siders themselves. He had little patience for sentiment, even the sentiment of those who were the intended beneficiaries of his reforms. Local residents took the brunt of his zeal in housing reform. As soon as he entered office, he demanded that the Tenement House Department begin enforcing the Multiple Dwelling Law. If landlords could not bring buildings up to code, their tenements would be torn down.[71] LaGuardia would grant no more moratoriums. His edict was: improve the buildings or vacate them.[72] And in 1934 to 1935, almost immediately after LaGuardia became mayor, the city oversaw the demolition of 900 buildings.[73] By May 1936, the expanse of vacant lots on the Lower East Side had tripled, rising from 200,000 square feet in 1934 to almost 650,000 by 1936.[74] Because of this clearance, the Lower East Side was experiencing a critical housing shortage by 1937. Of the 40,000 low-rent apartments demolished in New York City between 1933 and 1937, some 15,000 were on the Lower East Side.[75] A third of them had been demolished since 1935.[76] *The Real Estate Record* reported that rents had increased by 41.3 percent since 1934 and that vacancies on the East Side were now at a mere 5 percent. The year 1936 witnessed the sharpest drop in vacancies ever observed; between March and November, vacancies declined by 46 percent.[77]

Although some of the tenant organizers agreed with LaGuardia's policy, the severe shortage of low-rent housing caused considerable suffering. Tenants in buildings brought up to code usually had to move because of rent increases. In other tenements, where landlords could not or would not comply, owners simply lost their properties through foreclosures.[78] Despite good intentions, these methods of reform benefited few Lower East Siders and, at least in the case of remodeled tenements, ironically created more housing for white-collar residents and less for the poor.[79] In spring of 1936, the New York City Housing Authority tried to respond to this crisis by setting up a Vacancy Bureau to help relocate displaced households. The Bureau's 1936 survey found a net loss of 39 percent of vacant Lower East Side apartments. The primary reasons tenants moved were rent nonpayment or increases, the boarding-up of buildings, orders to vacate, renovation, and demolition.[80]

THE BIRTH OF PUBLIC HOUSING

In 1933, the federal government made money available to localities for slum clearance and low-cost housing. In February 1934, New York City created the New York City Housing Authority. Its first undertaking was the renovation of First Houses on Third Street between Avenue A and First Avenue. In December 1934, the city acquired from Vincent Astor eight tenement buildings on more than 53,000 square feet of land for less than $200,000. The Federal Emergency Relief Administration supplied money for work relief labor and materials.[81] Although the Housing Authority had planned to renovate the tenements, ultimately all were virtually rebuilt.

First Houses, formally dedicated on 3 December 1935, about one year after the opening of Knickerbocker Village, was the 'first government low-rental housing development in the history of the country.'[82] Rents were set at an average of $6.05 per room per month, still beyond the means of the poor. Skilled workers made up the largest number of tenants, followed by smaller numbers of unskilled workers, clerical workers, professionals and small merchants.[83] Furthermore, demand far outstripped supply. The New York City Housing Authority received 4,000 applications for 120 apartments. First Houses could accommodate fewer than three percent of those who applied.

Although the city congratulated itself for erecting First Houses, neighborhood people knew that it was a small victory indeed. After all, the project was less than a city block. An editorial in the *Henry Street Bulletin* expressed outrage at the limitations of the project:

> The housing situation is very acute. Instead of being cheered by the news of the opening of the Astor apartments on East 3rd Street, this department viewed with astonishment the talk of what a great achievement this was and how it will benefit the people of the Lower East Side . . . I believe it is merely to quiet the populace . . . to fill them with promises and hope. Is this another method used to suppress radical thoughts?[84]

Local merchants also complained about the First Houses, but for different reasons. Merchants associated with the *ESCN* had hoped to change the character of the East Side. Limited dividend housing such as Amalgamated Houses and Knickerbocker Village was as much government intervention as they wanted. The creation of First Houses seemed to solidify the working-class character of the area, thus undermining their dreams for a white-collar city.

Advocates of luxury and/or white-collar living on the Lower East Side, however, continued to remain optimistic, despite signs that their dream was not to be. In the years before the erection of the massive Vladeck Houses in 1940, they pressed forward on issues they hoped would aid their cause, such as the building of the East River Drive, rezoning the East Side, and widening streets. For instance, for eight years beginning in 1928, members of the Lower East Side Planning Association fought for rezoning laws. Finally, in 1936 the Mayor's Committee on City Planning and the Lower East Side Planning Association created a joint committee to come up with specific recommendations. They submitted their plan to the borough president in early 1937.[85] A public hearing was held in March 1938 to discuss rezoning 170 square blocks in the Corlears Hook section, an area that represented half the land on the Lower East Side. At the hearing, 400 private owners and members of the City Club pressed to rezone the entire area. Representatives from social agencies and tenant groups, including the Lower East Side Public Housing Conference, the American Labor Party, the East Side Tenants' Union, and several settlement houses opposed the plan as an impediment to the development of low-cost housing.[86]

The City Club was defeated. In July 1938, the city approved $300,000 for a municipally-financed slum clearance project on Corlears Hook. The editor of the *ESCN* finally acknowledged that 'all hopes for a medium-priced housing development in the immediate vicinity of Corlears Hook [have been] shattered.'[87] On 2 November 1938, plans were elaborated for a joint city and federally subsidized housing venture for 1,771 low-income families in the Corlears Hook area. The pages of the merchants' newspaper reflected anger and disappointment. With thinly veiled disgust, they said they hoped the project would be 'more successful than the NYCHA's so-called "First Houses," ' adding that they questioned whether more than a small fraction of the present tenants could be rehoused in the new project, considering that many in the immediate area paid less than $4 a room per month and were still on home relief.[88]

On 25 January 1939, the City Planning Commission voted to approve a plan to rezone this section of the East Side, slating only 42 percent of the contested land at Corlears Hook for exclusively residential use.[89] This victory was a pyrrhic one, however, since the LaGuardia administration lumped the Lower East Side merchants in with the rest of the Lower East Side in its call for slum clearance. It considered the local merchants, who had always held themselves aloof from the rest of the Lower East Side, as part of the East Side's problem, rather than its salvation. The proposed Master Plan shocked the merchants who protested vigorously against it. As created by the City Planning Commission in 1939, the plan slated virtually all of the East Side for slum clearance and low-rent housing. Merchants knew this plan would 'kill all chances for private construction.'[90]

The creation of Vladeck Houses was the final blow to the merchants' dreams for a very different Lower East Side. A survey by the Henry Street Settlement House showed that whereas 20,000 people had lived in Corlears Hook in 1910, by 1934 this number had dropped to 6,628. Living conditions in the Hook were dreadful; the area was the last stop for families who could no longer afford other Lower East Side shelter during the Depression. Rents were lower than those in Harlem and living standards, even for the employed, paralleled those of the unemployed because wages had dipped so low. Four years later the population had declined to under 5,000. By then a vast derelict population of elderly couples and single men inhabited the Hook, some in a Salvation Army shelter called 'Gold Dust Lodge' which housed 2,000 people a night. Even squatters in the Hoovervilles on vacant lots had to move when the city razed the many condemned buildings.[91]

Demolition of the Corlears Hook tenements finally began in May of 1939 and new construction commenced six months later. The project received over 19,000 applications.[92] By July 1940, the first 60 families moved into Vladeck City Houses and by November it housed 180 more. Although the city insisted that Vladeck was intended for displaced residents, 42 percent of the former residents of Corlears Hook were ineligible, chiefly because they were single or not citizens. Ultimately, less than one-third of the residents came from the immediate neighborhood.[93] Eight hundred families had been moved out of the area. One complained that 'the tenants here, they fought for housing. They were wrong. Now they can find no place to bury themselves.'[94] Nevertheless, many settlement and social workers considered Vladeck Houses a great victory for those who had pushed for public low-income housing on the Lower East Side. Despite the triumph of Vladeck Houses for low-income housing advocates, however, the Lower East Side still housed only two thousand families in public housing by 1941.

Housing conditions in the rest of the Lower East Side remained abominable. A 1940 Housing Survey in one subarea revealed 84 beds shared by 144 people. Of the 25 families visited, 11 still used outside toilets.[95] A report by the Citizens' Housing Council, which in 1941 examined 13 depressed districts in Manhattan, found the Lower East Side to be the most seriously depressed.[96] The community remained decidedly working-class, poor and ethnic, and continued to suffer from difficult living conditions. For example, as late as 1942, some 60 percent of the population was still receiving some type of relief.[97]

The fact that the Lower East Side would come to host many federally subsidized low-income housing projects insured that redevelopment of the neighborhood for wealthy and/or middle-class residents would remain the pipe dream of developers, urban planners, and local merchants.

Although significant planning for federally subsidized low-income housing occurred in the 1940s, the proposed projects did not open until almost a decade later. Thus, in late 1941 the New York City Housing Authority announced plans for the Jacob Riis and Lillian Wald Houses. However, it only acquired the Riis site three years later and the projects did not open until 1949. Construction of the Al Smith Houses began in 1951, seven years after the Housing Authority announced plans for it. Three other projects began construction in 1952. By 1955, subsidized housing had wiped out one-fifth of the Lower East Side's worst tenements, but these new buildings only masked deeper squalor. Although decent housing had been built for about 9,000 Lower East Siders, 40,000 still lived in dilapidated tenements.[98]

The composition of that population, however, was changing. After World War II, the Lower East Side continued to be home to Italians, Jews, and other eastern Europeans. But in addition, the neighborhood became the home of some of the half million Puerto Ricans who migrated to New York City after the war. By 1957, the rapidly growing Hispanic and black population totaled 25,000 of the area's residents, a trend which had important consequences for the future. Chapter 6 explores the effects of that population succession.

NOTES

1 *The New York Times*, 17 May 1931, Real Estate Section, XI, 2:5.
2 *The New York Times*, 23 January 1930, 47:1.
3 Joseph Platzker, 'Research Studies of Community Problems,' (New York, 1935), p. 10. Pamphlet in New York Public Library.
4 Ibid.
5 Helen Hall, *Unfinished Business: A Firsthand Account by the Former Director of the Henry Street Settlement* (New York: Macmillan, 1971), p. 15.
6 Ann Buttenwieser, 'Shelter for Whom? On the Route Towards Vladeck Houses, 1930–1940,' *Journal of Urban History* 12 (August 1986), pp. 394–6. My argument parallels much of Buttenwieser's, although she focuses more on the development of the waterfront.
7 Peter P. Cappel, 'The Dawn of a New East Side,' *East Side Chamber News* (henceforth *ESCN*), September 1929, p. 13.
8 *ESCN*, September 1928, p. 1.
9 *ESCN*, August 1928, p. 1.
10 'Creating New Apartments on Lower Second Avenue,' *The New York Times*, 2 June 1929, Real Estate Section, XI, 1:5.
11 H. I. Phillips, 'Moving New Yorkers Back to New York,' *Literary Digest* 101 (8 June 1929), p. 46.
12 Edwin Lahm, 'A Banker's Bold Analysis,' *ESCN*, July 1929, p. 7.
13 *The New York Times*, 7 June 1929, 46:3.

14 Mollie Keller, 'Defining the Metropolis in the Twentieth Century,' conference paper given at Association of Collegiate Schools of Planning, Buffalo, NY, 29 October 1988, p. 18.
15 Loula D. Lasker, 'Putting a White Collar on the East Side,' *Survey Graphic* 65 (1 March 1931), p. 585.
16 MARHO, 'Housing for Shelter or Profit?' A Guide to the New York Public History Project Slide Show on the History of Housing, April 1987, p. 12.
17 'A Close Up of the Regional Plan,' Box 22, Wald Collection.
18 George B. Ford, 'Regional Planning on the Lower East Side,' *ESCN*, March 1930, p. 11.
19 'Regional Plan,' *ESCN*, July 1930, p. 17.
20 Editorial, *The New York Times*, 1 July 1930, 28:3.
21 Regional Plan Association, 'The Lower East Side of Manhattan,' *Information Bulletin No. 2*, 20 April 1931, p. 6.
22 Frances D. MacMullen, 'Bad Slums that Remain a Reproach to New York,' *The New York Times*, 4 May 1930, Section 3, p. 10.
23 Buttenwieser, 'Shelter for Whom?,' p. 394.
24 Lasker, 'Putting a White Collar,' p. 588.
25 Lasker, 'Putting a White Collar,' p. 589.
26 Joseph Platzker, 'Streets of New York,' *ESCN*, November 1928, p. 11.
27 *ESCN*, September 1929, p. 7; *ESCN*, November 1928, p. 13.
28 *ESCN*, July 1930.
29 'Local Planning Dream Realized,' *ESCN*, July 1931, pp. 24–5.
30 MacMullen, 'Bad Slums'.
31 Harold Buttenheim, 'Housing,' reprinted in *ESCN*, May 1930, p. 16.
32 As quoted in *The New York Times*, 18 March 1932, 19:5.
33 *ESCN*, July 1930, p. 7; and 'Success of Lehman-Rabinowitz Coop Model Houses on Grand Street Celebrated,' *ESCN*, December 1930, pp. 14–15.
34 'Creating New Apartments on Lower Second Avenue,' *The New York Times*, 2 June 1929, XI, 1:6.
35 '7300 Families Seek Modern Apartments on Lower East Side,' *ESCN*, September 1929, p. 18.
36 Lasker, 'Putting a White Collar', p. 584.
37 Rose C. Feld, 'Opening a New Epoch in Housing for the East Side,' *The New York Times*, 26 October 1930, Real Estate Section, XX, 3:8.
38 Ibid.
39 Editorial, '$12 A Room,' *The New York Times*, 7 January 1930, 30:2.
40 George Stoney, 'Corlears Hook: The Land and the People,' February 1939, p. 35. Unpublished manuscript in East Side files, Settlements, Henry Street Settlement, Surveys, Seward Park Library file.
41 *Survey Graphic* (15 January 1931), p. 421.
42 'Low-Rent Flat Thrives after Two Years,' 20 February 1933. Clipping found in East Side Files, Apartments, Amalgamated Houses, Seward Park Library. The name of the newspaper is unintelligible, but is possibly *The New York Times*.
43 Thomas Compere, 'First of 100,000 in East Side "Mystery Land" to Move,' *New York Herald Tribune*, 13 April 1929, 7:1.

44 Alva Johnston, 'French Plans $50,000,000 "White Collar" East Side City,' *New York Herald Tribune*, 20 December 1931. Clipping in East Side files, Apartments, Knickerbocker Village, Seward Park Library.

45 Alva Johnston and Gustave Zismer, 'How Big Buying Was Concealed,' *New York Sun*, 19 December 1931, 35:1. See also *ESCN*, December 1931, p. 14.

46 *ESCN*, October 1934, p. 14, and *The New York Times*, 8 July 1934, X and XI, 1:3.

47 Editorial, *The New York Times*, 3 October 1934, 20:3.

48 As quoted in 'Knickerbocker Village Planned Four Years Ago,' *New York Herald Tribune*, 20 December 1931, V:1, p. 1 and 3, pp. 1–2. See also *ESCN*, December 1931, pp. 17–18.

49 *The New York Times*, 27 January 1935, Real Estate Section, IX and X, 2:3.

50 Aubrey Mallach, 'Knickerbocker Village Tenants' Association,' p. 31 in Heinz Norden Collection (Box 1, Tamiment Library). See also Mark Naison, 'From Eviction Resistance to Rent Control: Tenant Activism in the Great Depression,' in Ronald Lawson and Mark Naison, eds., *The Tenant Movement in New York City, 1904–1984* (New Brunswick, NJ: Rutgers University Press, 1986), p. 116.

51 *The New York Times*, 23 October 1934, 1:3.

52 *New York Herald Tribune*, 23 October 1934, 1:7 and 33:6–7.

53 See *The New York Times*, 24 October 1934, 23:8; 25 October 1934, 26:1; 28 October 1934, IV, 4:5; and 31 October 1934, 2:6.

54 Mallach, 'Knickerbocker Village,' p. 35.

55 *The New York Times*, 28 August 1935, 15:3.

56 *The New York Times*, 10 March 1936, 20:4; City-Wide Tenants Council Memo, Box 1, Norden Collection, Tamiment; and Nathan Ausubel, 'Hold Up The Sun! A Kaleidoscope of Jewish Life in New York,' unpublished manuscript, 1939, pp. 115–19, Federal Writers' Project Papers, New York City Municipal Archives. City-Wide was a federation of 25 local tenants' groups, including the East Side Tenants' Union, Knickerbocker Village Tenants' Association, Lavanburg Homes Tenants' Council, and the Lower East Side Public Housing Conference.

57 Editorial, *Henry Street Bulletin*, January 1936, p. 4, East Side file, Settlements, Henry Street Settlement, Seward Park Library.

58 Joseph Platzker, 'The Dawn of Knickerbocker Village,' *ESCN*, April 1933, p. 1.

59 'What Happened to 306 Families Who Were Compelled to Vacate Their Slum Dwellings to Make Way for a Large Housing Project,' conducted by the Lavanburg Foundation and Hamilton House, 1933, East Side files, Apartments, Knickerbocker Village, Seward Park Library.

60 'A Study of Low-Rental Vacant Dwelling Units in the Borough of Manhattan,' p. 15, Vacancy and Re-Housing Bureau Survey, 13 October 1938 to 11 November 1938, conducted by WPA. #665–97–3–20, New York Public Library.

61 Duane V. Ramsey with Abe Goldfeld, 'What Some Slum Dwellers Want in Housing: Findings of A Study in One Square Block in the Lower East Side,'

July 1935, p. 1, East Side files, Henry Street Settlement, Surveys, Seward Park Library.

62 Ibid., pp. 1, 4 and 8.

63 Michael Gold, *Jews Without Money* (New York: Avon Books, 1965), p. 105. Reprint of 1930 version.

64 Harry Shulman, *Slums of New York* (New York: Albert and Charles Boni, Inc., 1938), p. 119.

65 Ibid., especially pp. xv–xvii, 72, 76, 80 and 88.

66 Albert Kennedy, 'The Part of the Settlements in Cultivating Civic and Social Order,' Chapter 1 in 'The Interests of the Settlements in Housing, A Study Made in Connection with the Settlements Study Research Bureau – Welfare Council of New York,' March 1933, pp. 16–17, Box 22, RPA file, Wald Collection.

67 Progressive Mothers' Club Minutes, 24 January 1933, Box 210, file 3384, and 7 October 1937, Box 210, file 3388, Stuyvesant Neighborhood House Papers, YIVO.

68 Hall, *Unfinished Business*, p. 150.

69 See Thomas Kessner, *Fiorello H. LaGuardia and the Making of Modern New York* (New York: Penguin Books, 1989) for a full-scale study of this man, *passim*.

70 John D. Mollenkopf, *The Contested City* (Princeton, NJ: Princeton University Press, 1983), and Kessner, *Fiorello H. LaGuardia*, pp. 293 and 320–431.

71 Buttenweiser, 'Shelter for Whom?,' p. 405.

72 Joseph Platzker, 'Multiple Dwelling Law Changes to Cost $8,000,000,' *ESCN*, June 1936, p. 1.

73 Rebecca Rankin, ed., *New York Advancing 1934–35 Edition* (New York: 1936), p. 197.

74 *ESCN*, May 1936, p. 6.

75 Naison, 'From Eviction Resistance,' p. 120.

76 *ESCN*, October 1937.

77 *Real Estate Record*, 23 October 1937, Box 1, Heinz Norden Collection, Tamiment Library.

78 *ESCN*, April 1937, pp. 6–7.

79 George Stoney and Margaret Knepper, 'Can We Renovate the Slums? A Study of 54 Remodeled Tenements on the Lower East Side,' June 1939. Unpublished manuscript in East Side Files, Settlements, Henry Street Settlement, Surveys, Seward Park Library. The study found that in one completely modernized tenement, rents had increased 120 percent; the former tenants were forced out and white-collar workers moved in.

80 Vacancy Bureau, 'Comparative Study of Vacant Apartments on the Lower East Side Area,' March 1936, conducted by WPA project, no. 65–97–201. See 4 December 1936 letter from Vacancy Bureau, WPA and NYCHA Project, Box 17A2, folder 10, NYCHA Papers at LGA Community College.

81 'The Story of First Houses,' 15C7, Folder 18, NYCHA Papers, LaGuardia Community College. See also Kessner, *Fiorello H. LaGuardia*, pp. 327–30.

82 Rankin, *New York Advancing*, p. 196.

83 'Statistics on Tenants,' 7 October 1935, Box 15B2, folder 8, NYCHA Papers, LaGuardia Community College.

84 Editorial, *Henry Street Bulletin*, January 1936, p. 4, East Side files, Settlements, Henry Street Settlement, Seward Park Library.
85 Joseph Platzker, 'Rezoning Wins!' *ESCN*, January 1939, p. 1.
86 *ESCN*, '400 Owners Attend Zoning Hearing on March 16,' March 1938, cover; and 'Scores Argue over East Side Zoning Plan,' *New York Herald Tribune*, 17 March 1938, 17:2.
87 Buttenweiser, 'Shelter for Whom?,' p. 409, and *ESCN*, July 1938, p. 1.
88 *ESCN*, March 1939, p. 4.
89 Platzker, 'Rezoning Wins!'; see also *The New York Times* articles: 'East Side Chamber of Commerce Hails Move,' 26 January 1939, and 'Planning Board Votes to Rezone Lower East Side,' 21 March 1939. A clipping of the latter was found in East Side files, Zoning, Seward Park Library files. The source must be misidentified, since I could not verify in *The New York Times*.
90 *ESCN*, December 1939, pp. 10–11.
91 Stoney, 'Corlears Hook', pp. 36–9.
92 Editorial, 'Good Housing Helps Us All,' *The New York Times*, 18 July 1940, 18:3.
93 Buttenwieser, 'Shelter for Whom?,' claims that the figure was only one-sixth, although the NYCHA claimed one-third. See NYCHA Release, 12 November 1940, Box 3225, LaGuardia Papers, Municipal Archives.
94 Quoted in Joel Schwartz, 'Tenant Unions in New York City's Low Rent Housing 1933–1949,' *Journal of Urban History* 12, (August 1986), p. 423.
95 Henry Street Settlement Housing Survey of 1940, in FWP papers, Municipal Archives.
96 Sylvia Stark, *Ailing City Areas: An Economic Study of Thirteen Depressed Districts in Manhattan*, Citizens' Housing Council, May 1941, NYPL.
97 Stephen Goodwin, 'Jewish Communities,' *Jews of New York*, 7 January 1942, Box 3633, Jewish Communities – Goodwin, FWP, Municipal Archives.
98 *ESCN*, December 1941, December 1944, and October 1951.

Part II

The Process of Gentrification

The Great Depression had precipitously aborted efforts made in the 1920s to convert the Lower East Side to an enclave for middle-class residents. Although 'slum clearance' reappeared on the agenda after the end of World War II, it occurred within a drastically changed context and would utilize a new set of legislated mechanisms designed to achieve different goals. For the most part, the massive private investment that fueled the postwar housing boom avoided center cities. It was directed almost exclusively to suburban locations. In contrast, new residential construction in the inner city was confined almost exclusively to sites on 'slum land' that had been cleared for public housing projects or for middle-income housing partially subsidized by city, state, and/or federal funds. Whatever new housing was constructed on the Lower East Side fell within these categories.

The only other alternative to new construction on cleared land was to rehabilitate existing structures. The question was whether investors would find the old tenements of the Lower East Side attractive enough to encourage their reconstruction. They did not. First, most of the occupied apartments in the tenements were protected by rent-control regulations, which meant that tenants could not easily be evicted and replaced by a 'higher' class of renters. Second, the area contained few brownstones of intrinsic architectural appeal that would have attracted buyers interested in fixing them up for their own occupancy. Most structures were multi-family dwellings. Third, despite the low quality of the housing stock, prices were high, inflated by land values that could only be written down by urban renewal funds. So long as land costs remained high, the Lower East Side would offer no bargains to developers. That left 'ethnic succession' as the most likely prospect. The zone would continue to serve as a port of entry for newcomers to the city.

The four chapters that follow describe the process that attempted a total transformation of the East Village, even though the results fell far short of the hopes of investors. Chapter 6 examines the short-term revival of the zone as a port of entry for new migrants, notably from Puerto Rico. The failure of this strategy eventually led to a period of radical disinvestment, chronicled in chapter 7. Chapter 8 explores in greater detail the ensuing and intrinsically linked process of reinvestment and modest gentrification. In all of this, the city government did not play a passive role, but indeed sought to encourage certain outcomes and discourage others. Chapter 9 traces the role of city policies, particularly in the Koch era, to show how they affected the fate of the East Village in the 1980s.

Plate 6.1 Remembrances of Loisaida past
Source: Courtesy of Marlis Momber

6

Neighborhood 'Burn-out': Puerto Ricans at the End of the Queue

Christopher Mele

Neither the dream of retaining the children of turn-of-the-century European immigrants in a Lower East Side purged of ethnicity, nor its alternative of replacing the ethnic working class by professionals or even clerks from Wall Street, materialized in the postwar period of the 1940s and 1950s. For this was a time when young Americans were heading to the new suburban developments mushrooming on open farmland to accommodate the generation whose most lasting achievement was to produce the baby boom.

The adult children of parents who remained in the 'old neighborhood' refused to return home. Those who were veterans were assisted by liberal federal benefits, including the GI Bill of Rights which opened the social mobility path available through higher education, and special Veterans' Administration mortgage guarantees which, by reducing downpayments and subsidizing interest rates, opened the physical mobility path to home ownership. Once the war ended, this generation married quickly, founded new families, and collectively created new ways of life that were often snobbishly satirized as Babbitry transposed from small towns to suburban 'ticky tacky little boxes,'[1] or as life behind cracked picture windows.[2] These new ways of life were the antithesis of life on the Lower East Side. Their parents *may have* remained willingly in the old neighborhood, but for their children, clinging to their ethnic heritage was often embarrassing, even humiliating.

In the past, the Lower East Side had not depended on retaining the children of immigrants. Rather, population had been continuously replenished by new ethnic groups. Thus, the original Irish had been succeeded by the Germans who, in turn, were replaced chiefly by Italians and Jews from eastern Europe. Since the neighborhood's vitality depended on constant replacements, it was hit exceptionally hard when Congress curtailed immigration during the 1920s.[3] The effects were felt almost immediately in the neighborhood. Population on the Lower East Side began to drop, although enough children of the old immigrant stock remained to forestall complete neighborhood 'blowout.' When, in the postwar period, these children began to desert the city for the suburbs, vacancies piled up on the Lower East Side, requiring landlords to adopt new strategies to keep their buildings full.

To counteract declining demand, urban planners, property owners, business people, and merchants at first sought to modernize the neighborhood, to replace its obsolete and substandard housing, and to create an area that could compete with the suburbs for middle-class housing consumers. This strategy reflected real estate interests in that it was designed not to remedy the conditions of the poor who were living in blighted areas, but to recover profitability. It was thought that the best way to stem the flow of people and money to the suburbs was to demolish slum buildings and replace them with attractive, middle-class housing. However, because the scale of such a rebuilding effort was enormous and the access of private investors to the capital needed for carrying it out limited, rebuilding the Lower East Side came to depend on government subsidies.

The efforts of real estate investors to harness government policy to help them construct middle-income housing in inner-city neighborhoods were only partially successful. True, urban renewal succeeded in replacing some slums with middle-income developments, but government policies ultimately obstructed investors' revitalization plans by funding the construction of low-income housing. Despite this contradiction, many slum owners supported government programs of both middle-class renewal and publicly subsidized low-income housing, since these at least compensated owners for their land and the deteriorated structures on it.

However, the goal of redevelopment, namely, stimulating middle-class demand for central city housing, was ultimately defeated by the intensification of trends rooted in the prewar era. Even greater capitalization of the suburbs in the immediate postwar years and generous federal mortgage subsidies made suburban homes affordable to more people. Industrial relocation to the suburbs continued after the war on an unprecedented scale, draining jobs from the center city. These conditions exacerbated the growing obsolescence of the Lower East Side as a residential quarter.

THE 'QUICK FIX' TO OBSOLESCENCE: HOUSING PUERTO RICAN WORKERS

Middle-class redevelopment was neither as pervasive nor effective as real estate interests operating in the Lower East Side had hoped. After more than a decade of efforts to redevelop the slums, the area's housing market remained confined to low-income families and older white ethnics. The worsening conditions of the tenements, brought on by age and lack of upkeep, aggravated the situation of diminished demand. The enduring built form that had operated so effectively for urban real estate capital in the era of the great European migrations thwarted all postwar efforts to attract higher-income residents. New sources of low-income demand would have to be found.

The entry of unskilled and semiskilled Puerto Rican workers into New York City in the early 1950s served to make slums profitable again. Their entry into the neighborhood recreated the slum housing market of a half-century earlier. These workers were employed and resided in the inner city in a manner reminiscent of the turn-of-the-century European immigrants.[4] Entrepreneurial real estate capital responded to this new demand for low-income housing, and a speculative revival of interest in slum housing occurred in the first half of the 1950s. Speculators purchased heavily in areas such as East Harlem and the Lower East Side, where Puerto Ricans were most likely to settle.[5] Profits could be realized by rent gouging the vast number of newly arrived Puerto Ricans in desperate need of housing. Landlords in the Lower East Side (as well as in other slum areas of the city) further subdivided their tenement apartments, charging by the room and renting to several families. Many buildings contained only one toilet per floor, to be used by many families.[6] The quick profit derived from renting overcrowded and deteriorated living space was reminiscent of an earlier Lower East Side.

Revival of the slum, however, proved short lived and was replaced by an ensuing period of neighborhood 'burnout' – a widespread disinvestment of real estate capital that devastated large portions of the Lower East Side. This chapter explains why this shift occurred. It analyzes the dynamic relationship between the socioeconomic makeup of the new Puerto Rican residents and landlord investment strategies in the 1950s and 1960s.

Despite contemporary predictions that Puerto Ricans would replicate the American immigrant success story, the character of the Puerto Rican settlement in New York City was entirely different from that of the Europeans. The labor-market opportunities in the urban economy were transformed in the postwar era of sectoral economic change; manual labor was downgraded and deskilled, while white-collar positions were expanding. These factors converged to present new kinds of problems for the relationship between the low-income housing of workers in the Lower East Side and New York City's economy.[7] As the city's economic base restructured away from manufacturing, the function of the neighborhood's housing became marginal to the emerging growth sectors of the local economy: producers' and government services. Although this transformation had its roots in the early 1920s, the relationship between residence and employment that emerged in the 1950s and 1960s was radically different from that of the late nineteenth- and early twentieth-century 'slum.'

At the beginning of the century, the Lower East Side had functioned as a dormitory for the legions of workers who constructed the city and labored in its industries. In contrast, the integration of Puerto Rican workers in the city's employment base was aborted by the restructuring of the economy. Many of the new residents would become permanently poor (redundant workers[8]) and marginal to the city's economy. Thus, the prospects for continued profit making by tenement landlords deteriorated. When real estate investors discovered that the profits to be made by reinventing the slum were short lived, they responded by disinvesting. The residents of the Lower East Side paid the price of displacement in the widespread housing abandonment of the 1970s.

Puerto Rican Migration and Settlement Patterns

The formation of a Puerto Rican residential enclave on the Lower East Side did not replicate that of earlier immigrants – either in its trajectory of generational outward mobility or in residents' ability to mobilize power over neighborhood housing conditions. These paths, forged by the European immigrant experience, proved historically specific to them and to the social and economic conditions of the industrial era.[9] The Puerto Rican migration experience was different.

Unlike former mass migrations from Europe whose beginning and end dates are easily bracketed, Puerto Rican migration was spread out and more episodic. In 1940, there were still only about 61,500 Puerto Rican-born residents in New York City. Their numbers increased to almost 246,000 by 1950, to well over 612,000 by 1960, and by 1970 exceeded 800,000 (see table 6.1). Puerto Rican migration was affected by the legal status of the islanders as American citizens. In 1917, the Second Organic or Jones Act conferred citizenship on Puerto Ricans and thus eliminated quotas, waiting lists, and complex documentation. This lowered the social and economic costs associated with migration, since Puerto

Ricans 'burned no bridges' when they came to the mainland. It also meant that the migration flow was subject to sudden reversals. Migrants could – and many in fact did – return to the island and back again to New York, as required by personal or economic needs.

Table 6.1 Population of Puerto Rican origin living on the US mainland and in New York City, 1910–1970

Year	*Total on mainland US*	*Total in New York City*	*New York City's Puerto Rican population as percentage of mainland US Puerto Ricans*
1910	1,500	600	37
1920	11,800	7,400	62
1930	52,700	44,900	81
1940	70,000	61,500	88
1950	301,000	245,900	82
1960	892,500	612,600	69
1970	1,379,100	811,800	59

Source: Decennial censuses, as shown in Bureau of Labor Statistics Regional Report no. 46, p. 24. From Brian F. Earley, 'Puerto Ricans in the New York City Labor Market, 1970: A Structural Analysis' (doctoral dissertation, Fordham University, 1980)

The ability of Puerto Rican arrivals to carve out large neighborhood niches was hindered by the fact that migration was neither numerically overwhelming nor concentrated within a span of a few years. In addition, the mobility of New York Puerto Ricans to and from Puerto Rico and other destinations in the United States diluted any particular attachments to place. Post-World War II settlements in New York tended to be small, more numerous and differentiated, and dictated less by cultural ties to established Puerto Rican enclaves than by the availability of inexpensive vacancies. Consequently, except in East Harlem and parts of Brooklyn, Puerto Ricans never achieved the critical mass needed to overwhelm an entire neighborhood. The Puerto Rican settlement pattern was more piecemeal: initially a few apartments within a building, later a few buildings on a block, and eventually a few blocks in a neighborhood.[10]

The establishment of enclaves on the Lower East Side and in Chelsea followed this pattern. Although Loisaida (Nuyorican for Lower East Side) later emerged as a cultural and political center for Puerto Ricans living downtown, it was initially formed as a satellite barrio, highly sensitive to the ebb and flow of Puerto Rican population movements. At first, the Lower East Side took in the overflow from older core communities; new arrivals with few housing options settled in the cheapest housing in the worst condition. Many of these units were concentrated in the eastern blocks of the East Village and in the area just south of Houston Street (see table 6.2).

Table 6.2 Population of Spanish language or Hispanic ethnicity[a] in the census tracts of the East Village, 1960–1990

Census Tracts	*1960*	*1970*	*1980*	*1990*
Housing projects				
20	2,423	3,105	5,077	4,925
24	3,177	3,851	4,879	4,400
Non-project tracts				
22.02[b]	–	1,453	926	548
26 (0.01 and 0.02)[b]	5,510	6,876	3,070	2,613
28	2,362	2,746	2,540	3,191
30.02[b]	–	564	755	721
32	942	868	1,328	941
34	2,301	2,944	2,967	1,832
36.02[b]	–	426	711	501
38	1,258	744	1,152	1,032
40	2,461	1,357	1,564	1,030
42	[c]	[c]	162	141
Total	20,434	24,934	25,131	21,875

[a] Primarily Puerto Rican. Between 1960 and 1990 the Bureau of the Census periodically revised its categories on Hispanics. This table uses the definitions extant in each census year. See note to table 6.3.
[b] Prior to 1970, subdivision of tracts had not taken place.
[c] Not reported in 1960 and 1970.
Source: 1960, 1970, 1980 and 1990 US censuses

Contributing to the dispersion of Puerto Rican settlements were conditions of the postwar housing environment. Newcomers arriving immediately after World War II encountered a severe housing shortage. This shortage was compounded by the city's efforts to clear slums, which had intensified overcrowding in remaining low-income areas. Families living in urban renewal areas were displaced. In the process, a large portion of low-income housing on Manhattan's west side was eliminated; public housing construction in the East Harlem area erased several blocks of occupied tenements. Urban renewal thus displaced more poor families than could be accommodated either in existing slums or in new public housing projects. Urban renewal – nicknamed 'Puerto Rican Removal Plans' – shifted hundreds of Puerto Rican families from one slum area to another.[11] Families had little choice but to double- and triple-up with friends and relatives in substandard apartments, although some displaced Puerto Rican families were resettled in public housing. Public housing was not an option for the newest comers, however, since there was a two-year residency requirement for prospective tenants. Much to the advantage of slum landlords, government policies increased the demand for low-income housing by reducing its supply.

These experiences made it difficult for Puerto Ricans to organize a unified response to their precarious housing situation. Spatial deconcentration of Puerto Rican residents, resulting from their intermittent migratory patterns, their option to return to the island, displacement from their homes by urban renewal projects, and the unscrupulous tactics of landlords, inhibited the formation of the community-based self-help organizations that had been crucial in easing the transition for earlier immigrants. Strong Puerto Rican community groups eventually transcended these limitations, but most of the early groups organized around other issues. In more dispersed areas (and during the 1950s most Puerto Ricans lived in areas where they constituted less than half of the area's population), however, the formation of community-based organizations was uncommon. As Terry Rosenberg observed:

> Puerto Ricans have found scattered housing sites, perhaps a block, perhaps an apartment building, which were available to them . . . And while they have been restricted to recognized 'poverty' areas of the City, they have not been able to establish within these areas the ethnic group concentrations supportive of community projects and organizations.[12]

Organizations created in the 1940s focused primarily on cultural themes; few addressed economic and housing issues of living in New York City.[13] This changed as their numbers grew. The Puerto Rican Forum and the Congress of Home Town Clubs dealt with local educational issues. The Puerto Rican Family Institute, Aspira, and the Puerto Rican Community Development Project addressed poverty issues.[14] More militant groups surfaced briefly in the mid-to-late 1960s, raising Puerto Rican consciousness but having little success in bettering material conditions for the poorest Puerto Ricans.[15] New York affiliates of The Young Lords, a politicized youth gang from Chicago, were very active in social and political issues in Spanish Harlem.

Puerto Ricans living in smaller enclaves, however, were robbed of the potential political and economic capital gained from community organizations and their leaders.[16] In terms of housing, the connection between the lack of community organizations and low community power is clear. As their economic position worsened and the gap between their resources and rising rents widened, Puerto Ricans were ill equipped to withstand the effects of landlord disinvestment.

SECTORAL ECONOMIC DECLINE

The major difference between the experience of earlier immigrants and that of Puerto Ricans was the tighter economy the latter confronted. Initially, in the early 1950s, the economic situation for new arrivals was promising. The demand for labor that stemmed from the cut-off in immigration in the 1920s was amplified during and immediately after World War II. Wartime labor shortages in manufacturing in the industrial northeast and the rustbelt were largely filled by women and by African-Americans migrating from the south. In New York, the shortage of unskilled workers was also alleviated by Puerto Rican labor. The large migration wave of the 1950s corresponded to an increase in demand for workers to serve the expanding postwar economy. Migration was also facilitated by commercial airlines which began to offer cheap flights to the mainland.[17] Initially, Puerto Ricans did well in comparison to the general laboring population of the city, since their rates of labor force participation were higher than the city average. In 1950, for example, 76 percent of Puerto Rican males 14 years of age and older were in the labor force, as compared to 75 percent of the total male working-age population of New York City; 40 percent of Puerto Rican women were in the labor force, as compared to only 35 percent of the city's female working-age population.[18]

The demand for workers in low paying jobs was produced by the aging of the former immigrant population, and the lack, with the exception of the African-American migration from the south, of any notable labor migration since the early 1920s. Puerto Ricans increasingly found jobs in the labor market niche of center-city blue-collar positions left behind by the exodus of workers to new industries in the suburbs or by the occupational advancement of existing workers. Puerto Rican migration was viewed as crucial to salvaging New York industries that depended on inexpensive labor, such as the garment industry.[19]

Puerto Rican workers were employed largely in unskilled and often seasonal labor. In garments, for example, Puerto Rican men loaded and unloaded fabrics, operated heavy machinery, and delivered finished garments from factory floor to nearby showrooms. As the postwar demand for cheap labor swelled, firms stimulated the migration of more Puerto Ricans to the mainland. Several industries, including New York apparel firms, recruited Puerto Ricans in Puerto Rico, offering them jobs and placing them in housing. Government agencies encouraged migration as well. In 1948, the Migration Division of the Puerto Rican Department of Labor was formed to monitor the recruitment practices used by the numerous US labor contractors operating on the island. The division also maintained branch offices in New York and Chicago to facilitate employment placement. In New York, the Puerto Rican Commonwealth Office and the Mayor's Commission on Puerto Rican Affairs assisted in establishing air routes to San Juan and aided unemployed new arrivals by placing them in manufacturing jobs.[20]

The significant access to entry-level manufacturing jobs made by Puerto Ricans, however, was eventually curtailed by both the decline in and downgrading of manufacturing in the city.[21] After World War II, blue-collar manufacturing jobs, traditionally held by new immigrants, declined in number or were transformed into lower-paying 'deskilled' positions. Industries were leaving Manhattan for the suburbs or overseas. New jobs were almost exclusively in the service and governmental sectors. This deindustrialization eliminated the union footholds through which earlier immigrants had achieved socioeconomic and residential mobility.

Puerto Ricans bore the brunt of these economic declines. A large proportion were employed in exactly those industries most affected by restructuring. Forty-two percent of the Puerto Rican labor force worked in manufacturing in the 1950s. Between 1959 and 1969, manufacturing employment in New York City declined by 13 percent.[22] A declining number of light assembly jobs in plastic flower making, electric plating, costume jewelry preparation, and furniture making could still be found in nearby SoHo and Tribeca well into the late 1970s, but after that, manufacturing firms in those districts were displaced and their industrial lofts were transformed for new uses, such as upscale housing, art galleries, and boutiques.[23] Those industries had formerly recruited Puerto Rican labor from the Lower East Side. For example, in 1962, 48 percent of textile and apparel workers employed in loft plants in SoHo were of Puerto Rican origin.[24]

By virtue of their lack of seniority, Puerto Ricans often occupied the least secure positions in these industries. Garment making offers a very clear demonstration of the problems faced by Puerto Rican workers. Despite the gains Puerto Ricans made in capturing jobs in the garment industry and despite their numerical strength in union membership throughout the 1950s, the garment industry failed to provide them with the social mobility it had granted earlier immigrants. The industry was radically restructured. Positions were eliminated; work in less stylized and uniform garment production, such as underwear, brassieres and children's clothes, was eliminated as shops relocated offshore (ironically, many to Puerto Rico).[25] Production previously done in-house was farmed out to subcontractors to take advantage of significantly lower costs.

In addition, garment employers downgraded high-wage skilled and craft positions to semi-skilled positions which carried little chance for promotion. What were once considered entry-level jobs with potential for advancement were recast, with the consent of the International Ladies' Garment Workers' Union (ILGWU), as permanent low-wage positions. Historically, immigrants entered the labor market in low-wage and unskilled positions as pressers, cleaners, ironers, and shipping clerks. Through union membership and seniority, these workers gained increasing job security, structured wage increases, welfare benefits, and employment training. These positions, once dominated by Italians and Jews, had been important vehicles of their occupational mobility. Indeed, Jews and Italians had utilized the ILGWU and propitious labor rulings of the New Deal era to cement employment gains that translated to increased socioeconomic mobility.

But these gains were not passed on to the postwar rank-and-file members of the union, the majority of whom were African-American or Puerto Rican. The predominantly white-ethnic leadership of the ILGWU feared the restructuring that was occurring in the garment industry as a result of the standardization and decentralization of production. Their own positions would be lost if New York's garment industry folded or set up shop elsewhere. With this in mind, union leaders, without consulting the rank and file, negotiated a series of 'sweetheart' contracts with the apparel industry in the late 1950s and early 1960s.[26] ILGWU contracts negotiated in the 1950s reveal that the union embraced the strategy of maintaining low wages to forestall an exodus of the garment industry from the city. In his study of those contracts, Herbert Hill writes: 'Soon after World War II, the ILGWU adopted a policy of wage restraint that contrasted sharply with its earlier wage policy. This approach coincided with the rapid increase of nonwhites in the garment industry labor force.'[27]

Wages for unskilled labor in the garment industry fell drastically. Puerto Rican women, employed after 1950 in coat and suit making, an industry previously dominated by Italians and Jews, were hired as semi-skilled laborers and paid wages well below their predecessors.[28] Between 1960 and 1965, the real earnings of the rank-and-file members of the International Ladies' Garment Workers' Union (again, most of whom were Puerto Rican and African-American women) declined below the poverty level for New York City families, even though two wage contracts between ILGWU and garment employers had been negotiated. The complicity of what was historically the pathbreaker of immigrant socioeconomic mobility, the ILGWU, with the marginalization of Puerto Rican labor was pronounced.

The deskilling of labor was not unique to the garment industry; most labor-intensive manufacturing industries that remained in the city after 1950 initiated forms of wage-increase controls. Because wages no longer kept pace with the rising costs of living, many Puerto Rican workers became impoverished. As the relocation or closing of plants continued unabated in the 1960s and 1970s, even more were displaced. This shifting economic context – deindustrialization – in which the postwar Puerto Rican migration took place meant the elimination of a principal means of economic, social, and residential mobility.

Conclusion: The Declining Disposition of Housing

In the early 1950s, real estate capital in the Lower East Side saw a profitable future in the demand for low-income housing generated by yet another labor migration – the flow of migrants from Puerto Rico. The resurgence turned out to be a false revival with lasting consequences. Despite attempts by landlords to profit from this new wave of poor working-class migrants, their investments soon soured as they became proprietors of a neighborhood housing an economically idled population. The declining economic position of the vast majority of Puerto Ricans, their high rates of turnover, and their somewhat porous settlement patterns had profound implications for housing in the Lower East Side. The limited job opportunities for many of its residents isolated the Lower East Side from the expansion and growth of surrounding residential and business areas and marginalized the neighborhood from the fast-paced growth of financial, insurance, and real estate services in the city. The Puerto Rican population of the Lower East Side became trapped in a double downward spiral of poverty stemming both from its own economically disadvantaged labor-market position and from the increasing isolation of the neighborhood.[29]

Although Puerto Ricans never numerically overwhelmed areas of the East Village, they inherited a large part of it when non-Hispanics aged and then died off; the decline in non-Hispanics came not so much from 'white flight' as from the mortality of the aged eastern European immigrants. Census data from 1960 indicate that the non-Puerto Rican population in the neighborhood was basically old. There were very few children or adults in the child-bearing years. The aged were the remnants of the pre-1924 cohort of immigrants who had never left the neighborhood. By 1970 many of them had died.[30] By then, the population in the easternmost census tracts of the East Village consisted primarily of young Puerto Rican families with many children, whose incomes were well below the poverty level and who could ill afford higher rents. It was this shift in ability to pay higher rents – compounded secondarily by ethnic and racial discrimination by landlords – that set off the period of disinvestment.[31]

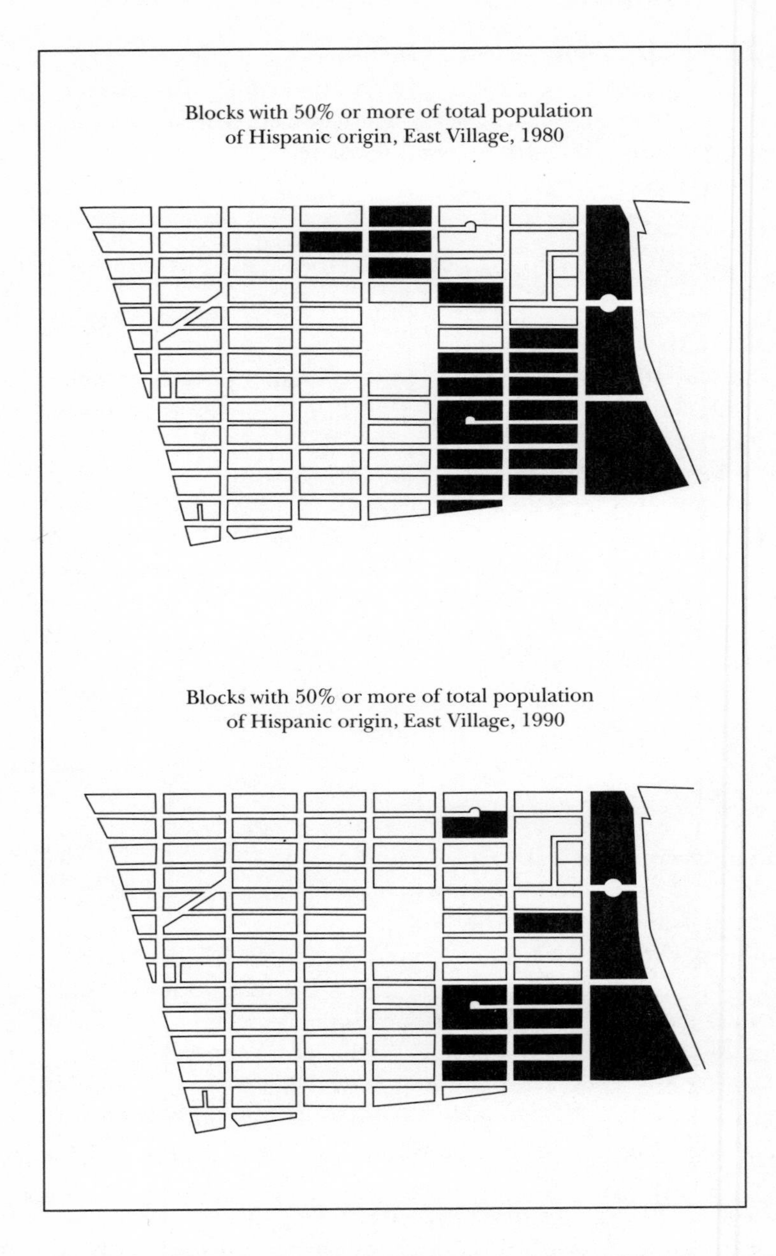

Figure 6.1 Displacement of Puerto Rican residents from the East Village between 1980 and 1990

Source: Computer-generated map by Christopher Mele, based on block data from the US Censuses of 1980 and 1990

Owners responded to the ceiling on profits brought on by the declining socioeconomic status of the residents by disinvesting. During the 1960s, the population thinned, due to Puerto Rican dispersal, return migration, and a drop in new migration from the island. The makeup of the remaining population shifted to those with meager economic resources and declining occupational prospects. Faced with declining demand and an impoverished pool of tenants, landlords disinvested in their properties by milking their rents and reducing upkeep. The consequence of real estate disinvestment through abandonment was the displacement of many Puerto Rican residents (see figure 6.1).

As the privately owned housing nearby was transformed – by abandonment in the 1970s and later by gentrification that pushed eastward in the 1980s (see chapter 7) – the housing projects would provide the most secure haven against displacement pressures that overwhelmed the adjacent blocks. Puerto Rican families came to dominate the Lillian Wald and Jacob Riis Houses, two large government-subsidized housing projects at the easternmost edge of the East Village. These projects, completed in 1949–50, had initially been populated by white working-class families. For example, of the 1,850 original resident families surveyed when the Lillian Wald Houses opened in 1949–1950, only 34 families were identified as Spanish (presumably Puerto Rican).[32] Between 1953 and 1956, however, the number of newly arrived and mainland-born Puerto Ricans living in the two public housing projects had increased by 150 percent (see table 6.3).[33] Today, four-fifths of the inhabitants of the two projects are Hispanic, mostly Puerto Rican.

In the decade of the 1970s, the economically-isolated community of Loisaida outside the projects was decimated, and the remaining residents fell victim to multiple social ills. The eastern blocks of Alphabet City

Table 6.3 Population of Spanish language or Hispanic ethnicity and as percentage of total population in the two public housing census tracts, 1960–1990

Census tracts	*1960*	*1970*	*1980*	*1990*
20				
Population	2,423	3,105	5,077	4,925
% Spanish language or Hispanic	31	44	77	81
24				
Population	3,177	3,851	4,879	4,400
% Spanish language or Hispanic	41	57	78	79

[a] The Census Bureau has shifted the meanings and names of categories from "Puerto Rican birth" to "Puerto Rican parentage" to "Spanish language" and, finally, to "Hispanic." As a result, the figures are only roughly comparable.

Source: US Bureau of the Census, 1950, 1960, 1970, 1980 and 1990

became among the poorest and most troubled in the city. Ironically, the devastation of the Puerto Rican community in the East Village prepared the ground for a successive period of attempted reconstruction. As land values and property prices plummeted, reflecting the neighborhood's despair, a new generation of investors entered the arena, seeking opportunities for profit. The next two chapters describe the sequence of neighborhood disinvestment and reinvestment that sought to gentrify the East Village.

NOTES

1 A mocking folk song of the times created by Pete Seeger.

2 The title of John Keats' condescending sociological study of life in the new 'Levittowns.' See his *The Crack in the Picture Window* (Boston: Houghton Mifflin, 1957).

3 The Johnson Act of 1921 reduced the flow of eastern and southern Europeans to the United States by limiting the annual number of new immigrants from given countries to 3 percent of their populations, as revealed in the 1910 census. In 1924, Congress amended the quota to 2 percent of their populations, as listed in the 1890 census. By 1929, Congress had capped new immigration to 150,000 persons annually. See, *inter alia*, Virginia E. Sanchez Korral, *From Colonia to Community: The History of Puerto Ricans in New York City, 1917–1948* (Westport, CT: Greenwood Press, 1983), p. 31.

4 Charles Grutzner, 'Fight on City's Slums So Far Losing Battle,' *The New York Times*, Sunday, 30 August 1953.

5 *Proceedings* of 'Puerto Ricans Confront Problems of the Complex Urban Society: A Design for Change,' a community conference sponsored by Mayor Lindsay, April 15–16, 1967, held at the High School of Art and Design, p. 115. A similar labor influx of southern blacks to New York set off housing speculation in neighborhoods of northern Manhattan and Brooklyn. In the Lower East Side, the newcomers were predominantly Puerto Rican. The average percentage of housing units occupied by non-white persons in all of the East Village in 1950 was 3.2; for tracts 20 and 24, containing the public housing projects, the average was 10.2; non-whites then constituted 16.2 percent of Manhattan's population. (Source: *United States Census of Population and Housing, 1950*.)

6 Graduate School of Public Administration and Social Service, New York University, *The Impact of Puerto Rican Migration on Governmental Services in New York City* (New York: New York University Press, 1957), p. 12.

7 This transformation from 'slum' to marginalized ghetto occurred in the urban cores of many North American industrial cities following World War II. See Loic J. D. Wacquant and William Julius Wilson, 'The Cost of Racial and Class Exclusion in the Inner City,' in W. J. Wilson, ed., *The Ghetto Underclass: Social Science Perspectives*, a special issue of *The Annals of the American Academy of Political and Social Science* 50 (January 1989), p. 11.

8 José Sanchez, 'Residual Work and Residual Shelter: Housing Puerto Rican Labor in New York City from World War II to 1983,' in Rachel Bratt, Chester

Hartman, and Ann Meyerson, eds., *Critical Perspectives on Housing* (Philadelphia, PA: Temple University Press, 1986).

9 David Ward, 'The Emergence of Central Immigrant Ghettoes in American Cities: 1840–1920,' in Larry S. Bourne, ed., *The Internal Structure of Cities* (New York: Oxford University Press, 1971).

10 Morris Eagle, 'The Puerto Ricans in New York City,' in Nathan Glazer and Davis McEntire, eds., *Studies in Housing and Minority Groups* (Berkeley: University of California Press, 1960), pp. 149–53.

11 *Proceedings*, p. 359.

12 Terry J. Rosenberg, *Residence, Employment and Mobility of Puerto Ricans in New York City* (Chicago: University of Chicago, Department of Geography, Research Paper no. 151, 1974), p. 50.

13 *Proceedings*, p. 169.

14 Active but not very successful. Very few publications on Puerto Rican organizations operating in neighborhoods in the 1950s refer to successful movements organized around social issues in general and housing issues in particular. On the contrary, contemporary activists were concerned that few such organizations existed. See Adalberto López (a Puerto Rican scholar raised on the Lower East Side), 'The Puerto Rican Diaspora,' in Adalberto López and James Petras, eds., *Puerto Rico and Puerto Ricans: Studies in History and Society* (New York: John Wiley and Sons, 1974).

15 López, 'The Puerto Rican Diaspora,' pp. 329–37.

16 Joseph P. Fitzpatrick, *Puerto Rican Americans: The Meaning of Migration to the Mainland* (Englewood Cliffs, NJ: Prentice Hall, 1971), pp. 57–8; Terry J. Rosenberg and Robert W. Lake, 'Toward a Revised Model of Residential Segregation and Succession: Puerto Ricans in New York, 1960–1970,' *American Journal of Sociology* 81 (March 1976), p. 1149.

17 Rosenberg, *Residence, Employment and Mobility*, p. 39.

18 United States Department of Labor, *A Socioeconomic Profile of Puerto Rican New Yorkers* (Washington, DC: US Department of Labor, 1975), pp. 62–3.

19 Clara Rodriguez, *The Ethnic Queue in the United States: The Case of the Puerto Ricans* (San Francisco, CA: R and E Associates, 1974), p. 121.

20 José Ramon Sanchez, 'Housing Puerto Ricans in New York City, 1945–1984: A Study in Class Powerlessness' (New York: doctoral dissertation, New York University, 1990), pp. 65–9.

21 See *inter alia*, Andres Torres, 'Labor Market Segmentation: African American and Puerto Rican Labor in New York City, 1960–1980,' *The Review of Black Political Economy* 20 (summer 1991).

22 United States Department of Labor, Bureau of Labor Statistics, Middle Atlantic Region, *Poverty Area Profiles: The New York Puerto Rican: Patterns of Work Experience*. Regional Report no. 19 (Washington DC: The Department, May 1971).

23 See, *inter alia*, chapter 2 of Sharon Zukin, *Loft Living: Culture and Capital in Urban Change* (Baltimore, MD: Johns Hopkins University Press, 1982).

24 Chester Rapkin, *The South of Houston Industrial Area: Economic Significance of Structures in a Loft Section of Manhattan* (study prepared for the New York City Planning Commission, 1963), pp. 38–40.

25 Robert Laurentz, 'Racial and Ethnic Conflict in the New York City Garment Industry, 1933–1980' (Binghamton, NY: doctoral dissertation, State University of New York, 1980), p. 239.

26 The bargaining terms of the ILGWU constitution allowed for exclusion of rank-and-file members from contract negotiations. Rank-and-file did not vote on this issue. Apparently, this was not a problem when the ethnic and racial backgrounds of the members and the leaders were identical. See Herbert Hill, 'Guardians of the Sweatshops: The Trade Unions, Racism and the Garment Industry,' in Adalberto López and James Petras, eds., *Puerto Rico and Puerto Ricans*, p. 387.

27 Ibid., p. 388.

28 Laurentz, 'Racial and Ethnic Conflict,' p. 240.

29 Sanchez argues that Puerto Ricans' housing conditions take their toll on the group's employment and class position. See his 'Housing Puerto Ricans,' p. 203.

30 Their places were partially taken by an influx of young whites. The exceptionally large cohort of unmarried 20- to 35-year olds of non-Puerto Rican parentage in 1970 reflects the appearance of a hippie population that concentrated in the East Village between 1967 and 1972. See George W. Carey, 'Hippie Neighborhoods and Urban Spatial Systems,' in Robert K. Yin, ed., *The City in the Seventies* (Itasca, IL: F. E. Peacock Publishers, 1972).

31 For a discussion of ghetto expansion and income decline, see David P. Varady, *Neighborhood Upgrading: A Realistic Assessment* (Albany: State University of New York Press, 1986), p. 10.

32 Survey of religious affiliations conducted September 1949 and January 1950 by Donald Walton, Minister of DeWitt Memorial Church, as cited in Leo Grebler, *Housing Market Behavior in a Declining Area* (New York: Columbia University Press, 1952), p. 147.

33 Sanchez, 'Housing Puerto Ricans,' p. 211.

Appendix to Chapter 6 The Other Side of the Coin: Culture in Loisaida

Mario Maffi

The Poet who today writes and prints, once only sang. But the Poet wasn't then an individual, but the community, and whoever could not sing verses would have had no other way to retain the data of his/her life.

Amadeo Bordiga, 1953

Maybe the masses receive their voice from the poet, maybe it is they who grant it, delegate it, and finally lose it.

Alessandro Portelli, 1992[1]

The history of Loisaida[2] cannot be told simply in terms of the dramatic process of its dispersal. Over more than a century, the entire Lower East Side experience showed that, however harsh, even desperate its living and working conditions might be, there was always day-to-day resistance on the part of its new residents – a stubborn creative response to chaos and misery that somehow made life endurable, nurtured several important sociocultural realities, and finally gave the area that laboratory-like quality it maintains to this day.[3]

In fact, as Bernardo Vega's memoirs or Jesus Colon's sketches clearly reveal,[4] life in Puerto Rican areas of New York was less fragmented and disorganized than is generally supposed. Puerto Rican enclaves on the upper West Side, in East Harlem, and in Lower Manhattan did manage to weave together a small effective network of coping institutions (clubs, newspapers, unions, and forums) and informal meeting places (stoops, rooftops, backyards, barber shops, *marquetas, botanicas*, and *bodegas*). In the complex dialectical process through which migrants became 'angled' by remolding anglo culture, these were the vehicles of tradition and information – the agents that held the community together when it was in the throes of adjusting to its new reality.

To this network of formal and informal community institutions must be added the written word. Among the individuals who figured large in this network were folklorist Pura Belpré, writers Julia de Burgos, Ramón Ruiz de Hoyos, Lola Rodrigez de Tio, and Jesus Colon, and *politicos*, such as Luis Moz Marín, Pedro Albizu Campos, and Bernardo Vega. But perhaps the most influential of all was the poet bard, Jorge Brandon, who 'carrie[d] his metaphors / in brown shopping bags / in steel shopping carts.'[5] These constituted decisive connecting links between generations, between a past of blue-collar work and a present of job displacement and population decline. Brandon, first with his *Teatro Ambulante* and then as 'the talking coconut,' carried on the tradition of the island's *lectores* (hired by cigar-makers to read aloud to workers) and *juegos florales* (beauty and poetry contests). He adapted to the new urban reality the figure of the oral poet who refuses to let his poetry be crystalized in print and who constantly remolds the collective experience of his countrymen in an ongoing monologue to be sung or told. In doing so, he acted as 'the sacred father-testament'[6] to the younger generations of Puerto Rican poets *en Nueva York.*[7]

Street gangs, that elementary form of aggregation for ghetto youth, also provided an important avenue to a new sociocultural identity. Developing out of a Chicago-based gang and modeling themselves after the Black Panthers, the Puerto Rican dominated Young Lords Organization established chapters in New York. In the late 1960s and early 1970s, the YLO had its headquarters on East Third Street in the Lower East Side; it shared the Christodora House (see Gordon, chapter 10) with other radical groups and operated a whole set of social services, from general culture courses given at St Brigid's Church to free breakfasts for hungry children. The street gang scene had effects that went well beyond the Young Lords Organization, which eventually disappeared with little trace.

Charas, Inc.,[8] a community center originally called 'The Real Great Society,' was born out of the confluence and politicization of two former gangs, the Chelsea-based Assassins and the Lower East Side Dragons. Charas immediately became involved in building, under the direction of architects Buckminster Fuller and Michael Ben-Eli, several geodesic domes in the area.[9] This was the beginning of an intense two-decade activity in community resistance and revitalization, in which Charas worked with groups such as Cooper Square, Adopt-a-Building, and several homesteading organizations. Charas also became involved in cultural expression – the painting of murals, photography, and productions of theater, movies, music and dance.

The local Young Lords Organization was also active culturally, most notably as an incubator for the poetry movement. Indeed, it was on the pages of *Palante*, the YLO's newspaper, that Pedro Pietri's 'Puerto Rican Obituary' was first published – a long, bitter moving poem-monologue that summed up the Puerto Rican experience *en la urbe*, in an ever precarious balance between yearnings and disillusionment, ethnic identity and big city allurements, traditional mores and beckoning status symbols.

> These empty dreams
> from the make-believe bedrooms
> their parents left them
> are the after-effects
> of television programs
> about the ideal
> white american family
> with black maids
> and latino janitors
> who are well train [sic]
> to make everyone
> and their bill collectors
> laugh at them
> and the people they represent.[10]

By giving literary voice to the new generations in New York, Pietri's work started the whole 'Nuyorican Poets' Experience' – Pietri himself, Miguel Algarín, Miguel Piñero, Tato Laviera, Lucky CienFuegos, Bimbo Rivas, Sandra María Esteves, Americo Casiano, Martita Morales, and others. And although not all of them actually *came from* the Lower East Side, the neighborhood played a central role in their experience.[11] In the mid-1970s, the opening of the Nuyorican Poets' Café on East Sixth Street, just off Avenue A, climaxed Loisaida's 'golden age,' its pregentrification flowering. It bespoke the fact that the community had by then reached rootedness in the neighborhood, and that this rootedness allowed it to nurture its own poets.

In works by the late Piñero ('so please when I die . . . / don't take me far away / keep me near by / take my ashes and scatter them thru out / the Lower East Side'[12]) and Rivas ('A Job / to feed the time I spend adrift / in search for substance in the street / Awake at three a.m. / not knowing where or when the end / will come to my disdain'[13]), one can feel the pulse of street life, the drama of everyday survival mingled with a vivid creative vision – the raw materials of life in the ghetto giving body and breath to poetry. Introducing the Nuyorican poets, Algarín wrote:

> The poet sees his function as a troubadour. He tells the tale of the streets. The people listen. They cry, they laugh, they dance as the troubadour opens up and tunes his voice and moves his pitch and rhythm to the high tension of *bomba* truth. Proclamations of hurt, of anger and hatred. Whirls of high-pitched singing. The voice of the street poet must amplify itself . . . A poem describes the neighborhood of the writer for the reader . . . The poems of this anthology are in the dance of the moment. The Nuyorican poets have worked to establish the commonplace because they have wanted to locate their position on earth, the ground, the neighborhood, the environment. These are the places that the poet names for his readers.[14]

And it is precisely in this strict relationship between the poet and his/her environment, the neighborhood-as-community, that the fascination of Nuyorican poetry resides.[15]

In those years, Loisaida began to speak its voice not only through poetry, but through the visual arts. The crumbling walls of the quarter's tenements erupted in an explosion of color. Mural artists, such as Eva Cockcroft, John Weber, James Jannuzzi, Susan Caruso-Green, Alfredo Hernandez, Tabo Toral, María Dominguez, Lee Quinones, Chico, Tomie Arai, Alan Okada, and several others, a rather multi-ethnic group, contributed their wall paintings which evolved into a pure Lower East Side style. Either by themselves, or in conjunction with Charas or CityArts, they created murals whose titles reflected their convictions: Afro-Latin Coalition, New Birth, The Wall of Respect for Women, Chi Lai/Arriba/Rise UP!, Seeds for Progressive Change, Women Hold Up Half the Sky, Crear Una Sociedad Nueva, Arise from Oppression, Baile Bomba, Homenaje a Don Pedro, La Lucha Continua. These beautiful art works grew directly out of the community's past and present, and by finding inspiration, materials, and types *in the streets*, were yet another expression of the kind of street culture that had always been typical of the neighborhood. What is more, they were *collective*, not only from a technical point of view (their conception and execution), but also in terms of content: they told the story of the whole community, often moving beyond the purely Puerto Rican boundaries to embrace all the communities that historically had comprised the Lower East Side. Other vital contributions were made by photographers, among them Marlis Momber who documented the mid-1970s flowering with passionate engagement (and whose photographs illustrate this book).

Nor were little magazines,[16] music festivals, and other community activities ignored. There were *bomba* 'concerts' at Charas and *salsa* dancing to 'A Band Called Loisaida,' as well as street fairs and fiestas. There were more political *cum* social and social-service activities – from the umbrella organization, Seven Loaves, to those of the Lower East Side Garden Coalition, Cooper Square, Pueblo Nuevo, etc. that composed the resistance front against the forces of gentrification and dispersal. It was not for lack of vitality that Loisaida's days were numbered.

The publication of the *Nuyorican Poetry* anthology and the birth of Loisaida as a name and a conception of community marked the climax of Puerto Rican experience in the East Village. The years that followed witnessed a veritable attack on Loisaida by the forces of gentrification, as the chapters in part II show. The community suffered first by distraction and then by dispersal. From the late 1970s on, it saw a veritable draining of precious individual and collective energies in the attempt to resist gentrification, and by the late 1980s, many exhausted fighters had defected by moving while others struggled against mounting odds to forestall collapse. Still, day-to-day resistance has not totally disappeared and individuals who had been among the protagonists of the mid-1970s flowering are still at work, albeit some no longer living in the area.

An intellectual turning point came between the late 1970s and mid-1980s, however, when Nuyorican poets began to move beyond the physical boundaries of Loisaida and the ethnic boundaries of Puerto Ricans. They joined forces with other Puerto Rican writers from the Bronx, Queens, New Jersey, and even Chicago and became part of a larger multicultural unit which included other Latino/a (chicanos/as, Central and South American) and Asian-American authors. In so doing, they confirmed the laboratory-incubator role that the Lower East Side always played on the American cultural scene. But paradoxically, this also tended to loosen their ties to the local neighborhood that had given them their impetus. They had little choice. The necessities of survival, the veritable siege conducted by real estate interests, the gradual dissolution of the community under attack, and the fragmentation of communal identity under so many pressures were being mirrored in a poetry that was becoming either more intimate and private or more general and universal. This shift is well illustrated in Pietri's evolution from *Puerto Rican Obituary* (1973) to *Traffic Violations*[17] (1983), an evolution from reality to surrealism, but it is also present in the work of Algarín and Laviera.

Something similar occurred in the murals. Mural painting continued on the Lower East Side throughout the late 1970s and early 1980s, but in recent years not only have the older huge works been neglected or erased, but the new ones reveal a similar shift. They *tend* to be more individualistic, both in terms of planning and execution and in terms of conception and themes. The neighborhood continues to spawn beautiful murals, but they are more intimate, personal, circumscribed – rarely epic and collective. And it is not accidental, given the rising drug and crime rates, that the most frequent format to have appeared in recent years is the 'Rest in Peace' one – murals commissioned to Chico or to other local artists by the family and friends of a deceased. The mural in memoriam of Bimbo Rivas, with its riveting eyes, is one of the most loving, and it constitutes almost an epitaph to an entire period of Loisaida history.

But the whole history of the Lower East Side shows that the spirit of creative resistance runs strong in the neighborhood and, like the Italian Karst rivers that suddenly disappear underground only to burst through again miles and miles away, always reappears. The reopening in 1990 of the Nuyorican Poets' Café on East Third Street off Avenue C, and the several social, artistic and political activities that are still going strong in the area are powerful signs of resistance and continuity. They may even be the beginning of a new stage in the Lower East Side's never-ending story.

NOTES

This appendix is in memory of Miguel Piñero and Bimbo Rivas.

1 Quotations are from Amadeo Bordiga, 'Fantasime Carlyliane,' *Il programma comunista* (1953), now in *Il battilocchio nella storia* (Torino: Editing, 1992); and from Alessandro Portelli, *Il testo e la voce. Oralità, letteratura e democrazia in America* (Roma: Manifesto Libri, 1992).

2 The late poet-performer-activist Bimbo Rivas wrote the poem 'Loisaida' in 1974 and the term was immediately taken up by the community as an apt symbol of its reality and struggles. See *Loisaida: Continent of Seven Colors* (New York: Taller Latinamericano, 1990); and Manuel Ramos Otero, 'The Point Blank Page,' *The Portable Lower East Side* (1991).

3 See Moses Rischin, *The Promised City: New York's Jews, 1870–1914* (Cambridge, MA: Harvard University Press, 1977); Irving Howe, *World of Our Fathers* (New York: Harcourt Brace Jovanovich, 1976); and Mario Maffi, *Gateway to the Promised Land. Ethnicity and Culture in New York's Lower East Side* (Amsterdam: Rodopi Publications; New York: New York University Press. Forthcoming.)

4 See César Andreu Iglesias, ed., *Memoirs of Bernardo Vega: A Contribution to the History of the Puerto Rican Community in New York* (New York: Monthly Review Press, reprinted 1984); Jesus Colon, *A Puerto Rican in New York and Other Sketches* (New York: International Publishers, reprinted 1982).

5 Pedro Pietri, 'Traffic Misdirector,' in his *Traffic Violations* (Maplewood, NJ: Waterfront Press, 1983), p. 103. (During the 1980s, Jorge Brandon lived for a time in a squatter-controlled building on East Eighth Street, before the city demolished the structure. Some squatters attribute the subsequent decline of Brandon's health to the 1989 eviction/demolition of that building. Note added by Christopher Mele.)

6 Tato Laviera, *AmeRícan* (Houston: Arte Público Press, 1985), p. 87.

7 Author's interview with Jorge Brandon, New York, 29 January 1991.

8 Still operating in a former school building on Ninth Street just east of Avenue B.

9 Syeus Mottel, *Charas: The Improbable Dome Builders* (New York: Drake Publishers, 1973).

10 Pedro Pietri, *Puerto Rican Obituary* (New York: Monthly Review Press, 1973), pp. 4–5. Reprinted by permission of Monthly Review Foundation: Copyright © 1973 by Pedro Pietri.

11 See Miguel Algarín and Miguel Piñero, eds., *Nuyorican Poetry: An Anthology of Puerto Rican Words and Feelings* (New York: William Morrow & Co., 1975); Eugene V. Mohr, *The Nuyorican Experience: Literature of the Puerto Rican Minority* (Westport, CN: Greenwood Press, 1982); Pedro López-Adorno, ed., *Papiros de Babel: Antologia de poesía puertorriqueña en Nueva York* (Río Piedras, Puerto Rico: Editorial de la Universidad de Puerto Rico, 1991); and Faythe Turner, ed., *Puerto Rican Writers at Home in the USA: An Anthology* (Seattle, WA: Open Hand Publishing, 1991).

12 Miguel Piñero, 'A Lower East Side Poem,' in his *La Bodega Sold Dreams* (Houston: Arte Público Press, 1980), p. 8.

13 Bimbo Rivas, 'A Job,' in Miguel Algarín and Miguel Piñero, eds., *Nuyorican Poetry*, p. 93.

14 Algarín and Piñero, *Nuyorican Poetry*, pp. 11, 181.

15 This same physical sense of place as foundation of a community can also be detected in several works by Asian-American authors of the Lower East Side. Speaking of Chinatown, for instance, Fay Chiang writes: 'These images still live on / in your streets / I pace them / their names imprinted / in my heart / Bayard, Mott, Pell, / Doyer, Bowery, Mulberry, / Canal, Division, / East Broadway, Henry, / Catherine / All hours of the day and night / I have coursed these streets / like the memories / coursing through my veins . . .' Fay Chiang, 'Chinatown: A Work-in-Progress Narrative Poem,' unpublished 1987, courtesy of the author. On these points, see Mario Maffi and Franco Minganti, 'City Maps and City Alphabets,' *RSA. Rivista di Studi Anglo-Americani*, Vol. 6, no. 8 (1990); and Mario Maffi, ' "Chi Lai, Arriba, Rise Up!" Some Remarks on Ethnic Writings in New York City,' in Hans Bak, ed., *Multiculturalism and the Canon of American Culture* (Amsterdam: VU University Press, 1993).

16 For example, *The Fourth Street 'i'* and *The Quality of Life in Loisaida.*

17 Pedro Pietri, *Traffic Violations.*

7

From Disinvestment to Reinvestment: Mapping the Urban 'Frontier' in the Lower East Side

Neil Smith, Betsy Duncan, and Laura Reid

The main point is that you want to be out on the frontier of gentrification. So you can't use the established financial institutions, for example, the banks. That's why you need the broker . . . You try to be far enough out on the 'line' that you can make a killing; not too far where you can't offload the building but far enough that you can buy the building cheap enough to still make money.

Steve Bass, Brooklyn developer, 1986

Many popular press accounts depict the geographical shifts associated with gentrification and urban restructuring through the highly resonant imagery of the frontier. City neighborhoods experiencing the gamut of related processes – residential rehabilitation, construction of new luxury apartments, the appearance of more middle- and upper-middle-class residents, the emergence of new boutique landscapes of consumption, and so forth – are envisioned as frontiers of a new time and place. The vivid ideological chords that suffuse this frontier imagery are readily apparent. As with all ideologies, however, there is generally a kernel of truth, and the ideology of the new urban frontier is no exception.

The kernel of economic truth here is that in neighborhoods undergoing rapid restructuring, there is indeed something akin to an economic 'frontier of profitability.'[1] Geographically as well as historically, the frontier represents a line dividing disinvestment from reinvestment. By disinvestment we mean the relative withdrawal of capital in all its forms from the built environment; reinvestment involves the return of capital to landscapes and structures previously experiencing disinvestment. Ahead of the frontier line, properties are still experiencing disinvestment and devalorization through the multifarious actions of landlords, owner occupiers, financial institutions, tenants, and the state. Over a number of years, relative or absolute disinvestment and devalorization result in the formation of a rent gap whereby the *actual* capitalized ground rent (or land value) under present use is substantially lower than the *potential* ground rent that could be appropriated at that location under a higher and better use.[2] Behind the frontier line, some form of reinvestment has begun to supplant disinvestment. Thus conceived, the frontier line represents the leading historical and geographical edge of urban restructuring and gentrification. This chapter examines the formation and spread of such a frontier line in the East Village, where residential rehabilitation of the classic gentrification sort has been occurring since the 1970s.[3]

Disinvestment in urban real estate develops a certain momentum that gives the appearance of being self-fulfilling. Historical decline in a neighborhood's real estate market provokes further decline, since the ground rent that can be appropriated at a given site depends not only upon the level of investment on the site itself, but on the physical and economic condition of surrounding structures and wider local investment trends. It is irrational for a real estate investor to commit large amounts of capital to maintain a pristine building amidst neighborhood deterioration and devalorization. The opposite process, sustained neighborhood reinvestment, appears equally self-fulfilling, for it is obviously irrational for a housing entrepreneur to leave a building in dilapidated condition amidst widespread neighborhood rehabilitation and recapitalization.

In the first case, investment in an isolated building may indeed raise its intrinsic value, but it does little to enhance the ground rent at the site and is in all probability unrecoverable, insofar as the neighborhood rent or resale levels will not sustain the necessary rise in the rent or price of the individual refurbished building. What benefits do accrue beyond the building itself are dissipated throughout a declining neighborhood. In the second case, the neighborhood-wide increases in ground rent that accrue from widespread recapitalization are only incompletely realized by owners of buildings who do not rehabilitate their properties, although of course, short-term speculative gains can be made by warehousing (keeping a building off the market until its price rises), flipping (buying a building in order simply to resell at a higher price), and other speculative practices that involve no significant reinvestment. (See chapter 8.)

But whatever the economic momentum established, this does not mean that neighborhood decline results from some irrational psychology among investors in real estate. Rather, sustained disinvestment begins as a result of largely rational decisions by owners, landlords, local and national governments, and an array of financial institutions.[4] These represent the major groups of capital investors in the built landscape and they experience various levels of choice in their investment strategies and decisions.[5] However disparate these individual decisions may be, they represent a broadly rational, if not always parallel or predictable, set of responses to existing neighborhood conditions.[6]

Whatever the dysfunctional social consequences provoked or exacerbated by disinvestment – deteriorating housing conditions, increased hazards to residents' health, community destruction, the ghettoization of crime, loss of housing stock, and increased homelessness – disinvestment is also economically functional within the housing market and can be conceived of as an integral dimension of the uneven development of urban places. Focusing on the relationship between housing demand and state policy, Anthony Downs makes this general point when he observes that 'a certain amount of neighborhood deterioration is an essential part of urban development.'[7] In addition to the effects of state policies, others have highlighted the role of financial institutions in disinvestment and redlining[8] and eventually abandonment.[9] The ultimate rationale for geographically selective disinvestment on the part of banks, savings and loan organizations, and other financial institutions is to restrict the effects of devalorization, economic decline, and asset loss to clearly circumscribed neighborhoods, and thereby protect the integrity of mortgage loans in other areas. Delimiting the geography of disinvestment serves to circumscribe its economic impact.

Some attention has also focused on the functionality of disinvestment from the point of view of landlords. While Sternlieb and Burchell have argued that landlords in declining neighborhoods, squeezed between decreasing rent rolls and increasing costs, are as much the victims of disinvestment as its perpetrators,[10] others have suggested a different picture. Salins argues that 'most of the present and future owners of this kind of property are there by choice, and are making money.' Market rationality, together with state policies, have 'led housing entrepreneurs to make money in ways that involve the destruction of the housing stock.'[11] Salins documents the process of 'graduated disinvestment' according to which building owners become 'increasingly exploitative of the property.' The building is 'milked' of its rent rolls while the landlord progressively reduces and may even terminate the payment of debt service, insurance, and property taxes; the performance of maintenance and repairs; and the provision of vital services such as water, heat, and elevators. In all likelihood the property also changes hands frequently, rarely with the benefit of traditional mortgage sources, before ending up in the hands of a 'finisher' who performs the final gutting of the building's economic value, up to and including the removal of fixtures and furniture which are scavenged for use elsewhere.[12] Physical and economic abandonment and arson-for-insurance are the eventual fate of many buildings.

Lake has corroborated this view with an intensive empirical examination of landlord tax delinquency in Pittsburgh.[13] He enumerates a variety of disinvestment strategies and notes that which one is selected depends on the type of owner (landlord versus home owner), the size of his/her holdings, the owner's perception of neighborhood property values, etc. Lake identifies a 'cycle of delinquency' whereby property maintenance, property value, and occupancy rates spiral downward in close relationship to each other.

At a more aggregate level, then, it is possible to view long-term neighborhood disinvestment as a necessary if not sufficient condition for the onset of gentrification. By establishing a rent gap, disinvestment creates the conditions for reinvestment.[14] But no matter how trenchant or self-fulfilling neighborhood disinvestment appears to be, the process is reversible; there is nothing natural or inevitable about disinvestment. Just as disinvestment is an active process carried out by more or less rational investors in response to existing conditions and changes in the housing market, so the reversal of disinvestment is equally deliberate. Any individual decision by an investor or housing developer to reverse direction and to embark on a course of reinvestment, rather than a disinvestment strategy, may result from myriad kinds of information and perceptions. Individual perceptions about changes in the neighborhood and in adjoining areas may contribute as much as real estate data from local real estate boards or chambers of commerce.

But assuming individual investors do not control the housing market in entire neighborhoods, successful reinvestment is contingent upon the broadly parallel actions of a range of individual investors. Whatever the individual perceptions and predilections of landlords, developers, and financial lenders, the reinvestment strategy reflects a rational collective assessment of the profitable opportunities created by disinvestment and the emergence of the rent gap. The more knowledgeable, the more perceptive, or simply the luckier investor may make the largest returns by responding more quickly, more accurately, or even more imaginatively to the opportunities represented by the rent gap, while the less knowledgeable, the less lucky, and the inappropriately imaginative investor may misjudge the situation, making lower profits or even sustaining a loss.

The focus of the present chapter is on the point of reversal where disinvestment in the East Village was succeeded by reinvestment between 1976 and 1985, and especially the geographical movement of this 'gentrification frontier.' There are a number of possible methods for identifying this turning point, using different data sets, but we suggest that none is as sensitive to the earliest phase as data on tax arrears.

An obvious indication of the economic turning point associated with gentrification is a significant and sustained increase in mortgage financing. Finance capital plays a critical role in the geographical division of urban space into recognizable submarkets and in place-specific disinvestment. Where an adequate flow of mortgage money is not forthcoming, the gentrification of a neighborhood can certainly begin but is unlikely to reach fruition. While mortgage data have been used widely by gentrification researchers,[15] it is not especially sharp as an indicator of *initial* reinvestment associated with the turning point.

The reason for this is suggested in the introductory quote from the Brooklyn developer. Much of the earliest gentrification activity is carried out by developers on the extreme edge of the economic frontier where traditional lenders are generally reluctant to invest yet. In advance of traditional sources, the actual funding mechanisms are diverse, often involve a variety of sources in some form of partnership, and are extremely difficult to trace. One common arrangement combines in partnership an architect, a developer, a building manager, a lawyer, and a broker. The first three of these will work on the actual conversion of the building, while the lawyer handles any problems regarding the deed transfer, loan arrangements, state subsidies and tax abatements, and any legal 'problems' resulting from the expulsion of existing tenants. All of the partners contribute financially to the project, and it is the function of the broker to secure additional private market loans on the basis of this seed money. Where building rehabilitation is organized in this manner, traditional mortgage data fail to reveal the date or dimensions of initial reinvestment.

A detailed survey of building conditions and an assessment of building deterioration levels might also reveal important information regarding the onset of reinvestment, but it is important to remember that reinvestment may begin substantially in advance of a building's physical upgrading. Indeed, in a detailed survey of displacement pressures in the Lower East Side, DeGiovanni found strong evidence that deterioration may actually be 'an integral part of the reinvestment process,' as landlords foster adverse physical conditions 'to clear buildings of the current tenants' before undertaking major repairs or resale.[16] Shifts in the physical condition of a building are better conceived as responses to economic strategies, rather than causes, and therefore provide at best a rough proxy for reinvestment. Similarly, increases in sales activity might simply indicate speculation or even intensified disinvestment, rather than the onset of gentrification.

In contrast, tax arrears data provide a very sensitive indicator of initial reinvestment connected with gentrification. Non-payment of property taxes by building owners is a common form of disinvestment in declining neighborhoods. Tax delinquency is, in effect, an investment strategy, since it provides property owners with guaranteed access to capital. Insofar as serious delinquency places ownership of the building in jeopardy through the threat of city foreclosure proceedings, we might expect that the extent of tax arrears in a neighborhood is highly sensitive to reversals in the investment landscape. When landlords and owners become convinced that substantial reinvestment is possible, they will seek to retain possession of a building whose sale price is expected to increase. Where buildings are seriously in arrears, this requires repayment of at least some back taxes, to prevent foreclosure by the city. Redemption of tax arrears can therefore function as an initial form of reinvestment. This position is supported empirically by Lake's findings in Pittsburgh; among owners of buildings with low to moderate assessed values, there is a clear correlation between their perception of increased property values and their intention to redeem their tax delinquency status.[17]

Tax delinquency thus lies on the fulcrum between growth and decline, expansion and contraction. Peter Marcuse made the first attempt to use New York tax arrears data to demonstrate shifts in investment patterns in a neighborhood threatened by gentrification.[18] He found significant evidence of turning points in several census tracts in the Hell's Kitchen neighborhood of New York City. The present research pursues this initial insight, applying the method to the transformation of the East Village after 1975.

Every city has its own specific procedures for determining tax delinquency and taking into public ownership buildings that surpass a certain threshold of arrearages. In New York City until 1978, foreclosure proceedings (referred to as *in rem* proceedings) could begin against buildings that were twelve or more quarters (three years) in arrears. The massive wave of residential disinvestment associated with the 1974–5 recession and New York City's fiscal crisis resulted in a rapid increase in delinquency rates. In response, a 1978 law, first proposed by Mayor Beame, made buildings eligible for *in rem* proceedings after only four quarters in arrears. (One- and two-family buildings and condominia were exempt from this change.) After four quarters in arrears, building owners have a grace period of a further quarter in which to repay taxes before the onset of *in rem* proceedings. For a further two years, owners can still redeem their buildings, but at the discretion of the city.

In practice, the city departments of Finance and of Housing Preservation and Development have rarely initiated proceedings against buildings that are less than twelve quarters in arrears, and although there are many complaints about the bureaucratic nature of the foreclosure procedure,[19] the city administration is reluctant to increase its already large stock of foreclosed and often vacant buildings, and so entertains a variety of repayment schemes from buildings owners. Many buildings are redeemed well after the twelve-quarter arrears threshold is reached without being foreclosed; others are redeemed according to individual installment plans; and still others are transferred from one owner to another with the purchase price incorporating the redemption of outstanding tax debts. Thus in practice, the cutoff point between safe and unsafe delinquency levels is not absolute but somewhat fluid.

City-wide property tax delinquency levels in New York City peaked in 1976 when over 7 percent of the city's residential buildings were in arrears – an extraordinary figure. After that peak, however, delinquency levels declined steadily, dropping to a 70-year low of 2 percent by 1986.[20] In the most immediate sense, the rapid decline in total arrears resulted from the easing of the recession, the overcoming of the fiscal crisis of the 1970s, and perhaps to some extent from the anticipation of the tighter 1978 law. But mostly it was due to the rapid inflation of real estate prices in the city from the late 1970s on.

Declining delinquency levels indicated a very significant reduction in disinvestment levels and a parallel trend towards reinvestment in previously declining real estate. Far fewer building owners were abandoning properties in the 1980s than in the 1960s and 1970s. This in turn was directly related to larger processes of urban restructuring, and to gentrification in particular.

Despite these reductions in overall delinquency, disinvestment still corroded a large section of the city's rental stock. Although here too there were significant reductions, the level of rental property delinquency remained high. In 1980, for example, 3.5 percent of the city's residential properties were in arrears, but this figure was dominated by some 330,000 rental apartments, fully 26 percent of the city's entire rental stock.[21] Although overall disinvestment rates declined, property tax delinquency became increasingly concentrated, both geographically and economically, in older neighborhoods dominated by large tenement and other multiple-unit rental housing stock. These represent the poorest neighborhoods destroyed by massive, systematic and sustained disinvestment over a period of three to seven decades: Harlem, Bedford Stuyvesant, Brownsville, East New York, the South Bronx, and the Lower East Side, including the East Village. Once home to more than half a million immigrants, the Lower East Side experienced intense disinvestment in the postwar period. Always Bohemian, the area began to experience gentrification in the mid-1970s, and by the 1980s had become a major target for reinvestment.

'One must realize,' wrote a local art critic, 'that the East Village or the Lower East Side is more than a geographical location – it is a state of mind.'[22] Indeed, the East Village was enthusiastically hailed in the 1980s as the newest artistic 'hangout' in New York City, drawing effusive comparison with Paris's Left Bank or London's Soho. In the gentrification of the East Village, art galleries, dance clubs, and studios have been the shock troops of neighborhood reinvestment, although the extraordinary complicity of the art scene with the social destruction wrought by gentrification is rarely conceded.

Touted as a 'neo-frontier,' the attraction of the East Village was attributed in the art press to its 'unique blend of poverty, punk rock, drugs and arson, Hell's Angels, winos, prostitutes and dilapidated housing that adds up to an adventurous avant-garde setting of considerable cachet.'[23] The artistic influx began in the late 1970s and was increasingly institutionalized after 1981 with the widely heralded opening of new galleries. The area has provided the setting as well as the subject of literally dozens of 1980s novels and several movies. But the romanticization of poverty and deprivation – the area's 'unique blend' – is always limited, and the neon and pastiche sparkle of aesthetic ultra-chic only partly camouflages the harsher realities of displacement, homelessness, unemployment, and deprivation in a neighborhood converted into a new frontier at the hands of gentrification.[24]

By 1980 the East Village, excluding the housing projects east of Avenue D, had experienced a population decline of 30.2 percent from 1970. In the same decade, however, median rents had increased between 128 and 172 percent in the area's eleven census tracts, universally higher than the city-wide increase of 125 percent. Fully a fourth of all households had incomes below the poverty line in 1980, but there was considerable variation by census tract (from 14.9 to 64.9 percent). In the absence of intercensal figures, it is possible to estimate population trends in the area between 1974 and 1986 by using data from the local gas and electricity company.[25] The number of accounts rose from 30,669 in 1974 to a peak of 31,516 in 1976 and then fell precipitously to 24,391 in 1982. Thereafter, it began to rise again, presumably as a result of gentrification; by 1986 there were 25,389 Con Edison accounts in the East Village. By 1990, for which new census totals are now available, the population of the East Village stood at about 50,000, indicating the completion of one cycle of decline and recovery.

Turning to disinvestment, the peak years of total tax arrears came in 1976 and 1977, when over 800 tax lots were in arrears; by 1986 this number had dropped to only 407. Figure 7.1 contrasts the history of disinvestment (total private market residential tax arrears) and population levels (as estimated from Con Edison accounts) between 1974 and 1986.[26] It indicates that although some redemption of tax arrears began after

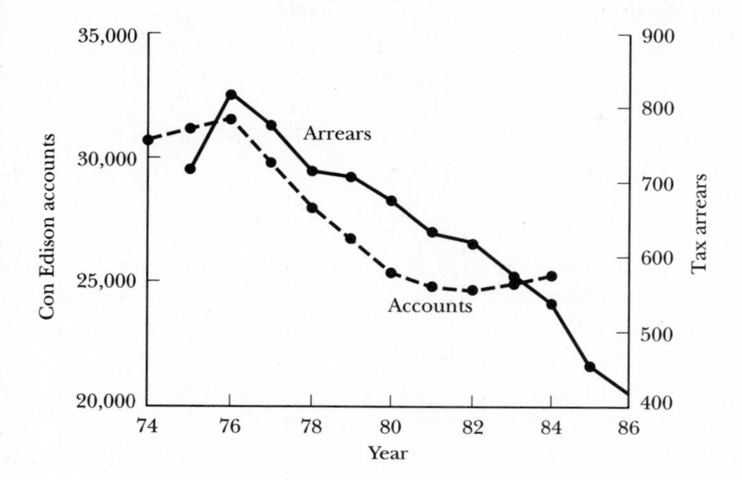

Figure 7.1 Change in total tax arrears and utility accounts in the East Village, 1974–1986
Source: Original graph by Neil Smith, Betsy Duncan, and Laura Reid. 'From Disinvestment to Reinvestment: Tax Arrears and Turning Points in the Lower East Side,' *Housing Studies* 4 (1989): 238–52

1976, it was not until after 1982 that the number of households began to rise.

Table 7.1 provides parallel data on vacancy rates. All of the census tracts experienced peak vacancy rates between 1976 and 1978, but by 1984 rates had dropped by half in virtually every tract. This suggests that there was a lag of perhaps six years between earliest reinvestment and repopulation. This offers further support for our contention that, in the gentrification process, economic shifts long precede demographic changes.

It would be reasonable to assume that the reinvestment in the East Village after 1976 was related in part to the imminent passage of the stricter tax delinquency law, but a broader perspective suggests that this had little immediate effect. Larger forces were at work. Furthermore, the data demonstrate considerable internal differences, geographically and historically, in the disinvestment and reinvestment processes.

Tax arrears data are collected by the Department of Finance and are available on the city's MISLAND data base. For each census tract, a summary is available showing the extent of arrears. Tax lots in arrears are categorized according to the severity of delinquency: three to five quarters in arrears; six to twelve quarters; and greater than twelve quarters in arrears. We can classify these as low, intermediate, and serious levels of delinquency, respectively. Table 7.2 provides data on serious residential tax arrears for the East Village between 1975 and 1984. Given the *de facto* threshold of twelve quarters before the initiation of *in rem* proceedings, low levels of arrears (three to five quarters) tend not to reflect sharp and significant changes in delinquency and redemption. However, arrears in

Table 7.1 Level and year of peak vacancies in census tracts of the East Village

Rank	*Tract*	*Highest % unoccupied*	*Peak Year*	*% unoccupied 1984*
1	26.01	25.06	1978	11.87
2	26.02	24.87	1978	10.53
3	22.02	21.11	1976	11.48
4	28	20.78	1976	5.59
5	34	16.24	1978	6.40
6	30.02	11.77	1976	5.20
7	36.02	11.77	1976	5.20
8	32	9.27	1976	3.77
9	38	6.98	1976	3.30
10	40	5.77	1976	2.38
11	42	4.50	1976	1.49

Source: MISLAND, Con Edison File

the intermediate (six to twelve quarters) and serious (twelve plus quarters) categories do reveal an interesting historical trend (see figure 7.2).

Until 1980 there was a clear inverse relationship between the number of buildings in the intermediate category and those in serious delinquency. Building owners would seem to have followed an obvious strategy: buildings were partially redeemed in 1978 and 1979 (bringing them back from the serious to the intermediate arrears category), presumably to avert the threat of foreclosure at the hands of a 1978 city-wide vesting as well as the new delinquency law. In 1980 a new wave of delinquency began, as about 170 properties slipped back from intermediate to serious delinquency. After 1980 the inverse relationship between serious and intermediate delinquency was suspended as both categories declined significantly.

Despite the national recession of 1980 to 1982, which seriously curtailed residential construction, the decline in disinvestment continued. Only with the threat of major foreclosure and vesting proceedings in 1985 was there a recurrence of the inverse relationship between serious and intermediate delinquency, but this was a ripple within a larger decline in overall disinvestment. This suggests that serious reinvestment in the East Village as a whole began after 1980, the year of peak levels in serious delinquency. Corroborative evidence comes from sale price data. Whereas median per unit sale prices for the entire Lower East Side rose only 43.8 percent between 1968 and 1979 (a period in which the inflation rate exceeded 100 percent), prices rose 146.4 percent (3.7 times the rate of inflation) between 1979 and 1984.[27]

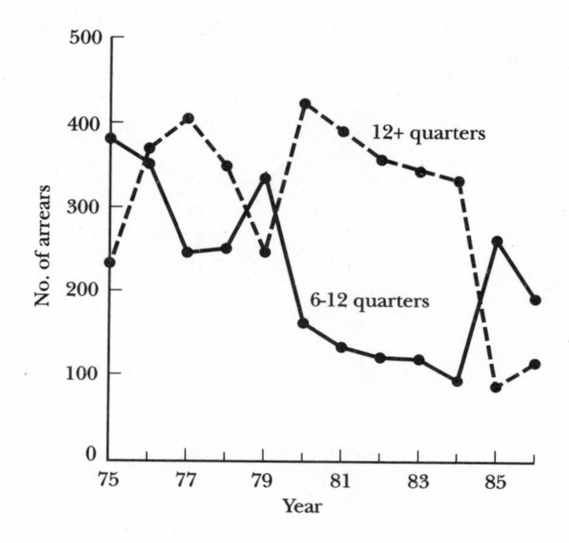

Figure 7.2 Trends in serious and intermediate tax arrears in the East Village, 1975–1986

Source: Original graph by Neil Smith, Betsy Duncan, and Laura Reid. 'From Disinvestment to Reinvestment: Tax Arrears and Turning Points in the Lower East Side,' *Housing Studies* 4 (1989): 238–52

In order to disaggregate the arrears data geographically and to identify the gentrification frontier, it is first necessary to identify the 'turning point' for each census tract. The turning point represents the year of peak serious arrears for each tract. Figure 7.3 provides four illustrations of this procedure. In Figures 7.3a, 7.3b and 7.3d, the turning points are 1980, 1982, and 1976, respectively. In tract 34, (Figure 7.3c), however, there were some 54 delinquent tax lots in 1976 and again in 1980; however, since our concern was to identify the date when disinvestment changed to sustained reinvestment, we took the later date as that tract's turning point. It is also apparent that intermediate arrears levels peaked prior to the turning points in serious delinquency. Leaving aside tract 42, where the number of arrears is too low to allow reasonable statistical comparison, in none of the remaining ten tracts did an intermediate peak follow the turning point in serious arrears.

Because of the small number of census tracts in the East Village, the identification of turning points was carried out for the entire Lower East Side, comprising 27 usable tracts. The earliest turning points came in 1975–6 and were generally on the western edge of the area. The latest were located in eastern tracts and occurred between 1983 and 1985.

Table 7.2 Trends in residential tax arrears, East Village, 1975–1985

Census tract	*Number of Quarters in arrears*	*Number of taxlots in arrears*											
		1975	*1976*	*1977*	*1978*	*1979*	*1980*	*1981*	*1982*	*1983*	*1984*	*1985*	*1986*
All	+ 12	241	369	402	344	244	417	385	352	338	324	79	107
22.02	+ 12	16	24	34	27	12	33	34	30	28	28	8	9
26.01	+ 12	39	72	87	66	53	88	76	71	73	73	10	11
26.02	+ 12	37	67	74	80	50	96	77	72	71	72	15	17
28	+ 12	40	57	64	49	34	50	44	43	42	38	5	14
30.02	+ 12	11	12	19	15	9	16	21	22	20	16	3	4
32	+ 12	22	27	30	26	24	44	44	37	35	39	19	23
34	+ 12	32	54	49	46	31	54	52	42	42	39	8	17
36.02	+ 12	14	18	16	15	11	14	14	12	10	8	5	3
38	+ 12	20	26	22	18	16	17	15	14	10	6	5	6
40	+ 12	9	12	7	2	4	5	8	9	7	5	1	3
42	+ 12	1	0	0	0	0	0	0	0	0	0	0	0

Source: Neil Smith, Betsy Duncan and Laura Reid, 'From Disinvestment to Reinvestment . . .,' *Housing Studies* 4 (1989)

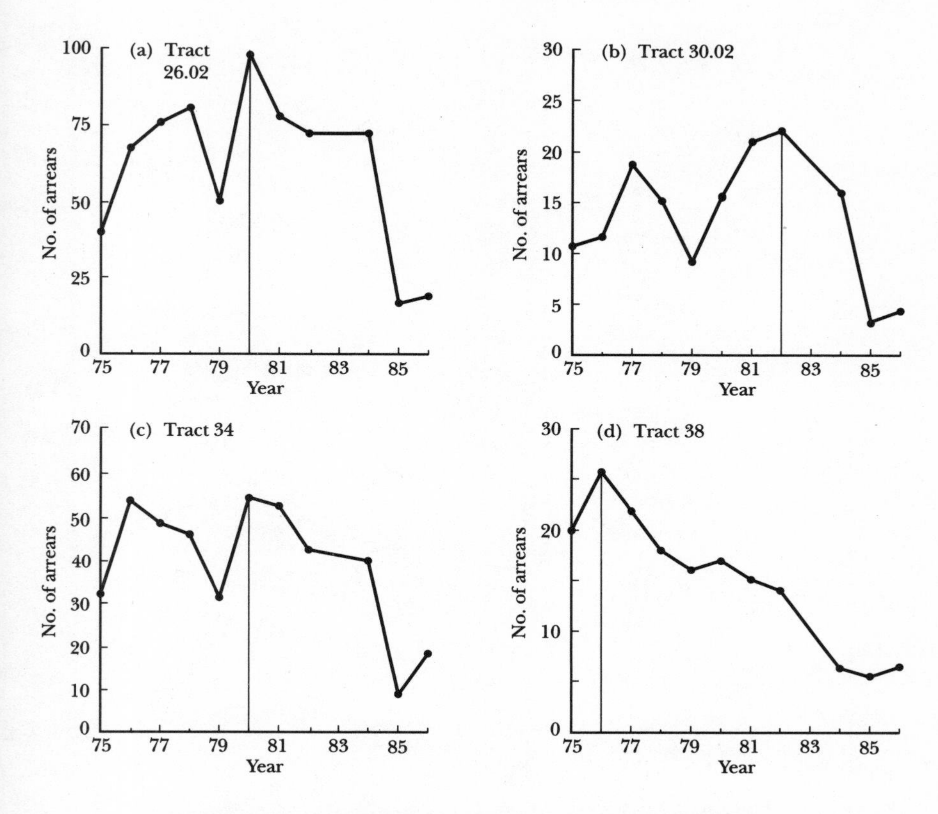

Figure 7.3 Sample turning points by census tract, East Village
Source: Original graph by Neil Smith, Betsy Duncan, and Laura Reid. 'From Disinvestment to Reinvestment: Tax Arrears and Turning Points in the Lower East Side,' *Housing Studies* 4 (1989): 238–52.

Every tract had experienced a turning point by 1985. The resulting geographical pattern of turning points demonstrates extreme statistical autocorrelation. The turning points were generalized into a chorographic map of the development of gentrification.[28] In figure 7.4, annual contour lines join points with the same chronological turning points.

By way of interpretation, where significant space intervenes between chronological contour lines, reinvestment is diffusing rapidly; steep contour slopes indicate significant barriers to reinvestment. The frontier is most evident where there are no enclosed contours (i.e., no peaks or sink holes). Peaks, with later years at the center of enclosed contours, represent areas of greatest resistance to reinvestment, while sink holes, with earlier years at the center, represent areas opened up to reinvestment in advance of surrounding areas.

The major pattern that emerges is a reasonably well defined west-to-east

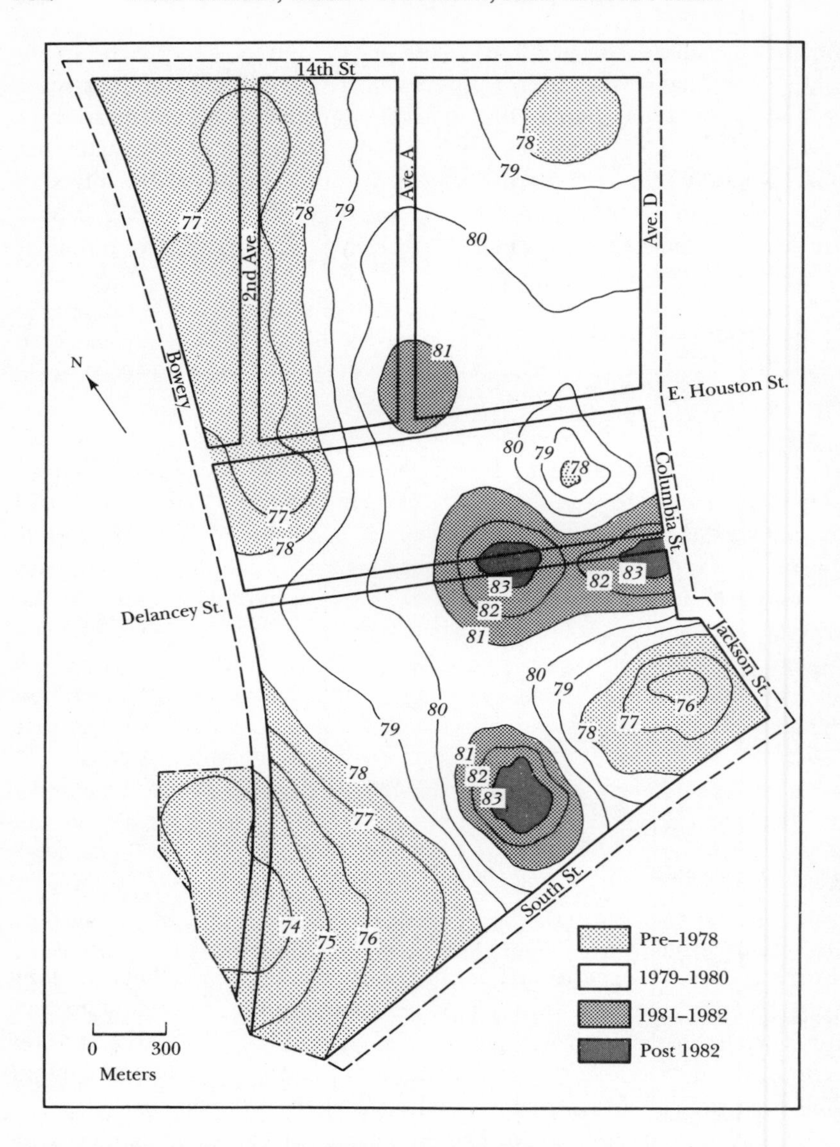

Figure 7.4 The shifting gentrification frontier in the Lower East Side
Source: Courtesy of Tony Lugo, computer-generated in Rutgers University, Cartography Laboratory

frontier line, with the earliest encroachments in the northwest and southwest portions of the study area. The reinvestment frontier pushes eastward until obstructed or slowed by localized barriers in the south and southeast. In geographical context, the data would seem to document a gentrification frontier advancing eastward into the Lower East Side from

Greenwich Village, SoHo, Chinatown, and the Financial District. Greenwich Village has always been a Bohemian neighborhood, but after some decline in the 1930s and 1940s, it began to experience gentrification in the 1950s and 1960s. SoHo's gentrification came a few years later but was essentially complete by the late 1970s. In Chinatown, an influx of Taiwanese capital in the mid-1970s, and later of Hong Kong capital provided the means for a rapid northward and eastward expansion of Chinatown (see Lin, chapter 2).

Barriers to the advancement of the frontier are apparent in several localized peaks, especially on East Delancey Street and on the southern edge near South Street. (Delancey Street is largely commercial. A wide thoroughfare leading to the Williamsburg Bridge which connects Manhattan and Brooklyn, its congestion, noise, and impassability may well have hindered reinvestment.) More generally, these peaks can be interpreted as demonstrating the limits of gentrification. The eastern and southern edges of the area are fringed by large public housing projects that have evidently acted as significant barriers. In addition, these nodes of resistance to reinvestment coincide with the traditional heart of the Lower East Side, where disinvestment continued as late as 1985, well beyond the 1980s economic recovery. This is also the poorest area, the last stronghold of a Latino population, and the focus of 'Operation Pressure Point,' a gentrification-induced police crackdown on drugs that began in 1985 – the year of the final turning point, as it happens.

There seem then to have been two distinct periods of reinvestment in the housing stock: the first between 1977 and 1979, especially in the western and northern blocks; and the second from 1981 until just after the 1987 financial crash. The later phase of reinvestment encompassed southern and eastern blocks, in addition to those already recapitalized in the earlier phase. It is important to bear in mind that reinvestment in the form of tax arrears redemption does not necessarily imply the kind of productive reinvestment that betokens gentrification and urban restructuring and might only indicate a speculative market. However, the reinvestment in the western and northern blocks in the late 1970s does seem to have been sufficiently sustained to have prevented a major recurrence of disinvestment in the recession of 1980–2. Visual evidence confirms that reinvestment in the area west of First Avenue has been longer in duration, more sustained, and more broadly based, whereas the census tracts in the east and southeast sectors continued to sustain the highest population losses (58 to 74 percent) throughout the 1970s, experiencing reinvestment only in the 1980s.

From 1975 to 1981, the profit frontier moved at an average speed of between 100 and 200 meters per year. It is important to add the caveat that this figure represents an averaging across a period in which the market was highly volatile. Further, these data cover only two short cycles of reinvestment and disinvestment; therefore, care must be taken in generalizing the conclusions. At the very least, it seems that the concept of an economic frontier in gentrifying neighborhoods would have to be amended to take account of the shifting pace of expansion. The diffusion of the profit frontier is potentially sensitive to external economic and political forces; it may be a stop-and-go process, more than a smooth progression.

The pattern of reinvestment in the East Village uncovered by our analysis adds flesh to the observable pattern of gentrification in the area. Observers agree that gentrification seemed to encroach on the East Village from its western border with the more established core of Greenwich Village. The area north of Fourteenth Street, including Gramercy Park but also Union Square farther to the west, had been the target of early redevelopment activity. Although Stuyvesant Town (a moderate and middle-income high-rise complex on the north side of Fourteenth Street farther to the east) may initially have hindered the southward diffusion of higher land values, once the process began, it may equally have acted as a northern anchor to the gentrification of the East Village.

By contrast, the southern and eastern blocks experienced deeper disinvestment, as suggested by their inordinately high vacancy rates. This area also borders on the core of the Lower East Side, south of Houston Street, where housing conditions are the worst in Manhattan outside of Harlem. Thus, reinvestment in the East Village began not in the area of deepest disinvestment and abandonment but on the borders,[29] where a killing could be made with little risk of being scalped, so to speak.

This analysis of reinvestment turning points and the resultant frontier of profitability is highly suggestive. The local complexity of the pattern and its deviation from a straight line diffusion process should come as no surprise; indeed, Frederick Jackson Turner, author of the nineteenth-century 'end of the frontier' thesis, was challenged on exactly this point, namely, that while the larger frontier line may have swept through, it left behind resilient pockets of frontier existence. As with the original frontier, the gentrification line is not so much a 'wall' of equal and continuous development, but a highly uneven and differentiated process.

That the gentrification process is uneven and discontinuous in time and space is emphasized by recent political and economic events. First, the severe national recession that struck in late 1989 may not have entirely halted gentrification in the Lower East Side, but it has led to a dramatic slowdown in reinvestment and, in all likelihood, some resurgence in disinvestment. In addition, the housing crisis of the late 1980s put a significant number of homeless people onto the streets and into parks of the neighborhood. Furthermore, a highly visible squatters' movement emerged. The resulting contest for public space, involving demonstrations, police riots, and evictions, suggests that as with the western frontier of the nineteenth century, the 'new' urban frontier is politically as well as economically defined.[30] The recession and the politicization of the Lower East Side and its housing market were also paralleled by a cultural shift, marked by a significant exodus of artists in the late 1980s.

All of these shifts have changed the form and dulled the trajectory of gentrification in the Lower East Side in the early 1990s. While it is by far too early to argue that the area is now 'suffering' long-term 'degentrification,' as some have claimed, the geography of disinvestment and reinvestment in the 1990s is by no means predictable. It seems likely, however, that the steep decline in housing prices after 1989 may well intensify disinvestment and, with it, the rent gap, potentially enhancing the opportunity for a later round of reinvestment and the conversion of the Lower East Side once again into a new urban frontier.

NOTES

This research was assisted by The National Science Foundation Grant SES87-13043. We would like to thank Fritz Nelson who assisted with some of the data analysis, and Tanya Steinberg and Valerie Preston who offered stimulating criticism and commentary. Tony Lugo and Michael Siegel assisted with some of the graphics. This chapter is adapted from an article that appeared first in *Housing Studies* 4 (1989), pp. 238–52, under the title 'From Disinvestment to Reinvestment: Tax Arrears and Turning Points in the Lower East Side.' Portions are reprinted with the permission of the publisher.

1 Neil Smith, 'Gentrification, the Frontier, and the Restructuring of Urban Space,' in N. Smith and P. Williams, eds., *Gentrification of the City* (Boston: Allen & Unwin, 1986), pp. 15–34.
2 By ground rent we mean the capital value paid for the use of land.
3 As elsewhere, such gentrification was preceded by a necessary amount of disinvestment. By focusing on the economic dimensions of gentrification and more specifically on the relationship between disinvestment and reinvestment, we clearly hold the movement of capital as central to explaining contemporary urban restructuring. This should in no way be construed as denying the importance of cultural, social, and labor-market changes in giving gentrification much of its form, significance, and specific local character. Especially in an area like the East Village, it is impossible to attain a comprehensive view of gentrification without integrating cultural and social with political and economic dimensions of change.
4 Calvin P. Bradford and Leonard S. Rubinowitz, 'The Urban-Suburban Investment-Disinvestment Process: Consequences for Older Neighborhoods,' *Annals of the American Academy of Political and Social Science* 422 (1975), pp. 77–86.
5 Clearly the state operates under a rather different set of constraints than do

private-market actors. Level of investment, type of building(s), age of structure, geographical and market location are all contingent – much more so for financial institutions and landlords than for the home owner whose economic investment is simultaneously a personal commitment to a home. Whether to relinquish real estate entirely in favor of other investments – stocks and bonds, money markets, foreign currency, stock and commodity futures, precious metals – is equally an option dependent upon expected rates of profit or interest. The economic effects of state policy are also differentiated according to building and neighborhood characteristics as well as location.

6 This assumption of limited rationality in individual disinvestment and reinvestment decisions should not be construed as a spurious endorsement of the neo-classical assumption of 'economic man.' We neither assume such an ideal individual, nor do we attempt to generalize about aggregate patterns of urban geographical and economic development from any such ideal type of individual.

7 Anthony Downs, 'The Necessity of Neighborhood Deterioration,' *New York Affairs* 7 (1982), p. 35.

8 David Harvey and L. Chaterjee, 'Absolute Rent and the Structuring of Space by Governmental and Financial Institutions,' *Antipode* 6 (1974), pp. 22–36; M. Boddy, *The Building Societies* (Basingstoke, UK: Macmillan, 1980); D. Bartelt, 'Redlining in Philadelphia: An Analysis of Home Mortgages in the Philadelphia Area,' mimeo, Institute for the Study of Civic Values, Temple University, 1979; J. M. Wolfe, G. Drover, and I. Skelton, 'Inner City Real Estate Activity in Montreal: Institutional Characteristics of Decline,' *The Canadian Geographer* 24 (1980), pp. 349–67.

9 George Sternlieb and Robert W. Lake, 'The Dynamics of Real Estate Tax Delinquency,' *National Tax Journal* 29 (1976), p. xvi.

10 G. Sternlieb and R. W. Burchell, *Residential Abandonment: The Tenement Landlord Revisited* (New Brunswick, NJ: Rutgers University Center for Urban Policy Research, 1973).

11 P. Salins, 'The Creeping Tide of Disinvestment,' *New York Affairs* 6 (1981), pp. 5–6.

12 G. Stevenson, 'The Abandonment of Roosevelt Gardens,' in R. Jensen, ed., *Devastation/Reconstruction* (New York: Bronx Museum of the Arts, 1980), p. 79.

13 Robert W. Lake, *Real Estate Tax Delinquency: Private Disinvestment and Public Response* (Piscataway, NJ: Center for Urban Policy Research, Rutgers University, 1979).

14 Neil Smith, 'Toward a Theory of Gentrification: A Back to the City Movement by Capital, Not People,' *Journal of the American Planning Association* 45 (1979), pp. 538–48; Neil Smith, 'Gentrification and the Rent Gap,' *Annals of the Association of American Geographers* 77 (1987), pp. 462–5; E. Clark, *The Rent Gap and Urban Change: Case Studies in Malmo 1860–1985* (Lund, Sweden: Lund University Press, 1987); B. Badcock, 'Smith's Rent Gap Hypothesis: An Australian View,' *Annals of the Association of American Geographers* 79 (1989).

15 P. Williams, 'The Role of Institutions in the Inner London Housing Market: The Case of Islington,' *Transactions of the Institute of British Geographers* 1 (1976), pp. 72–82; P. Williams, 'Building Societies and the Inner City,' *Transactions of the Institute of British Geographers* 3 (1978), pp. 23–34; Neil Smith, 'Gentrifica-

tion and Capital: Theory, Practice and Ideology in Society Hill,' *Antipode* 11 (1979), pp. 24–35; Frank DeGiovanni, *Displacement Pressures in the Lower East Side* (New York: Community Service Society of New York, 1987); R. Schaffer and N. Smith, 'The Gentrification of Harlem?' *Annals of the Association of American Geographers* 76 (1986), pp. 347–65.

16 Frank DeGiovanni, *Displacement Pressures in the Lower East Side*, pp. 32, 35.

17 Robert Lake, *Real Estate Tax Delinquency*, p. 192; Sternlieb and Lake, 'The Dynamics of Real Estate Tax Delinquency.'

18 Peter Marcuse, 'Gentrification, Residential Displacement and Abandonment in New York City,' Report to the Community Service Society (New York: Community Service Society of New York, 1984).

19 W. Williams, 'Rise in Values Spurs Rescue of Buildings,' *The New York Times*, 4 April 1987.

20 Ibid.

21 Salins, 'The Creeping Tide,' p. 17.

22 N. Moufarrege, 'Another Wave, Still More Savagely Than the First: Lower East Side,' *Arts* 57 (1982), p. 73.

23 W. Robinson and C. McCormick, 'Slouching Toward Avenue D,' *Art in America* 72 (1984), p. 135.

24 R. Deutsche and C. G. Ryan, 'The Fine Art of Gentrification,' *October 31* (1984), pp. 91–111.

25 As might be expected, Con Edison maintains rather accurate records on who is using their gas and electricity, and their data on the number of household hook-ups provide useful estimates of intercensal population trends. Data are available on an annual basis.

26 The Department of City Planning of the City of New York has compiled a centralized computerized database (MISLAND) covering a wide range of information about the city. The information is provided in a series of separate files. The arrears data are from the Property Transaction and Real Property Files (1987) and the vacancy data are from the Con Edison File (1987). For the latter, the figures include three categories of account: current accounts, accounts awaiting turn-on, and accounts in vacant buildings. The latter are active accounts; Con Edison defines multi-unit buildings as vacant if their vacancy rate is over 40 percent.

27 DeGiovanni, *Displacement Pressures in the Lower East Side*, p. 27.

28 The mapping was accomplished using a Golden Software package.

29 Peter Marcuse, 'Abandonment, Gentrification and Displacement: The Linkages in New York City,' in Smith and Williams, eds., *Gentrification of the City*, p. 166.

30 For an interpretation of the political and cultural economy of the Tompkins Square struggle in the context of gentrification, see N. Smith, 'New York City, New Frontier: The Lower East Side as Wild, Wild, West,' in M. Sorkin, ed., *Variations on a Theme Park: The New American City and the End of Public Space* (New York: Hill and Wang, 1992), pp. 61–93.

8

The Process of Gentrification in Alphabet City

Christopher Mele

As prices of investment properties in prime Manhattan neighborhoods have soared, buyers are now seeking worthwhile deals in such undervalued areas as the East Village . . . according to Peter Siegal, executive vice president and director of investment property sales at L. B. Kaye Associates, one of Manhattan's largest commercial and residential real estate and brokerage firms. 'The East Village, once transient in character, is being transformed into a neighborhood of young professionals,' notes Siegal. 'Investors are buying buildings primarily for rental purposes and are renovating vacant apartments. Properties on the avenues with retail space are the most valuable.'

'Investors Reported to Find "Good Deals" in Pocket Areas,' *Real Estate Weekly*, Vol. 35, no. 33. Wednesday, 22 March 1989.

A walk through Alphabet City in the mid-1980s already revealed the physical effects of gentrification that was encroaching on the neighborhood. Renovated Old- and New-Law tenements stood adjacent to vacant lots and burned-out buildings. Banners were hung in front of newly brickfaced buildings, advertising 'luxury units' with amenities such as terraces, gardens and laundry facilities. Young, mostly white and single students, artists, and a few professionals were already coexisting with earlier residents (latinos, hippies, and others) but under vastly better housing conditions, albeit paying significantly higher rents.

This was clearly a neighborhood in transition, but change was neither thorough nor pervasive; instead, revitalization was uneven and irregular. Signs of gentrification occasionally appeared in the least likely locations and in other places evaded what seemed to be the most plausible sites for neighborhood renewal. This strange hybrid of urban revitalization stemmed from the intersection of the interests of real estate capital with the distinctiveness of the East Village. There would be no prompt sweeping away of the neighborhood's past to be replaced by block after block of unvarying, renovated town houses.

This chapter traces the unique path gentrification took in the East Village in the 1980s. It describes the process of neighborhood restructuring from the perspective of real estate capital and its agents. Hoping to create newer and more profitable uses out of a working-class, economically strapped neighborhood, real estate investors sought to upgrade the built environment and alter the socioeconomic character of the resident population by displacing older and poorer residents and enticing newcomers. This process of reinvestment was by no means uniform, however, nor was it played out by the same set of actors with comparable economic resources. Instead, over time, a series of different forms of investment environments with associated risks was found. At successive stages, capital came from different sources and different actors entered and exited the investment game. This made real estate reinvestment a drawn-out but, to some extent, episodic process in which various forms of investment, different actors, and their different strategies dovetailed to transform the neighborhood.

We begin by laying out the logic of capital reinvestment in the East Village housing market, showing how successive waves of new capital set the foundation for the future shape of the area's physical and social landscape. This reinvestment eventually priced out existing small-scale 'mom and pop' owners while encouraging large real estate development companies to enter the local market. The arrival of these developers significantly altered the physical and social landscape of the East Village, but did not overwhelm it. As the financial stakes in the East Village became higher and plans for redevelopment multiplied, developers had to devise strategies to circumvent legal blockages to gentrification and to overcome the handicaps posed by the unique demographic composition of the area. How developers turned to atypical renters to fill their buildings is described at the end of this chapter.

Speculative Reinvestment in Alphabet City

At the earliest stage of development, when owners began to pay up tax arrears (see chapter 7), the first new actors in neighborhood reinvestment were the speculators – investors who purchased one or more properties solely for the purpose of quick resale at a profit. While this earliest manifestation of neighborhood renewal was not immediately visible in the landscape, the seeds of the physical changes that can be noted today, namely renovated apartment buildings, condos and co-ops, boutiques and expensive restaurants, are to be found in this process of reinvestment – a process that predated by a decade the actual physical alterations.

Speculation in privately held housing in Alphabet City originally overlapped with the period of widespread abandonment in which the dominant characteristics of the neighborhood – an epidemic of arson, drugs and crime – offered what seemed only the remote possibility of redevelopment and resettlement by a class of higher-income residents. During the 1970s, the southeasternmost blocks of Alphabet City (census tracts 22.02 and 26.01) experienced radical declines in their housing stock as landlords walked away from their buildings. A 1978 report commissioned by a local organization, Interfaith Adopt-A-Building, described this process of abandonment:

> In the process that leads to the kindling of buildings, landlords generally stop providing services which hastens the deterioration of the buildings and tenants move out. Drug addicts and adolescents are often hired as arsonists. The blocks destroyed by fires serve the interim purpose of becoming markets for wholesale drug commerce and related crime. As addicts and drug wholesalers begin to move into the block, they replace the families who speedily move out. Other criminally related commerce such as pimping, prostitution, and/or fencing and other rackets begin to blossom on the block; deterioration escalates and more fires are set. Eventually, the block is denuded of dwellings and residents, and the drug traffic lacking 'cover,' begins to move to another block. Such was the fate of East 11th, 10th and 6th Streets between Avenues B and C. These streets now contain less than half of the houses that were there even two years ago. They look like war ravaged towns and provide 'playgrounds' for the area's children, and shelter for addicts.[1]

Remaining in what was increasingly becoming a no man's land were Puerto Rican families, artists, activists, and students who had survived the decade of blight brought on by a lack of investment by landlords and the city. Some of the hardest hit areas bore testimony to the ravaging effects of neglect by private capital and city services. According to the censuses of 1970 and 1980, the number of year-round housing units in census tracts 22.02 and 26.01 declined by 50 percent in ten years, while the population in these tracts decreased by 58 and 65 percent respectively, considerably higher than the overall East Village decline of 27 percent.[2]

Yet out of these bleak and depressed conditions initial reinvestment germinated in the form of real estate speculation. That the area was bereft of capital meant that Alphabet City was well positioned for this. Potential investment opportunities were triggered by the extreme devaluation of buildings and land and the anticipated profit from an overflow of the growth in adjacent areas. Although they were entering a high-risk area, speculators in Alphabet City placed their hopes on a continued upswing in New York's economy and its real estate market, and on a continued eastward push of gentrification. The regional economy's shift toward corporate finance, insurance, and producer services was creating many new well paying jobs for Manhattan professionals, which stimulated a commensurate demand for good housing. Investments in the construction and conversion of cooperative apartments and condominia became increasingly lucrative, which, in turn, reduced the stock of affordable rental housing and fed the demand for newly renovated units in areas formerly deemed unmarketable. The earlier and extensive redevelopment of adjacent neighborhoods such as Greenwich Village and SoHo, which had undergone colonization by real estate investors in the 1960s and 1970s, placed the East Village in a strategic position for speculation. Considered in real estate parlance as a 'pocket area,' investors looked anew at the East Village, weighing its downtown Manhattan location, the demand for middle-income housing below the luxury market, and the bargain prices of property in the area.

Reflecting these changes, pioneer investment money began to flow into the area to take advantage of its depressed sale prices and low tax assessments. In the easternmost blocks of the East Village, the devalorization of land had reached the point where sale prices of property and tax payments were low enough to compensate for the risks of a possibly sour investment. As word of a 'good buy' caught on, the buyers' market grew crowded, and by the late 1970s and early 1980s speculators were buying up empty lots as well as deteriorated walk-ups and were reselling them within a few years, or sometimes months, at substantially higher prices. The number of properties bought and sold outpaced the sluggish sales activity that prevailed in the stark decade of the 1970s.

Since the logic of speculative investment is to procure profit by resale, not redevelopment, the rate of 'flipping,' that is, continued reselling of a single property within a short time at successively higher prices, was staggering. In a few cases, speculators sold their properties at two to three times the initial price. Table 8.1 shows illustrative sales transaction information for ten selected walk-up apartments within census tracts 22.02 and 26.01 in the early 1980s. Table 8.2 shows the increase in the percentage of market-available properties that were sold between 1980 and 1985, while table 8.3 shows their average sale prices.[3]

In the midst of what might be described as a 'speculative frenzy,' little actual transformation of the neighborhood – building renovations, new construction, and the presence of a new class of tenants – was evident. Since speculators anticipated that higher sales prices would be generated

Table 8.1 Sales transactions and assessment values for selected walk-up apartments in tracts 22.02 and 26.01, 1980–1987

Year of sale	*Sale price*	*Total assessed value*
LOCATION: TRACT 22.02		
Property 1		
1985	$ 30,000	$ 6,000
1987	$ 420,000	$ 18,700
Property 2		
1981	$ 85,000	$ 3,120[a]
1984	$ 135,000	$ 4,840
Property 3		
1982	$ 92,000	$ 3,000[a]
1986	$ 420,000	$ 5,260
Property 4		
1983	$ 70,000	$ 1,000
1984	$ 100,000	$ 1,000
1985	$ 180,000	$ 1,400
1987	$ 186,000	$ 3,680
Property 5		
1983	$ 84,000	$ 11,000
1985	$ 240,000	$ 17,000
Property 6		
1982	$ 15,000	$ 2,000[a]
1983	$ 36,500	$ 2,000
Property 7		
1983	$ 50,000	$ 1,500
1984	$ 170,000	$ 1,500
LOCATION: TRACT 26.01		
Property 8		
1981	$ 100,000	$ 41,400[a]
1983	$ 160,000	$ 41,400
1984	$ 1,220,000	$ 50,000
Property 9		
1982	$ 24,000	$ 10,400[a]
1983	$ 104,000	$ 10,400
Property 10		
1982	$ 65,000	$ 25,400[a]
1984	$ 215,000	$ 26,840

[a] 1983 assessment figure.

Source: *Sanborn Manhattan Land Book*, annually between 1983–1989

Table 8.2 Percentage of market-available walk-up apartment buildings sold in tracts 22.02 and 26.01, 1980–1985

Year	*Tract 22.02* (*n* = 28)	*Tract 26.01* (*n* = 23)
1980	14.2	8.6
1981	17.8	10.4
1982	3.5	8.6
1983	21.4	30.4
1984	28.6	39.1
1985	32.1	34.8

Source: Data assembled from the *Sanborn Manhattan Land Book*, issues of 1983, 1984, 1985 and 1986. Computations ours

Table 8.3 Average sales prices of walk-up apartment buildings in tracts 22.02 and 26.01, 1980–1985

	Tract 22.02		*Tract 26.01*	
Year	*No.*	*Price*	*No.*	*Price*
1980	4	$25,000	2	$61,500
1981	5	$70,000	3	$122,000
1982	1	$175,000	2	$44,500
1983	6	$63,160	7	$140,000
1984	8	$157,000	9	$382,833
1985	9	$223,625	8	$426,666

Source: Compiled from *Sanborn Manhattan Land Book*, 1983–1986. Computations ours

solely by a rebirth of the local housing market, no capital improvements were made. In many cases, especially in speculation on vacant lots, upkeep costs were nonexistent, which yielded even higher potential returns. The physical appearance of the neighborhood, therefore, remained fundamentally unchanged. But this stability was illusory. The net effect of speculative investment upon the direction of the community, although hidden, was critical, because it lay the groundwork for upgrading the housing market and had serious consequences for residential displacement.

The speculation phase was short and self-limiting. The increased sales activity drove up the hypothetical market value of properties whose owners were just 'sitting on' them. But as the returns that could be made from resale shrank, the speculators' market became saturated and exhausted. Only actual redevelopment of properties could yield further real estate profits in the neighborhood. By this time, city tax assessors had caught on to the increase in sales prices and began to raise assessed values. This further inhibited the speculative market. In the logic of investment, speculation played itself out and, in doing so, begat a successive investment opportunity for redevelopment.

SHIFTING FORMS OF OWNERSHIP: FROM 'MOM AND POP' TO LARGE DEVELOPERS

Speculators, whose activities drove up the costs of doing business in the East Village housing market, ushered in an era of more capital-intensive redevelopment and conditioned the market for the next generation of investors. As profits that could be made by 'sitting-on' unimproved properties and then reselling them declined in the crowded buyers' market, the atmosphere of investment shifted to the more costly venture of physically upgrading properties to capture tenants capable of paying higher rents. At this point, displacement pressures on the remaining tenants increased and the effects of gentrification became more visible on the landscape.

As the costs of entry into the neighborhood land market and the expense of doing business skyrocketed in the 1980s wave of speculation and increasing taxes, many 'mom and pop' owners were priced out of the market; they were replaced by real estate development firms. Because many East Village tenements are in poor condition, redevelopment is a costly venture, requiring financial resources greater than those needed for speculation and well beyond the means of many of the East Village's remaining small landlords. Municipal support to offset costs, in the form of tax breaks and discounts (many of which are granted only after construction has begun or has been completed), were available to building owners, but most small owners could not take advantage of these incentives because the costs associated with licensing, provision of architectural plans, and adherence to building codes were prohibitive. Development firms could.

The size and scale of the new development firms differed dramatically from the typical property owners who had dominated ownership in Alphabet City before speculation. The small landlords of the pre-gentrification phase were primarily petty capitalists who rarely held more than a few buildings. In contrast, the development firms were large and diversified. As can be seen from sample data presented in table 8.4, they tended to own other real estate not only within the neighborhood but in similar areas of the city, especially in Hell's Kitchen and Harlem, two other

Table 8.4 List of major property owners in the East Village and their holdings in other poor neighborhoods of Manhattan 1988

Using the Sanborn Real Estate Directory, a list was compiled of owners holding four or more recently purchased properties in the East Village. That list was cross-checked against the Real Estate Directory of Manhattan which lists individual owners and their holdings in the borough of Manhattan. Below is a sample of owners with extensive holdings within the East Village and other neighborhoods in Manhattan.

Martin Baumrind, owner

Lower East Side Holdings

207 East 5th Street	430 East 9th Street	436 East 9th Street
211 East 10th Street	512 East 12th Street	23 West 12th Street
329 East 14th Steet	221 Avenue A	125 First Avenue
127 First Avenue	242 Mulberry Street	

Midtown West

520 West 47th Street	522 West 47th Street	524 West 47th Street
526 West 47th Street	528 West 47th Street	

Peter Jakobson, owner

East Village Holdings

512 East 5th Street	514 East 5th Street	516 East 5th Street
518 East 5th Street	530 East 5th Street	532 East 5th Street
32 East 7th Street	34 East 7th Street	122 East 7th Street
62 East 11th Street	102 St. Mark's Place	128 St. Mark's Place

Harry Skydell/Hudson Park Management

Lower East Side Holdings

317–19 East 4th Street	704 East 5th Street	712 East 5th Street
299–301 East 8th Street	325 East 8th Street	355 East 8th Street
396 East 8th Street	398 East 8th Street	713–715 East 9th Street
525–27 East 11th Street	529 East 11th Street	626 East 11th Street
206 Avenue A	208 Avenue A	18–22 Avenue B
24 Avenue B	512 Broadway	195–203 Rivington Street

Spanish Harlem

334 East 96th Street	336 East 96th Street	338 East 96th Street
317–35 East 104th Street	235–37 East 105th Street	239–41 East 105th Street
244 East 106th Street	177 East 109th Street	179 East 109th Street
308 East 109th Street	272 East 11th Street	91 East 116th Street
93 East 116th Street	116 East 116th Street	447 East 116th Street
449 East 116th Street	274 West 116th Street	57 East 116th Street
166–68 East 118th Street	226 East 118th Street	228 East 118th Street
308 East 119th Street	2276–80 Third Avenue	2035 Third Avenue
2039 First Avenue	273–77 Madison Avenue	1520–24 Park Avenue
1546 Park Avenue	1629 Park Avenue	1630–36 Park Avenue
2143 Second Avenue	2145 Second Avenue	

Harlem and Upper West Side

80 West 105th Street	222 West 122nd Street	230 West 122nd Street
15–27 West 125th Street	362 West 127th Street	306 West 128th Street
308 West 128th Street	110 West 129th Street	34 West 131st Street
212 West 133rd Street	130–36 West 142nd Street	153 West 147th Street
144–46 West 144th Street	251–53 West 144th Street	303 West 142nd Street
207 West 148th Street	620 West 148th Street	602–10 West 149th Street
267 West 154th Street	540 West 159th Street	565 West 161st Street
575 West 161st Street	540–42 West 163rd Street	656 West 171st Street
521–23 West 180th Street	185–87 Audubon	117 Edgecomb
119 Edgecomb	121 Edgecomb	123 Edgecomb
125 Edgecomb	140 Edgecomb	157–59 Edgecomb
2367 Eighth Avenue	2367 Eighth Avenue	2742–44 Eighth Avenue
2790–92 Eighth Avenue	2739 Eighth Avenue	2795 Eighth Avenue
2798 Eighth Avenue	2859 Eighth Avenue	2895 Eighth Avenue
349 Lenox Avenue	351 Lenox Avenue	353 Lenox Avenue
355 Lenox Avenue	357 Lenox Avenue	357 Lenox Avenue
359 Lenox Avenue	360 Lenox Avenue	362–64 Lenox Avenue
366–68 Lenox Avenue	67 Macombs Place	307–09 Pleasant
2431–35 Seventh Avenue	2538–40 Seventh Avenue	2542–44 Seventh Avenue
2566 Seventh Avenue	20 Sylvan	

Source: Real Estate Directory Manhattan (New York: Real Estate Data, Inc., 1988)

neighborhoods undergoing gentrification. Their operations were facilitated by their in-house lawyers, maintenance and construction personnel, as well as access to capital such as institutional lending and second-mortgage financing.

In upgrading their newly purchased buildings or expanding their portfolio of holdings, developers were able to turn to institutional lenders for capital. Prior to 1980, commercial lenders had considered Alphabet City a high-risk area. An increase in lending activity by these institutions in the 1980s roughly coincided in timing with the arrival of developers. This was no accident. The redevelopment of areas adjacent to the East Village and the shift in typical ownership from individual landlords to developers lessened the risk considerably. Table 8.5 shows the increasing number of mortgages contracted in the census tracts of Alphabet City. The tracts have been divided into those east of Avenue B and those between Avenue B and First Avenue. This classification emphasizes the spatial unevenness of mortgage lending over time. Western census tracts adjacent to already gentrified parts of the East Village show an earlier and substantially higher level of mortgage lending than do those farther east. As adjacent blocks were redeveloped, commercial banks began to extend loans to areas formerly considered lending risks.

Table 8.5 Number of new institutional mortgages in Alphabet City census tracts, 1982–1985

Census tract	*Year* 1982	*1983*	*1984*	*1985*
Eastern tracts				
22.02	7	3	7	13
26.01	9	7	9	10
26.02	16	12	17	10
28	9	6	12	25
Western tracts				
30.02	4	4	10	10
32	42	25	27	43
34	25	39	61	62

Source: Survey Data Security Corporation. New York State Banking Mortgage Activity Reports, nos. 19 and 20

Greater accessibility to large amounts of capital opened up Alphabet City to the type of massive reconstruction developers had in mind. Increased capital made itself visible in the proliferation of condominia and cooperative apartments catering to successful artists, advertisers, publishers, and musicians who began to surface in the area in the 1980s. Their emergence was testimonial to the interesting and complex interrelationship between new forms of investment, outside investors, and the role of commercial lending institutions. Condominium and co-op conversions represented the culmination of a process rooted in speculation some years earlier. At that time, they had been only remote possibilities, and yet their appearance in the 1980s was clearly the product of speculative foresight.

Since condominium and cooperative conversions are time consuming and costly, it was chiefly large developers who followed this route. Conversion plans require both financial and legal resources before they can become effective. In order to stockpile rental units (warehouse) while continuing to pay upkeep expenses and taxes, developers require capital to finance the lengthy process of conversion. It is unlikely, therefore, that first-time or single-holding property owners can bear the expenses associated with non-eviction plan conversions.

If buildings slated for co-op or condo conversion are occupied by renters whose rates are state regulated, as most of the walk-ups in Alphabet City presently are, conversion is stalled by the legal protection enjoyed by current tenants. These legal protections restrain immediate conversion and therefore assist in curbing full-scale redevelopment toward luxury housing. One tactic used to circumvent these restrictions was to remove the apartments from the rental market. During the 1980s, the number of warehoused apartments – those that became or were 'made' empty and then renovated and withheld from the market in anticipation of conversion – increased dramatically in the East Village.

New York State Law requires that occupants of a certain proportion of apartments in a building must 'agree' to the conversion, which they can exercise by agreeing to buy their apartments. In neighborhoods like the East Village, however, few tenants had the financial resources to buy their units. Instead, owners wishing to convert their buildings kept vacated apartments empty, so that they could count them as having 'agreed' to the buy-out plan. Each unit warehoused in a particular building, therefore, was a step closer to conversion of the building. A study of warehousing conducted in 1985 by the New York State Attorney General's Office found that a significant number of unoccupied housing units were being kept off the market for the purpose of condominium and cooperative conversion.[4]

The social consequences of warehousing are many. Experts on homelessness contend that the warehousing of vacant apartments in New York City greatly contributed to the increase in the number of homeless, especially homeless families. Because they could not afford to purchase a condo or co-op even at the lower insider's price, many of the East Village's low-income renters were bought off or evicted.

Redevelopment Strategies in Alphabet City

Although co-op and condominium conversions grew more numerous in the 1980s, they never overwhelmed the East Village's available housing stock, even before the housing market collapsed in the late 1980s. Most of the upgrading that occurred in Alphabet City was aimed toward a market of young, single renters whose incomes were higher than those of existing residents. Legal, economic, and social barriers precluded the possibility that the neighborhood would follow an unswerving course toward luxury 'revitalization.' To make profits in local real estate, developers had to circumvent these barriers by devising new strategies for residential redevelopment that took into account the vagaries of the local market. Viewed in this way, the revitalization of Alphabet City in the 1980s for a new class of higher rent-paying residents was a process driven less by demand and more by the cunning of developers' relentless search for revenue. Dissecting the strategies investors used to circumvent the barriers to development provides evidence of the significant capacity of real estate actors to condition a depressed local housing market toward higher rents, even in the midst of legal opposition and market barriers.

Rent Regulations

Among the key factors that prevented a full-scale conversion of the East Village into a high-rent district were the laws protecting rent levels. Rent controls and renewable lease agreements obstructed the efforts of developers to upgrade units to higher rents or to convert them into cooperative or condominium units. Many tenement apartment dwellers in Alphabet City had resided for years in units protected by state-legislated rent controls and renewable leases. These rent regulations gave some protection to vulnerable populations. Holding on to rent-controlled or rent-stabilized apartments is a form of passive resistance to gentrifying pressures. Investors have long contended that the artificial market in rents created by controls interferes with the operation of a healthy housing environment in the city, one regulated by supply and demand. Studies have claimed otherwise: they indicate that decontrolled and destabilized apartments have, with few exceptions, been transferred to higher-income residents.[5]

Two renewable tenant bills govern the regulation of rents on apartments in New York City: the Emergency Tenant Protection Act of 1974 (EPTA) which was most recently renewed in June, 1991; and the Rent Stabilization Law of 1969 (RSL) which was renewed in April of 1991. These two bills cover existing rent-controlled and rent-stabilized buildings and govern the process by which apartments are decontrolled and destabilized. Each time the bills have faced the legislature for debate on renewal or expiration, strong efforts by housing proponents and general popular pressure for rent laws blocked efforts to overturn them. The trend however, has been, for greater numbers of apartments to be decontrolled and destabilized with time.

Developers had a keen interest in removing tenants from rent-regulated units in East Village buildings: some units with renewable leases still rent for as little as $90–150 per month. The existence of a large number of rent-regulated housing units slowed the pace of neighborhood redevelopment but did not arrest it. Instead, redevelopment took place gradually – apartment by apartment, building by building, and eventually block by block. The Community Service Society's displacement survey of 1984 found many apartments in the Lower East Side to be in various stages of gentrification *within* the buildings themselves.[6]

In the East Village, many leaseholders of rent-regulated apartments are Latinos on fixed incomes or receiving some form of public assistance. Thus, many of them, paying very low rents, live side by side with higher-income whites who pay more for their recently-renovated apartments. A 1989 survey of rents in a typical 18-unit walk-up in Alphabet City (see table 8.6) shows the wide range of rents that can coexist in a single building. The lower rents are accounted for by renewed leases protected from excessive increases by rent regulations, whereas the higher rents reflect either renovations, which allow for a higher rent increase than otherwise permitted under rent stabilization, or are accounted for by frequent lease turnovers.

Table 8.6 Rent roll for a four-story 18-unit walk-up building on Seventh Street between Avenues B and C

Apartment size/number		*Monthly rent, 1988–9*
One-bedroom	3A	Vacant
	2A	$256.11
	4C	$268.48
	4E	$281.80
	2E	$287.53
	3B	$333.39
	3E	$335.89
	4B	$346.19
	4D	$420.55
	3C	$468.60
	2C	$575.00
	3D	$739.68
	2D	$835.13
Two-bedroom	1B	Vacant
	1E	$173.56
	1C	$333.98
	1A	$450.00
	1D	$732.19

Source: New York State Department of Law, Real Estate Financing Bureau, January 1989

The range of rents within one building exposes the legal factors that slow the pace of redevelopment by preventing landlords from evicting tenants wholesale. To circumvent this restriction, developers have resorted to both illegal and legal means to empty their rent-regulated units. Illegal efforts, including turning off the heat and hot water in winter, renting to drug pushers who terrorize tenants, or torching emptied units, have frequently been used by the more notorious landlords in the East Village. Such illegal means have even been used to empty out entire buildings where most units are rent-controlled. Many existing residents, especially older Latinos, fail to register complaints of tenant abuse because of fear, language barriers, or a lack of information about where to go for assistance. Such tactics are no longer practical, once a number of units have been renovated for better-educated, higher-income and primarily white residents. Landlords must resort instead to buying tenants out, that is, offering sums at times in excess of $10,000 to induce tenants to move. For many low-income residents the amount is attractive. Yet with residents who obstinately refuse to move, there is no guarantee of immediately turning over a building's tenantry. Housing groups in the area have disseminated information in both Spanish and English, alerting residents to the dangers of evictions and buy-outs.

Once vacated, units may be renovated, often cheaply, and then placed on the market again, but at higher rents. By law, landlords may increase the rent of rent-regulated units after they have been vacated and structurally improved. Since higher rents can be charged each time a rent-stabilized unit is vacated and a new lease signed, East Village landlords target transient groups, such as single persons and students, who tend to move frequently.

Adding to landlord incentives to renovate their apartments and, in the process, rid themselves of rent-regulated tenants, are city policies that foster capital reinvestment in the housing stock (see next chapter). Amidst the abandonment of inner-city neighborhoods in the 1970s, both the city and the state sought ways to stem the outflow of real estate capital from declining neighborhoods like the Lower East Side. Incentive programs were enacted to assist landlords who claimed that punitive tax rates and regulated rents had made it unprofitable for them to reinvest in their properties. Temporary tax abatements and exemptions on a case by case basis were offered to owners who made capital improvements to their buildings.

These programs (J-51, 421-a, MCI and 1/40) encouraged improvements, such as new windows, furnaces and boilers, front doors, hallway renovations, brickfacing and intercom systems, which upgrade the value of the property. Some of these programs allowed landlords to pass on to their tenants part or all of the renovation and improvement costs. Acting as incentives for landlords to eliminate rent-regulated units, these policies placed low-income tenants in further jeopardy of displacement. In addition, since these programs are offered case by case, they have contributed to the unevenness of redevelopment within apartment buildings and within the entire East Village.

City-Owned Properties and Low-Income Populations

A second reason redevelopment occurred so unevenly in the East Village, however, was the disproportionately high number of city-owned abandoned and occupied properties in the neighborhood, as well as the large number of public housing units managed by the New York City Housing Authority. These forms of city-owned housing hinder pervasive redevelopment, either by serving as contentious spaces or by acting as pockets of low-income housing that could not be (easily) displaced. The city took control of many of the area's occupied and unoccupied apartment buildings in the late 1970s during the period of widespread owner abandonment. The majority of these properties are east of Avenue B (See figure 8.1).

As gentrification pressures increased, the disposition of the city-owned, officially unoccupied buildings and empty lots became a hotly contested issue. Clearly, the city and real estate interests preferred to have the buildings and lots auctioned off to private developers. A moratorium in force in the 1980s, however, prevented the city from doing so. Similarly, sweat equity monies, formerly provided to local housing coalitions which had homesteaded some of the city-owned buildings in the 1970s, were also cut off. While the fate of these properties was left hanging, as the city and local housing groups negotiated a settlement, groups of squatters and individuals opposed to gentrification illegally occupied and often rehabilitated some structures. By fall of 1987, the future of city-owned abandoned properties was resolved, for the time being, under the cross-subsidy agreement (see Sites, chapter 9 and Abu-Lughod, chapter 14), which gave both real estate and local housing coalitions a stake in the disposition of these city-owned lots and buildings.

Although large numbers of Hispanic residents were displaced from the private housing market by pressures of abandonment and redevelopment, a significant number of Puerto Ricans and Dominicans still reside in the area's city-owned and managed housing, both in the housing projects east of Avenue D and in city-owned tenements in the neighboring blocks between Avenues B and D. Most of the tenants in these buildings are on fixed incomes and rely on the city's below-market rents to maintain residences in the neighborhood. City-owned housing, then, has served as a buffer, preserving much of the ethnic and racial diversity of the East Village against the pervasive and somewhat homogenizing forces of gentrification.

For real estate interests, however, the presence of all these forms of city-owned properties reinforced the notion that, despite inroads made by speculators and developers, the East Village was not likely to succumb easily to a full-scale gentrification of the type occurring in other neighborhoods in New York or in cities such as Washington, DC, and Philadelphia. The prototypical 'yuppies' or 'Wall Streeters' have not shown much interest in settling in a district that contains so many city-owned and abandoned buildings and so disproportionate a share of public housing projects. In the strategy of gentrification, then, other types of consumers had to be found.

Figure 8.1 Map showing location of all city-owned properties in Community District 3
Source: Department of City Planning, New York City, *Atlas of City Property*, Vol. 3: Manhattan (New York: The Department, December 5, 1990)

Transient and High-Threshold Groups

The actual housing stock of the East Village – very small apartments in walk-up tenements – did not help in overcoming consumer resistance to a location in such close proximity to large-scale public housing projects. Developers therefore sought special classes of tenants willing to discount the larger environment. They found them in students attending the three major universities near the East Village and in single persons and/or members of 'alternative' cultures who were generally disinterested in or could not afford the amenities offered in typical gentrified neighborhoods. Both groups of newer residents were willing to pay substantially higher rents than the indigenous (largely low-income and Latino) residents. Thus, although they may not have been typical gentrifiers, they constituted a pool of potential tenants that developers began to tap.

Students attending the many schools in Lower Manhattan were attracted to the area because of its proximity to their campuses. Along Third Avenue, large dormitories for students of New York University, the New School for Social Research, and Cooper Union have been built; their concentration in a relatively small area adds to the youthful flavor of the East Village. In addition to living in the East Village, these students socialize, shop, and recreate there. The dormitories are a springboard for future tenants in the East Village and Alphabet City. Many, if not most, of these students will find apartments in the neighborhood, once they leave the dormitories. Since one of the key means for landlords to increase rents charged in regulated apartments is through tenant turnover, students constitute choice residents.

Other young single persons are attracted to the East Village for its downtown location and its reputation as a place receptive to alternative values and ways of life – an image developers have exploited in their attempts to market local housing. A significant number of homosexual males have taken up residence in Alphabet City, preferring and adding to the area's reputation as hospitable to nonconformists. Their presence, which is roughly equivalent in numbers to other subgroups moving into the area, repeats a pattern similar to the establishment of gay communities in Manhattan's West Village and Upper West Side, as well as enclaves in other American cities.[7]

These groups have other attributes that make them attractive tenants to developers. First, unlike the Latinos and older Ukrainians in the area who do not willingly relocate, students and counter-culture groups have no strong ethnic ties to the neighborhood. Overall, members of these groups demonstrate little long-term commitment to remaining in the neighborhood or in a single apartment within the area. Roommate turnover, job promotions and relocations, marriage, and the desire to live in nicer neighborhoods account for the high frequency of apartment turnover among these groups. Since frequent turnovers are an added bonus in that they permit landlords to raise rents, these high turnover residents are welcomed and, at times, sought out. Second, since many of these tenants double up in unstable roommate situations, their combined incomes allow them to pay rents that would be unreasonable for single-income households.

These transient groups also have a higher level of tolerance for the many social problems which, despite the changes occurring, continue to plague much of the Lower East Side. Students, for example, are not overly concerned with middle-class amenities such as frequent garbage pick-up, quality local schools, or convenient and elegant shopping facilities. Because of their limited economic resources and/or preferences for residing in 'alternative' neighborhoods, these groups endure above-normal levels of crime, noise, and drug-related problems. They are prime tenants, therefore, because they rent in areas that stereotypical gentrifiers avoid and, simultaneously, they imbue the area with an image of youthfulness and alternative cultures.

CONCLUSION

As gentrification progressed in the East Village during the 1980s, it became clear that it had limits. By 1989, just as *Real Estate Weekly* was trumpeting that the East Village 'is being transformed into a neighborhood of young professionals,' the bottom was falling out of the East Village real estate market. The process of gentrification that began during the 1970s, when landlords were walking away from their buildings, was aborting.

The pioneering speculators, who had made huge profits in the early 1980s by buying buildings at depressed prices and then reselling them without renovations, were no longer active in the East Village. By the early 1980s, the speculative phase was exhausted. Then, larger real estate firms entered the game, pricing out the 'mom and pop' owners and renovating buildings; their activities intensified displacement pressures on long-term residents. Using a variety of legal and illegal means, they enticed or forced the residents out of their apartments, warehousing the units until co-op or condominium conversion was possible. By the end of the 1980s, however, the demand for such co-ops and condominia sank – leaving many of these developers literally holding the bag. The failure of developers to complete the gentrification process was not due only to larger forces in the real estate market. Their activities were also inhibited by other more institutional factors (see figure 8.2).

Surface processes and effects

1970s	>Devalorization	>1970/80s	>Revalorization	>1980s
	Abandonment	**Speculation**		**Redevelopment**
Private rental market	Decline in low-income rent-regulated apartments through abandonment	Decline in low-income rent-regulated apartments continues		Decline in rent-regulated apartments through lease buyouts, evictions, warehousing, condominium and coop conversions
Built-environment	Deteriorated, 'burned-out'	No visible change		Renovations/ upgrading
Resident population	Declining minority, low-income	Continued decline		Declining low-income; rise in "high-threshold" groups

Subsurface processes and effects

1970s	>Devalorization	>1970/80s	>Revalorization	>1980s
Investment environment				
	Abandonment	**Speculation**		**Redevelopment**
	graduated disinvestment ("milking" of bulidings)	increased sales activity "flipping" increased sales prices		institutional lenders provide capital
Forms of ownership				
	Absentee landlords Mom and pop landlords	Speculators, Holding companies		Developers, real estate firms
	City of New York (*in-rem* program)		Moratorium on sales	

Figure 8.2 Model of the gentrification process in Alphabet City
Source: Original diagram by Christopher mele

The East Village's full-scale conversion to a high-rent district was inhibited by rent control and renewable lease laws protecting tenants and by the presence of low-income housing projects. These were only fragile barriers to displacement and gentrification, however. The neighborhood was eventually 'saved' in part by the same larger economic forces that initially had led to its gentrification.

NOTES

1 Interfaith Adopt-A-Building, 'A Portrait of the Lower East Side,' June 1978, p. 14.

2 In this same interval, the population of New York City decreased by 10.4 percent while nearby SoHo's population actually increased slightly.

3 The *Sanborn Manhattan Land Book* provides data on property transactions (building type, owners' names and addresses, assessment values on land and buildings, sales prices, and sale dates) for each lot in every block in Manhattan. Table 1 calculates the percentage of properties that were sold of the total number of market-available (not city-owned) properties in the given census tracts between 1980 and 1985. Table 2 gives the average sale price of walk-up apartment buildings sold per year in given census tracts.

4 New York State Department of Law, Real Estate Financing Bureau, report on conversions, January 1989, pp. 8–9.

5 George Sternlieb and James W. Hughes, *Housing and Economic Reality* (New Brunswick, NJ: Center for Urban Policy Research, Rutgers University, 1976).

6 Frank DeGiovanni, *Displacement Pressures in the Lower East Side* (New York: Community Service Society, 1987).

7 Glenn Albin, 'Swoon over Miami,' *Outweek*, 6 March 1991, pp. 36–7.

9

Public Action: New York City Policy and the Gentrification of the Lower East Side

William Sites

Gentrification pits a complex array of neighborhood residents and users in a fight over homes, profits, and public turf. In Manhattan's Lower East Side, such conflicts are often attributed to the area's heterogeneity, as diverse groups compete for the limited resources of one neighborhood.[1] But to fully understand gentrification, analysis must also focus on economic and political forces outside the neighborhood that set into motion the internal collision of rival claims.

When observers of neighborhood gentrification do look at 'outside forces,' they often misunderstand them. Thus, gentrification is often ascribed to a hodge podge of demographic, lifestyle, and economic factors. A typical scenario attributes gentrification to the large cohort of baby-boom professionals who, rejecting suburban living, became urban pioneers and saved moribund inner-city neighborhoods. *Time* magazine went so far as to suggest it was 'the hurly-burly pleasures of democracy – pluralism incarnate – that pulled Americans back downtown.'[2] Such interpretations are doubly problematic. They demean long-term inner-city residents, whose often-thriving communities are uprooted by gentrification. They imply, as well, a kind of consumer sovereignty on the part of 'gentrifiers,' or a free-market inevitability that operates without any political dynamic. In either case, the real connections between gentrification and the changing economic functions of American cities are obscured, and gentrification – like the market itself – is seen as beyond the reach of public policy. New York City government used precisely such an argument in the face of Lower East Side protests against gentrification. Said one city planning commission official in 1983: 'What I hear being implied is that public action is pushing people out. Public action is not – the city has no control over the private market.'[3]

'Public action' does, however, have considerable control over the market. While general economic forces and federal policies impel local development in certain directions, each municipal administration makes choices about how it will respond to those trends. It strengthens or weakens them. It distributes their benefits broadly or narrowly. It reduces or adds to the costs such trends impose on its most vulnerable citizens. It encourages development activities in one area of the city and discourages them in another. And in making these choices, municipal authorities use the policy and planning tools of local government to fulfill their own objectives.

This chapter locates gentrification within a broad set of inner-city development pressures brought on by changes in the economic functions of US cities. It argues that in New York City the Koch administration (1978–89) pursued a development strategy that favored large corporations and developers in a way that also furthered its own political interests. In doing so, the administration fueled market-driven development pressures that contributed directly and indirectly to gentrification in the Lower East Side. Local government, furthermore, actively sought to use its vast property holdings in the neighborhood to encourage gentrification, sparking a decade-long series of conflicts with community groups. Overall, the Koch administration heightened the costs of economic change for less-affluent New Yorkers, even as it failed to establish the conditions for balanced growth and enduring fiscal stability.

ECONOMIC CHANGE AND GENTRIFICATION

During the 1970s and 1980s, corporate reinvestment in many older American cities transformed their declining central districts into new business centers. A long-term pattern of economic growth based on the suburbanization of investment in industry and housing had reached maturity in the United States during the decades following World War II. It led to a slow but steady economic decline in the downtown areas of older American cities. Federal urban renewal monies for center-city reconstruction were dwarfed by national tax policies and spending priorities (such as home-ownership subsidies, highway construction, and military procurement) that further encouraged the abandonment of older cities.[4] While many areas of these cities remained neglected, real-estate revival in the urban core spurred gentrification in accessible and desirable residential areas.

By the mid-1970s New York was at a crossroads, faced with job and population losses, falling tax revenues, a decline in building construction, and substantial cutbacks in federal aid – and, consequently, a large municipal debt. While local political factors played a role, New York's fiscal crisis of the 1970s was in one sense a culmination of a long series of painful economic consequences.[5]

By the late 1970s and early 1980s, it became clear that economic restructuring had begun to redraw the postwar pattern of suburbanization and inner-city decline. American cities were increasingly transformed to suit the requirements of new forms of economic activity. While suburban development by no means halted, selective corporate investment refashioned central business districts (CBDs) into regional and, in the case of New York City, global command posts. Redevelopment of New York City's urban core enhanced its role as a corporate headquarters complex and fueled related business activities. Accordingly, it made up for some of the city's job losses through new employment opportunities clustered at the high and low ends of the income spectrum. Federal economic policies (deregulation, anti-unionism, and the subsidization of capital mobility) combined with cutbacks in urban assistance to further encourage the trend toward deindustrialization, service-sector growth, financial market hyperactivity, and labor-market polarization. The restructuring city was characterized by uneven economic and spatial development. Revival coexisted uneasily with blight and decay.[6]

Reinvestment spurred the growth of the corporate-complex service sector and a significant revival of the real estate market in the Manhattan core. Land values in the central business district (CBD) escalated, as did housing demand on the part of better-paid service workers, particularly for areas relatively near the white-collar job centers. However, the new corporate activity weakened the economic positions of centrally located manufacturers, traditional small businesses, and a growing stratum of poorer workers, and it did little to reverse disinvestment in many distressed non-core areas.[7] Taken together, these forces created the conditions for a market-led 'inner-city revival.'

From the early 1970s, a precipitous decline in private housing construction had combined with cutbacks in federal funding to funnel residential real-estate investment into the areas of rehabilitation and conversions. Whereas 1950s-style urban renewal had replaced some lower-income areas with higher-income housing, the government program eventually foundered on resistance to the direct displacement of the poor. Private 'upgrading' promised similar results without the political controversy associated with public-sector leadership or direct displacement.

The Politics of Fiscal and Development Strategy

The political complexion of New York City government and its approaches to economic development issues also shifted during the postwar years. A significant turning point was the mid-1970s fiscal crisis, whose resolution set the parameters for government reactions to the economic restructuring of the late 1970s and the 1980s. The Koch administration, in turn, was able to build a successful political coalition around the twin pursuits of economic development and fiscal austerity.

Throughout the 1940s and 1950s, the city's land-use policy had been the province of public administrator Robert Moses. As the head of a growth coalition fueled by federal and state money, Moses rammed through roads, bridges, parks, and urban-renewal housing developments. Along with projects by the Port Authority and David Rockefeller's Downtown-Lower Manhattan Association, Moses' planners refashioned the physical geography of New York City.[8] The urban social movements of the 1960s forced a significant reshuffling of these priorities, however. Under Mayor John Lindsay, an alliance between a portion of the business elite, Democratic Party reformers, and minority groups was welded together by federal funding. Development policy shifted away from Moses' 'slum clearance,' seeking instead to pursue neighborhood preservation and low-income housing along with expensive projects to promote core economic development.

By the mid-1970s, however, federal cutbacks, economic stagnation, and fiscal crisis spelled a new agenda. While their immediate goal was to banish the specter of municipal default, the emergency measures of the 1970s crisis also permitted extensive changes in the way New York City was governed. The supra-democratic powers given to financial watchdog agencies helped implement an austerity program, imposing many of the costs of the fiscal crisis on municipal workers and on less affluent citizens and neighborhoods in the form of decreased services.[9] In the process, crisis management also completed a shift in institutional influence away from the service-connected agencies (such as housing and anti-poverty programs) that were most susceptible to pressure by the general public.

Although the fear of imminent default eventually began to recede, the rhetoric and practice of 'fiscal politics' did not.[10] Enduring budget constraints, while often quite real, were also found to be a convenient means to deflect the demands of non-elite constituencies. In an increasingly accepted interpretation of the fiscal crisis, such groups (especially municipal workers and welfare clients) and the politicians who catered to them were held, in any case, largely to blame. Whereas banks and bond-rating agencies gradually became less visible arbiters of city government, their criteria for what made a good public policy remained.

Economic redevelopment and fiscal austerity were the linchpins of the local governing coalition led by Mayor Edward Koch. This ruling coalition successfully united the economic interests of business and its key organizations – the major banks and their governmental surrogates such as the Financial Control Board and the Municipal Assistance Corporation, large developers and their supporters, and, in a subsidiary role, municipal labor leaders – in a general program of fiscal parsimony and CBD growth.[11] The mayor's importance consisted in his ability to fashion a stable and powerful electoral base to support and carry out development strategies. Its ingredients were drawn from bountiful campaign coffers (filled with the help of real estate developers, who in turn became significant beneficiaries of economic development policy), political alliances with the remnants of the Democratic Party machine (in exchange for patronage and graft opportunities), and a weak and divided opposition. Sizable electoral majorities were solidified by a deft combination of personality, racially divisive rhetoric, and appeals to the benefits of fiscal solvency and economic growth.[12] Electoral and political dominance by the mayor assured stability and continuity in the governing coalition, which in turn enabled many growth issues potentially divisive to the coalition to be negotiated and settled outside the political arena.

Under Koch, local government was restructured to promote economic development in an age of increased corporate mobility and federal cutbacks. The administration's purported development strategy was to allow 'natural forces' (businesses) to do what they did best, with the principal role of government being 'to get out of the way.' In this view, just as an unnaturally intrusive administration had discouraged private enterprise and thus led to the fiscal crisis, one that knew its proper role would allow business to create a 'true economic renaissance.'[13] In practice, fostering natural forces involved quite a lot of government activity, selectively applied.

The administration created new economic development programs to court and retain (non-manufacturing) corporate facilities. It relied on loan and tax-incentive programs and zoning changes to promote business activity and intensive redevelopment in the Manhattan CBD, and it mounted a series of large commercial development initiatives, such as South Street Seaport, the Javits Convention Center and 42nd Street Development Project. Local government during the Koch years altered the development planning process and housing policy as well, changes that furthered the use of local government to assist private development. In short, the development strategy under Mayor Koch was not simply to rely on the private market. Rather, it was to adapt the instruments of public authority to help fuel the market – a market which, as we have seen, was restructuring New York City in highly uneven ways.

In a seemingly unpropitious period marked by intense competition between cities for corporate investment, the Koch administration thrived politically by coupling its development program with fiscal austerity. Its success was partly attributed, of course, to New York City's special position in finance, the leading sector in the international economic order of the 1980s. Yet the local alliance between government and business flourished, not simply by striving to subordinate politics to the new economic reality as it claimed, but also by depicting that reality in a way that furthered its own economic and political agenda. Thus, on the one hand, New York was trumpeted far and wide as having (at last) a receptive and robust business climate. On the other hand, that climate had to be made to seem fragile and easily reversible, for only fragility justified very generous concessions to mobile corporations and to the government's elite supporters. To business, the city was presented as a place where economic growth was assured, without the burden of rising demands from the populace that usually accompanied growth. To that populace, the administration painted a future that could be thrown in jeopardy by the least sign of corporate relocation plans or by any more than minimal benefits for lower economic strata.

In a July 1982 advertising supplement in *Forbes*, for instance, the mayor proclaimed that 'the City's remarkable recovery and aggressive pro-business policy have effected a turnaround . . . Our public-private partnership has worked to create a true economic renaissance.'[14] Yet shortly thereafter, the administration, pressured by the Financial Control Board, was imposing funding cuts on all agencies and demanding wage concessions from municipal unions to cope with budget deficits. In 1984, amidst a remarkable economic boom that resulted in greater local tax revenues than expected, the mayor again tried to hold back wage increases. At the same time, the administration announced that most of its Lower East Side properties would have to be sold to private developers to raise scarce money that might later be used to subsidize low- and moderate-income housing.[15]

The coupling of business renaissance and popular austerity not only secured the city administration widespread support in the business community, but it also marginalized development alternatives, obviating the need to articulate and defend the chosen strategy in terms of social costs, benefits, and contributions to the public good. Unexamined were forms of leverage the administration might have used to spread the fruits of the 'renaissance' – both to diversify the economic base and to assist the poorer half of the city.[16]

DEVELOPMENT POLICY AND PLANNING

The Koch administration did not formulate a comprehensive plan to fulfill its development objectives. Instead, it relied heavily on the use of tax incentives to fuel business and real estate expansion. Municipal agencies tended to use policy-planning instruments – powers over zoning, development impacts, and the use of public resources – in a flexible, negotiated fashion. Development projects that were legally mandated to pass through a public land-use review process did require a kind of *ad hoc* planning, encouraging adaptation of the planning process to make it more receptive to administrative goals. In such cases, plans were increasingly 'predeveloped' by developers and city officials, packaged with an agreed-upon set of public amenities, and shepherded through the land-review process by top city administrators.

After 1976 the city government established economic development programs that used loans and tax incentives to court and retain (non-manufacturing) corporate facilities and spur real estate values in the Manhattan core. The ostensible rationale for using tax-incentives to motivate businesses to remain in or relocate to New York was job creation. In an age of increased corporate mobility, analysts agreed that special efforts would need to be taken to protect and expand the city's job base. It was not always clear how successfully the Koch administration's loan and tax-incentive programs were in accomplishing this goal. Often, the recipients of tax breaks were not required to create a specific number of jobs; when they were, their failure to fulfill that commitment did not always affect their subsequent access to public subsidy. Nor did city officials seem to be concerned with what jobs were created, who would fill them, or whether subsidizing job creation in large firms might reduce jobs in small businesses.[17]

Although Manhattan office construction rebounded after the fiscal crisis, for a time private housing construction remained at very low levels.[18] The Koch administration therefore used tax incentives to promote sorely needed housing. Much of that new construction was luxury housing supported by ten-year partial tax exemptions under the 421a program, initially intended to promote moderate- and middle-income housing. According to one study of 421a projects approved between 1981 and 1983, the average rent per unit exceeded $1,100 and ten large Manhattan developers received three-fourths of the $103 million in tax exemptions.[19]

Also significant was the city's J-51 program of tax exemptions and abatements for housing conversions and rehabilitation. City officials argued that the program served to increase both the tax base and the supply of habitable housing. A 1981 study by City Council President Carol Bellamy, however, suggested a long-term loss of up to $1 billion in revenue from J-51 tax breaks for conversions that in many cases would have taken place without subsidy.[20] The program also had the effect of subsidizing the depletion of low-income rental units, partly by encouraging the conversion of Manhattan's stock of single-room-occupancy hotels, traditionally the housing of last resort for poor single men.[21]

Beyond tax incentives, the administration's use of other policy tools in conjunction with its planning capabilities gave its role in development a more interventionist cast. The planning process during the Koch years involved privatizing much project initiation and coordinating planning (more accurately understood as deal making) through the mayor's office. Development plans, when not simply permissible 'as-of-right,' were worked out between developers and city officials, excluding other civic actors from the process. One community board chairperson complained that some *developers* were more open to community participation than the administration was. In at least one project, South Ferry, the administration refused to release any information about the bids that had been solicited. 'We felt the bids – the models and the drawings and the ideas – belonged to the developers who had prepared them,' said the city official in charge of the project.[22]

One Lower East Side plan, worked out between developer Samuel J. LeFrak and the City of New York to develop housing on an urban renewal site near the Williamsburg Bridge, became public knowledge only after the city council representative from the area happened to hear about it. The administration then released only part of the agreement, withholding a memorandum that contained special terms advantageous to the developer. When questions were raised about the propriety of a single bid, the administration solicited other bids but cautioned that it was unlikely to receive one as attractive as the LeFrak proposal. It did not, and the LeFrak Organization was re-designated the developer for the site.[23]

The administration defended its predevelopment method, at least in part, by pointing to the concessions that were wrested from developers in exchange for public resources or zoning variances. These concessions usually came in the form of either financial proceeds from the sale of public land or the private provision of public spaces and services (or 'exactions' as they are called). Such trade-offs came to be criticized on economic grounds alone. The Office of the State Comptroller, for example, estimated the financial value of public amenities in one audit sample to be less than 5 percent of the market value of the bonus floor area granted to developers.[24] Beyond their cost, the content of exactions was also challenged. Since no explicit government plan had established a priority list of local needs and clear mechanisms to fulfill them, how was the administration or the public to determine whether the concessions made by the developers were those most needed by the city? Several other cities with strong real estate markets (notably Boston and San Francisco) developed policy formulas linking development to the production of low- and moderate-income housing. In New York, however, a 1984 mayoral study rejected such 'linkage' policies.[25]

Since projects could be hindered by outside environmental review, outer-borough political interests, legal challenges, or neighborhood and public opposition that surfaced during the land-review process, much of the mayor-centered planning process was devoted to navigating development packages through the complex process of political ratification. The Department of City Planning, for example, rather than being concerned with overall land-use planning, usually confined itself to studies of specific zoning changes and project impacts; these were often criticized for soft pedaling potential adverse effects.[26] Because larger public input was excluded from earlier phases of the planning process, it would normally gain a hearing only at the points of ratification (such as the neighborhood community board or the Board of Estimate). By this time the significant parameters of projects were more or less in place, and civic and community groups perceived their only avenues to be to approve projects, attempt to scuttle them, or press for minor changes. Increasingly, these groups sought to halt city-approved land deals in the courts, hitherto a venue used more often by developers seeking relief from municipal restrictions.[27]

Taken as a whole, the various policies and planning initiatives of the Koch years served market-dictated development, but this was hardly a simple process of letting the 'natural forces' of the market run their course. The administration itself played a leadership role in development, one that was distinguished from that of developers not by its greater concern with larger public goals but by its ability to use public resources and institutions to assist private development. As a result, the planning process and its policy instruments, including tax incentives, zoning variances, and exactions, served to subsidize businesses and developers and to exclude the wider public.

Gentrification and City Policy

The Koch administration's development strategy had important spatial consequences for key Manhattan business district areas (Lower Manhattan,

East Midtown and, later, West Midtown). The dense clustering of redevelopment sites quickly generated rising land values and housing demand in nearby residential areas. These gentrification pressures were welcomed by city government which complemented its development efforts with housing policy measures designed to encourage redundant private reinvestment in neighborhoods such as the Lower East Side, without safeguarding against its harmful effects.

Gentrification was viewed as a positive revitalization of poorer neighborhoods. The city planning department's one major study of private reinvestment (focusing on the Upper West Side and Park Slope areas) concluded that reinvestment had improved housing conditions, stemmed deterioration, strengthened neighborhood commercial areas, and increased assessed values. While conceding the possibility of displacement, the study did not attempt to measure it.[28] And yet, a strong link between gentrification and displacement had been established as early as the late 1970s. Peter Marcuse estimated that between 10,000 and 40,000 New York City households were displaced by gentrification each year.[29] In the Lower East Side, a 1984 study found 'substantial pressures for displacement' in the form of excessive rent burden, overcrowding, building deterioration, and tenant harassment by landlords.[30]

City government's encouragement of gentrification, therefore, opened it to charges of subsidizing displacement. Critics often focused on the administration's various tax-incentive programs. The J-51 program eliminated low-rent housing units and, along with the 421a tax incentives, served to hyperinflate property values in or near gentrifiable neighborhoods. During the early 1980s, the Lower East Side, for instance, was surrounded by districts where 421a construction was substantial, relative to other areas of New York City. The J-51 program included between 10,000 and 15,000 units of Lower East Side housing as of March 1984.[31] When in 1983 the state legislature decided to exclude certain districts from J-51 eligibility, the city administration insisted that the Lower East Side remain included.[32]

Another thrust of local housing policy during the 1970s and 1980s was to weaken the rent-regulation system. Rent control and rent stabilization came under stronger attack from a newly reorganized and elite-directed stratum of small- and medium-sized property owners.[33] After 1981 the Rent Guidelines Board, appointed by the mayor, awarded yearly rent increases that outpaced inflation during a period when real renter incomes declined. The effects of a weakened rent-regulation system were most pronounced in neighborhoods such as the Lower East Side, which combined decayed housing with gentrifying prospects. In those areas, reinvestment and in-migration created a market demand able to support residential rent increases higher than the city-wide average. Gentrifying areas also experienced dramatic increases in commercial rents. In the early 1980s a sudden rise in the demand for Lower East Side retail space, especially art galleries, drove commercial rents from roughly $6 per square foot to as much as $20 to $30 per square foot.[34] During the same period, the mayor led a successful effort to oppose a City Council bill authorizing commercial rent arbitration.[35]

The combination of regulatory inaction and housing subsidies spurred gentrification in many New York City neighborhoods. Granted, private reinvestment in economically depressed areas raised property values and boosted tax assessments. In the Lower East Side it also increased the supply of habitable housing and promoted property upgrading – but only after further deterioration to empty buildings of their poorer tenants.[36] Gentrification achieved its economic successes by replacing poorer residents with a higher class of occupants; displacement was an inevitable consequence of uncontrolled private reinvestment.

The administration's attitude toward gentrification mirrored its approach to large-scale development. Private reinvestment in declining neighborhoods, seen as uniformly benign, was also portrayed as precarious – not because of the boom-and-bust irrationality of the private real estate market, but because substantial public intervention to channel the benefits of gentrification or protect its victims might 'create disincentives to upgrading.'[37] Outside the administration, on the other hand, planners developed alternatives to both abandonment and uncontrolled gentrification. The early 1980s witnessed credible proposals for controlled neighborhood reinvestment.[38] And in the Lower East Side, as we shall see, community groups developed their own blueprint to tap the surging reinvestment in that neighborhood to benefit poorer residents.

Lower East Side and the Struggle Over City-owned Housing

The converging forces of economic restructuring, Manhattan redevelopment, and a less profitable lower-income housing market set the stage for gentrification in the Lower East Side. In 1979, the market in neighborhood real estate started to quicken, and by the following year the first wave of entrepreneurs began to make their mark in the Lower East Side.[39] A significant cultural component was provided by young white 'marginal gentrifiers,' many of whom, drawn by affordable housing and a thriving countercultural community, fed into an East Village arts scene that was inflating in tandem with property values.[40] The neighborhood's political identity, on the other hand, remained one that had been forged by a long and combative history of housing conflicts; the interests of long-time residents continued to find political expression in a loose alliance of neighborhood groups, some of which were well practiced in tenant organizing and the inventive use of public protest. As in-migration was swelled by less-marginal gentrifiers, and as property speculation fueled the private housing market, the various interests of investors, neighborhood groups, newer residents, and city government itself all collided over the issue of city-owned properties.

The bulk of the city's *in rem* housing stock had been acquired during the wave of owner abandonment in the 1970s. By 1987 in the Lower East Side alone, an estimated 500 buildings and lots were in the administration's hands.[41] With the advent of private reinvestment in the Lower East Side, these parcels became the object of a fierce contest of wills. For real estate investors seeking profits in the Lower East Side, the properties represented an extraordinary opportunity to construct or rehabilitate market-rate housing. Tenant and neighborhood groups, on the other hand, saw the city-owned stock as an invaluable resource for the creation of community- and tenant-controlled housing for lower-income residents. (Indeed, before the reawakening of the private market in the area, the administration itself had encouraged such efforts, albeit fitfully.[42]) Such groups also feared that the sale of *in rem* properties for market-rate housing would further accelerate gentrification and displacement.

For the administration, its Lower East Side properties were both burden and opportunity. In one respect a fiscal albatross, they not only consumed substantial operating expenses (which the city held partly in check by notoriously low standards of upkeep), but also represented an ongoing loss in property taxes.[43] However, as the Lower East Side housing market began to show genuine profit-making potential, the sale of *in rem* parcels to developers promised to save expenses, generate new tax revenues, and assist gentrification – all at the same time. Yet neighborhood opposition also mounted, as the costs of gentrification became clearer.

The result was that city-owned properties in the Lower East Side came to be a complex and enduring political problem for the administration. On the one hand, fiscal priorities, dovetailing with larger development and housing aims, predisposed the administration to sell its properties. Yet pressures from the community to retain the properties for lower-income housing remained sufficient to keep them off the auction block. For an administration determined to extend its housing and development policies to a neighborhood that remained particularly hostile to them, the emerging stalemate was a challenge to its political resourcefulness. Its response consisted of three major initiatives: the alternative management programs, an artists' housing proposal, and the cross-subsidy plan.

In the wake of the 1970s fiscal crisis, city government attempted to auction off *in rem* housing, but the auction process, plagued by financial improprieties and low success rates, proved politically unviable for most Lower East Side properties. A partial change of strategy was reflected in 1978 in the transfer of management of *in rem* properties to the newly reorganized Department of Housing Preservation and Development (HPD).[44] HPD's task was not simply to manage properties, but to regenerate tax and rental revenues from slum housing and, using federal community-development funds, to revive the private market in slum areas. The agency developed a diversified approach to city properties (especially those in 'salvageable' slums such as the Lower East Side) focused on the narrow goal of returning them to the private market. The department did create a Division of Alternative Management Programs (DAMP) that adopted genuinely innovative rehabilitation programs, such as low-income tenant co-ops and housing managed by neighborhood groups, but it then proceeded to reshape and restrict these programs to complement its larger development and housing policy to fuel the market.[45]

Therefore, rather than developing explicit neighborhood plans based on community needs, the housing department emphasized further neighborhood gentrification and its own fiscal interests. Such was the case with the Tenant Interim Lease (TIL) program, a system of low-income tenant cooperatives, initially the most successful alternative management program in Manhattan. By 1982, the administration had pushed through changes in resale rules to help gentrify TIL buildings. As it became clearer that private investment was reviving the Lower East Side real-estate market, however, the city cut back its alternative management programs in the area, ignored increasing numbers of applications from community groups for *in rem* buildings, and evicted homesteaders as squatters.[46] Meanwhile, HPD had recruited private real-estate managers to run its properties to increase their rent yield. The agency also demolished vacant (or forcibly vacated) *in rem* buildings, ostensibly because they were unsound or serving as drug dens. The effect was to replace potential sources of low-income public housing with vacant land more attractive to private developers.

In 1982 HPD also sought, through the land-review procedure, to privatize some of its vacant housing stock under a proposal for an Artists' Home Ownership Program, AHOP. This program was represented by the mayor as a chance for artists to 'help fight abandonment and decay on the Lower East Side and to renew the strength and vitality of this community' in a way that would also prevent 'avaricious landlords' from profiting.[47] In fact, the program did involve private developers, as well as artists with incomes substantially higher than the neighborhood average, and was strongly opposed by many local groups and artists. Despite approval by the area's community board, AHOP was voted down by the Board of Estimate in 1983, following a well mobilized opposition campaign led by these groups. Borough President Andrew Stein subsequently conceded the need to make membership on Community Board 3 more widely representative of neighborhood interests.[48]

Drawing on a formula that had successfully revived Manhattan's SoHo district, AHOP was an attempt by the administration to cobble together a pro-gentrification coalition that would weaken resistance to privatizing city-owned housing in the Lower East Side. In SoHo, a novel confluence of loft conversion, downtown arts frenzy, and strategic city intervention had resulted in widespread gentrification and, eventually, the displacement of small manufacturers and homesteading artists alike. (The mayor had become so excited by the prospect of artists as sure-fire gentrifiers that in 1979 he even suggested the SoHo formula for the South Bronx.[49]) The more modest Lower East Side AHOP proposal was even less promising than SoHo's. The New York City arts community had grown wary after the SoHo experience. A number of Lower East Side artists, in fact, were active in neighborhood anti-gentrification groups, and even downtown art-world fixtures began showing discomfort over the role of the arts in gentrification. In defeating AHOP, neighborhood groups succeeded in linking together housing and arts constituencies – at least temporarily – into a counter-coalition to oppose publicly sponsored gentrification. Viewed at the time as a significant political setback for the mayor, the AHOP debacle also left the administration cautious about initiating new proposals for city-owned housing in the area.[50]

By 1984 gentrification had further accelerated. The private market was now drawing long-term investors and widespread rehabilitation without direct public subsidy. The Lower East Side Joint Planning Council (JPC), a coalition of neighborhood groups, presented its own plan to Community Board 3. Noting the strong private market, the JPC plan argued for inclusionary zoning (which would have required market-rate developers to also create lower-income housing), greater tenant protection from displacement, and the use of all *in rem* properties for low- and moderate-income housing.[51] Several large demonstrations showed considerable neighborhood support. Faced with a credible and community-supported alternative, city government responded with a vague and hastily assembled 'cross-subsidy' proposal that addressed only the third issue raised by the JPC plan. According to the plan then set forth by the city, the sales proceeds from market-rate development of 80 percent of the *in rem* properties would be earmarked to rehabilitate future subsidized housing in the remaining properties.[52] Community Board 3, now less compliant, was sympathetic toward the thrust of the JPC plan, versions of which it endorsed in June 1984 and May 1985. The administration, however, showed little interest in negotiating concessions to the board, and over the following two years both plans languished. Statements by local officials and real estate brokers continued to urge privatizing *in rem* properties for market housing and warned that capital flight to more cooperative neighborhoods was imminent, unless neighborhood groups capitulated.[53]

The confrontation over cross-subsidy distilled a conflict between two visions for the Lower East Side. The administration's proposal offered a subsidy component that, while not negligible, was small enough not to impede the plan's larger economic effect – fueling gentrification. The internally generated subsidy bolstered the political claim that the city supported economically mixed housing in the Lower East Side, while at the same time freeing it from a major financial commitment to create or preserve low-income housing. The initial JPC plan, based in part on non-market-defined community needs, was an attempt to tap the booming private market in a way that would also compel city government to guarantee a place for substantial numbers of traditional neighborhood residents. Community Board 3's version of the plan eventually offered a 50/50 split – half of the *in rem* properties to be sold for market-rate housing, which in turn would subsidize the other half for low- and moderate-income units. Beyond the plan's provisions, however, the mere fact of its emergence demonstrated an articulate demand by the neighborhood to participate in the planning process. The administration's announcement of the original cross-subsidy proposal, and its reluctance to negotiate with the community board, indicated the political obstacles the neighborhood faced.

Meanwhile, in the private housing market gentrification was proceeding slowly but steadily. Large institutional investors (Bank Leumi, Chemical Bank and, especially, Citibank) plus 'long-term players' such as Kalikow Realty were now active in the area.[54] Finally, in early 1987, Community Board 3 was invited into serious negotiations with HPD which was now politically more responsive to the need for subsidized housing. By October of that year, the two sides had signed an agreement for a modified cross-subsidy plan. The accord permitted the sale of *in rem* vacant land for the private development of 1,000 market-rate housing units in exchange for the creation of an equal number of publicly funded low- and moderate-income units in empty *in rem* tenements.[55]

Yet implementation of the plan has lagged. In early 1988 the administration's separate proposal for builder Samuel J. LeFrak to develop the Lower East Side urban renewal site was revealed. Community Board 3 opposed the proposal because it promised no low-income housing and had been assembled without the board's participation. When cross-subsidy then came to a standstill, board members publicly accused HPD of holding the plan hostage to the LeFrak proposal.[56] Once cross-subsidy began to move forward again, the community board, responsible for setting up the institutional structure to manage the plan's lower-income units, struggled with its new role. After further modifications, the Lower East Side cross-subsidy program finally began in 1990 to rehabilitate the first of its projected 1,000 subsidized apartments.[57]

In retrospect, Lower East Side resistance did not halt gentrification nor did it create strong safeguards against displacement. Demands for curbs on the 'upscaling' of the area's *privately* owned housing – or at least for a modest channeling of its profits into creating more subsidized housing – were successfully resisted by the administration. Factional strife between neighborhood groups, which had always been present, predictably came to the fore, now that implementation of a concrete plan was the issue.[58] Nevertheless, the most striking feature of the Lower East Side experience was that an administration which was supportive of uncontrolled gentrification had been driven to take an unusually direct and visible role in pursuing it. Unable to dispose of its properties quickly, HPD was forced by well-organized neighborhood groups to pursue its interests in the spotlight. As a result, the administration was compelled to negotiate over alternatives to the unreflective use of public resources for private profit.

Public Action: The Koch Years and Beyond

Struggles in the Lower East Side during the 1980s stemmed from more than the neighborhood's internal 'contrasts and contradictions' or the clash of 'so many different constituencies.'[59] Gentrification, I have argued, originated in changes in the larger urban economy that were managed by local government in ways that benefited the city's economic and political elites. The Koch administration's city-wide policies, coupled in the Lower East Side with efforts to privatize public-housing resources, constituted a significant and damaging form of 'public action.'

Cities and their governments are prey, of course, to forces beyond their control. Dependent on mobile corporate investment and on public resources controlled at the national and state levels of government, US cities must attract and retain investment to generate development, jobs, and revenues. What kinds of investments and jobs, which types of development and where they are channeled, what sources of revenue and how to allocate them – these are questions over which local governments, despite their vulnerability, exert considerable influence. The Koch administration maintained that the best answers to questions of development would be found by the market; its policies, however, involved the use of municipal authority and resources to foster market outcomes. Shunning broader participation, planning devolved into an expedient apparatus for harmonizing the interests of developers and top officials. The result was economic resurgence, balanced budgets, and an impressive building boom in the urban core – followed by stagnation, fiscal crisis, and a glut of unused Manhattan office space. Development was not linked consistently to general public benefits. And gentrification, bringing much-needed reinvestment to poorer neighborhoods such as the Lower East Side, was fiercely opposed because it was not being channeled to upgrade the neighborhood for its residents.

The onset of recession near the end of the Koch years brought a forceful reminder of the power of larger economic forces to shape neighborhoods. In the wake of the Wall Street uncertainties of October 1987, the Lower East Side real estate market lost considerable allure.[60] New restaurants and shops continued to sprout, but so did boarded-up storefronts. Rents remained high but were compelled to pull back from the stratospheric levels of the mid-1980s. Landlords bravely asserted that money still could be made there, and yet the negotiated cross-subsidy plan's market-rate housing component drew little interest from investors. After a decade of rapid economic change, the Lower East Side seemed afflicted with what one anthropologist has called 'stalled gentrification.'[61] While many neighborhood advocates welcomed the respite, their issues of concern – shortages of affordable housing, a thriving drug trade, conflicts over public space – remained unresolved. Clearly, uncontrolled neighborhood *investment and disinvestment* – seeming opposites – both spell instability, displacement, and conflict.

Meanwhile, the election of David Dinkins as mayor in 1989 brought an end to the Koch era, though not necessarily to its policies. Dinkins assembled a diverse electoral coalition: one that included blacks, Hispanics, and white liberals; reform and regular Democrats; municipal unions and neighborhood groups, as well as business executives and major developers.[62] Candidate Dinkins promised to supplant the racial divisiveness of the previous decade with new sensitivity and mutual respect. Community groups in the Lower East Side anticipated a better relationship with City Hall – and, indeed, some were not disappointed.

Yet the heterogeneity of Dinkins' electoral coalition and the haziness of the candidate's vision augured an eventual post-election dilemma. Because recession and fiscal crisis left scant public resources with which to accommodate the coalition's multiple interests, the turning point arrived sooner, rather than later. The Dinkins campaign had not combined its message of 'racial healing' with a critique of the special powers and priorities of banks and bond-rating agencies nor with an alternative set of development and planning initiatives. These programmatic silences, when coupled with what one prominent supporter called the mayor's success in 'demobilizing the coalition that elected him,' left Dinkins with little political room for maneuver in the face of the bond-rating agencies' demands for wage and service cuts.[63]

By the end of its first 18 months in office, the Dinkins administration was pursuing a fiscal approach indistinguishable from that of the Koch years – except by a strange coupling of harsher austerity with expressions of sympathy for its victims. The social consequences of the anticipated cuts in municipal services promised to be alarming. Dinkins's re-election prospects were already being questioned.[64]

A more fundamental question concerns what kinds of political pressure from New Yorkers would be required to compel a local administration – whether headed by Dinkins or his successor – into resisting the priorities of the fiscal monitors. Also unclear is the degree to which Koch's successors will duplicate his leadership role over local development activity. As economic recovery begins to shimmer on the horizon, pressures will again mount to take public action to promote development and neighborhood reinvestment. The form such action takes will depend, in some measure, on the prevailing interpretation of the previous decade.

NOTES

1 Lisa Belkin, 'The Gentrification of the East Village,' *The New York Times*, 2 September 1984, VIII: 1; Steven A. Holmes, 'A Neighborhood Battle: Apartments or a Park,' *The New York Times*, 18 December 1989, **II**:3; John Kifner, 'Worlds Collide in Tompkins Sq. Park,' *The New York Times*, 31 July 1989, I:1.

2 Spiffing Up the Urban Heritage,' *Time*, 23 November 1987, pp. 76–9. See also many of the academic treatments in *Back to the City: Issues in Neighborhood Renovation*, ed. by Shirley Laska and Daphne Spain (Elmsford, NY: Pergamon Press, 1980).

3 Stephen Daly, 'The Shape of its Future Splits East Village,' *The New York Times*, 20 March 1983, VIII: 14.

4 David M. Gordon, 'Capitalist Development and the History of American Cities,' pp. 21–53 in William K. Tabb and Larry Sawers, eds., *Marxism and the Metropolis* (New York: Oxford University Press; second edition, 1984); William K. Tabb, 'Urban Development and Regional Restructuring, An Overview,' in Larry Sawers and William K. Tabb, eds., *Sunbelt/Snowbelt: Urban Development and Regional Restructuring* (New York: Oxford University Press, 1984); Michael Peter Smith, *City, State, and Market: The Political Economy of Urban Society* (New York: Basil Blackwell, 1988), chapter 1.

5 William K. Tabb, *The Long Default: New York City and the Urban Fiscal Crisis* (New York: Monthly Review Press, 1982), pp. 69–88.

6 Ibid., pp. 89–106; Bennett Harrison and Barry Bluestone, *The Great U-Turn: Corporate Restructuring and the Polarizing of America* (New York: Basic Books, 1988); Susan S. Fainstein, Norman I. Fainstein, Richard Child Hill, Dennis R. Judd, and Michael Peter Smith, with P. Jefferson Armistead and Marlene Keller, *Restructuring the City: The Political Economy of Urban Redevelopment* (New York: Longman, 1983).

7 John Mollenkopf, 'Economic Development,' in Charles Brecher and Raymond D. Horton, eds., *Setting Municipal Priorities, 1984* (New York: New York University Press, 1983); Robert Ponte, 'Manhattan's Real Estate Boom,' *New York Affairs* 8 (1984), pp. 18–31.
8 Robert A. Caro, *The Power Broker: Robert Moses and the Fall of New York* (New York: Vintage Books, 1974); Kenneth T. Jackson, 'The Capital of Capitalism: The New York Metropolitan Region, 1890–1940,' in Anthony Sutcliffe, ed., *Metropolis, 1890–1940* (Chicago: University of Chicago Press, 1984); Norman I. Fainstein and Susan S. Fainstein, 'The Politics of Urban Development,' *City Almanac* 17 (April 1984).
9 Tabb, *The Long Default*, pp. 21–35.
10 Norman I. Fainstein and Susan S. Fainstein, 'Economic Restructuring and the Politics of Land Use Planning in New York City,' *Journal of the American Planning Association* 53 (spring 1987), pp. 245–6. On fiscal politics, see Martin Shefter, *Political Crisis/Fiscal Crisis: The Collapse and Revival of New York City* (New York: Basic Books, 1985).
11 Major business groups included the Chamber of Commerce and Industry, New York Partnership, Economic Development Council, and the Citizens Budget Commission. The important development boosters were the Citizens Housing and Planning Council and the Real Estate Board of New York. See Shefter, *Political Crisis*, and Jim Sleeper, 'Boom and Bust with Ed Koch,' *Dissent* (fall 1987).
12 Shefter, *Political Crisis*; Fainstein and Fainstein, 'The Politics of Urban Development;' Albert Scardino, 'They'll Take Manhattan,' *New York Times Magazine*, Part 2, 7 December 1986, p. 35.
13 City of New York, 'New York City: An Economic Renaissance,' advertising supplement to *Forbes* (5 July 1982), pp. 63–4.
14 Ibid., p. 63.
15 Joyce Purnick, 'Freeze on Hiring Imposed by Koch; He Cites Economy,' *The New York Times*, 5 October 1982, I:1; Michael Goodwin, 'Koch Is Expecting City Tax Windfall,' *The New York Times*, 5 October 1984, I:1; Belkin, 'The Gentrification.' The proposal to sell Lower East Side properties (the so-called cross-subsidy plan) is described below and in chapter 14 this volume.
16 Edward G. Goetz, 'Type II Policy and Its Mandated Benefits in Economic Development,' *Urban Affairs Quarterly* 26 (December 1990), pp. 170–90; Fainstein and Fainstein, 'Economic Restructuring'; Sleeper, 'Boom and Bust'; Russell W. Baker, 'Bye Bye Bodega,' *Village Voice*, 17 October 1989; Todd Swanstrom, *The Crisis of Growth Politics: Cleveland, Kucinich, and the Challenge of Urban Populism* (Philadelphia: Temple University Press, 1985), chapter 10; Peter Dreier and W. Dennis Keating, 'The Limits of Localism: Progressive Housing Policies in Boston, 1984–1989,' *Urban Affairs Quarterly* 26 (December 1990), pp. 191–216.
17 Mollenkopf, 'Economic Developments'; Glenn von Nostitz, 'New Tax Program Is the Same Old Giveaway,' *City Limits* (April 1986), pp. 33–4; Doug Turetsky, 'Industrial Aid,' *City Limits* (April 1986), pp. 20–3.

18 Peter Marcuse, 'The State of the City's Housing,' *City Limits* (August–September 1985).

19 City of New York, Department of Housing Preservation and Development, *HPD Handbook of Programs*, October 1984; George Sternlieb and David Listokin, 'Housing,' in Charles Brecher and Raymond D. Horton, eds., *Setting Municipal Priorities, 1986* (New York: New York University Press, 1985). The study of 421a rents and exemption values is cited in Frank Domurad, 'Where Tax Dollars Went,' *City Limits* (August–September 1985), p. 27.

20 Domurad, 'Where Tax Dollars Went,' p. 26.

21 Robert Hayes, 'The Mayor and the Homeless Poor,' *City Limits* (August – September 1985), pp. 6–9.

22 Scardino, 'They'll Take Manhattan,' p. 35.

23 Alan Finder, 'Koch and LeFrak Agree on Plan for 1,200 Middle-Income Units,' *The New York Times*, 29 February 1988, I:1; Alan Finder, 'LeFrak's Offer Allows Chance for Conversions,' *The New York Times*, 2 April 1988, I:27; Alan S. Oser, 'Using Condo Sales to Assist New Rentals,' *The New York Times*, 10 April 1988, X:9; 'LeFrak Wins Development Right,' *The New York Times*, 26 May 1988, II:5; Lisa Kaplan, 'Seward Park Court Fight to Stop LeFrak Land-Grab,' *People's Press* (June 1989); Elaine Chan, 'Seward Park Battles: Court Dismisses Suit Against LeFrak,' *Peoples Press* (March 1990). In the end, LeFrak let his option drop.

24 State of New York Office, of the State Comptroller, Office of the State Deputy Comptroller for the City of New York, *New York City Planning Commission Granting Special Permits for Bonus Floor Area* (New York: 15 September 1988), p. MS-3.

25 W. Dennis Keating, 'Linking Downtown Development to Broader Community Goals: An Analysis of Linkage Policy in Three Cities,' *Journal of the American Planning Association* 52: 2 (spring 1986).

26 John Mollenkopf, 'City Planning,' in Charles Brecher and Raymond D. Horton, eds., *Setting Municipal Priorities, 1990* (New York: New York University, 1989); Fainstein and Fainstein, 'Economic Restructuring.'

27 H. V. Savitch, *Post-Industrial Cities: Politics and Planning in New York, Paris and London* (Princeton, NJ: Princeton University Press, 1989).

28 City of New York, Department of City Planning, *Private Reinvestment and Neighborhood Change*, issued March 1984.

29 Peter Marcuse, 'Abandonment, Gentrification, and Displacement: The Linkages in New York City,' in Neil Smith and Peter Williams, eds., *Gentrification of the City* (Boston: Allen & Unwin, 1986), p. 163.

30 Frank F. DeGiovanni, *Displacement Pressures in the Lower East Side* (New York: Community Service Society of New York, 1987), p. vi.

31 City of New York, Department of City Planning, *Housing Database: Public and Publicly Aided Housing in New York City: 1985 Update Volume*, pp. 18–19.

32 Domurad, 'Where Tax Dollars Went.'

33 Victor Vainio, 'Landlords Meet, Organize Against "Oppression",' *Tenant* (January 1984); William Rowen, 'The Big Rent Fix,' *City Limits* (August–September 1985); Ronald Lawson, 'The Political Face of New York's Real Estate Industry,' *New York Affairs* 6: 2 (1980), pp. 88–109.

34 Rosalyn Deutsche and Cara Gendel Ryan, 'The Fine Art of Gentrification,' *October 31* (winter 1984), pp. 91–111; Douglas C. McGill, 'Art Boom Slows in the East Village,' *The New York Times*, 25 July 1987, p. 13.

35 Rowen, 'The Big Rent Fix'; Baker, 'Bye Bye Bodega.'

36 DeGiovanni, *Displacement Pressures*; Marcuse, 'Abandonment, Gentrification and Displacement.'

37 City of New York, Department of City Planning, *Private Reinvestment*, p. 126.

38 See, for instance, Robert Schur, 'Holding the Line in the Neighborhood,' *City Limits* (June–July 1981); and Peter Marcuse, 'Gentrification, Abandonment and Displacement: Connections, Causes, and Policy Responses in New York City,' *Journal of Contemporary Law* 28 (1985), p. 195.

39 Richard Goldstein, 'The Gentry Comes to the East Village,' *Village Voice*, 19 May 1980, p. 18; Tom Robbins, 'The Changing Face of Norfolk Street,' *City Limits* (June–July 1981); DeGiovanni, *Displacement Pressures.*

40 See Anne Bowler and Blaine McBurney, 'Gentrification and the Avant-Garde in New York's East Village,' *Realm Working Paper No. 4* (New York: New School for Social Research, Aug. 1989). The term 'marginal gentrifiers' is taken from Damaris Rose, 'Rethinking Gentrification: Beyond the Uneven Development of Marxist Urban Theory,' *Society and Space* 2 (1984), pp. 47–74.

41 Janet Abu-Lughod, 'Tompkins Square,' *Realm Working Paper No. 1* (New York: New School for Social Research, December 1988) based on official print-outs by addresses; City of New York, Department of General Services, Division of Real Property, *IPIS Database* (February 1991).

42 'HPD's "Child" Matures: Rehabs Set to Start,' *City Limits* (November 1978).

43 Harry DeRienzo and Joan B. Allen, *The New York City In Rem Housing Program: A Report* (New York: New York Urban Coalition, January 1985), p. 43.

44 Steven Katz and Margit Mayer, 'Gimme Shelter: Self-Help Housing Struggles Within and Against the State in New York City and West Berlin,' *International Journal of Urban and Regional Research* 9: 1 (1985); Harry DeRienzo, 'The Public Housing New York City Didn't Want,' *City Limits* (August–September 1985).

45 Ronald Lawson, 'Tenant Responses to the Urban Housing Crisis, 1970–1984,' in Ronald Lawson and Mark Naison, eds., *The Tenant Movement in New York City, 1904–1984*, (New Brunswick, NJ: Rutgers University Press, 1986), p. 241.

46 Tim Ledwith, 'Lower East Side Tenants: Squatters or Homesteaders?' *City Limits* (November 1981); Leslie Bennetts, 'Lower East Siders Assail Proposal to Destroy Drug Trade Buildings,' *The New York Times*, 22 July 1982, **II**:5; Rob DeRocker, 'Housing Agency Plans to Auction In Rem Holdings,' *The Villager*, 27 May 1982.

47 Leslie Bennetts, '16 Tenements to Become Artist Units in City Plan,' *The New York Times*, 4 May 1982, II:6; Grace Glueck, 'The Mayor's Lower East Side Story: Tenements into Co-ops for Artists,' *The New York Times*, 11 August 1981, III:9.

48 Marshall Berman, 'A Struggle to the Death in Which Both Sides Are Right,' *Village Voice*, 12 July 1983; Richard Goldstein, 'Why Artists' Housing Went Down,' *Village Voice*, 22 February 1983, p. 41.

49 The gentrification of SoHo is treated in Sharon Zukin, *Loft Living: Culture and Capital in Urban Change* (Baltimore: Johns Hopkins University Press, 1982). The mayor's suggestion for the South Bronx is reproduced in Chuck Delaney, 'Lofts for Whose Living?' *City Limits* (October 1981), p. 20.

50 Goldstein, 'Why Artists' Housing Went Down,' p. 41.

51 'This Land is Ours,' *City Limits* (June–July 1984), pp. 20–2; Lower East Side Joint Planning Council, 'This Land is Ours: A Strategy for the Preservation and Development of Affordable Housing on the Lower East Side' (March 1984).

52 Joyce Purnick, 'Property Sale is Key to Plan to Renew Lower East Side,' *The New York Times*, 25 July 1984; 'Furor Over City's Lower East Side Scheme,' *City Limits* (August–September 1984), pp. 7–9; Bonnie Brower, *Missing the Mark: Subsidizing Housing for the Privileged, Displacing the Poor* (New York: Association of Neighborhood and Housing Development, Inc. and the Housing Justice Campaign, August 1989), pp. 29–30. See chapter 14 for a fuller account of the final outcome.

53 'Lower East Side Real Estate Profile,' *Real Estate Newsletter*, Manhattan edition, 16:51 (4 November 1985); 'Developers and Rehab Specialists Vie for Lower East Side Properties Not Controlled By City,' *Real Estate Newsletter*, Manhattan edition, 18:2 (24 November 1986); Janet White, 'Real Estate Resurgence Continues in East Village as Property Values Soar,' *Real Estate Newsletter*, Manhattan edition, 19:2 (23 November 1987).

54 Ibid.

55 Memorandum of Understanding between Manhattan Community Board 3 and City of New York's Department of Housing Preservation and Development, 30 September 1987.

56 The accusation, on which the HPD commissioner declined comment, is reported in Alan Finder, 'Lower East Side Housing: Plans and Conflict,' *The New York Times*, 14 May 1988, p. 33. The Seward Park Extension Urban Renewal Site, where the LeFrak development was to be located, had been the focus of controversy for over two decades. In 1967, 90 Old-Law tenements were demolished under a plan to construct moderate- and middle-income housing on the site. Neighborhood groups were bitterly divided over the plan and by a subsequent concession from Mayor Lindsay's administration to build low-income apartments for some of the site tenants who had been displaced. The LeFrak proposal, after having reopened the controversy, appeared to have been abandoned by 1991, leaving the future of the site again undecided. For a political analysis of the earlier conflicts, see Sophie Gendrot and Joan Turner, 'Ethnicity and Class: Politics on Manhattan's Lower East Side,' *Ethnic Groups* 5 (1983), pp. 79–108.

57 See chapter 14 for more details.

58 Robert Fox, 'Cross-Subsidy: An Overview and Update,' *Lower East Side News* **I**:1 (February 1990); Steven Vincent, 'Waiting for Glasnost: Grassroots Democracy on the Lower East Side,' *Lower East Side News* I:1 (February 1990).

59 Belkin, 'The Gentrification'; Kifner, 'Worlds Collide,' B:5.

60 Peter Grant, 'The Lower East Side: "It's All Going to Come Up One Day",' *New York Observer*, 14 March 1988.

61 Brett Williams, *Upscaling Downtown: Stalled Gentrification in Washington, DC* (Ithaca, NY: Cornell University Press, 1988).

62 Frank Lynn, 'Dinkins Team: Old Hands Join a Few Newcomers,' *The New York Times*, 4 November 1989, p. 29; Sam Roberts, 'Dinkins Gaining Support Among Business Executives,' *The New York Times*, 26 September 1989, II:1.

63 Sam Roberts, 'Gadflies of Today Parcel the Blame among Old Allies,' *The New York Times*, 1 July 1991, II:1.

64 And indeed, Dinkins did lose to Giuliani in the mayoral race of 1993.

Part III

Contesting Community: the Issues and the Protagonists

The people of the Lower East Side may have been victimized, but they have never been merely the passive victims of outsiders. As we have seen, many of the latter had 'designs on' or 'plans for' the area. Planners and developers came and went with remarkable regularity. Occasionally, strong city officials intervened directly, most notably Robert Moses (who is still a neighborhood anathema to many old-timers), or more regularly indirectly, as they did in the 'incentive' era of Koch. But the results they achieved on the Lower East Side were always less than they had hoped for. To some extent, the problems were just too large and too complex to be 'fixed,' either by private agents (whether settlement workers or real estate magnates) or by government officials (from the few well-intended, such as Mayor John Lindsay, to others, typically less benign). But to some extent the plans of outsiders were always confounded and sometimes defeated by the sheer intransigence of Lower East Siders of all stripes. Passivity was not their strong suit.

In part III we demonstrate this by looking first at a number of recent controversies that have resulted in conflict and sometimes even in violence. In conflict situations, events look different to the various protagonists. Rather than place ourselves 'above' the conflicts, we have tried in the next few chapters to capture this indeterminancy. The section begins with the viewpoint of a middle-class progressive academician who has lived just opposite Tompkins Square Park for over two decades. Her account unwittingly reveals some of the dilemmas of being politically committed while also being a property owner. The section then moves to a collage that tries to reconstruct a picture of recent conflict in the area – based upon direct observations, interviewing, newspaper accounts, and amateur video recordings. While this may not be a balanced or 'truthful' description of recent battles over the neighborhood, it is more detailed and specific than the usual shorthanded accounts of neighborhood conflicts. The truth *is* in the details, for only they can capture the complexity of the shifting subgroups and alignments in the neighborhood. The three anti-gentrification perspectives that have diverged in the past few years are those of the homeless, the squatters, and the housing reformers.[1] The three chapters devoted to these groups – each done by a different researcher sympathetic to the group studied – attempt to capture the viewpoints of these community actors with very different diagnoses of causes and different interests and visions of solution. The efficacy of each group's efforts to shape the future is evaluated in the concluding chapter.

NOTES

1 The term 'housing reformers' is somewhat misleading. Indeed, almost every institutional 'actor' in the Lower East involved with the housing question

would like to be classified as a 'reformer.' Our treatment is not exhaustive. Among the many community organizations we do *not* discuss specifically are Cooper Square, Goles (Good Ole Lower East Side), Rain, Charas, etc. Unable to do justice to the complexity of organizations on the Lower East Side – a suitable topic for another book – we have chosen to focus on the framers of the cross-subsidy plan because of its centrality to the topic of this book. We are very conscious of the fact that we are missing an important analysis of the internal political organization of the local Latino community. Our attempts to locate a researcher able and willing to work in this community ended in failure; the absence of the Puerto Rican voice remains a defect of our analysis.

10

A Resident's View of Conflict on Tompkins Square Park

Diana R. Gordon

For more than twenty years I have lived on the north side of Tompkins Square Park, in a neighborhood where intense and varied conflict over public questions is the norm. Recurring subjects of dispute include the ownership, occupancy and use of private and public space, the control of individual (and animal) behavior, and the role of regulatory authorities like the police and parks departments. Contests have involved a range of disputants:

- Resident vs resident on the individual level – for example, should dogs be allowed in the park, and if so, should they be leashed?
- Resident vs resident on the group level – for example, anarchists and yuppies fight over whether the city should enforce rules about drinking and sleeping in the park.
- Resident vs representatives of the state – individuals and groups, such as neighborhood, housing and development organizations or religious leaders, conflict with the police or community board concerning the use of force or a park curfew.
- Resident vs non-resident land owner or landlord – in a general movement to resist gentrification, residents fight both private and public landlords.

Underlying these contests are deep cleavages of personal and social morality, the meaning of community, the nature and power of rights, and the proper role of the state.

In this chapter I provide some background on the history of conflicts in the area and present three cases of neighborhood conflict that occurred within a two-block radius of the northern half of Tompkins Square Park, examining their dynamics more as a resident observer than as a social scientist. I end with a discussion of three possible explanations for why conflict persists in this neighborhood of the Lower East Side.

My 'insider's view' of the conflicts during the period between 1960 and 1990 arises from my limited perspective and is by no means comprehensive. It leaves out the large range of group conflicts that involve my lower-income neighbors who live farther back from the park. These neighbors are more intensely involved with the use of city-owned properties, organizing against drug dealing on their streets and in apartments, controlling police violence and intrusion, demanding better municipal service delivery, and setting local standards for public education.

Instead of analyzing these conflicts, I will provide both generalizations and a mouse's-eye view, based on my own involvement in three episodes of conflict that have arisen since the mid-1960s: the fight over uses of Christodora House, a large building on the east side of the park; the dispute on my block over the arrival of Project Contact, a drug program run by the Educational Alliance; and the conflict over the tent city of homeless people which sprang up in Tompkins Square Park in 1989. My cases all concern land-use disputes, not surprising in an area where space is at a premium and where escalating housing costs push even middle-class people out of the city. Residents' claims in the conflicts often have a strongly moral flavor; the righteousness of the claimants or those whom they represent has shaped resolutions as much as need, right or efficiency.

Tompkins Square's history reflects many themes of American urban social history – settlement by working-class immigrants and migrants, continuing conflict over scarce resources, and the effort of elites to impose various kinds of discipline on the 'lower' classes.[1] Tompkins Square was one of the five public squares built following the original grid plan for Manhattan. Although it was created by draining and filling in a swamp in 1834, it never served as the playground for gentry who were expected to inhabit elegant homes surrounding the park. Instead, German and Irish immigrants working in the new shipping industry lived in tenements to the south and east of the park.[2] Their protests against joblessness, which they took to the park in 1857 and 1874, were forerunners of later activism.[3] In January 1874, municipal police attacked 7,000 workers and their families who had gathered in the park to press for public aid for the unemployed, arresting 46 and causing many injuries. Samuel Gompers, who later was to found the American Federation of Labor, was present and described the police action as 'an orgy of brutality.'[4]

The animus behind the police riot of 1874 reflected a general disdain for immigrant workers. Some 'more assimilated' Americans perceived immigrants as an ignorant mob holding dangerous foreign ideas. Such a perspective also informed the turn-of-the-century social reformers who tried to introduce immigrants to 'civilizing' influences through camps, schools, and recreational activities. They hoped their efforts would pacify restless dissidents and transmit northern European culture to those Lower East Side residents who came from southern and eastern Europe.[5] Tompkins Square Park became a center for many of their services for adults and children. (The northwest corner continues to be the site of the first Boys' Club in the United States, founded during this period.)

The conflicts of the late twentieth century, like those of earlier times, often stemmed from resistance to far-away domination of basic resources such as work, housing, and public space. During the years I have lived in the East Village, the uses and control of residential and recreational space have been continuing sources of tension. Defiance of official social control is still met with official violence. I moved into the neighborhood shortly after the Memorial Day riot of 1967, when the police took their nightsticks to 'flower children' in the park. More recently, I have observed the clashes of 1988 and 1990, when the police beat people who resisted their orders to vacate the park and its bandshell.[6]

Resident-to-resident conflict also predates the 1960s, although it is harder to trace. *Call It Sleep*, Henry Roth's great novel of the Lower East Side, set in the first decade of the twentieth century, conveys the violence of crowded, angry people struggling to reach across barriers of language and culture. Race and class are new cleavages dividing Lower East Side residents today, but the messages of suspicion and outrage my neighbors send to one another sound in some ways like those of Roth's characters.

CHRISTODORA HOUSE

Towering over Tompkins Square in the mid-1960s was a nearly empty, 16-story city-owned building, built in 1928 as a 'skyscraper settlement house.' Originally, reformers had hoped that this residential hotel of 240 light, pleasant rooms on the top floors would generate enough income to support the community activities in the floors below, which housed a paneled library, a concert hall, a large swimming pool, a gym, and classrooms.[7] Sold to New York City in 1947 when rent control made the building's varied uses uneconomical, Christodora House had gone into decline, and by the 1960s only a small portion of it was in use as a welfare center and storage space. Dilapidated but sturdy, in the spring of 1967 it became the focus of residents' desire for a community center that could house athletic and cultural activities, buying clubs, and training programs.

A small group named itself the 'Committee for a Tompkins Square Community Center' and appointed a young, black, Spanish-speaking man named Bob Collier to head the campaign. He began negotiating with officials of the New York City Parks Department, which controlled all recreational uses of city-owned property, for the right to use a room at the Christodora to serve as a community-center office, as well as for a reopening of its pool and gymnasium.

The diversity of neighborhood people who got involved in this project was as striking as the energies and enthusiasms of the group planning the community center. The wife of a local doctor collected donations of paint from neighborhood hardware stores. Neighborhood youths painted the office and the gym. A local artist planned to hold children's art classes in the building, and a former circus performer was interested in starting a juggling and acrobatics program. Politicians went out of their way to express support for the effort, particularly after the 1967 Memorial Day weekend riot when police came in swinging in answer to a complaint that hippies were sprawled on park grass during a rock music festival. Lorraine Miller, a local lawyer who had made an unsuccessful bid for State Assemblywoman, interested Manhattan Borough President Percy Sutton in the project and brought the Lower East Side's city council member to visit the building.

But the Parks Department and the Urban Task Force set up by Mayor John Lindsay to keep the lid on low-income neighborhoods during the long hot summers of the late 1960s, could not keep their promises of supplies and personnel for a modest program. The pool cost too much to fix; pool cue replacements and chalk could not be purchased because they were not listed on the standard Parks Department requisition forms; and the department was simply too centralized and too traditional to support unplanned neighborhood capital projects. While brahmins of Mayor Lindsay's city government held ideas about decentralizing authority and shaping programs to fit neighborhood needs, neither Lindsay's young Turks nor the agency's old-line bureaucrats could shift the balance of power between government and citizens.

For their part, the residents kept escalating their demands. Initially seeking a couple of rooms for a community center, residents developed larger ambitions of making municipal government work for them and of testing the value of fundamental political participation. Broadening the scope of demands created raised expectations for 'citizen participation' in decisions about how public goods would be used. The Parks Department officials had wanted to provide a limited range of services that would marginally increase opportunities for recreation in the Tompkins Square area. The Tompkins Square Community Center workers, however, wanted help in building a permanent institution, a symbol of their dreams for improving and integrating the community.

Even without the facilities and services they thought they had been promised, the small band of community workers, high school drop-outs, and housewives began to operate a variety of activities, such as basketball, karate, and tutoring, in the lower floors of the Christodora House. Community meetings were held in the building during the evening and small steps toward harmony and community in the neighborhood were taken. One night, informal negotiations between Puerto Rican gang leaders, members of a hippie group called the Diggers, and heads of various community projects resulted in a 'peace treaty' among the gangs and between the gangs and the hippies. On Thanksgiving, *The New York Times* reported that local merchants and community organizations had contributed free food for a dinner at the center, and that 'the hippies and Puerto Ricans, who have been antagonistic in this hippie enclave of the East Village, joined in the feast in apparent friendliness.'[8]

But this was a fragile and fleeting achievement. Clashes between various factions of residents and between supporters of the center and city officials became more frequent and acrimonious during 1968. Six months after he took over leadership of the Tompkins Square Community Center, Bob Collier was publicly revealed to have been released on federal parole the previous year, having been convicted of conspiracy to bomb the Washington Monument, the Liberty Bell, and the Statue of Liberty as a means of drawing attention to the oppression of blacks. The revelation undermined his authority. Although a private donor was found to provide his salary, the Civil Service Commission refused to approve his appointment. The information also strengthened the pre-existing doubts of more conservative members of the Tompkins Square community about his chaotic organizational style and the way he managed building activities. It was alleged that the building was harboring drug addicts and revolutionaries, an image based on credible reports of glue sniffing by truant adolescents in the basement and the open distribution of Black Panther literature and circulars recruiting cane-pickers for the Cuban Venceremos Brigade. In addition, careless representations by city officials about how they would try to help with the center were interpreted as unkept promises by frustrated community residents. This ongoing clash culminated in a disastrous struggle over whether to give a group of community residents legal control over the whole building.

This sad tale is too complicated to recount fully in this space. Briefly, a mayor's aide had agreed to get the relevant city agencies – the departments of Real Estate, Parks, and Public Works, and the Urban Task Force program – to consider leasing Christodora House for a nominal sum to a board of governors composed of a representative group of community residents. After the board was formed, the aide signed a letter setting out the respective duties of the city and the board, which the Tompkins Square residents interpreted as conveying binding promises, despite a final sentence which read: 'Finally, my involvement with the project is contingent upon the understanding that the Board of Governors is a functioning representative group from the Tompkins Square community that could supply the funds needed to maintain and operate the building.'

Not only did the city not keep its 'promises,' but in February 1969 police from the Ninth Precinct raided the building and forcibly closed it, enforcing an eviction notice from the city Department of Real Estate. The city's stated reasons for the raid were the mess in the gym caused by the remains of clothing donated for the 1968 Poor People's campaign and the continuing deterioration of the physical facility, e.g., the elevators had broken down and some of the repairs made by community residents had not withstood hard use. But the police broke furniture and confiscated files in the raid, suggesting that other motives were present. In interviews with city officials conducted shortly afterward, no one even pretended that the mess in the building was the real reason for shutting down the center.

Although the city insisted that a long-term lease of Christodora House with a community group was still possible, after the raid the community's leverage with the city was weakened and the factionalism which had always been a community problem became insurmountable. The board of governors collapsed almost immediately, and the city rejected a successor group, claiming that it represented only the 'radical fringe' in the area. A third committee, drawn from a broad range of grassroots groups and stable service organizations of the Lower East Side, fared somewhat better, but was able to obtain only an 11-month lease from the city, with the stipulation that during that period both parties would work toward a longer-term arrangement.

The shifting leadership of the movement to take over Christodora House and the lack of assurance that the building would belong to the community made it very difficult for residents to raise the money needed. The Department of Real Estate, in conjunction with involved community organizations, prepared a 35-year lease for the approval of the city's Board of Estimate (a body composed of the Mayor, the City Council President, the Comptroller, and the five Borough Presidents, now superseded) which had the final word on leases of more than one year. After several votes to postpone consideration of the lease, the Board of Estimate finally voted in late 1970 to table the proposal indefinitely, thwarting hopes for community control held by both the Tompkins Square residents and by some of the mayor's men.

[illegible] the final decision (or the non-decision that con-st[illegible]rmal level) came from policy makers far from the sit[illegible] were unable and probably unwilling to evaluate the [illegible]'s capacity to deliver on its promise to build a neighborhood institution. The threat of further politicization of the neighborhood was more real to the Board of Estimate than the prospect of new services and recreational activities, and that body exercised its distributive role to exclude Tompkins Square as a constituent power base.

The Christodora House struggle may have been a precursor of the conversion of the Tompkins Square neighborhood from a predominantly working-class enclave to a target of gentrification without a strong community capacity to resist. The city sold the building in 1975 for $62,500 to a Brooklyn real estate developer who specialized in subsidized low-income housing. The building changed hands twice more, selling for almost $3 million in 1984, even though it was undeveloped and more dilapidated than ever. In 1987 it became a luxury co-op, subsidized by tax abatements that probably cost the city more than the amount even the most aggressive community resident had requested for the center. The developers demanded one million dollars for the penthouse apartment, which Cher was rumored to have purchased.

The economic 'improvements' of the area through gentrification have not brought with them efforts to develop a community center, although in a move that some neighborhood activists contend is a form of pacification by the city government, the Department of Housing Preservation and Development has granted control of other buildings to artists and social service providers for non-political ventures.

Project Contact

During the early 1970s, one of the dominant forms of community involvement in New York City neighborhoods became the block association. Organized by individual home owners and tenants, but sometimes supported with modest foundation grants or city grants and services, the associations deal with a wide range of issues, from public safety (neighborhood watch programs) to block amenities such as trees. Sometimes the groups address more intangible yearnings for community and communication by sponsoring such activities as parties and athletic events.

Many of these block associations collapse after an early burst of enthusiasm for democratic neighborhood organization. Initial projects are completed, ongoing projects take more commitment than anticipated, or people discover they don't like their neighbors well enough for sustained participation in social activities with them. Perhaps some members acquire an uneasy sense that block associations deflect demands for real neighborhood change.

Conflict can play a major role in creating and sustaining a block association. On the Lower East Side, this seems to be the norm. In early 1975, a nearly-defunct block association was given new vitality when a social service organization bought a vacant brownstone on the north side of Tompkins Square Park to house a non-residential drug treatment program for adolescents and adults. This perceived threat to public safety and property values mobilized the largely white, middle- and working-class residents of Tenth Street between Avenues A and B to fight Project Contact and its sponsor, the Educational Alliance. (Educational Alliance had originally been founded by German-American Jews in 1893 to educate, acculturate, and contain the immigrant masses flowing into the Lower East Side.)

Almost as soon as Project Contact had purchased the brownstone, a property owner on the block organized several tenants and owners to protest the projected use of the building. To mobilize more supporters, they called a meeting in the nearby Boys' Club where angry residents protested that the Alliance had not told them of its plans for the building. They worried that property values might decline if it were known that drug abusers came to the block every day. They also worried that program participants would purse snatch and be a bad influence on the neighborhood's children, even though a park full of drug dealers posed a far more likely threat to residents. They planned to complain directly to Educational Alliance officials and to try to get the city to withdraw its grant for operating Project Contact. They discussed instigating city investigations into possible health and building code violations of Project Contact that could delay or even defeat the planned use of the building.

Not everyone on the block was in sympathy with the positions of the project's opponents. At a second meeting, a hastily organized opposition group appeared. This faction argued that while the Alliance had shown a poor sense of community relations, little evidence existed that social ills would result from the project, and that opposition to the program was probably unwarranted or at least premature. This second group was made up of residents who tended to have more formal schooling and were more liberal politically than the program's opponents, and the cultural gaps between the factions soon became chasms that added intensity to the already highly charged issue of the drug treatment program. Nonetheless, the move to oppose Project Contact was defeated in that second meeting, and the group proffered the project a provisional welcome. Those attending the Boys' Club meetings decided they should revive the block association to provide both a means to channel complaints to the Educational Alliance and a democratic forum for defusing the antagonisms among residents which sometimes threatened to erupt into violence.

The decision to revive the block association and use it to negotiate with Project Contact brought with it a contest for leadership. Not surprisingly, the two candidates for president were at loggerheads over what position the block association should take on Contact. After they got into a fist fight on the sidewalk outside the meeting where the vote was scheduled, a third compromise candidate was hastily nominated and elected. He proved to be both a strong force for conciliation and an energetic proponent of other roles for the block association. He was able to express the neighbors' concerns when Project Contact participants went up on the roof to smoke, but he also threw himself into steering the block association toward social activities that would minimize the conflicting interests of people on the block and stress their commonalities.

Despite its disputatious birth, the block association quickly became an integrating force in the neighborhood. For three years it sponsored a community square dance, complete with cake decorating and other contests, and it continues to hold a pot luck supper at Christmas. Starting in 1978, it organized an annual art show which has become a substantial enterprise (now run by a spin-off organization); it was held in the park every June (until the 1991 park closing). It has also provided social services in emergencies. When a fire severely damaged a building on the block, the group organized the neighbors to offer temporary shelter and storage for the tenants; block association members also met with the absentee landlord of the building to dissuade him from abandoning it.

On the surface it would appear that the institution-building of the block association served to depoliticize the original issue of Project Contact's presence on the block, and therefore to weaken the 'conservative' faction's claims for cleanliness, order, and the maintenance of property values. But subsequent events suggest another conclusion. With the weakening of the most local units of the Democratic party structure in New York City, both the executive and the legislative branches of local government have tapped neighborhood associations as important sources of political intelligence and recipients of political favors. As increasingly credible representatives of neighborhood concerns, however unrepresentative they may actually be of the residents, block associations have acquired access to politically powerful people and institutions, especially when they form coalitions. A sign of the rewards of this development can be seen in the June 1990 meeting of the Tompkins Square Park Neighborhood Coalition, held at the same Boys' Club where the initial meeting to protest Project Contact was held. The coalition called on the city to enforce Parks Department rules about noise, drinking, and sleeping in the park. About twenty police officers attended the meeting, parking several police vans ostentatiously at the entrance of the building. Blue police barricades created a corridor from the sidewalk into the auditorium, even though only about 150 people could fit into the meeting space. The message was clear. The conservatives had been able to mobilize the local governmental authority.

Tent City

On 14 December 1989, a day of freezing temperatures, police officers and Parks Department employees took down about 45 plastic tents and makeshift shelters in Tompkins Square Park that housed some 90 homeless people. The number of park residents had recently been diminishing, down from the 300 who had lived in the park the preceding summer. Large Parks Department trucks hauled away tons of old clothes, building materials, and debris. Teams of parks workers raked up the refuse left behind, trying to make the park usable once more for other members of the neighborhood (see Greshof and Dale, chapter 12).

Neighborhood reactions to the sweep, which had been rumored for weeks, were very mixed. A small group of protesters in the park booed the workers and shouted 'Sieg Heil' at the commander of the Ninth Precinct. Some neighborhood residents did not come out to protest but, angry at the city's general unwillingness to take long-term measures to address the housing crisis of low-income New Yorkers, believed the homeless should be allowed to stay in the park. Others were sympathetic to the plight of the homeless but felt that the interest of the community as a whole in the use of this public space outweighed the needs of the homeless. Still others were unambivalently glad to see the tent city demolished, arguing that the homeless brought addiction and prostitution with them. They asserted that many of them were actually anarchist squatters, that is, 'voluntary homeless' with a political agenda, rather than 'truly needy people.'

This diversity of views had sparked community conflict for many months before the sweep. Civic and block associations were internally divided over whether or not to ask the city to act, and what to ask it to do. Community spokespersons interviewed by the media reported the facts in such divergent ways that less involved residents could not figure out what was going on in their own neighborhood. Heavy police protection became necessary to maintain minimal order at meetings of the community board and its parks subcommittee after a self-proclaimed anarchist group threw cat feces during one dispute. Sidewalk conversations between long-time neighbors became increasingly strained because it was impossible to avoid taking a position on the homeless in the park.

The conflict among neighborhood groups had many dimensions. Beyond the question of the homeless in the park was the larger issue of social and legal ownership of the neighborhood. Some saw gentrification as an immediate cause of the park problem and a future threat to their own housing security. Others hailed gentrification as the most promising force for 'revitalization' of the community – enhancing their property values, making the streets safer, and holding back the immigrant tide. In an odd twist, the long-term residents who were working-class Ukrainians, Poles and Italians seemed more likely to support what they sometimes called the 'new neighborhood' than the more middle-class artists and professionals who moved in before the gentrification wave of the 1980s and might have more in common with the new gentrifiers.

Both sides struggled to appropriate legal concepts to their political and moral battles. The white working-class residents drew on formal notions of law and rights to argue that the homeless should be evicted from the park and that heavier police guard should protect the property interests of people in the Christodora House – the co-op that had become the hated symbol of yuppie invasion to the homeless and their champions. The longer-term professional people – some of them 1960s activists settled into calmer middle-aged social concerns – were more likely to be vaguely concerned with fairness and the definition of a new right to housing, and were consequently without a practical program to resolve the current conflict.

In the weeks before the 1989 sweep, the anger of those most antagonistic to the people in the park became very focused. Memos left on every doorstep argued that the law was not being enforced in the park. An appendix to the longest memo set forth park rules regarding the use of benches, camping, fires, dumping, among other things. Together, the memos transmitted the underlying message that park residents were filthy, disgusting, and dangerous. The memo writers wanted to defend themselves against offensive sights, smells, and immoral influences, using the language of park rules and regulations; but their claims were no more legitimized than those of the homeless advocates, who argued for a universal right to shelter.

EXPLANATIONS

Why should conflicts arise and remain salient so consistently in the East Village? In what follows, I argue that out of three overlapping explanations, the most useful may be one which centers on the tensions arising from migration to the area.

Hypothesis 1: Demographics as Destiny

The first hypothesis suggests that endemic mutual hostility generates out of the diversity of the population, which is heterogeneous ethnically, economically, occupationally, and politically. Of the ten subareas of Manhattan studied in a 1987 housing and vacancy survey, the Lower East Side was one of four areas with substantial percentages of at least three different racial or ethnic groupings, including white, black, Asian, and Hispanic.[9]

Several months before the 1989 sweep of the homeless, *The New York Times* described the park as a reflection of the neighborhood:

> where elderly Poles and Ukrainians hold down their benches on the west side, while younger Puerto Ricans, blacks, Cubans and Jamaicans come in from the blocks to the east . . . Skateboarders, basketball players, mothers with small children, radicals looking like 1960s retreads, spikey-haired punk rockers in torn black, skinheads in heavy work boots looking to beat up the radicals and punks, Rastafarians with dreadlocks, heavy-metal bands, chess players, dog walkers all occupy their spaces in the park, along with the professionals carrying their dry-cleaned suits to the renovated 'gentrified' buildings that are changing the character of the neighborhood.[10]

The increasingly varied economic positions of those who participate in neighborhood conflicts have given rise to very different stakes among activists, particularly since the mid-1980s:

- the poor families and young singles are most concerned with preserving low-income housing;
- the artists add to that concern an interest in preserving the area's diversity and color;
- the long-term, middle- and working-class home owners prize general stability and keep an eye on real estate values;
- the new yuppie residents value order and the conventional esthetics of an urban neighborhood with amenities;
- the homeless, including a sizable group of squatters, while only occasionally heard in public debates, are a constant reminder to the rest of the neighborhood that housing is scarce and the social welfare 'safety net' is porous. Within that group, the anarchists dramatize political defiance of the state as it both constructs and constricts that net.

With such a variety of stakes in the neighborhood, solidarity seems likely to be elusive. But how is conflict generated? Do the demographics of the community's population create a dynamic of conflict? Or do significant outsiders such as the police, developers, planners, and the media respond to the polyglot needs and demands of residents in ways that generate conflict? The heterogeneity hypothesis seems useful but incomplete.

Hypothesis 2: the Custom of the Neighborhood

Another explanation lies in the cultural and historical traditions of the area, with its extensive network of tenant organizations and community groups. I have already pointed to the legacy of conflict from the 1870s and later Tompkins Square riots, as well as to the way settlement houses contained and organized neighborhood protest. The strength of this explanation is evident in the pride residents take in their ability to organize meetings and protests at the drop of a hat. Social welfare professionals refer to the area as the most organized in the city, and this characteristic stems from a century of experience, encouraged by community organizers from earlier eras.

But this hypothesis, resting on custom as the catalyst for social action, is also incomplete. It accepts the custom of organization and social conflict as a given, needing no explanation.[11] But why did the tradition of conflict develop? Is an underlying rationality at work in the generation of conflicts, rather than an instinctive tendency of residents to follow past practices? The demographic makeup of the neighborhood has changed a great deal since the Tompkins Square riot of 1874 and the paternalistic control of social reformers at the turn-of-the-century. Yet the social dynamic has prevailed. Something more is needed to explain the stimulus, timing, and evolution of conflicts.

Hypothesis 3: an Identity of Impermanence

A third hypothesis, which I favor, is a conflict theory. The Lower East Side in general, and the Tompkins Square area in particular, is constantly changing and perceives itself to be perpetually under siege from invaders of one kind or another – in this sense, it is the Sicily of Manhattan. The very nature of the neighborhood is continually contested. From the military that used Tompkins Square Park as a parade ground after the Civil War to the art entrepreneurs who lined the streets with limousines in the early 1980s, occupation seems the norm. Most recently, the poor, minorities, and clergy have voiced the persistent suspicion that public and private elites intend to develop luxury housing and chic boutiques for white-collar workers in a neighborhood seen as the last 'undeveloped' area near Wall Street.

The working-class Lower East Side has been a neighborhood of transition and transience for most of its history. It achieved an identity as a point of entry and exit even before the wave of immigration from eastern and southern Europe began around 1875. The initial population of Irish and German workers lived in hastily-erected tenements built in the 1840s and 1850s on the side streets surrounding the park. The nationalities and cultures (and now, the economic status) of new arrivals have changed, of course. Puerto Ricans came after World War II, Dominicans in the 1970s, and Asians and yuppies most recently. But the image and the reality of an identity of impermanence have prevailed. Where perhaps it might be possible to find relatively fixed cultural characteristics in wealthier neighborhoods, the Lower East Side is identified primarily in terms of its continual state of flux.

This quality creates a special kind of political geography. By definition, residents of this area are themselves invaders, only slightly less outsiders to one another than those who are perceived as succeeding to their turf. And how can their turf be claimed, if it is defined as always in transition? In other neighborhoods, residents can resolve many problems based on their mutual and unstated understanding of established avenues and strategies of influence. The parallel is perhaps the way government and business interact in policy making, with explicit bargaining less common than an unstated reciprocity which serves to organize production and allocate resources.[12] Problems that other neighborhoods absorb, overlook, or handle by a mutual exchange of benefits, become head-to-head controversies around Tompkins Square. Groups in the Lower East Side must first establish their standing to make a claim, even before they can assert the claim itself. Those responding to the claim, similarly, are likely to explicitly or implicitly challenge the claimant's authority. The two-step problem-solving process results in innovation, not routine, with all the risks that implies.

It is easy to see conflict in this environment as a manifestation of alienation, but I have come to the conclusion that it is also an expression of community. When residents fight back against external forces such as the police, they build solidarity, at least momentarily. And at least some of the fights among the residents have tightened social bonds in the neighborhood by providing opportunities for communication. Lower East Siders are proud of their fights. They complain about landlords and cops and dog-owners and junkies as though someone were going to listen to these complaints, even when past experience suggests their plaints will be ignored.

Even now, with the odds against them, residents of the Tompkins Square area are organizing to fight gentrification with still more demonstrations and meetings and teach-ins. Their vision is of a neighborhood where recent immigrants, artists, youth, the poor, and working people can find space, shelter and privacy for a reasonable price. Such an identity is surely worth fighting for.

NOTES

1 Herbert Gutman, 'The Tompkins Square Riot in New York City on January 13, 1874: A Re-examination of Its Causes and Its Aftermath,' *Labor History* 6 (winter 1965), pp. 45–70.

2 Marci Reaven, 'Tompkins Square: Past and Present,' unpublished paper accompanying exhibit sponsored by the Municipal Arts Society, New York City, 1989. But see also Reaven and Houck, chapter 4.

3 Bill Weinberg, 'Legacy of Rebellion: Tompkins Square and the Lower East Side,' *Downtown*, 14 February 1990. The original source cited by all scholars remains the article by Gutman, 'The Tompkins Square Riot.'

4 Gutman, 'The Tompkins Square Riot,' p. 55.

5 Cary Goodman, *Choosing Sides: Playground and Street Life on the Lower East Side* (New York: Schocken Books, 1979).

6 I missed the June 1991 closing of the park because I was overseas at the time.

7 Diana R. Gordon, 'The Sixteen-Story Misunderstanding,' in Diana R. Gordon, *City Limits: Barriers to Change in Urban Government* (New York: Charterhouse, 1973).

8 *The New York Times*, 24 November 1967, p. 50. See also Craig Unger, 'The Lower East Side: There Goes the Neighborhood,' *New York* magazine, 28 May 1984, pp. 32–41, which depends on this.

9 Michael Stegman, *Housing and Vacancy Report: New York City, 1987* (City of New York, Housing Preservation and Development, 1988), Table 7.4.

10 *The New York Times*, 31 July 1989, p. B1.

11 Robert Kidder, *Connecting Law and Society* (Englewood Cliffs, NJ: Prentice Hall, 1983), pp. 51–5.

12 Charles Lindblom, *The Policy-Making Process* (Englewood Cliffs, NJ: Prentice Hall, 1980), pp. 72–6.

Plate 11.1 Political activism in the East Village
Source: Courtesy of Marlis Momber

11

The Battle for Tompkins Square Park

Janet Abu-Lughod

Some points in space seem to perpetuate their mystique far beyond what chance would predict. Certain cities, for example, occupy spaces that time and time again tend to be singled out as sacred sites. Archaeologists probing the depths of the earth discover strata of holy space shaped by successive peoples whose religions have changed but whose religious edifices are layered one above the other. In much the same way, albeit with respect to more profane activities, certain urban spaces serve a recurring function – as places for protest. One thinks immediately of Bastille Square in Paris, Hyde Park in London, and Independence Square in Philadelphia. In Lower Manhattan a few sites have come to be associated with politically charged protest: the park in front of City Hall, Union Square (which has hosted speeches, rallies and labor mobilizations), and Tompkins Square Park.

It is often difficult to explain exactly why *these* spaces and not others should be singled out as protest sites. A *sine qua non*, and a characteristic of all of them, is that in the densely built-up city they offer sufficient open space to permit large crowds to assemble. Second, they are *public* spaces. Government ownership gives people the *right* to be there, without running afoul of private property restrictions.[1] But at the risk of seeming too mystical or romantic, one must also acknowledge that these zones are also *symbolic* spaces, deriving significance from historic precedents. Participants in later protests may recall earlier struggles and have their collective resolve strengthened by the connection, through social memory, to past battles.

Today, this symbolism is often reinforced and intensified by the mass media. The press associates certain highly visible and well publicized events with specific places which become emblematic of certain political positions. Thus, Central Park's recurring Earth Day celebrations continue to be linked symbolically to the 'love-ins' of the 1960s, and one can think of other instances where organizers intentionally select a 'space of celebration' to make sentiments more vivid. In the iconography of New York, Tompkins Square Park has become enshrined as a place for 'outrageous' behavior, where violation of middle-class proprieties serves (and is seen to serve) both shock and protest functions. Persons joining such protests know this. The spectators who come to watch expect this. And the press has merely to mention that an event occurred there[2] to evoke pre-existing sympathies or animosities.

Most events in Tompkins Square Park, however, have been peaceful affairs with small ripple effects. Relatively modest in scale, they have been met with enormous tolerance, not only by fellow park users but by the police and employees of the Parks Department. Given those precedents, events that in more upscale neighborhoods might be viewed as anathema were accepted as perfectly normal, day-to-day behavior in Tompkins Square Park. What needs to be accounted for, then, is not *why* events of

Plate 11.2 Organizing another protest in Tompkins Square Park
Source: Courtesy of Marlis Momber

various kinds have periodically occurred in Tompkins Square Park, but rather, why *certain* 'outrageous' events have been tolerated whereas others have not, and even more significantly, why certain previously tolerated forms of behavior or events became, *at certain moments in the history of the neighborhood*, the focus for crackdowns, sanctions, and confrontations. Given the social law of inertia, the time-line along which most trends proceed is pretty steady. Occasionally, however, this long-term time (*la longue durée*) is interrupted by 'explosive time': historical moments when time and space compress so dramatically that, in the crucible of its compression, new trends and new coalitions evolve or are revealed. Revolutions are the most large-scale of these moments of explosive time, but local protests can also take place in explosive time.

The most significant moment in 'explosive' time in the recent history of the East Village occurred between 1988 and 1991, bracketed by the 'police riot' of August 1988, when officials attempted but failed to impose a night-time curfew on park use, and the denouement in June 1991, when some 300 police, barricading all adjacent streets and surrounding the park with 8-foot high metal fences, finally achieved that end by closing the park entirely for more than a year.[3] This chapter reviews that explosive engagement, asking *why here and why now?* As we shall argue, the most convincing explanations are to be found not in the characteristics or even in the behavior of the protesters, for these have tended for a long time to be relatively constant in quality if not in specifics, nor solely in the changing issues of contention. Rather, the deeper causes that transformed normal protest into riots and battle-like confrontations must be sought in the dialectic between internal forces and the outside arena. Because of this, we must look to larger social causes which give rise to the *specific* issues over which protests are registered and to the climate of the contest.

Our contention is that the forces of urban 'law and order' are mobilized against protest (or indeed used to intensify it) *only* when special motivation exists to buttress the interests of some players with a given stake in the area – either as residents, investors, or officials. Because of this, an analysis of the confrontational events themselves can help us in reaching a deeper understanding of the forces that have been transforming the East Village and its larger region, the Lower East Side.

Although Reaven/Houck and Gordon (in chapters 4 and 10) have both chronicled earlier protests and controversies in the park and its surrounding area, by far the largest and most violent confrontation in recent times was the one that pitted an estimated 400 police officers against hundreds of residents, visitors, and onlookers the night of 6 August and the early hours of 7 August 1988. Not since January 1874[4] had so massive and conspicuous a battle taken place in the fractious space of the Lower East Side. Covered extensively by the New York news media, it was also played up in the national press which focused the country's attention, for a brief moment at least, upon this otherwise unpublicized area.

While treated as a single event in the media, its meaning was embedded in a far more complex and prolonged struggle whose roots lay in the process of neighborhood gentrification that had been going on for at least a decade and a half (see chapters 7, 8, and 9 by Smith et al., Mele, and Sites). Reactions to this process by such key actors as the 'homeless,' the 'squatters,' and the 'housing reformers' are presented in later chapters which lay out the deeper causes of the controversies. Before these can be understood, however, we need to reconstruct the sequence of events that led up to the Saturday night battle of 6–7 August 1988 and trace what was revealed in its aftermath. The repercussions of the 'riot' are still being felt.

The 'Scene' and Preliminary Skirmishes

The summer of 1988 was a hot one in New York. The month of July had broken records for the sustained number of days with temperatures in the 90s. The tenements of the Lower East Side, notorious for their lack of adequate ventilation and their antiquated wiring, were particularly unbearable in heat, and the low incomes of most residents precluded air conditioners. Furthermore, even those fortunate enough to own air conditioners were only intermittently served, since the eastern area of Manhattan south of Fourteenth Street had routinely lost power in the worst summer overloads.[5]

In these circumstances, Tompkins Square Park had become an outdoor 'living room,' not only for nearby residents but for those from a wider sending zone. Especially on weekends, the bandshell in the park was a popular spot, with rock groups and other entertainers performing before overflow crowds. The audience was not simply drawn from the neighborhood; many others, disdainfully dubbed the 'bridge and tunnel' thrill-seekers from the suburbs and outer boroughs, drifted between the commercial and open-air clubs in the vicinity.[6] The 'scene' at these clubs does not begin until quite late, and the crescendo of sound tends to build in the early morning hours. There is some club-hopping, quite a bit of street conviviality, and often, patrons wandered into the park to enjoy the planned and unplanned concerts and 'happenings.' Much of the action is on the western edge of the park, along Avenue A.

The noise generated by such gatherings was one reason why some residents were asking the police to intervene. But some pressures to 'clean up the park' were also coming from those who sought to evict the small town of 'homeless' whose population had swelled modestly, especially after the city began to evict the homeless from other more 'upscale' locations. However, 'the problems of noise and litter caused by the overflowing Avenue A bars [were] not new,' as William Ney pointed out,[7] nor was the suggestion that a curfew be imposed on the park unprecedented. For several years running, certain residents in the neighborhood had complained about the noise, and in response the 'police and Parks Department [had] proposed that a dusty law on the books requiring all city parks to close at 1 A.M. be enforced,' even though 'no one on the Lower East Side [could] remember ever seeing the park closed at night.'[8]

Despite its animation, the melange of park users was not particularly menacing. Tompkins Square Park had always been famous for the diversity of its clientele and enviable for its remarkable capacity not only to tolerate but to absorb such variety. A sympathetic *New Yorker* correspondent noted that by summer, 'the ongoing party and the settlement of the dispossessed had noticeably fused. The result was a mild commotion, a bit boisterous but no threat to anyone.'[9] Clearly, however, *some* people felt threatened, although at the time the focus was still on noise, not on homelessness. A loose coalition was forming.

During the prior ten years, the visible manifestations of gentrification had been moving eastward from Third Avenue, gradually reaching the solid buildings abutting the park at Avenue A (see Smith et al., chapter 7). A new 'class' of residents – somewhat older, wealthier, and not necessarily sympathetic to the 'youth scene' – was available to join forces with those long-standing residents who lived in the East Village before the hippie invasions of the 1960s, the punk invasions of the 1970s, and the hard rock scene favored in the clubs, and who had earlier opposed those waves. The issue that unified this otherwise disparate set was their opposition to noise.

In spring 1988, the Avenue A Block Association demanded community board support for more police, enforcement of noise ordinances, and the imposition of a curfew. At a well attended meeting of CB3 on 15 June 1988, a representative of the AABA proposed closing the park at night. The complaints from AABA were acknowledged by park committee chair Ann Johnson (who was later elected chairperson of CB3) who entered the item as 'new business,' which meant that it could not be acted upon that night. According to Ney, there was no general support for a curfew:

> Community Affairs Officer Johnson was attending for the local police and spoke against closing the park . . . Philip VanAver . . . a member of the Park Committee, and also of the Friends [of Tompkins Square Park] . . . reminded the group that the closing had already been rejected as an option by the community at large. He suggested that another town meeting should be called . . . This was the final meeting of the summer . . . Because the

> issue had not been calendared . . . it could not appear on the 28 June agenda [of the full board].[10]

In the vote recorded that night (25 yes, 0 no, 4 abstentions), the Community Board instructed Danziger to prepare a letter in support of AABA's request for greater police presence in Tompkins Square Park between midnight and 6 a.m. *but AABA's request for imposition of a curfew was decisively rejected.*

Despite this clear lack of community support, on 11 July Captain MacNamara of the local precinct announced the Police Department's decision to enforce the closing law. However, even after that order was issued, the regulation was applied inconsistently. The police continued to tolerate the homeless in the park after the closing hour. Given this ambiguous situation, there seemed to be no urgency to mobilize the community against the closing. Indeed, it was not until 31 July that any organized protest against the curfew took place. This 'protest' was in the form of a concert by several of the rock bands in the area. The concert-cum-protest drew a crowd of about 300 people who scuffled with police when the latter arrived in force after midnight. 'Nightsticks and bottles flew, people on both sides were injured, arrests were made.' The police, badly outnumbered, withdrew.[11]

A few days later, Deputy Chief Darcy hosted a meeting at the Manhattan South District Headquarters of the Police Department. Present were MacNamara plus four other representatives of Precinct 9, two representatives from the mayor's office,[12] one representative each from the offices of elected officials Manfred Ohrenstein and Miriam Friedlander [Councilwoman Friedlander had already left on vacation], four board members from CB3, two CB3 staff members (including Martha Danziger, the paid District Manager), the head of the Manhattan Parks Department, five members of the Avenue A Block Association, and Betsy Newman, representing the Friends of Tompkins Square Park, who seems to have crashed the session.[13] Neither Ann Johnson nor Van Aver were invited, so that no one from the neighborhood who wanted the park to remain open was actually asked to attend.[14] It is especially significant that no one from the CB3 executive board was present; instead, it was persons with strong real estate interests[15] who attended. The question of who drew up the guest list remains unanswered, but the question of what the meeting's consequences were does not.

The Police Department took the meeting as an invitation to vigorously enforce a curfew. Ney reports that on 5 August, the night before the riot, Father George Kuhn of St Brigid's Church,[16] noticing significant concentrations of police in the park, was told by Captain MacNamara that 'the noise problem had apparently gotten out of hand [and] that the community had met and agreed that the park must be closed from one AM till six.' When Father Kuhn pointed out that the demonstration was not scheduled until the next day, as clearly indicated on the large banner stretched above a park entrance, MacNamara responded that the department had made a mistake. But it appeared that the police were actually rehearsing for the next night.

> 'We can't afford to lose this one,' Captain MacNamara told him. 'If we lose this one we might as well pack up and leave town.'[17]

Needless to say, they did not pack up, but returned in force the next evening.

New York Times reporter Michael Wines[18] dismissed the conflict that occurred the next night between hundreds of 'young people [*sic*] and 450 police officers' as basically non-political, rooted instead 'in a less gripping social schism: a feud between the area's sleepless over-30 residents and younger, noisier revelers on the streets outside.' However, Wines then refuted his own simple-minded diagnosis of a generation gap by acknowledging some of the complexity and dynamism of the situation. He noted that in the

> confluence of . . . police interest in the noise . . . and the appearance of fringe groups who adopted the curfew as a cause of protest . . . a dispute over loud radios grew into a war over treatment of the homeless, the civil rights of park-goers and allegations of a city plot to help real-estate developers purge the neighborhood of its poorer and less stylish elements.

He quoted skinheads and punks as complaining: 'It's the yuppies moving in on us . . . It's like we scare the rich people.' And certainly, other groups leafletting the neighborhood called upon the community to protest the curfew, which they diagnosed as related to the gentrification of the area by young professionals. Wines quotes one as saying: 'The police are just there to patrol for the real-estate interests. It's the rich against the poor, and the poor are just going down the drain.' The events of the night of the riot offer considerable evidence for this reading of the situation.

Robert McFadden's account confirmed the complexity of causes but argued that gentrification was the basic issue:

> As rising rents have displaced the historic culture of artists, musicians, social rebels and poor people, new and more affluent residents have made their presence felt and a backlash of resentment among long-standing residents has piqued the feud.

The imposition of the curfew was seen 'by many residents and others . . . as one more imposition, like rising rents and other unwanted changes.'[19]

THE RIOT ITSELF: SEQUENCE

It is always difficult to reconstruct explosive events such as 'riots.' For one thing, because the violence extends over considerable space, as that evening's events did, no single observer can see all. Secondly, observers are essentially viewing the event through their own value perspectives, interpreting what they see, as well as seeing it. Such filters make even the most 'objective' views somewhat biased. I have tried to reconstruct the sequence of events from several key sources: newspaper accounts by journalists who were actually present on the scene or who interviewed a large number of persons who were; interviews I conducted after the events; and, most importantly, the unedited four hours of on-the-spot videotape filmed by local resident Clayton Patterson.[20]

C. Carr's article in the *Village Voice*[21] was perhaps the most detailed and graphic of the many journalistic accounts of the early stages of the action:

> It started before midnight . . . Near the entrance [to the park] at 8th Street and Avenue A, a plump balding man in a tie-dye exhorted about 100 punks, politicos, and curious neighbors . . . "Yuppies and real estate magnates have declared war on Tompkins Square Park" . . . [There was an] aura of latent violence. Even so, who could have predicted the police riot to come within the hour . . . At midnight . . . the motley demonstrators had begun trooping defiantly around the paths [of the park] with their "class war" banners . . . [past the bandshell which the police were using as headquarters] . . . Protesters marched by, chanting that hell no, they wouldn't go . . . It was 12:30 Saturday night, a peak traffic hour on the avenue between Alcatraz, the Wah-Wah Hut, 7A, and the Pyramid – when, as a rule, skinheads and spiky heads hang out at the curbside, neighbors go to-and-froing, and the peddlers set out their tattered goods . . . But on this night, people were lining the park between 7th and 8th as if waiting for a parade . . . [Ringleaders shouted] "It's our fuckin' park!"

Then, the police put on their riot helmets. By then, some in the crowd were throwing bottles, some firecrackers were set off, and one could hear shouts of 'yuppie scum.' Carr continues:

> About 12:55 . . . the mounted police suddenly charged up Avenue A . . . radiating hysteria . . . They were sweeping 9th Street and it didn't matter if you were press or walking home from the movies or sitting on your stoop to catch a breeze . . . The cops seemed bizarrely out of control . . . They'd taken a relatively small protest and fanned it out over the neighborhood, inflaming hundreds of people who'd never gone near the park to begin with. They'd called in a chopper. And they would eventually call 450 officers.

This account is essentially confirmed by Clayton Patterson's videotape, which offers the most detailed sequencing of the escalation of the riot.[22] The filming begins at about 11.45 p.m. on that steamy evening. The park was well populated by a markedly unmenacing crowd: young men and women (some in conspicuous punk attire) ambling in a relaxed way, couples strolling hand in hand. There was much 'milling' and very little apparent organization, although one heard an occasional firecracker, some low-keyed chanting, and police whistles in the background. A small group of demonstrators paraded slowly, their chants of 'No police state' and 'It's our fuckin' park' competing with mixed strains of music rising from other parts of the park. Intermittent blasts of police whistles can be heard, although at this point no policemen are visible; one also heard noisemakers of the type one might blow on New Year's Eve. All in all, it was a pretty boring 'scene,' with most people just standing around, laughing, talking.

The police who, with their patrol cars and wagons, have begun finally to mass along the perimeter of the park look decidedly uncomfortable. They are joined by mounted police whose horses circle slowly outside the park. More police arrive shortly after midnight, but the general atmosphere remains calm and quiet. The crowd is not 'mean' or angry.

Suddenly, the police sirens sound off, triggering a more animated response from a crowd that closes ranks. Tension mounts. The old anti-Vietnam war chant, 'Hell no, we won't go,' is picked up, led by what appear to be remnants of that earlier movement (mostly men about 40, wearing headbands, bolero jackets, etc.). A fugue of antiphony begins. The ranks of impassive mounted police, some with their badge numbers covered, start to close in toward the park. They are met with a stepped up chant of 'No park curfew!' and then, fresh-faced girls chime in, 'It's our fuckin' park.' Nevertheless, the general tone is still party-like. Marchers pass the camera, showing their banner which reads 'Gentrification is Class War,' and someone shouts to the police: 'Get the horse-shit out of the park,' a suggestion that elicits laughter from the crowd. But it is getting closer to 1 a.m. and the mood has become much more tense.

The camera pans to people's faces, showing that some are getting worried if not frightened. A number of people peel off and leave the scene. On the other hand, the sound track picks up a bright-toned 'This is great fun!' suggesting that not all are apprehensive about what might occur should the police seek to enforce the curfew. Heightened sirens signal the arrival of more police cars. Police are mingling with pedestrians on Avenue A (at the western edge of the park), trying to convince them to leave. Then, a phalanx of patrolmen lines up around the park, facing outward to the streets, while other officers try to disperse the crowd.

Now, for the first time, one sees evidence of organization, leaders, people in charge giving directions. Someone shouts the order, 'Go back in the park!' An ugliness settles over the police, who have now lined up in their riot helmets. It is matched in the crowd, which taunts the police with escalating shouts of 'It's our fuckin' park; you don't live here!' Prepared banners are moved to the frontline. Their messages read: 'The Park Belongs to the People;' '1988 = 1933;'[23] another adds the word 'REVOLT' to the basic 1988 = 1933; and the largest banner of all, 'Gentrification is Class War.' In short, now that the banners are massing, it is clear that there has been prior preparation and planning. There is also direction. In response to the chant 'climb over the fence,' people begin to scramble back into the park.

It is now a little before 1 a.m. and the police have closed in. The mounted police charge into the crowds.[24] The scene is brutal. The camera shows police beating people; a prone figure in the street is being viciously kicked by several policemen. The horses are galloping in all directions and police sirens reach a crescendo as more police cars arrive. Over the loudspeaker comes the demand 'Clear the streets!' followed shortly thereafter (as the mounted police chase people onto the sidewalks) by the bizarre demand to also 'Get off the sidewalk!' People scatter to avoid the flying nightsticks as foot police attack without apparent provocation, screaming 'Go home!' The streets are now emptying, leaving the injured to hobble off. Things grow quieter.

By now, the outside of the park is fairly deserted, except for the police cars, horses and foot patrolmen (and women) massed along the edges of the park. The stores at the park's perimeter have all been shuttered closed; only the bars and one convenience store are still open and lit. The police continue to clear the streets, but the remaining crowds are so thin that several officers are able to gang up on single victims. Four throw a young boy off his bike and rough him up.

By about 15 minutes after 1 a.m. the violence steps up drastically. Stragglers are pursued mercilessly. There is a sad view of a wounded young man, curled to fetal position, who has just been beaten by two policemen. He turns plaintively to the camera and says in a heavy accent that he is Russian. He clearly doesn't understand what is going on. Other bloodied bystanders are being cradled and led away by friends. The scene has become distinctly ugly. One hears explosions (shots? more firecrackers?) and more sirens, sees more police cars, and everything is drowned out by the flashing lights and screams of a helicopter scooping low over the park.

Some protesters later barricade the narrow side streets that run westward from the park, and the police, with equal determination, use force to disperse them. Over the sounds of battle, the soundtrack picks up a faceless voice saying, with considerable insight one must admit, 'This is a real estate conflict.' The composition of the crowd has changed markedly over the course of the hour. Not a single punker can be seen and the protest 'organizers' are pretty much invisible; they are evidently still in the park. Along the west side of Avenue A, a rubbernecking crowd of young, middle-class white observers has emerged from the bars and clubs to watch the 'action.'[25] There are also more blacks and Latinos, arriving from the east.

The character of the action also shifts. A young woman, speaking in a softly modulated tone, enjoins: 'Everyone, sit down in the street.' Young well dressed kids, one by one, join the sit-in until about 30 seated figures block the street; behind them mass others drawn from a wider social spectrum. The police are ranged to face the 'kids,' but keep their distance. They are visibly disarmed, especially when the 'kids' sweetly sing 'This Land is Our Land.' There are now many observers and only a few 'players' – the college students who now chant, in beautifully enunciated 'cultured' tones, 'Piggy, piggy' and 'We want our park.'[26] After a stand-off in which the air hangs with perplexity, the 'innocents' stand up and some, hands in the air, approach the police lines in an unmenacing way, saying, again in perfect diction, 'All we want to do is to go into the park.' This crowd has apparently not witnessed the earlier violence, since it seems to consist of a new and good-humored population. A bearded guitarist is singing a spiritual. A group of (mostly black) men quietly sings 'We Shall Overcome.'[27] The polite chanting of 'We want our park' continues, interspersed by more hostile calls of 'Police, go home!'

But the chaos ebbs and flows, as the camera catches both 'hot spots' and places where people are ambling. Inside a local convenience store, thirsty participants are buying drinks, some selecting their favorite beverages, others choosing bottles that will make good weapons. Meanwhile, the battle lines are redrawn – with the police and people each massing at opposite ends of Avenue A. People are chanting louder and faster. A woman who has been injured is being cradled in the lap of a female friend who shouts 'Give her air, get away, don't touch her until the ambulance comes,' and later we see her carried on a stretcher into the ambulance.

It is at this point that a local priest, who has been cooling out the crowd and especially the diverse young men and women (some blond, some black, some Latino, two Krishna followers) who have formed a subset around him, interposes himself as go-between, crossing back and forth from the protesters to the police officers to gain a compromise. He reassures the youth that there will be a meeting next week so that they can present their views. 'Don't worry,' says the priest, 'It's gonna happen.'[28] Other speakers urge 'reason,' saying things like 'This is so stupid,' 'It just plays into their hands.' We overhear snatches of conversation: 'We need to have peace.' 'Residents in the area do not like violence.'

'Rents are going up.' 'Housing is a problem.' 'There are rich and poor, blacks and whites [in the neighborhood]. People need to have a place; the park defuses tensions.'

While the discussions among neighbors and the dialogue between the priest and the police continue, Rome is burning. The demonstrators' shouts are growing louder, and attempts by the priest and others, now using a bullhorn to address the crowd, to cool things down, fail. Bottles are thrown, and one overhears the police directive: 'Keep them past the store to keep them from getting more bottles.' The sounds of breaking glass can be heard. The large confrontation is imminent.

Now the mounted police line up their horses, and foot police mass, putting on their riot helmets. Their expressions have changed from fatigue and boredom to smiles and excitement: they are clearly getting 'turned on.' They advance against a shouting and chanting crowd which now contains more punks, blacks and Puerto Ricans and is largely male. The filming deteriorates immediately, so it is clear that the film-maker himself is running fast as the police attack anyone handy. The police shout 'Move! Move!' and bloodied victims retreat. The injured are being helped by small clusters of demonstrators who are backed against the walls. A young white couple ministers to an African-American man with a bad head wound from which blood flows copiously; they get him to remove his shirt which they use to staunch the flow. In the meantime, someone has run to call an ambulance and, in an act of supreme irony, a solicitous policeman comes over to see if he can be of any help! The contradictions of the evening are manifold and become more so.

Even the moderating priest admits he can't get 'them quiet tonight.' He says to the police, 'It's not going to calm down tonight until you get your artillery out of here!' Others shout: 'No curfew in the park;' 'Why were we pushed out of our homes?' while the proprietor of the Pyramid Club, blood streaming down his face, begins the chant 'We have the park: Demonstrations *every night, every night.*'

The tensions are noticeably defused by the arrival, in elegant civilian clothes, of the head of Metropolitan Police South, who takes command. Does he order the police to leave? It's hard to know, but the mounted police inexplicably turn their horses around and retreat north on Avenue A. The demonstrators sneer and slowly advance after them, applauding and shouting 'Every night!' A group marches behind its banner that reads 'Gentrification is Class War,' their fists raised. By now the crowd is advancing quickly and jubilantly, shouting '*Go home*!' after the retreating police, to which one participant appends, 'And clean up the horse-shit.' People feel they have triumphed. They re-enter the park from Avenue A and amble past the bandshell, smiling. Then someone shouts 'Let's get the Christodora!'

A small group assembles at the front door of the Christodora House. Unaccountably, no one has locked it from inside. A few from the group enter the lobby and throw large tree plants onto the sidewalk. Shouting 'Die, yuppie scum,' the crowd crashes police barricades into the lobby. 'We know who you are!' 'Die, yuppie scum. This is what they did to the people,' they shout as they bring out more plants from the lobby. Participants are looking hostilely at the building, scanning the windows for frightened occupants. The last act in this night's drama makes the meaning of the events crystal clear. The demonstrators post their banner, the one that reads 'Gentrification is Class War,' on the facade of the Christodora House – the deeply resented emblem of neighborhood change. The 'riot' is over.

Between August 1988 and June 1991, the community was in turmoil. The aftermath and consequences followed logically from the battle lines drawn up the night the community struggled against the city over who would control the park. The coalition of community groups, temporarily united by their anger at what they considered unwarranted police interference and brutality in August 1988, would gradually unravel in the years that followed.

Analysis of the Events of August and Their Immediate Aftermath

An event of such scale and public character could not be swept under the rug. Investigations of what many in the neighborhood still refer to as the 'police riot' of August 6–7 were not long in following. Complaints of widescale police abuse of power, concealment of identifying badges, and excessive use of force were made on the legal level to the Civilian Review Board.[29] Within a week of the riot 81 complaints of police brutality were filed, one of them by Harris Pankin, a 28-year-old rock singer and acknowledged squatter[30] who later became an active member of the 'Task Force on the Tompkins Park Riot' organized by the community board.

The community board also took the community's grievances to an indifferent mayor. A few days after the event, some 15 members of Community Board 3 met with Mayor Koch and numerous city representatives and police brass. In response to the mayor's request for information, Philip Van Aver began to tell the story, starting with the community-wide meeting in 1987 that had rejected the curfew option. The mayor, visibly bored, interrupted the account and afterwards, the mayor's press secretary simply repeated the official line – that the community said it wanted the park closed![31]

The following day, CB3 chair Ann Johnson, who had opposed the curfew, went on vacation, leaving Luis Nieves (the former chair), Louis Soler (the first vice chair) and Martha Danziger (the paid manager) in charge. On 12 August:

> Ms. Danziger called Mr. Soler . . . at ten in the morning, and told him a press conference had been organized for two o'clock that very day . . . [at] the CB3 office . . . Danziger later informed Soler that [Antonio] Pagan[32] had things well in hand and would read the statement and answer the questions . . . Mr. Pagan, simply a member-at-large . . . [and] not even a member of the Executive Committee . . . [was] part of the BASTA Group . . . a group of Lower East Side co-op and landowners [that opposed locating homeless shelters in the East Village]. The officers and membership of BASTA overlap with that of the 1st Street Block Association, and the organizations share office space. Martha Danziger is a member of the 1st Street Block Association.[33]

Mr. Soler arrived at the office as the press conference began. There was some confusion, but Antonio Pagan presided and read his statement calling for a curfew, which some have suggested was written by Martha Danziger. Months later, after the summer vacation, the full board of CB3 issued an official denial that it had ever voted in support of a park curfew. The Pagan-BASTA statement that had been read at the August press conference was reissued in mimeographed form and distributed, clearly marked as a 'Minority Report.'[34]

While all this was going on in the community, the police were conducting their own self-criticism which focused less upon the unwarranted violence of their response than the tactical errors they had made. Commissioner Ward's 'post-mortem' concluded that police has not behaved according to the lessons they had learned from the 1960s. A sidebar to a *New York Times* account of Ward's 10 August press conference listed ten major errors the police claimed to have made. None questioned whether excessive force had been used. The exclusive focus on tactics was obvious:

1. The police should have closed Avenue A to traffic.
2. The mounted police had been brought in too soon after a group sat down in Ave. A.
3. The helicopter stayed too long, thus attracting more crowds.
4. Setting up the temporary police headquarters in the park was a mistake because it required reinforcements to go through the crowds to reach it.
5. There was no evidence that the crowd had to be dispersed on Ave. A to let trapped motorists by.
6. Very few arrests were made.
7. The rooftops should have been secured.
8. 'Apparently, no senior officer was in charge of coordinating assignments . . .'
9. The ranking officer at the park 'may have' left his post at a crucial time to go to the bathroom at Manhattan South headquarters on 21st Street.

10 The usual communication chain apparently failed, and top officials were not notified of the riot until the worst of it was over.[35]

These self-criticisms were scarcely the type that community leaders, outraged by what they perceived as police brutality and 'overkill,' wanted to hear.

Confronted with official indifference, the people of the East Village returned to public action. A peaceful rally in Tompkins Square Park was planned for the following Saturday. One organizer said it was planned by a 'very loose' coalition of groups and individuals while another stressed that its purpose was to 'channel any negative energy into more positive creations.'[36] The event, which had a 1960s feel, began quietly enough:

> On Saturday August 13, after a 'languid' morning with homeless people sleeping on benches, old men playing cards and cityworkers and volunteers sprucing up the park, the day's loosely planned events began at midafternoon with a three-block march of about 100 people from Cooper Union Square to the park to protest the violent police role . . . Chanting "March with us! Free the park!" and "Koch is the puppet of landlords and bankers," the protesters . . . marched along St. Mark's place . . . Then at a bandshell . . . speakers criticized the police, Mayor Koch, Police Commissioner Benjamin Ward and the gentrification of the area around the park . . . During the rally, held under a banner proclaiming "Gentrification is Class War," some people watched a television screen showing a videotape of 1960's riots in the United States.[37]

A more sympathetic observer, C. Carr, writing in the *Village Voice*, was even more explicit about the 'love-in' quality of the opening events. She noted that although 13 August would end in confrontation:

> it was born in a mellowness worthy of the Summer of Love. In the morning, several people planted a tree . . . Farther in, someone had spread clothes over benches, free for the taking. A table near the bandshell with flyers about squatting . . . had a plate of free sandwiches, and shortly after noon people lined up at lunch tables, the food donated by area grocers.[38]

But an undercurrent of rage simmered, the issue being '*housing: homeless crowding the parks and streets while apartments remain empty until they are sold at prices no one native to the area can afford.*'[39] In what may have been the first hint that 'homelessness' was to become as big an issue in the neighborhood as the park curfew had been, a Woodstock teepee was set up and an invitation extended for anyone to stay in it for the night. Whereas earlier in the day folk singers with guitars had played 1960s themes, including 'This Land is Our Land,' by night time:

> the skinheads began to appear . . . [and] the music was turned up and piped through amplifiers to the hard acid beat of the 80's . . . At least 20 hard-rock

> groups, *all booked long before last week's violence* [my emphasis], wailed away until about 11 P.M.[40] when the concert ended peacefully.[41]

Carr's account picks up the rest of the evening's story. After cleaning up the park, at 11 p.m. people began a march to Washington Square Park; within five minutes the march was flanked by a contingent of police who jumped off their buses in full riot gear.[42] But, as another journalist observed, both police and protesters exercised caution, 'determined to avoid a return of the bottle throwing, name calling and club swinging that touched off bloody clashes the previous week-end.'[43] The 90 helmeted officers, reinforced in Washington Square Park by 80 more, kept their tempers and their distance.[44]

It was only after the marchers returned to Tompkins Square at 11.45 that trouble began. The demonstrators tried unsuccessfully to remove the barricades around the park. They waved their 'Gentrification is Class War' banner and chanted, 'The people! United! Will never be defeated!' Carr's account continues.[45]

> Gradually they [the protesters] dispersed. It was nearly 1:15 before I realized what was happening on Avenue B. The flag-bearing protesters stood in the park entrance over there, yelling at the cops and the Christodora . . . [around which] helmeted cops [had] created a box formation, closing all . . . streets and forcing the demonstrators into the park. [The police picked off people to arrest.]

Again, the symbol that best stood for the underlying causes of neighborhood tension was the Christodora House.

MEANINGS AND THEMES OF EXPLOSIVE TIME: 6–13 AUGUST 1988

Three themes are interwoven in the accounts presented above. One is economic, a second political, and the third cultural. Each had its own symbols. During the weeks of confrontation with the city, they were blended together, which gave to a large fraction of neighborhood residents a coherence which would begin to erode in the next months. The clear divide between 'us' (the neighborhood as a whole) and 'them' (the mayor, the police, the parks department, all viewed as in league with the 'gentrifiers'), so apparent in August 1988, would eventually become fuzzy, as divisive issues successively detached groups from the coalition. As we shall see, each detachment frayed an alliance that had been forged in the time of police confrontation.

The basic economic theme was gentrification, which included not only resentment of the speculators and large developers who were colonizing local space, but the subsidiary themes of abandonment and arson (which were held jointly responsible for the loss of affordable housing), opposition to landlords and 'profiteers' who were warehousing empty apartments, and support for homesteading and, to a lesser extent, tolerance of squatting, which was rationalized, at least by the squatters themselves, as the rightful confiscation and dedication to live human use of property that capitalism had killed. The general theme of the resultant loss of affordable housing was connected with the increase in homelessness in New York and led to sympathy for the growing population of the homeless who had been establishing themselves within Tompkins Square Park.

The symbols of these economic themes were to be found primarily in the banners displayed during the two confrontations with the police, of which the most obvious was the one that read 'Gentrification = Class War,' and in the by-now routine attacks on the Christodora House as the most tangible proxy for profit-seeking developers. They were also to be seen in the new level of concern for the homeless and the new level of tolerance for the jerry-built shelters which the homeless had begun to construct in Tompkins Square Park – out of tents, cartons, plastic dropcloths, and discarded corrugated tin – after the battle over the curfew had been won.

The political themes were no less visible. Allusions to the police state and the Vietnam War were frequent both during the demonstrations (*viz.*, the banner of '1933 = 1988,' the chants of 'Hell no, we won't go,' and of 'The people! United! Will never be defeated!'[46] and the showing of videotapes from the 1960s the afternoon of 13 August) and afterwards, as the various task forces, organized under the aegis of Community Board 3, sought to keep alive the complaints about police brutality and to call for disciplinary action. The political opposition between 'our neighborhood' and Koch's administration and the police, now bracketed together as supporters of gentrification and enforcers of law and order, developed these themes further. By this linkage, the political issues were elided with the economic ones. Many argued that after years of tolerance, police activity was being suddenly and radically stepped up in the area to 'clear the ground' for further gentrification. At the rally of 13 August this theme was made explicit in the chant, 'Koch is the puppet of landlords and bankers.'[47]

The final theme was of cultural and lifestyle oppositions. It is in this connection that the controversy over 'noise,' music, and even dress codes, must be viewed. The call for a curfew was seen as more than a call for a moratorium on music; it was a call to protect the neighborhood and the park from 'scary' people. A 75-year-old woman who had lived in the neighborhood for 46 years was quoted by McFadden as saying, 'At night, the weirdos come out with those funny hairdos. We want to sit in peace . . . but they play their instruments and use their four-letter words. It's very disconcerting for old people.'[48]

While this statement captures two extremes of lifestyles that coexist in the East Village, it by no means encompasses the multiple cleavages that eventually fractured the unity the riot of 6–7 August and its more mellow 'aftershock' the following week had achieved. Although the 'punks' to which the old woman alludes may have been the focus of *her* worries, other groups existed whose values were even more 'threatening' to the remaining neighborhood residents who, whether they supported 'gentrification' or its antithesis of 'affordable housing,' still believed in property rights. These were the self-styled 'squatter/anarchists'[49] and the homeless who, by 1990, were increasingly linked together in people's minds.

The squatter/anarchists distinguished themselves from the other participants in the August events, claiming to represent a counter-culture that went deeper than purple hair, minimalist art, or acid rock. And they, too, drew connections between economics, politics, and culture. Michael Wines,[50] scarcely a sympathetic observer, gave voice to this underground group who contended that:

> the police who swept down the park's trendy Avenue A [on 7 August] . . . missed the roots of the protest altogether . . . [which they say] are nearer the unfashionable Avenue B side . . . in a small and shadowy community of urban homesteaders, ecologists, fringe rock bands and revolutionary priests whose lives revolve around political action.

Wines calls them an 'unconventional lot – sporting nicknames like Jerry the Peddler and John the Squatter,' and uniting 'survivors of the 1960s anti-war protests' with 'dropouts from 1980s materialism.' Claiming to have interviewed Frank Morales[51] and other self-proclaimed squatters, Wines paraphrased their view that although they had lent 'impetus' to the Tompkins Square protests on 31 July and 6–7 August, they had neither planned a confrontation nor expected the massive police retaliation. Nevertheless, they argued that such a confrontation was inevitable, sooner or later, because there 'is a class war between the richer, backed by the police, and poorer residents of Loisaida and similar areas.'

The second group whose violations of property norms were perhaps even more threatening were the homeless, whose numbers in the park increased dramatically after 1988, once the curfew had been lifted. In the eyes of some, the squatters and the homeless became increasingly linked together, although only the squatters seem to have been unambivalent about and pleased with the association. The 'homeless' were adopted as a 'cause' by the anarchist/squatters who often joined them in the park encampment, especially when it was rumored that an eviction was imminent. At least some of the homeless were apprehensive about being too closely associated with the squatters. While they welcomed the squatters' support, they feared that their own ability to maintain a *modus vivendi* with 'the authorities' (the police and Parks Department personnel with whom they interacted daily and on whose forbearance they depended to stay in the park) might be jeopardized by too close an association with a group that seemed intent on baiting and defying those authorities.[52]

The Coalition Unravels

The moment during the summer of 1988, when a united front galvanized in the East Village to oppose gentrification, the curfew, and police brutality, and when this united front was overwhelmingly expressed by the appointed representatives to Community Board 3, was a brief one. The subsequent intra-community struggles revealed how much more complex the structure of neighborhood power was in the multiplex and changing zone around Tompkins Square Park. In the aftermath of the riot, not only did existing cleavages become more visible, but the cleavages themselves underwent realignment, coalescing into different patterns.

In the literature supporting empowerment and neighborhood self-determination, such complexities and unstable alliances have tended to be glossed – as if there existed a simple opposition between 'the people of a neighborhood' whose 'wishes' should be respected, and the larger political (city-wide) and economic (real estate development) forces arrayed against them. While during the hot summer of 1988 this dichotomy was not totally false, the simple binary power structure apparent at that time was only temporary. Later events revealed ambivalences and dialectics, requiring us to reconceptualize how community power structures operate in diverse neighborhoods such as the East Village.

While it would be possible to classify the diverse neighborhood actors and their opinions on many dimensions and with respect to many issues, in the chapters that follow we concentrate on two issues which have organized the central debates in the area in the past few years, and we summarize the positions taken on them by four crudely defined 'interest groups.'[53] The two major basic issues are 'affordable' housing' and the 'homeless,' both terms standing for complex and embedded conditions specific to the East Village.

THE ISSUES

Affordable Housing, Squatting and Demolitions

The trajectory of housing/squatting conflicts over affordable housing began earliest, triggered by the 15 years of neighborhood gentrification efforts described in part II of this book. By the mid-1980s it was the dominant controversy in the neighborhood, thrust to the foreground by opposition to the Lefrak Project (see Sites, chapter 9) and by the subsequent strengthening of Joint Planning Council representation on the community board. Between 1986 and 1988, local debates raged most furiously over housing issues and the meetings of Community Board 3's Housing Committee were particularly lively and well attended. These debates climaxed and then subsided, once the Housing Committee obtained its 'Memorandum of Understanding' from the Koch administration on the cross-subsidy plan (see chapter 14 for later developments). After that, the issue receded from public discussion, superseded by private negotiations between representatives of the community board and relevant city agencies over *which* specific city-owned tenement buildings would be included in the affordable housing subsidized rehabilitation program. Since according to the Memorandum of Understanding, the city was 'permitted' to sell its vacant lots for a profit to developers wishing to build market-rate housing in return for subsidizing tenement rehabilitation by non-profit mutual housing associations, *the city now had a vested interest in converting its worst buildings into empty lots.*

It is in this context that squatter evictions and tenement demolitions must be understood. After signing the Memorandum of Understanding in 1987, the city stepped up its campaign to remove squatters from the abandoned tenements it owned. Although the authorities had earlier closed up most buildings' entrances and windows with cinder blocks, squatters had gained access to these potentially livable structures and were fixing them up. Estimates of the number of buildings occupied by squatters and of the number of squatters involved in these occupations range widely and wildly.[54] (See Van Kleunen, chapter 13.) Regardless of the exact numbers, a few of these occupations generated considerable controversy.

The most publicized cases occurred in April and May of 1989 when two six-story city-owned tenement buildings occupied by squatters (316 East Eighth Street and, across the street, 319 East Eighth Street) were eventually demolished by the city, but not without considerable opposition. The New York Buildings Department claimed the structures were unsafe, although residents claimed that the buildings had functioning utilities, that the residents had invested considerable money in fixing them up, and that the buildings were sounder than adjacent ones.[55] Residents wanted the city to serve them official eviction notices. HPD, which 'owned' the structures, claimed that the buildings were legally 'vacant' and therefore could be demolished without prior legal action. At 10:30 a.m. on 1 April police acted to remove the squatters from 316 East Eighth Street and by early afternoon a demolition crew was already tearing down the building. Frustrated protesters vented their anger on the Christodora House just around the corner. According to *The New York Times* account, 'rocks were thrown through the building's glass lobby doors and the window of a second-floor apartment, and a bag of garbage was dumped in the lobby.' Nine protesters were arrested. On 20 April the City Building Department, despite letters from two Pratt Institute architects and a licensed contractor that the building could be rehabilitated, declared the tenement across the street at 319–21 East Eighth Street unsafe. On 2 May when demolition crews arrived to tear it down, however, they were met by protesters who spilled urine on the crew and pulled down their scaffolding.[56] By evening, 200 protesters who had gathered at the scene faced off against 300 hastily dispatched police officers; 16 persons were arrested.[57] Demolition was temporarily halted when lawyers obtained a restraining order from a State Supreme Court Justice,[58] but this order was overturned during the night by another judge. Three days later, on 5 May more than 200 police officers blocked off the entry to Eighth Street to keep observers and protesters on the park side of Avenue B. They formed a solid phalanx in front of the Christodora House to protect it from harm and guarded the bulldozers that razed the remainder of the building.[59]

Throughout the rest of 1989 and afterwards, evictions of squatters proceeded apace, albeit with much less fanfare, except for the dramatic squatter occupation of an abandoned four-story school house at 269 East Fourth Street (the so-called ABC Community Center). Many observers attributed the decline in interest and support for the squatters to the wedge that had been driven between housing reformers involved in the cross-subsidy project and the squatters. These two groups were increasingly locked into a zero-sum struggle *over the very same properties*. (See chapters 13 and 14 for a fuller discussion.) But another part of the wedge was over the issue of the homeless population living in the park.

The Tent and Bench Dwellers in the Park

The trajectory of the park/homeless controversy began later and took a different course. After the 1988 'police riot,' Community Board 3 organized a special task force to ventilate the community's anger at police brutality. Once it became evident that only a few indictments would grow

Plate 11.3 Demolition of a squatter-occupied building on Eighth Street
Source: Courtesy of Marlis Momber

out of the post-mortem investigations[60] and that no changes would be made in top administrators of the police department, the task force turned its attention more and more to the issue of neighborhood control over park usage. Gradually, the activities of the task force merged with those of the CB3 Park Committee, especially when it became clear that the Parks Department was making plans to 'renovate' Tompkins Square.[61] Suspicious that redesign would be used to facilitate police surveillance and 'military control' and thereby permit enforcement of a curfew or worse, the CB3 Park Committee insisted that the community be consulted on any planned renovations and that such plans be submitted first to the board for its approval. Although the Parks Department declined full disclosure, those portions of the renovation that had earlier been supported by CB3 did go ahead without incident. The community had insisted that the bandshell remain and that renovations be done in stages, so that most of the park would remain open. The improvements to the basketball courts and wading pool area on the northern end of the park and the installation of elegant new playground equipment at the park's periphery were approved by the community and were in place and use by 1990.

But the issue of community control over the park was increasingly superseded by the issue of the 'homeless' who were making the park into their home. Both of these themes came together in June 1991, when the

Parks Department, supported by a large police force, finally evicted the park residents and closed off almost all of the park for renovations – even though their plans had never been approved by, much less disclosed to, the community board. This story will be told more fully in the next chapter. Here we might give only a few highlights of the two-year campaign against the people living in the park.[62]

In the aftermath of the summer 1988 riot, enforcement of the park curfew was only desultory. This 'tolerance' (coupled with heightened intolerance in nearby parks) encouraged a growing number of homeless persons to settle in Tompkins Square Park. By early July 1989, their numbers had increased to about 200, and some residents had ingeniously constructed makeshift shelters to protect themselves and their possessions from theft and the elements. This tolerance was suddenly rescinded. On 5 July 1989, some 250 police officers descended on the park to evict the homeless, while Parks Department workers used sledgehammers and axes to demolish some 40 structures that had been built.[63] The park was temporarily closed off by police to prevent protesters from interfering with the operation, but this did not prevent 30 from being arrested on that occasion.

By then, some of the homeless men were becoming more sophisticated in linking their expulsions to housing and gentrification:

> Several homeless people squatting amid the ruins said the raid was part of a concerted effort to drive them from the park because their presence hurt property values. Richard DuPont, an unemployed carpenter and park resident for one year noted: "Within five years, the East Side will be just as preppie as the West Side. You got people paying $2,000 a month in rent, and they don't want this eyesore."[64]

Once the pressures let up, however, the homeless encampment began to recover to 'pre-sweep' proportions and the issue again came to the fore in community debates. But by then a new set of voices was heard, and they expressed considerably more exasperation with the conditions in the park.

Before the fall of 1989, public discussions about the expanding encampment of homeless in the park were dominated by individuals and groups sympathetic to the settlement. But in October 1989 a special public hearing to 'advise' the CB3 Park Committee was held at Village View Houses at Sixth Street, a block from the park. The large turnout of some 150 persons, many of whom had hitherto not been much involved in local controversies, was clearly the result of careful organization by a faction that supported eviction of the homeless. However, very few among the evening's many speakers called unambiguously for eviction. And in the vote taken at the end of the meeting, the chair was merely instructed to recommend to the CB3 Board that it call for greater enforcement of laws already on the books: namely, those against use and sale of drugs, unauthorized fires, litter, etc. At that meeting, however, the Parks Department may have tipped its hand. Jack Linn, Assistant Parks Commissioner, 'suggested' that the park would be closed for 12 to 18 months for total renovations. To illustrate his remarks, he drew a 'hypothetical' plan for such changes on the meeting-hall's blackboard.[65]

This session was followed on 24 October 1989 by a very animated and acrimonious general meeting of CB3, held at Catherine Street in Chinatown. Prior to the 6 p.m. meeting, supporters of the homeless assembled in Tompkins Square Park for a protest march to Catherine Street. The usual banners reading 'Gentrification is Genocide' and 'Stop the War on the Poor' were evident, and it is alleged that an American flag was burned. The opening part of the meeting itself was periodically interrupted by audience shouts of 'Fascist' and 'It's *our* fuckin' park.' Speeches[66] by radical activists and local homeless argued vehemently against reinstating the curfew and even threatened to re-enact the riot of August 1988. Lack of discipline and tensions between CB3 members and dissident speakers erupted into a tug of war over the microphone, in the course of which the cord was broken; debate continued over the substitute PA system provided by the demonstrators.[67]

By then, the meeting was clearly out of control. The chairperson had taken to standing on top of the board table in a futile attempt to restore order, City Council member Miriam Friedlander was engaged in a shouting match with hecklers in the audience, eggs and other objects[68] were thrown, and there were isolated physical scuffles. At 7 o'clock, more than a dozen riot-equipped police entered the hall, interposing themselves between the audience and the board members seated in their usual place at the front of the auditorium. After 20 minutes of noisy protests that included chants such as 'Curfew, try it! We'll have another Riot!' and 'Pigs, out of the meeting!' the police withdrew. In the subsequent closed session, 15 board members voted to recommend that the park remain open around the clock (i.e., against eviction of the homeless), 7 voted against the resolution, and 6 abstained. (The remaining 22 members were absent.)

Nevertheless, on the afternoon of 6 November Parks Department workers demolished some 20 tents in the southeast corner of the park near Avenue B and confiscated the occupants' belongings, claiming that the zone was a 'shooting gallery' for drugs.[69] And about one week later, on 15 November at the Community Board 3 meeting held at Public School No. 20 near the park, some 500 persons heard Friedlander and Parks Commissioner Harry Stern outline a plan to remove the tent city from the park.[70] A 'help center' would be established with city funds and personnel to provide medical help and counseling for relocation. The newspaper account quoted Friedlander as calling the plan 'humane,' and quoted Linn as saying that 'everyone is hoping people will voluntarily leave the park when they are made aware of the available alternatives.' Although some residents spoke in support, neither the homeless nor their supporters were enthusiastic. A park resident was quoted as saying:

> We won't accept this. Three weeks will pass and we will take back the park. How can anyone think they can take just three weeks to rectify a situation like this? If they want to help us, let them give us a building, and we will help ourselves.

Although this plan to help the homeless bore little fruit and protests against evictions continued to be mounted, support for the homeless began to erode. *New York Times* correspondent John Kifner attributed this to a deterioration in the physical conditions of the park:

> The park is a remarkable sight. Ragtag huts and tents, many of them surrounded by garbage or piles of grocery carts or other odd possessions, now dot the . . . park. Smoke drifts from fires set in trash barrels . . . [R]aggedly dressed people mill about. The other day a man who had built a lean-to around the park bench he slept on was grilling and selling kebabs from his perch.[71]

Not all abandoned the homeless, however. The four churches in the vicinity continued to oppose tent removal until empty buildings in the neighborhood could be made available as alternative shelters. And Kifner quoted Father Kuhn of St Brigid's as saying: 'It's not a pretty scene . . . It's connected with the [city's] . . . crisis of housing, of drugs. Because we have no housing, there is a park that is not pretty.'

Taking courage perhaps from the decline in support for the homeless, however, on 13 December an officer from the local police precinct made the rounds, warning the homeless that they would soon be evicted,[72] an operation that began the next morning at 9 a.m. when some 90 homeless in 45 shelters were given fifteen minutes' warning to pack up their belongings.[73] About 80 'peace officers' of the Parks Department, dressed in green park ranger uniforms, supported by 90 maintenance workers, 20, then 40, and finally 70 uniformed police, as well as plainclothes officers, participated[74] in the sweep. Photographers were supposed to record possessions too heavy to be easily removed, so they could later be returned (which they were not), and five garbage trucks and another five flatbed trucks were used to haul away the debris from the structures. They proved an insufficient number. Resistance was largely symbolic;

about 20 of the structures were set afire by their owners, the blazes swiftly put out by the fire department.

At the December 'sweep,' Parks Department officials insisted that they had no plans to close the park or keep the homeless out. Inspector Julian was quoted as saying, 'If they want, the homeless people can come back later with blankets and sleeping bags. They just won't have the structures.' These successive sweeps never did clear the homeless out of the park, as will be seen in chapter 12. Only the Draconian action of 3 June 1991, which closed the park down completely for the 'renovations' hinted at by Jack Linn 20 months earlier, put a halt to the encampment.

THE MAJOR CONTESTANTS

The four major local 'groups'[75] taking somewhat different positions on these issues have been: the white working-class residents of European background and their allies; the housing activist reformers; the radical counter-culturalists; and African-Americans and Latinos.

The first position is supported chiefly by relatively conservative 'white ethnics,' including a few home owners but mostly long-term renters in the area. They tend to be older and female, although their spokespersons are usually male. They are primarily interested in neighborhood safety and stability and share with long-term middle-class residents a positive view of neighborhood revitalization, so long as it does not displace them from their rent-controlled apartments or make their own housing 'unaffordable.'[76] For them, Tompkins Square Park is a valued neighborhood amenity which they do not mind sharing with their fellow residents, even those quite different from themselves, so long as these other groups do not interfere with their safety or access. For many years they tolerated the existence of a limited number of people living in the park, seeking only to be partially insulated from them, visually and interactively. This group is sometimes viewed by more liberal and/or radical elements in the community as the 'natural,' albeit sometimes unwitting, 'ally' of the gentrifiers, both developers and newcomers of greater wealth. To the developers, the older ethnics represent the 'respectable' population that does not need to be replaced to 'upgrade the neighborhood.' To the new gentry, they offer the ethnic ambience that enhances the illusion that they have moved into a vital, interesting urban neighborhood of the type fast disappearing from American cities.[77]

Faction two may be characterized as 'liberal reformers,' some of whose members date back to the early homesteading movement in the neighborhood, some even earlier. The closest this faction comes to having a united front is the Lower East Side Joint Planning Council, which is a weak coalition of smaller neighborhood groups (often with interlocking directorates), most of whom support the goal of affordable housing, although they may differ as to the best means to obtain it. As is common in local community organizations these days, the principal actors are middle-class, white, and female, although they cooperate easily with others who do not share these characteristics. Some of the leaders are exceptionally well grounded and sophisticated in the intricacies of housing and city planning[78] and are sincerely dedicated to preserving at least part of the housing stock in the East Village for residents of low and moderate income. Self-avowed pragmatists, they have skillfully negotiated agreements – with agencies of the city government for the cross-subsidy housing program that is now helping to rehabilitate city-owned tenements in the area,[79] and most recently, with banks, non-profit organizations and foundations which are needed to provide the additional capital to convert these structures into decent and affordable housing. Most 'housing activists' never supported the park curfew and some have defended the homeless on humanitarian grounds, consistently opposing their eviction from the park until decent and suitable (that is, non-shelter) alternative housing can be provided. However, they were eventually 'turned off' from the issue because of what they perceived to be a growing alliance between the homeless and the 'less-respectable' faction among the squatters. They accuse the squatters, with whom they have come into increasing conflict over the disposition of city-owned tenements, of simply 'using' the homeless for their own ideological ends.

The third faction, held in contempt by the first two, might be termed the 'radical dissidents,' although far less neutral words – ex-hippies, extremists, and even 'crazies' – are applied to them by members of factions one and two. But as noted above, they prefer to call themselves anarchists and squatters.[80] The squatter/anarchists' attitude toward the homeless is strongly favorable, since the former tend to view them, perhaps unrealistically, as the vanguard of a revolution that will eventually overthrow the cash nexus of capitalism. They are often as contemptuous of the housing reformers as the latter are dismissive of them. They characterize the cross-subsidy program as a 'sell out' to the establishment, and they perceptively recognize that once the city deeds their tenements over to mutual housing associations, it is they who will be displaced.

And finally, there are the blacks and Latinos in the housing projects, in the remnants of Loisaida, and, up to June 1991, in the park itself. It is hard to know exactly how they fit into community power struggles. The project residents seem to be relatively uninvolved in the area housing battles since, if they once had a stake in that housing, they lost it long ago. The remaining residents of Loisaida seem mostly demoralized: some continue to move away; others support the cross-subsidy plan in the hope that crumbs may come their way; and others, perhaps unrealistically, have placed their faith in Antonio Pagan, whom they helped elect, as a potential representative of *la raza*. They are conspicuously absent from community task forces, CB3 special committees, and their voices are seldom raised at the general community board meetings that periodically invigorate debate. And finally, there are the homeless, most of whom are black and Latino men. While a few have become active participants in community discussions,[81] most chose to keep as low a profile as possible, in the hope that by lying low, they would also be allowed to lie nightly in the park.

In the chapters that follow, we focus on the three groups whose needs and goals have framed the community controversies in the four years between the 'riot' of August 1988 and the reopening of Tompkins Square Park in August 1992: the homeless, the squatters, and the housing activists. In these chapters, the various authors present the conflicts through the 'eyes' of members of their groups, albeit not uncritically.

NOTES

1 That the space must be public, if it is to be covered by Bill of Rights' guarantees of freedom of assembly, is clear. This is one reason why we should be concerned over the substitution of 'quasi-public' space in shopping centers and malls for truly public space. While activities in the open spaces of shopping centers and malls are presumably 'free' and open to all, such spaces are essentially 'private property' and thus cannot be used, by right, for public protests.

2 For example, during a time when the homeless were occasionally using the US flag to defend their turf, *The New York Times* published a picture of a flag-burning in another park of New York. The caption, significantly, referred instead to Tompkins Square Park which, in this instance, had nothing to do with the event pictured. Reference to Tompkins Square Park did, however, evoke an intended heightening of 'revulsion.'

3 To be more accurate, three small areas remained open but with limited, police-controlled access: a renovated active sports area on the northern end of the park, a renovated playground for children on the northwestern edge, and a tiny dog run entered from Avenue B. Despite this closing, the symbolic character of the ghost park remained. In the aftermath of the Los Angeles explosion over the verdicts in the Rodney King beating, New York experienced only minor repercussions. The major response was a march of perhaps 500 persons, mostly high schoolers, from Times Square down to Lower Manhattan. By the time the march reached Washington Square Park, only about 200 participants remained, and they had left little damage in their wake. At Washington Square, they were met by participants in a May Day demonstration coming from the East Village. Only after the two groups joined did the demonstration become more explosive – trashing buildings and breaking shop

windows before terminating at Tompkins Square Park (field notes: Andy Van Kleunen). Postscript: The park, duly renovated, was reopened in late August of 1992 and, despite weekly small protests and a few arrests, the police have thus far been successfully enforcing a night curfew.

4 See the brief account in chapter 4 by Reaven and Houck.

5 It may have been a triage choice at Con Edison's electric station at Fourteenth Street and the East River that sacrificed the Lower East Side to keep power flowing to middle-class zones farther north.

6 Set near or around the park were various music clubs, such as King Tut's Wah-Wah Hut, Alcatraz, Pyramid Club.

7 Quotation is from William Ney, 'Tompkins Square Police Riot,' *The New Common Good*, September 1988, p. 1.

8 Ibid.

9 See *The New Yorker*, 22 August 1988, p. 18 (unsigned).

10 Ney, 'Tompkins Square Police Riot,' p. 7. Two members of Community Board 3 later claimed in interviews I conducted with them that no full meeting of the board ever did occur on 28 June and that even if there had been an alleged directive by some board members to support the curfew, it would not have been valid; interestingly enough, no one has ever been able to find minutes from the purported board meeting.

11 Ney, 'Tompkins Square Police Riot.'

12 At that time, David Dinkins was still Borough President of Manhattan.

13 The latter, who claims that she learned of the meeting only by accident, expressed the opinion that the meeting had been secretly called and was a put-up job.

14 Ney, 'Tompkins Square Police Riot,' p. 9.

15 Such as Wachtel, LaLumia, Sicklick, and Piorkowska. See Ney, 'Tompkins Square Police Riot,' p. 11. The case of Krystyna Piorkowska is an interesting one. In public meetings in the neighborhood, this owner of a small number of rental buildings has often clashed with members of both the 'reformist' and 'radical' factions in the neighborhood. If the Christodora House is often the lightning rod for anti-gentrification sentiments, K. P. is often the scape-goat for anti-gentrifier animosities.

16 George Kuhn, pastor of St Brigid's Church that faces the eastern side of the park, has long been a quiet but determined force in the neighborhood, protecting and assisting the homeless with food distributions while trying to keep tempers cool on all sides. Increasingly militant in the past few years, he has been arrested for leading small demonstrations and has recently brought suit against the city for closing the park without a prior environmental impact study.

17 As quoted in Ney, 'Tompkins Square Police Riot,' p. 11.

18 See Michael Wines, 'Behind the Park Melee, A New Generation Gap,' *The New York Times*, 8 August 1988, p. B2.

19 Robert D. McFadden, 'Park Curfew Protest Erupts. . . ,' *The New York Times*, 8 August 1988, pp. A1, B2.

20 Clayton P. is a local resident of Canadian origin who has lived in the East Village since the 1960s. Proprietor along with his wife of a small local store

that makes and sells decorated beanies, Patterson is also an amateur maker of videotapes, primarily intended as promotional advertising for a number of rock groups in the neighborhood. Politically committed, he began to use his camera to document events in the neighborhood. He recorded the complete four hours of police-neighborhood confrontation the night of August 6–7, a tape which constitutes crucial evidence for at least a portion of what transpired that night.

21 C. Carr, 'Night Clubbing,' *Village Voice*, 16 August 1988, pp. 10, 17. Quotations have been taken from p. 10.

22 The following account is taken from my detailed notes on the entire Patterson tape. I viewed the tape twice in a public setting (where the responses of the sympathetic audiences were as revealing as the tapes themselves); many viewers were clearly reliving the events. I also reviewed excerpts in more private settings, since REALM sponsored the preparation of a one-hour edited version suitable for wider distribution. I am grateful to Clayton for his cooperation. Patterson's tape was so damaging to the police that they made an attempt to impound it, but he resisted and provided only a copy (which he claims was tampered with when it was in police custody). His tape was eventually instrumental in the indictment of six police officers on criminal charges and has been used as evidence in a number of lawsuits against the city stemming from the August 'police riot,' as the event is commonly referred to in the neighborhood.

23 The slogan of the 'Missing Foundation,' often seen as graffiti in the neighborhood, along with the rock group's symbol, an inverted martini glass with two diagonal slashes, signifying 'the party is over.'

24 The first time I viewed the videotape was in a bare hall in the East Village, where 150 people, many involved in the 'movement,' had assembled. The audience reactions were uninhibited. It was clear from their responses that many were actually reliving the experience of that night. People booed at the police, cheered when the crowd prevailed, laughed to release their tensions when they could. The hall itself was decorated with two banners that had survived the riot. One read 'No Curfew, No Police State,' the other was simply '1988 = 1933,' an unveiled reference to the rise of fascism in Germany.

25 They seem to lack the good sense to get out!

26 For me, it evoked the early moments in the Kent State protest.

27 This seems now to be everyone's symbolic syncretism, a syncretic religion for a syncretic neighborhood.

28 Later revealed to be the promise of a meeting between community organization leaders and the police within a few days, a meeting that never took place!

29 This was originally an all-police body formed in 1953 to handle civilian complaints but had been reorganized as a panel of civilians after the Harlem and Bedford-Stuyvesant riots of 1966. In 1985 it was revised to include six civilians named by the mayor, and six executives of the Police Department named by the police commissioner. For more details, see *The New York Times*, 12 August 1988, p. B4. Needless to say, the board handed down few indictments against the police and there were no convictions.

30 James Hirsch, 'Complaints Accuse Police of Wild, Random Brutality,' *The New York Times*, 12 August 1988, p. B4.
31 William Ney, 'After the Fact,' *The New Common Good*, September 1988, p. 13.
32 Pagan's name will continue to surface. He later supported the eviction of the homeless from the park, challenged the 'housing reformers' over rehabilitation of local buildings, and finally, taking advantage of the redistricting of the city mandated by the new city charter, defeated Miriam Friedlander in the next election for City Council. This was his first bid for power.
33 Ney, 'After the Fact,' p. 15. The acronym BASTA (sp. for 'enough') is derived from 'Before Another Shelter Tears Our Community Apart.'
34 Field notes from meeting of the Tompkins Square Riot Task Force and documents distributed in fall 1988.
35 Todd S. Purdum, 'Lessons of 60's Forgotten in Park Riot,' *The New York Times*, 11 August 1988, p. B22. It is significant that in the park closing of 3 June 1991, the police avoided every one of the 'tactical errors' its post-mortem had identified almost three years earlier.
36 Dennis Hevesi, 'Rally in Tompkins Park to Protest Police Action,' *The New York Times*, 12 August 1988, p. B4.
37 Robert D. McFadden, 'One Week After the Clash, Protesters Hold a Quiet Tompkins Sq. Rally,' *The New York Times*, 14 August 1988, p. 39.
38 See Carr's 'When the Rainbow is Not Enough: People's Park: Round Two,' *Village Voice*, 23 August 1988, p. 11.
39 Ibid, my emphasis.
40 Carr, in ibid., says the music ended promptly at 10 p.m.
41 Hevesi, 'Rally in Tompkins Park.'
42 Carr, 'When the Rainbow is Not Enough,' p. 12.
43 James Barron, 'Tompkins Square Protest is Marked by Restraint,' *The New York Times*, 15 August 1988, p. B3.
44 Ibid.
45 Carr, 'When the Rainbow is Not Enough.'
46 C. Carr, reporting on the 13 August march to Washington Square Park that followed the concert in Tompkins Square, noted the resurrection of this older political chant from the 1960s. See p. 12 of her 'When the Rainbow is Not Enough.'
47 Robert McFadden, 'One Week After the Clash.'
48 Ibid.
49 These terms, although often linked, are not synonymous. The free application of the term 'anarchist' in the East Village perhaps deserves explanation. Whereas in 'mainstream' society this term is used, if ever, as dismissive or pejorative, in the East Village a segment of the population identifies itself by this name and has come to be referred to in this manner by friends and foes alike. In the rest of this chapter we follow the neighborhood's usage, with no political judgment implied. But see chapter 13 for a fuller discussion.
50 Michael Wines, 'Class Struggle Erupts Along Avenue B,' *The New York Times*, 10 August 1988, pp. B1, B5.

51 Whom he described as a 38-year-old former Episcopal priest heading a group of squatters. (See Van Kleunen, chapter 13, for more information.)

52 The link between the squatters and the homeless also posed a problem for the liberals who opposed gentrification and supported affordable housing and a non-curfewed park. And many of the homeless did not share the squatters' anti-property views. Most of the homeless were not opposed in principle to private property; they just couldn't afford to amass much of it or afford to pay rent to owners of private property! (See chapter 12 for more details.)

53 In this analysis, we are ignoring those with pure (and absentee) economic interests in the area – namely, large developers, financial institutions, and to some extent, landlords.

54 Maria Laurino, in 'It's a Great Big Room, That's the Way We Live,' *Village Voice*, 6 September 1988, pp. 10, 15, cites Frank Morales as the source for an estimate of 1,000 (but perhaps this refers to the entire city) and unidentified 'community residents' as the source for an estimate of 50.

55 For information on the April 1 demolition of 316 East Eighth Street, see Lisa Foderaro, '9 Held in Protest Near Tompkins Square Park,' *The New York Times*, 2 April 1989; and Sarah Ferguson and Dean Kuipers, 'An Eye for an Eye: Squatters Attack Christodora After Loisaida Demolition,' *Village Voice*, 11 April 1989. For details on the 2 May altercation, see Scott Ladd and T. J. Collins, 'Demolition Project Starts, Stops,' *New York Newsday*, 3 May 1989; James McKinley, 'Melee Site Quiet, But Police Stand Guard,' *The New York Times*, 6 May 1989; and Sarah Ferguson, 'Squatters' Victory? Protestors Piss Off Demolition Crew – For Now,' *Village Voice*, 9 May 1989.

56 Sarah Ferguson, in *Village Voice*, 9 May 1989.

57 James McKinley, Jr., 'Melee Site Quiet.'

58 Ladd and Collins, 'Demolition Project.'

59 Field notes of 5 May and McKinley, 'Melee Site Quiet.'

60 In the end, only six indictments were handed down and none of these officers was found guilty.

61 Park 'renovations' and conflicts between the city and neighborhood over design had often followed violence in the Tompkins Square area. (See chapter 4 by Reaven and Houck.)

62 The following accounts are based upon field notes by the author and New School graduate students taken at the meetings on 19 and 24 October 1989, and on newspaper accounts, including the following: Chris Flash, 'Community Board 3 vs Tompkins Square Park,' in *The Shadow* (an anarchist free paper), October 1989; 'Police Called to Meeting on Tompkins Park,' *The New York Times*, 25 October 1989; and a *New York Post* editorial on 27 October 1989. I am grateful to Chris Mele for abstracting and organizing these and other materials in our research files, which facilitated writing the next section.

63 See, *inter alia*, James McKinley, Jr., 'City Moves to Clean Up Tompkins Square After Raid,' *The New York Times*, 7 July 1989; Timothy McDarrah and Gene Ruffini, 'Park Squatters Swept Up and Out,' *New York Post*, 6 July 1989; Nick Ravo, 'As Homeless Rally, Police Patrol Tompkins Square Park,' *The New York Times*, 9 July 1989; and Nick Ravo, 'Tensions Ease in Tompkins Park Protest,' *The New York Times*, 10 July 1989.

64 As quoted in James McKinley, Jr., 'City Moves.'

65 This was exactly 20 months prior to the actual execution of his hypothetical plan, which was estimated to require his announced 12–18 months!

66 The usual routine for a community board meeting is that the closed deliberations of board members are preceded by brief remarks made by community residents who must sign up in advance to be allowed to speak.

67 Much of this description is drawn from field notes taken by Dorine Greshof that evening, supported by field notes taken by Andrew Van Kleunen and Christopher Mele.

68 Including, some say, a bag of blood or feces.

69 'Parks Officials Raze Tompkins Square Tents,' *The New York Times*, 7 November 1989.

70 Our chief source here is James Barron, 'Removal of Tompkins Square Homeless Is Set,' *The New York Times*, 16 November 1989. For more details, see chapter 12.

71 See John Kifner, 'Neighborhood Attitudes Shift as Park Declines,' *The New York Times*, 8 December 1989.

72 John Kifner, 'Tent City in Tompkins Square Park is Dismantled by Police,' *The New York Times*, 15 December 1989. Another account can be found in Jessie Mangaliman, 'Park Workers Level Tent City,' *New York Newsday*, 15 December 1989.

73 Field notes by Dorine Greshof.

74 Observed by eight photographers and three lawyers, as well as a handful of passersby and a few 'researchers.'

75 The word 'group' is really not accurate, since a group is more organized and interactive than what we have in mind here. Many people in the neighborhood remained unaligned, although most had opinions on the issues. As in all communities, only a relatively small percentage within these 'opinion' categories are actively involved in local politics, attending meetings. or participating in demonstrations, or even supporting or opposing them. And within that subcategory are persons who actually do form groups, in the sense that they see each other frequently, confer together to plan strategies, and play prominent roles as spokespersons or behind-the-scene actors in getting things done.

76 Here their interests diverge from those of the gentrifiers, particularly purchasers of renovated co-ops and condominia. The latter's investments depend upon rising rents in the neighborhood. I should acknowledge here my disagreement with the characterization of this group by Diana Gordon in her chapter 10 above.

77 This group was also important in supporting anti-drug sweeps of tactical police units, the curfew on the park, and, although it might try to conceal it, removal of the homeless.

78 A few are trained architects or planners.

79 About which more later.

80 It is necessary to distinguish between 'squatting' as a literal legal condition and the 'ideology of squatting' – that is, a commitment to a larger set of

values rejecting the legitimacy of property 'ownership.' I am using the term 'ideological squatter' here to denote that it is more a commitment to an ideal than descriptive of actual housing tenure. Some 'actual squatters' may just be homeless persons or undocumented aliens financially and/or legally unable to sign leases, whereas some 'ideological squatters' may actually be paying rent on regular apartments, without jeopardizing their political 'credentials' as advocates of squatters' rights.

81 A 'spokesperson' from the homeless had become a standard token at most community meetings and his remarks were usually applauded.

12

The Residents in Tompkins Square Park

Dorine Greshof and John Dale

Observers following events in Tompkins Square Park were hardly surprised when, at 5 a.m. on 3 June 1991, the authorities forcibly removed from the park about 175 homeless men and women, many of whom had been there for years. This population had survived a two-year campaign to evict them – a campaign that involved periodic demolitions of their shanties and milder but persistent bureaucratic harassment by Parks and Police Department personnel. The park, against the expressed wishes of the neighborhood, was to be closed for at least a year so that it could be completely 'renovated.' Critics were angered that an estimated six million dollars was to be spent on 'closing and renovating' Tompkins Square at a time when the city was experiencing a fiscal crisis and homelessness was increasing. Journalist Sarah Ferguson called closing the park the most expensive way to get a homeless-free park.[1]

Why did the city's earlier attempts to establish a homeless-free park fail whereas its most recent strategy apparently succeeded? And how had the counter-tactics devised by the homeless confounded earlier campaigns to force them from the park? This chapter explores how the homeless formed a symbiotic alliance with anarchists, squatters, and other groups opposed to gentrification in the East Village, and attributes their final removal to the political defeat, perhaps only temporary, of anti-gentrification forces. As chapter 11 noted, the homeless were neither the initial nor fundamental issue in the political contestations that closed Tompkins

Square Park. Their presence in the park emerged only belatedly as a political issue within the context of the larger battle over gentrification.

Between the winter of 1989 and the spring of 1991, the co-authors of this chapter observed activities in the park almost daily and talked at length with many of the park's users. At least one of us was present at every major altercation or eviction involving the homeless. We interviewed city officials and spoke casually with residents whenever something 'was up' in the neighborhood. We also attended most community meetings when residents debated what policies to adopt toward the homeless in the park. What we observed was a complex and dynamic process of 'political' negotiation over time, one that shaped and reshaped social relations within the park and that transformed its physical geography. While saddened by the final removal of the homeless, we were not surprised when that long anticipated event occurred. What surprised us most was the remarkable resilience of the 'community of homeless' which had survived earlier attempts to dislodge them.

HOMELESSNESS AND GENTRIFICATION IN THE EAST VILLAGE

One of our first observations was that the term '*the* homeless' was both inaccurate and an oversimplification. Many residents of Tompkins Square Park rejected the label 'homeless,' since they saw themselves as actively making homes. Furthermore, we found it difficult to generalize about the participants. Park residents had varying degrees of residential commitment to their 'homes,' had different reasons for settling there, and were engaged in a variety of often conflicting activities. And finally, despite the stereotypes of parks officials, the 'community' was far from a random collection of transients. Over time, residents had developed a complex system of spatial segregation, were adjudicating disputes among themselves, and had forged a set of survival skills that prolonged their occupation of the park.

The presence of 'homeless' people living in Tompkins Square Park in the late 1980s was not a new phenomenon. The Census of 1980 had recorded some fifty persons in the park that year, mostly white males.[2] According to the next census, this population had increased to over 200 and its composition had changed; by 1990 most were black and/or Hispanic. The number of whites remained stable (32 in 1980 and 34 in 1990) whereas the black population rose from 17 to 108 and that of Hispanics from 8 to 80. In both census years, the typical resident was an unattached man. Women constituted only 6 percent of all residents at both times, and in neither year were there any families with children.

Parks Department officials complained that one of the problems they faced in 'managing' Tompkins Square Park was the wide fluctuation in population and what Assistant Parks Commissioner Jack Linn referred to as 'the constantly changing cast of characters.' According to Linn's view of the situation, Tompkins Square Park was only one stop among many throughout the city and beyond for a predominantly transient population that has been estimated in the tens of thousands in New York City alone. Linn argued, with some validity, that even if alternative housing could be found for all current park residents, their places would soon be taken by others.[3]

The problem of homelessness is certainly larger than Tompkins Square Park. By the late 1980s, public concern over what to do about the homeless and frustration with the city's failure to handle the problem were escalating. Also escalating was the political consciousness of the homeless themselves. In New York a public demonstration at City Hall in December 1988 drew thousands of homeless people and their supporters to protest Mayor Koch's housing policies. A year later, a national housing demonstration in Washington DC stimulated the formation of New York's 'Tent City,' an organization by and for homeless people. This organization was later active in Tompkins Square Park.

Just before August 1988, about 200 people had been living in the park,[4] mostly sleeping in the unsheltered bench area along its northern edge, where smaller numbers had been for years. Their presence was decidedly peripheral to the heated exchanges over whether the city should enforce a curfew. Although Tompkins Square Park was the only city park without a curfew, which gave people the legal right to spend the night there, the homeless were not the only park users who benefited from a park without a curfew. Action-seeking youth from a wide sending area and local counter-culture groups, which often sponsored the music performances in the park's bandshell, also gained. The 'anarchists' and 'squatters' (see Van Kleunen, chapter 13) were the first to link a curfew-free park not only to their right to mount performances but to the right of the homeless to stay in the park. They challenged the proposed curfew on the grounds that 'the city is just trying to keep the homeless from staying in the park.'[5] Most newspaper accounts at the time dismissed this accusation as a typical example of anarchist paranoia; they denounced the performers for trying to shift the blame from the real source of conflict (their loud music) to the problem of the homeless, for which no one had a solution. Without completely accepting the anarchists' construction of events, we must admit that they were not only defending the right of the homeless to remain in the park, but were also strategically attempting to widen their base of support against the curfew. The anarchists may also have benefited from the presence of park residents in ways that media analysts did not recognize. The presence of the homeless in the park, especially after they began to construct makeshift shelters, focused the attention of pro-gentrification forces in the East Village on control of Tompkins Square Park, which tended to distract attention from the squats and may have slowed down the city's efforts to evict squatters.[6] Other groups, while not actively encouraging the homeless to settle in the park, were sympathetic to and in some instances supportive of their needs. Individuals from the neighborhood often conversed with certain park residents and nearby restaurants frequently distributed food. Local and even distant churches (Emmaeus House, for example, located in upper Manhattan) periodically visited to offer food and living alternatives.

Many East Village residents, however, expressed considerable ambivalence, especially about the more permanent structures that began to appear after the reprieve of August 1988. A local artist expressed this ambivalence well. Since 1989 she had been photo-documenting the structures built by the park's homeless. Explaining that she had matured during the 1960s, like many of her East Village friends she considered herself fairly 'liberal' and sympathetic to the homeless. She thought the homeless deserved better accommodations than city shelters. However, she felt that the homeless should not be allowed to live in the park because they interfered with its use by other residents. She observed that many residents were torn between empathy for the homeless and frustration at being denied use of one of the few green spaces in the area.[7] This ambivalence came out clearly in the remarks of Lower East Side residents who attended the rancorous Community Board 3 meeting held just after the park's closing. While unhappy with the situation, many East Villagers blamed not the homeless for usurping the public space of the park, but various city officials and policies for failing to offer a decent alternative. However, other East Villagers were more concerned to establish a homeless-free Tompkins Square Park, and their position became increasingly vocal at community meetings between the 1988 riot and the park's closing.

These changes in attitudes cannot be explained by any dramatic increases in the park census. While the number of persons living in the park fluctuated quite dramatically between 1988 and 1991, it never exceeded 300 and was under 200 at the time the park was closed. The city, therefore, could not legitimately claim that it closed the park in June because the homeless population had suddenly escalated. Rather, it was responding not only to the increased pressure being exerted by gentrification forces in the neighborhood, but also to its own growing frustration at the failure of its earlier attempts to clear the park. In addition, real estate developers had begun to blame the tapering off of gentrification and even the collapse of speculative values in the East Village on 'the homeless crisis in the neighborhood.' They joined local property owners in voicing a stronger NIMBY ('Not In My Back Yard') opposition – not only to the park dwellings but to local shelters, charging that the presence of the homeless and the institutions serving them posed a serious threat to local economic development and home values.[8]

Mayor Dinkins was also under attack for indecisiveness in solving the city's mounting problems. Whether or not these issues were accurately identified, they led to mounting pressures to remove the homeless from the park.

Early Attempts to Remove the Homeless

After a year of relative quiet in the aftermath of the 1988 riot, during which shelters became increasingly elaborate, the city made its first eviction attempt. On 5 July 1989, personnel from the Parks and Police Departments evicted about two hundred park residents and demolished some 40 shanties, declaring that they violated an ordinance forbidding 'tents and structures in the park.' City Council member Miriam Friedlander denounced these actions, complaining that 'the City Administration cannot solve the homeless problem with such sneak night attacks on the homeless in Tompkins Square.'[9] Indeed, they could not. Within a month, approximately 300 homeless were again living in the park.

Opposition to their presence was organizing, however. At an extremely heated community meeting on 18 October 1989, at which squatters were noticeably absent and groups of newly organized older 'ethnics' were present in large numbers, residents complained that the 'homeless' had 'taken over' the park and were preventing its use by non-homeless. (It was at this meeting that Parks Department representative Jack Linn first revealed plans to renovate the park in three stages, beginning at the northern end where the majority of shanties and park dwellers were concentrated, but then proceeding southward to encompass the rest of the park.) By a loud voice vote, participants demanded stricter enforcement of existing rules in the park, but even they *did not call for eviction of the homeless.* Nevertheless, on 15 November Miriam Friedlander announced that all structures and shanties would be demolished, but only after assistance had been given to residents. She gave assurances that evictions would not take place until outreach services had been provided through the new Tompkins Square Park Multi-Service Center which Borough President David Dinkins and Council member Friedlander initiated on 20 November 1989. *The New York Times* quoted Friedlander as defending the initiative as 'a humane plan that gives consideration to the people who live in the Park.'[10]

Most park residents demurred. When the plan for the 'help center' was announced at the November meeting, Keith Thompson, a well known spokesman for the homeless and a Tompkins Park resident, stood up and shouted, 'I tell you this, Miriam Friedlander, we're not going anywhere. We're staying in the park until we get affordable housing.' Although Jack Linn later claimed that 90 people had been relocated through the Help Center, park residents denied this vehemently. The homeless viewed the outreach service as a master plan to get rid of them. The anarchists and squatters, claiming to know what 'enforce the rules' and 'renovation' meant, had posted a flyer at the park entrance at Avenue B and Ninth Street immediately after the meeting of 18 October:

> Defend the Park: Hands off the Homeless!
> Bring food, pots & pans, blankets, wood and construction materials
> Tonite and all through the winter to Tompkins Square Park!!!

Some squatters began to sleep in the park, to show solidarity with the threatened population.

Nevertheless, when the demolition of the shacks finally took place on 14 December there was no serious resistance. The shacks were destroyed but occupants held on. About 10 persons moved into the garden of Trinity Church at the corner of Avenue B and Ninth Street, and by nightfall 20 more had returned to the benches. After midnight, fires, permitted by a special emergency court order, were again burning in the park. People began to reorganize their territories and reassemble their personal belongings. About 50 persons were back in the park the day after the sweep, even though the temperature had dropped to 10 degrees.

The park looked desolate. Some of the benches were partially protected and people huddled together around big fires. They slept in the daylight sun to avoid freezing to death at night. Some moved to squats in the neighborhood. The scene of their destitution aroused neighborhood sympathies. Some residents from the neighborhood brought food (mostly cookies, chips, popcorn, and cakes) and provided clothing, blankets, and sleeping bags. More and more neighborhood residents became involved, even participating in formal protective 'watches.' On 23 January when the temperature was only 3 degrees, the belongings of Al (one of our best friends in the park) were confiscated by the 'parkies.' A woman living on Avenue A saw everything from her window; she called a local radio station to report that 'at this moment, the Parks Department is taking someone's bed away in Tompkins Square Park.' Al was grateful, saying, 'I'm glad that at least someone looks after me.' Despite this basic charity provided by local residents, local churches, and soup kitchens, the park's open spaces emptied out. By January 1990, most of the people remaining in the park had sought shelter in the bandshell and bathrooms.

But as the weather improved, the Tompkins Square Park population regained its previous proportions. The census count at the end of March 1990 found 225 people in the park, and by summer of 1990 the nightly head-count had risen to 300, the same total Jack Linn had reported at the 18 October meeting. Thus, the population and the number of shelters had recovered to the levels reached between 'sweeps.' Thereafter, they fluctuated with the weather and with the actions of the city. Throughout the winter of 1991, the population living in the park ranged between 100 and 150. When the weather improved in the spring, they were joined by another hundred or so. From mid-April until 1 June 1991, the population stood at about 225, although residents were being warned that the Parks Department planned another sweep.[11] In fact, more than 50 people left just one day before the final closing of the park, so that only about 175 persons remained to be dislodged the next morning.

THE CHANGING PHYSICAL AND SOCIAL SPACE OF THE PARK

Just as the number of homeless living in the park was affected by the city's repeated attempts to evict them, so also were the areas of the park in which they established proprietary rights. To understand how this geographical transformation occurred and how the social organization of the homeless changed over time, one needs to visualize the physical layout of the park before its closing.

A recreational zone extends all across the northern third of the park, surrounded by a high chain-linked fence. This zone is divided into three subareas: on the east are basketball and handball courts; the middle section contains a fountain and wading pool; and on the west is a hard-surfaced recreational space which serves variously as a 'theater' for performance artists, a rink for skateboarders, and a playing field for informal games of catch, baseball, and football. BMXers and even kids with remote-controlled cars use this space when it is not otherwise occupied. This area was renovated in 1990, with the full support of the community board. Two other renovations were made at the same time, namely, the playgrounds with their brightly colored and indestructible iron-pipe climbing jungles and swings, one located in the southeastern corner of the park, the other on the west side just south of the active recreational zone. A large sign announces that these are off-limits to all but children and their guardians. Park rules also restrict access to the designated dog run, just north of the playground on the southeast corner, to all but dogs and their owners.

Between the fenced recreation space and the Park House (located centrally along the park path equivalent to Ninth Street) was an area park residents affectionally called the DMZ ('de-militarized zone'), since theoretically, all park users and subgroups of homeless shared access to it. Chain-link fencing surrounded this quiet sanctuary, which had been popular with a small coterie of newspaper readers and coffee sippers. The homeless, though rarely more than a few at a time, used to steal a quiet moment in the DMZ, but, for the most part, park guidelines established in 1990 encouraged them to stay on the southern end of the park.

But the park's physical appearance and social geography in the spring of 1991 had evolved considerably from what it had been only two years earlier. In August 1989, before the approved renovations were underway, 'shanties' had clustered along the northwestern edge along East Tenth Street and in the park's southwestern corner at the intersection of Seventh Street and Avenue A. Park residents had also built shanties along the periphery of the park, both inside and outside the park's gate. By then, the fountain was no longer in operation, but its associated wading pool was popular among park residents for bathing and laundering. The poorly equipped playground areas were not restricted to children and their custodians, and park residents freely lunched and napped there. Also, the dog run was then located on 'the Hill' – a gently sloping grassy mound at the park's center that had allegedly been formed from dirt excavated from the bandshell's foundation in 1965.

The city's renovation of the northern section of the park began to change the social organization of the homeless encampment and their relations to non-park users, and after the first shanty demolition in the summer of 1989, the homeless were regrouped toward the southern end of the park. Nevertheless, many areas remained open to them. Throughout the two-year period of study, the bandshell (an imposing high platform stage enclosed by three solid sides and a full roof, located in the middle part of the southern edge of the park)[12] accommodated fairly large numbers of sleepers, shopping carts, and piles of cans or clothing when it was not being used for concerts and performances. In addition, the park's bathrooms had become the almost exclusive preserve of park residents, although there were often conflicts over access since those wanting to sleep in the stalls often prevented others from using the toilets for more customary purposes.[13] In addition, drug users moved to the bathrooms in winter when they could no longer use the summer screen of rich park foliage to hide from police surveillance.

But mixing between the homeless and other park users was common. The southwestern end of the park continued to house the chess tables where elderly European men spent long hours playing chess, smoking, and drinking. Bench space scattered throughout the park, when not converted to shelter by park residents, accommodated local teenagers (often inaccurately referred to as 'punks' and/or 'skinheads'), younger 'anarchists,' college students, a dedicated group of Ukrainian friends often referred to by other park users as the 'Eastern Bloc Alcoholics,' and others. And there were always those who held up the park gate and fence around the perimeter by leaning against it, congregating mostly near Avenue A to watch the pedestrian parade of East Village patrons.[14] Fence leaners included loiterers, panhandlers, housing activists with sign-up sheets or literature, and even police officers. Occasionally, joggers lapped the park's perimeter.

Raising a Home in the Park

Tompkins Square Park's various, overlapping areas were not only differentiated in terms of the physical space users occupied, but also in terms of the social relations that developed in them. Both underwent a sequence of subtle (and sometimes not so subtle) shifts over the two-year period. Within the park, these shifts entailed considerable negotiations among the diverse groups that made up the homeless population. Like the differences between homeless and non-homeless users, the differences among park residents were occasionally marked by tensions that could erupt into conflict.

Park residents differentiated themselves along two axes: (1) the degree of their residential commitment to Tompkins Square Park; and (2) their interests and activities within the park. Fitting the Parks Department's stereotype, some residents were clearly transients, briefly taking a seat on a park bench or staying overnight or for a few days on their way to somewhere else or using the park as a temporary refuge when they had had a fight with their families.[15] However, many of the park residents we got to know were relatively settled, having spent many years in the park. From their perspective, their long-term presence represented a bona fide residential commitment. 'Junior,' also called 'The Mayor' (of Tompkins Square Park), was a black man in his middle fifties who had been living in Tompkins Square Park for seven years. When we got to know him he was occupying a small section of the bench area on the park's southern end. Knowing he had been included among the 'homeless' in a Parks Department head count one day, he expressed his resentment at being considered 'homeless': 'The park *is* my home, but most people don't want to accept that fact. Society tells us that if you don't got a house, you don't got a home. I *got* a home. You're sitting in my living room.' He had a point. The term 'homeless' often did not accurately apply to a good portion of Tompkins Square Park residents. The existence of permanent structures within the park gave testimony that at least some of the residents were not transients. They fully intended to stay in place.

Especially by the summer of 1989, one would have been justified in describing the park as a shanty *settlement* for the formerly homeless, similar to the favelas and bidonvilles associated more with third world cities than with an American metropolis. The makeshift homes were gradually becoming more elaborate and personalized, reflecting each builder's sense of privacy and order. The park benches served as foundations. Metal shopping or canvas mail carts, covered by blue plastic tarpaulins, provided the basic building materials for the creation of alternative living spaces. These structures became increasingly permanent and contained neatly piled possessions, mostly the revalorized discards of residents and store owners around the park. The new 'neighbors' cooked on fires stoked in metal trash cans and washed their clothes in the park's wading pool.

The 'homeless' who were making homes for themselves had some common interests that created a basis for cooperation and community. First and foremost, they had a common interest in keeping the park open and in ensuring their right to remain. The perpetual fear that they would be evicted or that their shanties would be demolished if 'park order' broke down forced them, despite their differences, to maintain order. Those who stayed only briefly in a larger circuit of their transient itinerary were perhaps less committed, but they too cooperated to preserve a low profile. Most women and girls, for instance, used the park only now and then. As their stories revealed, they were usually in transition from one intolerable living condition to another. They viewed the park as a necessary, albeit temporary, accommodation rather than a permanent shelter. In addition, some young women used the park's spaces to escape from parental supervision or as a place for illicit activities. Teenagers frequently used the park's bathrooms and bandshell to smoke or shoot up drugs.

Over time, the homeless developed a strong sense of territoriality, virtually 'privatizing' the public space they had come to occupy. They not only asserted their rights to individual sites, constructing their shelters on them, but also over their collective space, first protecting the clusters of shanties built along the park's perimeters and then, once such dwellings had been regrouped after the December 1989 eviction, establishing their rights over the single large south central area ceded to them. The new pattern of concentration transformed the relationship between the park residents and their Lower East Side neighbors, yielding a new *modus vivendi*. Physical segregation of the homeless paradoxically permitted a normalization of relations. Local residents felt freer to use park facilities, especially the newly renovated recreational spaces in the northern end. Brief conversations between some neighborhood people and the homeless occurred more frequently. Some park residents explained that they somehow had to 'show everyone that the homeless could use the park without keeping others from using it too.' During 1990, there was little conflict between the homeless and other park users.

The relationships of the homeless among themselves also changed as a result of their relocation. Now that they were more concentrated, they had to devise ways to organize themselves and to defuse any tensions that might arise from their differing interests and activities. Informal 'zones' began to be labeled. By 1990, for instance, park residents had established a 'theft-free zone' around 'The Mayor's spot' near 'The Hill.' This was clearly distinguished from another area where heavy drug users congregated, which some residents derisively labeled the 'substance abuse zone.' In addition, park residents referred to a section of benches located on either side of the park thoroughfare linking Ninth Street as the 'safety zone,' because Parks Department employees and police officers cruised there regularly and night lighting offered extra protection to those, like the elderly, who were particularly vulnerable to violent attack.

Practicing such exclusionary zoning among themselves helped park residents reduce conflict and isolate potential problems. For instance, many of the homeless believed that drug use was a problem, in part because it might be used as a pretext to evict them all from the park. In 1989, 'Little Haiti,' named after the ethnic origin of its occupants, was located at the southwest corner of the park along Seventh Street; it was reputed to be a drug-infested area. According to Thomas, who lived for three months on the park's bandshell:

> A reason for the current problems is the attitude of some homeless groups in the park. Little Haiti turned people off. It has led to stigmatization of homeless people in the park, and in general. The same for the Ukrainians in the park. They hang out near the chess tables and drink all day. They are alcoholics and in this sense are substance abusers too. They add to the problems.[16]

Thomas' understanding that park residency was tenuous and contingent on responses from the neighborhood was shared by many of the park residents, as was their determination to avoid visible conflict that might be used to justify another eviction. Park residents reached unspoken agreements with park personnel and enforced discipline on their own. For example, in November 1990, a new park employee, driving a department pick-up truck, trashed the contents of a canvas mail cart parked in front of the bandshell. Someone living in the bandshell threw a bottle at the truck, angering the new employee who turned his truck around and gunned it toward the bandshell. The front of his truck clipped the mail cart which he had just emptied.[17] Before violence could escalate, three other park residents not living in the bandshell rushed to the scene to pacify the outraged bottle thrower. Five others went immediately to the Park House to file a formal complaint. One of the Parks personnel apologized for the mistake, explaining that the new employee was not yet familiar with the informal rules governing the everyday management of Tompkins Square, which tolerated the presence of possession-filled shopping carts. However, some park residents suggested that the 'parkies' had imported this new employee on a one-day assignment in order to 'test the winds.'

Park residents occasionally used their self-management in a more aggressive way to dissociate their collective identity from the activities of 'skinheads' and anarchists. Renaldo, a park resident who endured the two demolitions of 1989 and left the park only in the final hour of the 1991 closing, told us how he and other residents handled a group of 'skinheads' – teenagers with shaved heads and radical behavior – who had begun sleeping in the park. The newcomers came in late at night, drunk, and made so much noise that many of the park residents complained they could not get to sleep; residents feared that the youths would get everyone else into trouble. One night, a group of park residents surrounded their tents. Renaldo described the brief but effective confrontation. 'We told them that if they didn't leave we'd make them leave. And that was the end of it. They left that evening.'[18]

Thus, many of the homeless learned to self-consciously monitor their use of the park and their interactions with neighborhood residents and park authorities to fend off negative images of themselves in the media and political debates, and thus to prevent other groups from justifying their removal from the park. At first the homeless learned to posture themselves blamelessly in their interactions with non-resident park users in order to avoid negative attention. Later, they used this same politics of self-discipline offensively.

While all shared a common interest in mutual protection, subgroups of residents also evolved from shared interests and activities. The 'can collectors' constituted one such group. Refuting the stereotype that the homeless are a dependent and lazy population, these men were highly mobile and active. They rose early in the morning and worked late, returning cans for cash sometimes as far away as the southern tip of Manhattan. Can lore was central to their conversations. At night they would park, cover and tie their shopping and mail carts together, and then 'talk cans,' sharing their very specialized knowledge and language.

> "What are you doing with those *Blatz?*" [cans of a cheap beer not eligible for deposits that one can-collector was throwing into a discard pile]

"You don't know where to take these?"

"You mean you can get money for those?"

"Yeah, just crush 'em up – you know where to turn in flat aluminum, don't you?"

"Yeah, but not Blatz."

"Hell, they ain't gonna read 'em when they're crushed up!"

"I guess that's true . . . I guess they can't. I like that!

Other park residents were involved in the politics of homelessness. Although this was a relatively small group of about 30 people, members were vocal and had extensive contacts outside the park's boundaries. They defended the construction of shanty settlements as a viable alternative to the city's hated public-shelter system, arguing that life in Tompkins Square Park was safer, more peaceful, and provided a greater sense of community than any city shelter. None, however, preferred living in the park to a decent affordable room: they all supported low-income housing and opposed gentrification of city neighborhoods. After the national housing demonstration in Washington DC in October 1989, a group of homeless people formed 'Tent City' to register political protests against the city's housing policy. By exposing homelessness in the public arena they hoped to convince the city to provide more housing. Although their immediate goal was to keep the park open for the homeless until alternative shelter space could be made available, their wider preoccupation was with gentrification as the cause of the loss of low-income housing. They saw the park, therefore, as the first battle field against gentrification.

The 'Tent City' people formed an alliance with the anarchists and other housing activists in the neighborhood. Although some developed strong ties to the squatters, they preferred the park to living in abandoned buildings. Some saw themselves as the 'vanguard' of Tompkins Square Park residents and could not understand why their co-residents would not join their larger struggle. But even if they had been able to mobilize all park residents solidly behind their program, it is unlikely that their resistance could have stood up to the final attack on the park that was mounted in June of 1991. Indeed, it was their allies, the 'squatter/anarchists,' who created the *casus belli* that eventually dislodged them from the park.

Razing a Home and a Park

The last act began with the so-called Memorial Day 'riot' the night of 27–8 May 1991, and culminated when, a few days later, the homeless were unceremoniously evicted and the police barricaded the park. The 'cause' of the riot had a familiar ring. Not only did it occur on Memorial Day week-end (as had an earlier one between 'flower children' and the police in 1967), but it was again associated with a rock concert in the bandshell, organized by local squatters and activists. The assembled crowd 'exploded into violence . . . [in reaction] to police harassment of one of the young homeless men who had taken up residence in the park . . . [T]he anarchists occupied Avenue A, blocking traffic, overturning garbage cans and lighting bonfires.'[19] The police took this as the opportunity it had been waiting for and the homeless had most feared.

Although the residents in Tompkins Square Park had been expecting another park sweep and had been practicing non-violent forms of resistance, they were not prepared for the massive attack that occurred on 3 June. They were awakened to the sight and sound of perhaps 300 riot-geared police officers marching in formation toward their 'homes' from all sides of the park. The situation was a rout. Renie left the following frantic message on our telephone answering machine: 'Something's going down here at the park! Looks like we're outta here. [Deputy Mayor] Lynch was here talking last night, and I had gotten the impression we'd have another day to clear our stuff. I gotta pack!' Junior compared the event to the final scene in *Butch Cassidy and the Sundance Kid*, when hero-outlaws Redford and Newman were surrounded by a hundred Mexican soldiers. Although seven people were arrested for refusing to leave the park, four of them also charged with resisting arrest, none was from among the 175 homeless people who decided to stay until the final call: 'Everyone out!'

That day, New York City Parks Commissioner Betsy Gotbaum announced in front of local TV crews at the park that she took complete blame for 'the chaotic condition of the park' and added that she intended to rectify matters.[20] She enumerated the three options the Community Action Unit, a committee comprised of parks, police, human resources and City Hall officials, had considered to restore 'social order':

1 They could close the park down, clean it up, and re-open it with a nightly curfew enforced by the police.
2 They could sponsor an early morning sweep to remove shelters occupied by the squatters.
3 They could clean up the park in stages to keep the homeless on the move.

To park residents, Gotbaum's last two options were already familiar. Both had already failed. Early morning sweeps (option 2) had been implemented in July and December of 1989, but without lasting results. The plan to clean up the park in stages (option 3) had been initiated in 1990 when renovations began on the northern third and the homeless were re-segregated elsewhere, but that plan had also failed to yield a 'homeless-free' park. Now, Gotbaum's option 1 was being followed, even though it had earlier been rejected. David Dinkins had given orders to 'close the park down, clean it up, and re-open it with a nightly curfew.' Renovations were expected to take some 18 months.

The cost of exercising that option was a serious erosion of trust between the community and city government. In essence, the city abandoned any attempt to work through Community Board 3. The police had always had more than enough brute force to control local protests. However, it had sought local community support for its actions. Not only had the community failed to support its prior shanty demolitions, but Community Board 3 had vigorously opposed closing the park. This 'social network of resistance' had effectively confounded the city's earlier attempts to establish a curfew and to remove the homeless. The administration now had to override a decision of its own creation.

Given the city's decision to move despite local opposition, the residual coalition between the homeless and their more radical supporters was powerless to resist the heavy display of police force. Like the homeless, who subsequently relocated on vacant city lots between Avenues B and D along Seventh, Eighth and Ninth Streets, the squatters and 'anarchists' could not challenge the police physically. Once the homeless were forced from the park, the original social network of resistance was disempowered and protests proved futile. Such protests on behalf of the absent homeless were soon abandoned.

By closing the park to all, against the recommendation of the local community board, the city had angered a broader spectrum of residents who for a short time voiced their outrage in unison with the anarchists and squatters. Chants of 'police state' were joined, even by those who had formerly opposed the presence of the homeless in the park.[21] But this newly forged network of resistance soon dissolved. Whether as the result of true political compromise or as the final step in a plan that may have anticipated (even banked on) such a community response, the city offered immediate concessions. They reopened certain areas of the park – the playgrounds for children, the dog run, and the recreational facilities along the northern end, although they also imposed a 9:30 curfew. At the same time, however, the bandshell was demolished and the homeless were legally prevented from returning. By summer's end, the protests and demonstrations gradually dissipated.

THE AFTERMATH

The non-violent departure of the homeless and their failure to participate in the summer's gradually de-escalating protests did not reflect acceptance of defeat; they simply had no time to waste because they had to set up new homes. Many moved directly to two vacant city-owned lots east of Avenue B. One, located on Ninth between Avenues C and D, accommodated 25 structures housing from 50 to 70 homeless people, whereas at the time of the park's closing there had been only five structures there. This lot was the site of a thriving drug trade that attracted, among other people, non-homeless teen-aged girls in the early morning and evening. The second lot, named 'Dinkinsville' by its new occupants, was located on Eighth Street between Avenues B and C. In a space a third the size of the Ninth Street lot were crowded another two dozen makeshift structures. Occupants of both shantytowns were predominantly but not exclusively black and male. One distinguishing feature (which impressed many photo-journalists) was the improvised sidewalk shower whose illegal attachment to an adjacent fire hydrant was dismantled each evening. But sanitation problems plagued the settlements. Several Portosans (portable toilets) were placed on the lots by local community groups, but money soon ran out and their rental had to be discontinued. The strength of the homeless also ran out.

A banner draped along the chain-linked fence around one of the relocation lots had read: 'Tompkins Square Park in Exile. The Homeless Aren't the Criminals. The System Is.' A resident interpreted this message for us: 'Most of us have better places to go, far away from here . . . but we choose to stay here together . . . where we cannot be made invisible.' But, indeed, they were eventually 'made' invisible. In September, the police forced the disbanding of these alternative settlements and most of the former residents of Tompkins Square Park had to find alternative crevices in the city's interstitial spaces in which to hide. Some moved to other empty lots farther east near Avenue D, but the social community that grew up in the park and that we observed for more than two years no longer exists.

NOTES

1 Sarah Ferguson, 'Tompkins Squares Everywhere,' *Village Voice*, 24 September 1991, p. 29.

2 At first we were inclined to dismiss this number as a typographical error but now we believe, given the characteristics of these 50, that park residents were indeed enumerated by census takers in tract 32, block 101 (1980 census).

3 Interview conducted with Jack Linn in June 1991. The situation of the homeless did not improve under the Dinkins administration. In September 1991, *The New York Times* (see Thomas Morgan, 'New York Admits Failure of Homeless Family Effort,' *The New York Times*, 18 September 1991, p. B3) cited predictions by city officials that 6,000 families would be living in the shelters

by June 1992, breaking the 1987 record set during the Koch administration. During the same month, Nancy Wackstein, the frustrated director of the mayor's Office on Homelessness and SRO Housing, announced her resignation.

4 Joann Wypijewski, 'Tompkins Square Park,' *Zeta Magazine* (November 1988), p. 86.

5 Telephone interview with John Mensing in July 1991. Mensing, sympathetic to the anarchists' agenda, participated in negotiations with Bill Lynch during the park closure which helped influence a non-violent removal of the homeless from the park, once the plan to close the park had become decidedly unpreventable. Mensing thought that the anarchists had purposefully attached themselves to the homeless issue – unsure if the tactic would benefit their agenda to resist gentrification but seeing nothing to lose, and potentially confounding the city's attempt to establish a curfew in the park. He found our argument too calculated. He did not see the anarchist move as a diversionary tactic to prevent the city from focusing on their squats, but rather emphasized the anarchists' genuine concern for the way a curfew would negatively affect their use of the park.

6 Interview with Jeff Wengrofsky in June 1991. A later interview (July) with 'Manny,' a squatter on East Seventh Street, both confirms and complicates this analysis. Manny claims that while many of the more thoughtful anarchists understood this diversionary effect, most anarchists were 'unfortunately' more motivated to act instinctively against authority, without thinking beyond the significance of that end in itself.

7 Interview with Margaret Morton in May 1991.

8 As shown in the chapters on gentrification, there were deeper causes of this 'collapse.'

9 Press release, entitled 'Friedlander Condemns Police Action in Tompkins Square,' dated 6 July 1989, distributed by the office of council member Miriam Friedlander.

10 James Barron, 'The Removal of Tompkins Square Homeless is Set,' *The New York Times*, 16 November 1989, p. B4.

11 At an all-day meeting held in a hall on St Marks Place on Sunday 2 June to discuss the problems of housing in the East Village, one of the representatives from the park's homeless community announced soberly that residents expected eviction within 48 hours. He also announced that residents were being trained in forms of non-violent resistance (Abu-Lughod field notes), although when the sweep came early the next morning, they had no opportunity to put these skills into practice against more than 300 police officers.

12 Demolished on 27 August 1991, after the park was closed.

13 Perhaps this fact helps shed more light on the park residents' dilemma than the usual moral condemnation of human excrement found throughout the park grounds during and just prior to shanty demolitions and the park's closing.

14 Who, in turn, furtively watched them!

15 The few women in the park tended to fall into this category.

16 Racial tensions might have played a role here, but they were not simply white versus black. The older Ukrainian residents were very anti-homeless, since their bench space was under threat by the homeless. The tensions between the homeless and Ukrainians were especially complex.

17 The inexperienced 'parkie' was later cited for reckless driving by a police officer who had been called to the scene.

18 Interview with Renaldo Valentino, a park resident, in May of 1991.

19 Bill Weinberg, 'Tompkins Square Park as Police State,' in *Downtown*, no. 249, 19–26 June 1991.

20 Field notes of 30 May 1990.

21 Field notes from the 18 June meeting of the community board. Even Miriam Friedlander used the word 'outraged' when she addressed the meeting.

13

The Squatters: A Chorus of Voices . . . But is Anyone Listening?

Andrew Van Kleunen

LOWER EAST SIDE SQUATTER COMMUNITY STATEMENT

Who We Are, and What We Believe

We are young and old, black, white, Latino, and Asian, families and singles. We are people of the Lower East Side. The majority of us are low income people. We can no longer afford the skyrocketing rents in our own neighborhood.

We believe housing is a basic human right for all people without exception . . . Governments are not addressing the problem in any realistic or humane manner. Therefore we have taken charge of this important area of our lives: housing. Along with $\frac{1}{4}$ of the world's population, we have moved into vacant, unused land and buildings . . . Through our own resources and creativity we are rebuilding structures left abandoned by the city for years. We have developed a great sense of pride, community, and vision which happens when a group of people begin to reclaim their lives and powers. We've proven through squatting that we can provide immediate, safe housing for people who live in the buildings while working on them . . .

We believe it is criminal for homeless men, women, and children to suffer in dangerous shelters, on the streets, or doubled up in crowded apartments when there is plenty of vacant housing. We believe that in a crisis of homelessness as today's, it is right and necessary for homeless people to seize available housing for themselves and their families. We believe Tompkins Square Park, and all parks, should be places where homeless people can sleep until permanent housing exists for the homeless in NYC. No curfew in Tompkins Square Park! We will fight any forced removal of homeless people into military facilities now being renovated for use as shelters outside the city.

We believe the city must be stopped from selling off our vacant land for luxury development that only a few can possibly afford. The vast majority of local people are, in fact, low-income people. Therefore, we demand an overall plan be developed for the Lower East Side by the people of the Lower East Side.

We believe squatters and tenants must work together to prevent more people from being forced out of the neighborhood by evictions, co-opping, arson, higher rents, etc.

Access to our buildings is not and never will be limited by racial or ethnic discrimination. As a whole, our buildings are and will always continue to be racially and ethnically integrated.

We have a viable housing program that provides truly affordable housing at a fraction of the cost of all other methods and programs . . . As resident caretakers of our buildings, we will maintain these properties as permanent low-income housing, affordable to anyone, to be passed to future generations for their welfare. Therefore we are committed to the creation of a united position and a unified agreement among all squats to protect our buildings, to allow us to speak with one voice, and to guarantee that our buildings and apartments can never be made commodities to be sold or rented for profit.

We are organized to prevent evictions by any governmental or non-governmental body. By defending our homes, we defend the fundamental right of all people to have decent, affordable homes.[1]

'We Will Not Surrender Our Land or Our Homes.
We Will Not Disappear or Cease to Exist!'[2]

No discussion of the last decade's events on the Lower East Side would be complete without a word from the neighborhood's 'squatter community.' A disparate collection of approximately 500 people living in some 20 vacant buildings scattered throughout Loisaida,[3] the squatters provide an alternative voice (or, more accurately, 'voices') to local debates that extend far beyond controversies around their own occupation of abandoned tenements: the fight against gentrification, the closing of Tompkins Square Park, the recurring police brutality in the neighborhood, the eviction of poor street peddlers from local sidewalks, the city's demolition of buildings (usually squatters' homes) in order to assemble land for sale on the open market. Every one of these local struggles would have played out differently had it not been for the presence of the neighborhood's squatter community.

But such activism has earned the squatters more than their share of critics. Not only have they come into direct confrontation with the Police Department, HPD, City Hall, and the federal government, as well as with locally interested 'conservatives' ranging from real estate investors to right-wing politicians, but the squatters have also become embattled with local 'liberal' institutions like the Joint Planning Council (JPC), which the squats accuse of 'selling out' the neighborhood. They chide these liberal cadres for being more concerned with 'keeping their socially conscious organizations in business' than with defending Loisaida's low-income residents. Such pointed critiques, when added to the squatters' occupation of buildings which JPC organizations have been eyeing for their own projects, have sown a good deal of resentment between these two anti-gentrification groups.

But the squat community has drawn its most damning criticism for those extreme occasions when some of its more radical members have contributed to the neighborhood's most infamous and explosive eruptions: the 'riots' around the park, the heated shouting matches at community board meetings, etc.[4] Reporters, city officials, local elites, and even many community residents have relied on such extreme episodes to construct a distorted and condemning stereotype of the entire squatter population: namely, that they are a reckless gang of young, outspoken, white 'self-styled anarchists' from middle-class suburbs who have little regard for the sensibilities of other Lower East Siders and whose political agenda is reducible to the launching of empty bottles at the police in an attempt to 'smash the State.'

Surely there are members of the squat community who resemble a less extreme version of this 'anarchist' stereotype. It might also be said that the squatters' movement has its definite 'anarchistic' qualities. But to characterize the Lower East Side's 500 squatters as a homogeneous band of 'anarchists' (especially in the pejorative manner in which that label has been used by squat opponents) is categorically incorrect. Not only does such a depiction cloud our recognition of the diversity of people who have moved into Loisaida's vacant buildings, but it also prevents us from assessing the variety of motives that have prompted such a wide range of people to take this 'radical' action in the first place. Uninformed acceptance of the stereotype precludes an understanding of the way in which the 'labeling' of the squats has succeeded in promoting the interests of a once marginal, but now increasingly influential, conservative minority in the Lower East Side community.

It was one of the latest 'attacks' on the squats by a few members of this prodevelopment minority that prompted a cross-section of the squat population to come together and compose the 'Squatters Community Statement' excerpted above.[5] It was intended to 'set the record straight' about who the squatters are and why they believe that squatting is vital to the preservation of Loisaida and the housing of its people. Their hope was to clarify their goals to the local public, so that they might forge a progressive alliance between the squats and other Loisaiders: primarily with the neighborhood's homeless and low-income residents, but also with those liberal housing advocates who were willing to acknowledge the political and practical legitimacy of a squatter presence on the Lower East Side.

Along some similar lines, this chapter is intended to expose some aspects of the squatter movement which rarely enjoy the light of public scrutiny. Before we can fairly evaluate the squatters' motivations, we need to examine the history, the composition, and the beliefs of the movement in a manner not presently allowed to us by popular stereotypes. Based on observations and discussions with a variety of people from the squat community,[6] this preliminary report is meant to project some of the voices of the squatters' movement, so that other anti-gentrification constituencies on the Lower East Side might recognize the opportunity (and the necessity) for serious dialogue with their squatter neighbors.

The Recent History of Squatting on the Lower East Side

It is difficult to discuss when and how squatting started on the Lower East Side, since people have been establishing 'unauthorized' homes on city-owned and private property in Loisaida for decades, if not centuries. To go back just a few years, during the 1960s and 1970s numerous vacant tenements, office buildings, and factories in Lower Manhattan were occupied by artists, musicians, and counter-cultural types (the 'hippies' and 'yippies') looking for 'free space' to pursue their crafts and alternative lifestyles. Illegal 'crash pads,' where people took over vacant buildings for anywhere from a few nights to a few years, were common during that time. Also during that era, radical political organizations like the Puerto Rican Young Lords were very active in Loisaida's Latino community. The Lords were well known for organizing large-scale occupations of vacant buildings in 'el Barrio' in upper Manhattan and attempted some smaller-scale building seizures on the Lower East Side as well.

Land clearance for urban renewal, governmental neglect of tenement housing, and capital disinvestment in Loisaida throughout the 1970s only swelled the stock of abandoned housing units available for such spontaneous housing strategies. For example, early in that decade some local people occupied several Lower East Side buildings which had been vacated to make way for urban renewal. These squatters had intended to stay only temporarily in these buildings until reconstruction commenced. But when they and other community residents learned that the new housing planned for those sites would not be offered to local people (e.g., two buildings were designated as nurses dormitories for an expanding hospital in the area), Lower East Siders demanded that the buildings be permanently given to their illegal occupants.[7] In another case, two vacant *in rem* buildings on Fourth Street were taken over and rehabilitated by a group of politically active and recently immigrated Puerto Rican men. After they had brought their families over from 'the island,' these squatters successfully negotiated with the city government for legal title to their buildings. Many of those families still live there today, testaments to the neighborhood's 'squat' heritage.

Also during this period, the Lower East Side's 'homesteading' movement found much of its inspiration in the defiant illegality of squatting. The city's homesteading program, which granted legal title and financial assistance to prospective owner-occupiers willing to rehabilitate abandoned city-owned buildings, was established in the late 1970s only after illegal occupations such as those mentioned above had multiplied to an alarming level throughout the ghettos and barrios of New York.[8] Even after the homesteading program was established, the city was reluctant to offer title and funding to low-income applicants, and usually did so only after a group of homesteaders had illegally asserted *de facto* 'ownership' of a property. Thus, there remains to this day a certain philosophical connection between current squatters and some of the Lower East Side's long-time homesteaders.[9] Squatter relations with formal homesteading *organizations* (RAIN and LESAC), however, have cooled amidst growing competition over the neighborhood's remaining vacant buildings.

Another effect of the 'blowout' of Loisaida was the increased number of occupied tenements which, after their tax delinquency and vestment by the city, were placed under the charge of HPD's Office of Central Management. Under this inefficient city bureaucracy, many of these occupied buildings became unlivable. Those tenants who did not leave stopped paying rent to the city and began to run the buildings themselves, in some cases joined by newcomers who collaborated with them to service and renovate the properties. This had been the situation in three adjacent *in rem* buildings near Avenue D where, after a few years of HPD's management, only 10 of the 62 apartments were still occupied.[10] In 1981, after tenants had made some progress in rehabilitating and reoccupying the buildings, HPD brought eviction proceedings against all the residents, claiming that their unauthorized actions had made them all 'squatters' – the term used in tenant-landlord court for lawbreakers who have illegally appropriated someone else's property.[11] As the legal battle between the squatters and the city wore on, some 46 organizations, including members of the JPC, rallied to the squatters' side. Regardless, by 1986, after years of court rulings and appeals, it seemed the Avenue D occupants were facing imminent eviction. But by then, a new and growing constituency of Lower East Siders was already mobilizing to join the Avenue D cause. They came from the new wave of squats that had sprung up throughout the neighborhood since 1985.

This new generation of squats differed somewhat from its predecessors. For one, the new squats housed a significant number of white inhabitants, both from the Lower East Side and elsewhere. But these were hardly white islands in the Loisaida sea. In fact, the squats were quite heterogeneous, exhibiting the same kind of diversity that can be seen in today's squat population.[12] Some of the new squats also exhibited an expressly radical political orientation that had not been evident earlier. This new consciousness might be traced to the context in which these squats were founded: the surge of homelessness in New York during the 1980s and the accelerating efforts of the Koch administration to gentrify the Lower East Side (see Sites, chapter 9). Hence, squats established during this post-1985 period were seen not only as places to live, but also as bases for a new movement of community-based direct action which could challenge the displacement of low-income New Yorkers and the transformation of Loisaida.

Arising from this new local squatter base was the 'Valentine's Day Committee for Housing Justice,' a coalition of squatters not only from Loisaida but also from the South Bronx and other areas of New York. The committee's immediate objective was to mount a proactive defense on behalf of the three Avenue D squats. On 14 February 1986, members of the committee attempted to occupy HPD's central offices, demanding 'amnesty' for the three buildings.[13] The action clearly signaled to the city and the Joint Planning Council that a new and more confrontational actor had entered the fray.

Frank Morales, an Episcopalian minister, was one of the squatters from the South Bronx who participated in the Valentine's Day Committee. He eventually resettled in one of the squats that comprised an entire 'squat block' on Eighth Street just east of Tompkins Square – what some squatters call the 'mothership' of the current movement.[14] In a recent interview, Morales reflected on political aspects of the squat scene at that time:

> 319 and 327 East 8th were the first ones on the block. 319 was already going, and then 327 was opened up by a bunch of people, including folks from New York, San Francisco, Rome, Berlin, etc. That became a real hot-bed of ideology. It was a great building . . . highly political. Every night, it was a beehive of activity. People from all over the country and the world were coming there. And there were meetings, and new crews were going out to open up new buildings. And the politics were around 'Spatial Deconcentration.' [See below.] It was on everybody's lips . . . 'Spatial Deconcentration is Forced Relocation!' . . . The Valentine's Committee was very clear in its focus. It was two things: An affirmative OFFENSE strategy: TAKE BUILDINGS. So we organized groups. People made pamphlets on how to open buildings up. And a bunch of squats opened up all over the place. And there was a DEFENSIVE strategy: 'EVICTION WATCH.' Once a month, all the buildings would get together and link up. This group would not constitute itself as an authority over any of your buildings, but would be a place where people could link up. Why go to an Eviction Watch meeting? Because if the cops come to your building, and you shout, and nobody even knows you because you don't come to any collective meetings, nobody's going to be able to defend you! And people generally liked to come to the meetings. They were festive occasions. You got to see people from the other buildings. If you needed a buzz-saw, you could find somebody with a buzz-saw. Those first couple of years, that defensive network functioned very effectively, such that we called out people to defend buildings at least a dozen times prior to 1988. In fact, the defense of the park [in August 1988] was due, in part, to the base that had been generated

> by three years of work [defending our buildings]. That's why when people shouted 'Curfew!' there was immediately a crowd at the park.

How did the other housing groups react to this new radical presence in the neighborhood? At first, there seemed to be an unspoken understanding between the squatters and the JPC that each would 'do its own thing.' Although each had misgivings about the other's tactics and agendas, there still seemed to be enough room for them to stand on the same side of the issues regarding housing affordability and gentrification. In 1985–6 the number of squats in the neighborhood was still small and the stock of vacant buildings was large enough to limit friction between the two groups over project sites. Furthermore, the JPC (through Community Board 3, on which it had recently won expanded representation) was still negotiating with the Koch administration over the cross-subsidy plan, which it believed could slow City Hall's prodevelopment plans.

Squatters cite incidents from the mid-1980s when there was even something close to *collaboration* between the squats and the housing organizations. Leaders from a JPC affiliate might come to a squat in the middle of the night to enlist the squatters' 'expert assistance' to scare away a suspected vandal from one of the organization's vacant 'homesteads.' Similarly, there were times when JPC executives joined in the fight to prevent the city's forced eviction of one of the newer squats. John Mensing, a former 'anarchist' squatter from East Fifth Street, recounts the following:

> We were having a squatters benefit party at 'Neither/Nor' on New Year's Eve in 1986, and the city and the police decided to move on the Fifth Street building that same night. And somebody ran over to the party and said, 'The police are coming to Fifth Street!' So a bunch of people ran over there. And somehow [one of the well known executives of the JPC] wound up over there as well . . . And as the police were about to kick us out, she went up to the cops and said, 'You cannot do this!' And they said, 'Well, who are you?' And she said, 'I AM THE COMMUNITY! . . . This is a community problem and we'll deal with it. We don't have any need for you.'

After losing its court battle against the Avenue D squats, the city had begun to step up its use of force to remove Loisaida's squatters. Local liberals, although unwilling to come out in support of squatting *per se*, spoke out against the city's invasive and militaristic tactics.[15]

Thus, the squatters and the JPC could identify some common enemies. But the housing organizations' willingness to negotiate with City Hall was becoming a point of increasing tension between the two groups. Some of these earliest confrontations occurred around specific housing proposals, when JPC organizations sought sites already occupied by Loisaida residents. Such plans included the forced eviction of Adam Purple and his 'Garden of Eden,' and the attempted destruction of La Plaza Cultural.[16] In both cases, squatters accused the non-profit developers of consciously siting their projects on 'seized land,' while acres of nearby vacant lots went unclaimed.

But the most pointed squatter clashes with these organizations began in 1987, after the JPC and CB3 announced their final accord with City Hall over the 'Cross-Subsidy Plan' (to become known as the '50/50 Plan'). The squat community condemned the JPC's 'deal' with the city: the sale of Loisaida's vacant lots to real estate developers as a means to generate funds for JPC housing projects that would evict squatters from their buildings. Frank Morales reviewed some of their objections:

> In community board meetings, we would say, 'The 50/50 plan fuels gentrification!' Because you can't have a market-rate condo on one lot, and then take some money from that condo and build low-income housing next door to it, and expect that 10 years from now everything is going to be the same, that there isn't going to be continual [inflationary] pressure on that low-income house . . . But the Joint Planning Council accepted this compromise, basically playing into the hands of the government, which had pressured and bribed and extorted and squeezed some of these groups. You know, 'We'll get you this grant . . . but you'll have to do this and that' [to 'sell' this plan to the neighborhood]. Rather than saying, 'Not one bit of land for private speculation and condos!' . . . these groups would tell us, 'But the money's not there, and therefore we had to make this compromise, and 50% is better than none.'

Squatters not only felt that this was self-serving on the part of the JPC. They also believed it was a dangerous mistake, increasing the dependency on the state from which these advocate housing groups would not be able free themselves. General discomfort with the cross-subsidy plan not only distanced the squatters from the JPC, but served to weaken the progressive alliance among some constituent JPC groups. And it was through these widening gaps in the local anti-gentrification front that a coalition of landlords, conservatives, and what the squatters would call 'poverty pimp' organizational leaders would later rise.

While some squatters would charitably characterize the cross-subsidy plan as a typical liberal 'mistake' rather than as a purely vindictive move against the squats, all were adamantly opposed to a new development plan proposed by, among others, Antonio Pagan, director of the LES Coalition for Housing Development and one of the conservative fringes of the JPC. The new proposal called for five JPC organizations to be granted 'site control' of 30 buildings on the Lower East Side, to be redeveloped through corporate 'tax credit' monies brokered by the Local Initiatives Support Corporation (LISC) and the Enterprise Foundation. At the fall 1990 meeting of CB3, when it was announced that the board had already approved the LISC/Enterprise proposal without any public debate, the squatters were horrified: at least eight of their buildings were included in the properties to be put under the control of Pagan's organization![17] Pagan and his allies had long been open about their wish to eliminate Loisaida's squats, and the squatters quickly mobilized to expose what they viewed as a cynical use of a housing program to satisfy an anti-squat vendetta. It was in order to counteract the stereotyping that Pagan and others were using to isolate the squats from their potential allies in the community that the squatters composed their 'Community Statement,' quoted at the beginning of this chapter.

WHO ARE THE SQUATTERS?

This brief historical review suggests that the unauthorized occupation of vacant buildings on the Lower East Side was not new nor was it brought to Loisaida by a band of 'reckless anarchist outsiders.' Rather, the present squatter population had accumulated since the early 1970s through several 'generations' of squat buildings. A wide variety of races, ages, family types, class backgrounds, places of origin, and agendas of both a political and practical nature have been involved in squatting. The following is only a partial list of some of the characteristics that can be found among current residents of Loisaida's squats.[18]

- Whites, Blacks, Latinos, Asians.
- Men and women, boys and girls.
- Senior citizens, younger adults, college and high school-aged youth, kids and babies (some of them born in the squats).

- Homeless people who had been living in the streets, the shelters, local vacant lots, or Tompkins Square Park.
- Former rent-paying tenants abandoned by their landlords, who then took charge of their buildings.
- Immigrants and other low-income families who could no longer stay doubled-up in local apartments.
- Working-class adults who landed in NYC without a place to stay or who could not continue to meet rising NYC rents.
- Young people, some of them from middle-class and upper-class backgrounds, who rejected their parents' lifestyle and came to the Lower East Side in search of a less bourgeois existence.
- People who had 'fallen through the cracks' of the state welfare system – pensioners who could not get into subsidized housing, recovering substance

abusers reluctant to go back to the drug-filled shelters, single men who did not qualify for a government apartment.
- People with their own small businesses, people with low-paying or temporary employment, street peddlers, unemployed people, and people not looking for work.
- Artists, musicians, poets, writers, and other individuals who have consciously chosen a profession/lifestyle which does not yield the salary needed to rent a Manhattan apartment.

- Punks/cultural 'anarchists,' including members of local hard-core bands.
- Communal nurturers who want to raise their families in a politically and environmentally conscious setting.
- Craftspersons who want to create their own living/work space.
- Professionals who have left their jobs in search of a less alienating way of life.
- Europeans who squatted in their home countries and are seeking a similar life in the US.
- Political Anarchists,[19] Communists, Yippies, general anti-authoritarians, radical populists, liberals, and other representatives of the factionalized left.
- People without any strongly developed political views.
- Politically-inspired free thinkers, psychedelics, New Age metaphysicists, and loyal 'Rainbow Gathering' participants.

Of course, this variability is not distributed evenly throughout the neighborhood's 20 squats. Some squats tend to be more homogeneous, such as those founded by African-Americans and Latinos before 1985, or, conversely, the newest squats opened by younger 'punk anarchists.' But in between are those buildings that have endured out of the post-1985 squat struggles. Not only were these buildings diverse in their original composition, but over time these squats and their neighbors have been able to bridge some of their social and cultural differences, opening the way for increasing numbers of local tenants and homeless people to become squatters in these buildings as well.[20]

THE MOTIVES OF THE 'MOVEMENT'

Not surprisingly, members of this diverse population have claimed a variety of *personal motives* for squatting on the Lower East Side. These differences have made it difficult at times to maintain active 'movement' solidarity across even the majority of the neighborhood's several hundred squatters. However, there are certain essential principles on which most squatters agree; these have been sufficient to align the squat community and periodically mobilize them into action.

Defense of the Squats

The first and most basic common goal is to *defend the squats*. All squatters live in constant fear of invasion and forced eviction from their homes. The 'eviction watch' network is designed for mutual protection from the city government and others who would threaten their buildings. Art Cabrera, a single father from Brooklyn who lives with his children in a squat and operates a one-man construction business out of his van, gave a recent example of the solidarity building of squat defense:

> The position of 'No Evictions' . . . it's a lot of commitment to say, 'I'm not going to let the cops come in and throw you out.' We warded off an eviction just last week, down at this squat called 'Pest Squat,' what used to be the old Tent City building. By the time we got there, HPD and the police had thrown them all out. They had all their stuff out on the sidewalk . . . about 8 or 10 young punks who had been living there since the spring. Within two hours, we had everybody back in the building and the doors secured. We talked to the workers, and told them, 'This is an illegal eviction . . . blah, blah, blah,' and the workers told the HPD people, 'This is an illegal eviction, you don't have the proper paperwork, and we don't want to get in the middle of this thing.' Because as the thing went on, more and more people were coming, and it was getting heated. And the cops were just intimidating the shit out of these kids . . . Those kids never thought that they'd be back in that building. But they are. And out of that comes all different other types of social relationships: friendships, working relationships, and solidarity. I see those kids on the street now, and that incident just upped their solidarity. And a lot of those kids, for whatever reason – their anti-authoritarianism, or whatever – they're now down to defend these buildings. My building, their building, whatever. They're a valuable force, those 'punks' . . . believe it or not.[21]

Another squatter related a story of active mutual support that paints the squat community in stark contrast to the inattentiveness found in many inner-city neighborhoods:

> The other night, some skinheads went into a squat building on *x* street at about 4 o'clock in the morning. They had baseball bats. This was right after one of the recent 'riots.' So, somebody came by on a bicycle, alerting everybody . . . By the time we got there, there were about 100 people milling around. Now, if it had turned out to be serious, I would have immediately come back and said, 'Hurry up there! There's problems.' I would have gone around to everybody's door with my hammer, and pounded on it and told them, 'Get down there quick. They need us.'

The premise of 'no evictions' is not only an important base of squatter solidarity. It also offers a potential connection between the squats and the low-income tenants and homeless people living in Loisaida. Squatters have been discussing the expansion of their defensive network to include low-income tenants, mom and pop stores, shantytowns, park residents, and others vulnerable to eviction who might join in a mutual 'community defense' to prevent each other's displacement.

Defense of 'Squatting'

'Defense of home' is one simple tenet of the movement that is reasonably accessible to local observers. However, there are deeper motives that loosely unite Loisaida's several hundred squatters and which require some further explanation. Squatters justify squatting *per se* not only as a legitimate activity to gain their own housing, but as a way to meet the needs of poor people in Loisaida and throughout New York City. While there is more variety of interpretation around these issues than would be found around the clear-cut position of 'no evictions,' three basic defenses of the merits of squatting recurred in some recent discussions.

'Squatting is the most immediate and resourceful way to create desperately needed low-income housing.'

So argued Karen (a pseudonym), a single mother taking care of two young children, who has lived and worked in the Lower East Side for the past 20 years, the last six of them in squats:

> What [HPD and the JPC] label as 'low-income' is . . . well, it's not me. I can't pay what they are calling 'low-income rents.' Basically starting at like $500 for a studio. I mean, anyone can call 'low-income' anything they want. But what are the rents? Can somebody making minimum wage afford to live there? Can a mother on welfare afford to live there? Can senior citizens getting Social Security afford to live there? Well, no. 'Low-income' doesn't cover them. We have to make another bracket for them. 'Low-income' means $18,000 [annual income] or less. So people making $18,000 a year can afford one of their apartments. But what about the people that make $7,000 a year, or $10,000 a year? They can't![22] The only real low-income housing being developed in this area are the squats!

Pete and Beth (pseudonyms) are an older married couple. He has a small disability pension. She earns a little money from her paintings, which include portraits of people who used to live in TSP. When they moved to the neighborhood in the mid-1980s, they realized that they were ineligible for almost every subsidized housing program on the Lower East Side. As they told it:

> Finally, we were accepted into the RAIN homesteading program. But we really couldn't afford that building. We were actually living in a squat on Eighth Street while we were working on our building in the RAIN program. We had to lie about where we lived! But we needed a place to stay right away. And it takes a long time to finish one of those homesteads . . . When we got burned out of Eighth Street, that's when we realized that even if we were on Section 8 in the homestead, we would have had only a hundred dollars a month left over to live on. We couldn't do it. So we moved over here [to this squat] . . . And a lot of these homestead buildings are having trouble now, because the sponsors are cutting back on the funds. This is one area where we in the squats have an advantage over them.

Squatting is thus seen as an effective housing strategy to meet the needs of an increasing number of poor New Yorkers underserved not only by the private market but by the government-sponsored housing system.

Lower East Side squatters also claim they can rehabilitate buildings more cheaply and quickly than non-profit organizations. Eric Rassi lived in a cramped basement cubicle in Chinatown before he moved to his squat. Skilled in construction, he complained about the present system of housing production:

> If they [the JPC] are going to be waiting for money to come in from the government before they do something with these buildings, then they'll never solve the problem, because they're spending $100,000 a unit. For instance, our building would cost them at least $1.2 million to renovate. Now, this is a tenement building. It's 25 foot wide. There are 12 apartments. And I don't think it should require more than a million dollars to renovate this building, especially when we're doing it for about $75,000 total. And we're removing it from the commodity system. If you get a lot of this type of housing into a land trust (which we plan for this building), and people living across the street find out that we're not only paying $100 a month to live in the building, but that with that kind of money we can renovate the entire building in a matter of a couple of years, the guy across the street sitting in a $800 studio is going to wonder why he's paying $800 a month.

The immediacy of squatting becomes especially important for the neighborhood's homeless people. Eric pointed out:

> We've had people living out on the streets of New York for ten years. And these guys are just waiting to come in and be put to work and be given the right to live in their own space. You can bring 5 or 6 guys from the park. (they're ready to work) . . . and have a 2 year renovation, giving them apartments, and opening another 7 apartments at the same time for families who are doubled up in the neighborhood.[23]

Countering charges that squatting in a vacant building is not a viable option for families with children, certain squats have already instituted 'family plans' in which other squatters in the building work with a family to renovate an apartment while parents and children remain in their present home. Hence, squatting can become a housing option for an increasing number of Loisaiders.

Finally, squatters ask *how long* the housing proposed by the JPC for development under the cross-subsidy and LISC/Enterprise plans will truly remain 'affordable?' As Morales argued above, squatters believe that low-income housing developed in the same space as upper-income housing and then left to the private market will eventually inflate in price. Squatters also point out that 15-year 'buy-out' options – which allow a sponsor to pay off his mortgage to the government in order to release the building from resale restrictions on the open market – will make affordable housing only temporary.[24] In contrast, squatters want to remove their low-income units permanently from the commodity system.[25]

'The squats are barriers to state-sponsored dispersion of poor inner-city residents and the gentrification of their neighborhoods.'

Squatters generally feel that there is something very wrong with a government that will not spend money to house the homeless, and yet will deploy hundreds of armed police into a neighborhood to evict people from a building they are trying to fix up. Hence, most squatters are very skeptical about any actions by government, a sentiment stressed by local radical thinkers who situate the gentrification of the Lower East Side within a larger strategy to depopulate and 'manage' poor black and Latino inner-city neighborhoods. Their thesis about 'spatial deconcentration' has been one of the main political statements of the post-1985 movement.[26]

According to them, the strategy of 'spatial deconcentration' arose out of efforts by the federal government during the late 1960s to analyze why the urban black and Latino ghettos of this country had recently rioted so violently against poverty. In 1967, President Johnson convened the National Advisory Commission on Civil Disorders (otherwise known as the Kerner Commission) to develop national strategies to prevent the recurrence of such uprisings.[27] In 1968, the Commission issued its recommendations,[28] which ranged from involving more community people in discussions of city policies (the 'Neighborhood City Hall' concept, which Mayor Lindsay, a Commission member, eventually instituted as a precursor of community boards)[29] to improving police tactics in ghetto neighborhoods.

It is the last two chapters of the Kerner Report, authored primarily by HUD consultant Anthony Downs, that have attracted the most attention from squat activists. In these chapters Downs outlined two possible strategies to restabilize America's inner cities. One, the 'enrichment choice,' would enhance education, employment, and welfare opportunities in ghetto areas in order to vault more blacks and Latinos into the less turbulent stratum of the middle class. Downs saw this approach as beyond the realm of short-term possibility, and thus stressed the adoption of his second more immediate housing strategy: the 'integration choice.' The premise of the second strategy was that the best way to prevent non-whites from protesting their poverty in urban ghettos was to disperse them from these explosive 'spaces' and relocate them in higher-quality housing projects scattered outside the city.

Downs elaborated this thesis in his 1973 book, *Opening Up the Suburbs*.[30] Essential to the strategy was a redistribution of poor minorities to achieve 'middle-class dominance' in both suburban and inner-city neighborhoods. As for the redevelopment of black and Latino ghettos, Downs suggested that 'new means of comprehensively "managing" entire inner-city neighborhoods should be developed to provide a more effective means of withdrawing economic support from housing units that ought to be demolished,' and that 'relatively few small-scale physical capital investment projects should be placed in decaying inner-city areas until incomes there are raised and dispersed economic integration is underway.'[31] Once these neighborhoods had been 'sufficiently deconcentrated,' city governments could then proceed with 'large-scale projects that create entirely new neighborhood environments' that would attract enough 'non-poor residents . . . to produce an economically integrated environment with middle-class dominance – as required for true viability.'[32]

Shortly after Downs had published his book, a very similar policy seemed to have been instituted in New York City. The proposed program of 'planned shrinkage,' as championed by NYC Housing and Development administrator Roger Starr, called for both the targeted reduction of municipal services – housing development, building code enforcement, fire protection, sanitation, etc. – and the accelerated demolition of vacant housing in the city's already deteriorated poor black and Latino neighborhoods. The intent was to catalyze the physical destruction of these already depressed communities, so that their poor residents would move out; the city could then 'land bank' these areas for massive redevelopment in the future.[33]

Many Lower East Side squatters are convinced that government concern over inner-city rebellions, federal housing policies to deconcentrate low-income populations, the coincident 'shrinkage' and eventual 'blowout' of the Lower East Side, and the city's current efforts to demolish Loisaida's vacant buildings and squats in order to make way for luxury housing are all connected. They view the gentrification of the Lower East Side not merely as an economic process fueled by profit making but as a state-sponsored strategy of social control over poor people and people of color.[34]

By seizing land and mobilizing a movement within these once abandoned spaces, squat activists see themselves as creating both physical and political impediments to these 'state-management' strategies. Squatters likewise perceive 'compromises' like the cross-subsidy plan as the culmination of the government's 1960s strategy to co-opt local progressives and to use government-funded community organizations as buffers against local insurgency.[35] Indeed, the cross-subsidy's plan to repopulate the Lower East Side with a mix of middle- and low-income people sounds to many squatters like a thinly veiled effort by the state to assert 'middle-class dominance' over the neighborhood. (See chapter 14 for a different view of cross-subsidy.)

'Squats are autonomous spaces of both personal and collective empowerment.'

Many squatters ironically agree with one claim made by JPC representatives that 'they had no choice' except to negotiate a deal like the cross-subsidy. The squatters point out that when these groups abandoned their early efforts to organize local residents and began to concentrate on servicing government contracts, they lost an empowering base among the people of the community. While buildings stood empty, the housing reformers told Loisaiders to be patient – that they would get apartments as soon as the JPC and CB3 had reached an accord with the city. In distinction, the squatters claim to have taken the fight for affordable housing straight to the community's residents, emboldening them to create their own homes without waiting for a 'benevolent' handout.

Hence, people living in the squats feel that the *empowering* aspects of squatting have enriched them two-fold. Classes of usually exploited individuals (the poor and homeless, women, substance abusers, etc.) have discovered within the autonomous spaces of the squats a chance to reassert control over their own lives. And from such experiences of *self-empowerment*, these individuals have discovered the path of *collective empowerment* as well. People who would not have identified themselves as 'leaders' or 'activists' have, through squatting, found the common resolve to help lead the fight for popular control over the Lower East Side. Several anecdotes speak to its effects. For example, Valentin (a pseudonym) is a young Latino who, upon his arrival in New York, wound up sleeping in Tompkins Square Park. In the park, he met the members of 'Tent City'[36] and, in the fall of 1989, joined their occupation of a vacant school building on East Fourth Street. The building was to become the controversial 'ABC Community Center,' a squatter-run residence with space for community meetings, drug counseling, and free classes in subjects ranging from GED equivalency to construction skills.

> The ABC building had originally been occupied by some young anarchists. They weren't really doing anything with the building. Then Tent City came in. We got together with the anarchists and some others [squatters, political groups, church groups, etc.] and organized the building by floors. Tent City took the second floor and secured the first floor. The anarchists who were already there took the third floor. Positive things really started happening there. People who had been having real problems started to develop leadership qualities. Some were finally getting past their substance abuse. It was giving them a chance to make something of their lives. Things were really open there, as far as who could come in and participate. That wound up being a real liability for us . . . But we had some really good meetings, some with as many as 125 people. At one point we had about 40 people living there. Things were really coming together . . . But it seemed that the word got out that we were really becoming organized, really moving towards some level of self-determination. When we heard that the community board was discussing what was going to be done with the building, we started showing up in force to the CB meetings. But when we left for a meeting, the cops showed up and tried to force the others out of the building. Eventually, they did force us out.[37]

Just as squatters create their own housing, so they can use these free spaces to provide services for themselves and the surrounding community without being beholden to the state. Karen argued that this empowers women.

> The way apartment buildings are set up, it's really isolating for the families. The mothers go crazy, the kids go crazy, and you don't have any help. In the squats, we have the space to establish . . . communal daycare with a kitchenette, etc. We could set it up so that it would be easier on the women, to give them a chance to do things during the day that they usually can't do when they have the kids . . . The way that the needs of women could be met in squats is very, very radical. I really believe in direct action of the people. There were periods when mothers in this neighborhood used to organize their own daycare centers. When I moved here in 1972, there were parent cooperative daycare centers all over the place . . . But then the government came along and said, 'Wow . . . you know, all you have to do is get into our program, and we'll find somebody to operate your daycare center, and we'll give you this and that . . . and all you have to do is send in a proposal.' Well, some groups did it and some groups didn't. But once you did that, it destroyed the cooperative nature of the daycare . . . And then you had all the rules and regulations that you had to follow if you were going to get the funding. And the City would tell you, 'You have to have this, and you have to have that . . . otherwise you are illegal.' Now it's illegal for parents to have daycare! The only daycare centers that are allowed are the ones that have all of these things [for which] you need lots of money. Therefore, mothers solving their own daycare needs is not possible. You wind up being in this totally dependent situation, where you just have to plead for a daycare center. Well, as far as the problem of

> space, we've got it. Women in the squats have the space and ability to start up a center in one of our buildings in a week's time.

PROSPECTS FOR THE MOVEMENT AND THE FUTURE OF LOISAIDA

The squatters' movement, while small, is well mobilized and its members are committed to squatting. But what are the movement's prospects for mobilizing other Loisaiders to join their efforts? Any new alliance of the various anti-gentrification constituencies in the neighborhood will depend in part upon how the community reacts to the government's latest use of force to control neighborhood spaces. In the past, police battalions and wrecking crews advancing on local squats generated a tentative unity among squatters, liberal JPC leaders, and some community residents. In the same way, the recent show of force in the closure of Tompkins Square and the growing fear of similar plans for the squats and homeless settlements east of the park may generate sufficient dissidence among Loisaiders to forge a squatter-influenced counter-alliance. Frank Morales discussed one such possibility when I spoke with him shortly after the park was closed:

> We now have the opportunity on the Lower East Side to again advance the resistance [against Loisaida's transformation] . . . What is called for is the creation of a popular organization on the Lower East Side: one that is composed of these various [anti-gentrification] tendencies; one that has a platform in support of squatting and direct action, in support of fighting gentrification and opposing warehoused apartments, in support of pressuring the government for money to build housing – in other words, both the Anarchist line [autonomy from the State] and the line of the Communists and others [pressure for State redistribution of resources]. These various approaches [could be pursued] through a constellation of local groups working around food, shelter, and clothing issues: the predominant issues of concern in poor communities. All these possibilities exist. But we're at the point now where if we don't organize around such a goal soon, we could see a steady deterioration of this [mobilizing potential] at the hands of this current fascist repression.

It is still too soon to determine if anything resembling such a 'united popular front' will materialize on the Lower East Side. However, current misperceptions of the squatter movement have heretofore left emotional distance between the squats and some of their potential allies. Squatters have thus begun to examine how they will bridge this gap.

Squatters and Loisaida's Poor and Homeless Residents

A main claim of squatting's legitimacy is its identification with the struggles of the low-income people of the Lower East Side. But to what extent have the poor and homeless of Loisaida been able to identify with the squatters? The answer is mixed. As a measure of success, squatters claim their relations with their immediate neighbors are warm. Art Cabrera gave one example:

> Our relationship with our neighbors has been very good . . . mostly on the social level. I found these tree trunks, and I put them out in front of the building. Every night of the week, you see who's sitting out there. Old folks from the other side of the street [from Pagan's Section 8 buildings] come over, and we're talking with them, hanging out, getting to know their kids. And the local teenagers hang out over here. We're trying to get a better rapport with them. The building next door . . . it's kind of a homestead. They're real supportive. A woman who has been in the neighborhood for 15 years lives in this little building in back of us. She says, 'Well, you know . . . you guys are in good shape, because the matriarch of the building across the street, the old Puerto Rican woman who sits out front all the time and nods to everybody, she likes what you're doing' . . . And the Latinos on our first floor – they're Columbian, a family and a single guy – they want to finish the first floor so that they can bring people in from the neighborhood, to show them what we're doing. One of the guys is a pretty good artist. He wants to use his space as a studio where he can display his stuff and other people's stuff from the community.

At the immediate level of daily squat life, community residents can relate to the hard day-to-day work of the squatters – people who are struggling to create homes in a vacant building that the city had previously allowed to be a danger to their block. Of course, cultural and language differences between the still significant number of whites in the squats and local Latinos continue to persist. But with time has come a growing familiarity between squatters and their neighbors. And with the growing number of community residents now living in squats, the chances for cooperative ventures between squatters and others have improved considerably.[38]

But while many Loisaiders can identify with what they see of squatting at what we might call the 'building' level of the movement, the neighborhood's reaction to some of the movement's 'activist' aspects (that is, its campaign to mobilize the larger Lower East Side community in order to confront the State and Capital around the issues of gentrification, Tompkins Square Park, etc.) has been far more uneven.

Dave Tompkins has observed the squatters' movement from a variety of perspectives within this context. An African-American resident of Loisaida since the late 1960s, Dave lived in a rented room in an apartment on Ninth Street until 1989 when his building 'went co-op' and he was forced into the streets. Dave moved down the block to Tompkins Square where he lived and helped to organize the park's residents until their June 1991 eviction. He now lives in a squat barely a block away from his old apartment. Dave reflected on the potential for an activist coalition between Loisaiders and the squats:

> Most Lower East Side people didn't mix with the squatters. The squatters were 'outsiders' to us. I'm not saying this in any pejorative sense . . . It's just that the squatters tended to stay within their own type of community. When I was living in the park, that was when I first really got to know any squatters. Before then, when I was living on Ninth Street, all I saw [them to be] was people dressed in black walking by. All I knew was that they were outsiders. Can the squatters organize this community? . . . The squatters are a legitimate force here. But, personally, I think what they ought to do is just live their lives, be respectful of the community, and help them in a genuine sense. The analogy would be if a white guy come up to me and says, 'Hey Brother!' and gives me all these different hand shakes. In the old days, that would be a sign that he was 'down.' But now, you just don't trust people who give you that. It's too much. So I think the squatters shouldn't try so hard. Just go ahead and do what they're doing, and let time take its toll. Because the squats are multi-faceted. So with time, like at our building, people see us working, they see a mixture of people in the building. I know a lot of people in the community, and they're supportive of that. An example . . . Look at the latest flyer that came out [about re-opening the park]. It depicts violence. Now how are you going to get the Lower East Side, the regular folks – and I know, I've been one of the regular folks – to come out in response to that kind of message? That's not the way . . . There's many different factions here in this community. So what you have to do is address each person's fear. It's a multi-pronged thing. But when the revolutionary anarchists want to do their thing, they want you to know straight up, 'This is how I want you to see it.' They want to beat you over the head with it. They might be right about what's going on! But you have to entice people to get involved.

Many squatters would not adopt Dave's hesitancy towards mobilizing the people of Loisaida. But his reservations do recall concerns that have been raised by some squatter activists regarding the contradictory perceptions of the squat movement held by the people of the Lower East Side. Surely, squatters recognize their own efforts at both the 'building' and 'activist' levels of their movement as being integrally related. However, there seems to be an incongruity between the positive acknowledgment of the squat buildings by their immediate neighbors and the larger Lower East Side community's general disassociation from squatter 'activism' in the neighborhood as a whole.

Generally, day-to-day life in a squat building – the chores of renovation, the communal aspects of living and working together, the challenge of sharing a politically charged space with other individuals of varying backgrounds and viewpoints – requires a real commitment to *cooperation across diversity*. If squatters in the same building do not find a common ground upon which to act collectively, they may be left without a home.[39] However, nothing (at least not until recently, perhaps) has forced the squat population to develop a *binding* consensus *outside* the walls of their buildings. The 'anarchistic' organization of most inter-squat collective actions[40] and the increasing diversity of the squat population have heretofore distracted the squat community from reaching a broad agreement on how to mobilize other Loisaiders.

As a result, a sometimes confusing array of messages and organizing styles has been emitted by the squats' various political tendencies. Predictably, the squatters with the most notoriety – usually those who want to counter the 'war on the poor' in Loisaida with a similar 'militaristic' response against the state and its police agents – have come to represent to the community the entirety of the squatters' agenda: a controversial prospect that has not been well received by many of Loisaida's poor and homeless people heretofore.

Not only have such internal inconsistencies strained the squatters' efforts to maintain both autonomy and solidarity within its ranks, but they have also made the squat population liable to distortion and division by some of their critics. While defending some of their more militant comrades, Pete and Beth also convey some of the tensions and vulnerabilities that have accompanied their movement's centrifugal nature.

> *Pete*: Basically our [the different squatters'] politics are not all that much different. Except, for example, that my wife and I tend to try as much as possible to go through political and legal channels to fight something, while somebody else might say, 'Let's go down and throw bottles at the pigs!' (Chuckles) We've got the same goal in mind, but we have just a slightly different way of going about it.
>
> *Beth*: Like some people [the Community Board, etc.] will talk about 'good squatters' and 'bad squatters,' but who is to say, 'You're a good person, you deserve a house, but this other one doesn't'? Who gave them the right to judge? . . . Now, politically, some of these kids are too hot-headed for me. They're leading the vanguard at the riots and stuff like that. But I might have done the same at their age. And they're idealistic, they've got all this energy. To them, they're doing right. I can't go around and say, 'You're wrong because you're doing this.' I'm not the judge. They're fighting for what they believe in.

Nevertheless, a growing number of squatters are questioning how they can achieve squat/neighborhood collective action if the community's impression of the squats continues to be determined by the public actions of only a segment of their membership.

Squatters and Other Community Organizations

Squatters are partially responsible for the lack of clarity with which they have regulated their popular image. But it is their opponents who have seized this opportunity and magnified the now well-known negative stereotypes. For example, Antonio Pagan's Democratic Action Committee posted the following signs[41] throughout Loisaida during his run for City Council, seeking to scapegoat squatters for the community's problems.

> SQUAT YUPS GET FREE RENT, SPACE, ELECTRIC, GAS, WATER.
> WHAT GET YOU!
>
> EURO TRASH IN THE SQUATS.
> AMERICANS IN THE LOTS.

Local right-wing interests, such as the Democratic Action Committee, have used slanted representations of the squats in an attempt not only to alienate community people from the squatters, but also to ride the resultant reactionary fervor to a new position of influence within Lower East Side politics. Rising from what was once a marginal conservative faction on the JPC and CB3, Pagan's subsequent upset over progressive incumbent Miriam Friedlander (the official who had appointed the liberal JPC representatives to the community board in the mid-1980s)[42] now raises questions about the continuing influence of these liberal housing advocates in their ongoing negotiations with the city government.

Pagan's election also prompts speculation about whether some of these liberals will now choose to look past their differences with the squatters in order to join forces against this rising prodevelopment faction. Many squatters feel that there is room for collaboration between themselves and those JPCers willing to accept the squats' presence on the Lower East Side. Some churches, political organizations, and housing groups have come out publicly to support the squatters' fight against the LISC/Enterprise initiative. Some squatters have also discussed the need for a more flexible and varied approach to community-based planning in Loisaida, one that would include a wider range of housing types – including both squats and the government-funded projects pursued by the JPC.[43] Such an approach could benefit the JPC by decreasing its reliance on public funds and strengthening its links to an empowered and mobilized population able to challenge City Hall. In turn, the JPC's experience in creating land trusts and mutual housing associations could assist squatter aspirations in these areas.

These are all possible bases for the generation of a truly united popular front in the defense of the Lower East Side. But time is running out. As Frank Morales mused: 'If we don't reach this new level of struggle . . . then we'll go through a protracted gentrification of the Lower East Side. And by the year 2000, our neighborhood will become housing for Wall Street bankers . . . so that they can shoot down to their thieves' den.'

NOTES

1 From a flyer distributed throughout the Lower East Side in the fall and winter of 1990–1.

2 A popular squatter banner, seen on much squat literature and at many street demonstrations.

3 This is the squatters' own estimate of the size of their community. A group not amenable (either practically or philosophically) to census counts, there has been no definitive enumeration of the squat population. A further ambiguity is who constitutes a 'squatter.' If we include people who have built shacks on vacant lots, or those who occupy vacant buildings but are not known to the squatters' movement, or tenants who have lived for years in a local apartment without paying rent, or even people who have illegally created community gardens and parks on city-owned land – all of whom have been called 'squatters' by the government – there are many more than 500 people 'squatting' on the Lower East Side.

4 Much of this criticism follows the misperception that everyone who participated in the escalation of these events was a squatter. Not only does such a characterization ignore the essential role that squat opponents (the police, certain members of the community board, etc.) played in these confrontations, but it also overlooks the whole range of non-squatting activists who took the side of squatters and homeless people in these clashes.

5 This occurred in the fall of 1990 in reaction to Community Board 3's vote in favor of the LISC/Enterprise proposal (see Abu-Lughod, chapter 14).

6 Though I have attempted to talk to as broad a cross-section of squatters as possible, my conversations with 'punk' and/or expressly 'anarchist' squatters have been insufficient to be presented at this stage of the research. While their general viewpoint is certainly included in this chapter, I feel it proper to acknowledge this shortcoming and intend to address it in future installments.

7 Joseph Kahn, 'The Squatters of New York,' *New York Post*, 8 August 1970. See also Lisa Jorgenson, 'New York's Squatters: Vanguard of Community Control?' *City* (fall 1971), pp. 35–8.

8 Doug Turetsky, 'Rebels With a Cause?' *City Limits* (April 1990), pp. 12–15; and Seth Borgos, 'Low-Income Homeownership and the ACORN Squatters Campaign,' in R. G. Bratt et al., eds. *Critical Perspectives on Housing* (Philadelphia: Temple University Press, 1986), pp. 428–46. Although the city had to be pressured to sanction low-income homesteading on the Lower East Side, it was more willing to *initiate* the type of 'homesteading' that had been used by other east coast cities to attract upwardly mobile 'pioneers' into such 'up

and coming' neighborhoods. See 'The Homesteading Pitch,' *City Limits* (March 1981), pp. 23–5.

9 Some squatters even use the terms 'squatting' and 'homesteading' interchangeably. For example, a squat which houses some of the earliest and most radical members of the local squatter movement recently changed its painted facade from an embattled banner identifying the building as the 'Frontline' squat to a plain black wall with the words 'The (numerical address) Homestead.' Likewise, the squatter-produced 'how-to' manual, *Survival Without Rent*, recommends (on p. 7) that prospective squatters use the term 'homesteading' when trying to explain what they are doing to the general public. Use of the term 'squatting,' which takes its inspiration from the politically oriented housing movements of Europe and the third world, was even a point of mild contention during the formative stages of the post-1985 movement on the Lower East Side; some building occupiers felt more comfortable with the less provocative label of 'homesteader.' But the 'squat' language was eventually adopted by all in order to create a collective identity for the local movement.

10 Tim Ledwith, 'Lower East Side Tenants: Squatters or Homesteaders?' *City Limits* (November 1981), p. 16.

11 This negative connotation to the 'squatter' label (one usually associated with junkies, drug dealers, etc.) has caused some Lower East Side squatters to question why they should use for themselves a derogatory label used by their opponents. In the case of the Avenue D buildings, the occupants vehemently insisted that they were not 'squatters' (in the city's sense of the word).

12 Not only was there a mixture of whites and local people of color within these squats, but there were also a number of formerly homeless African-Americans and Latinos who had found out about the buildings through squatting 'workshops' conducted by Lower East Side activists in homeless shelters and housing advocacy conferences throughout the city.

13 Spencer Rumsey, 'Burn, Baby, Burn' *East Village Eye* (April 1986), pp. 8–10. See also the rejoinder to Rumsey ('Who Let This Guy In?') from the squatters of 327–9 East Eighth Street (May issue of *East Village Eye*, 1986), p. 13. The Avenue D squats eventually triumphed over HPD's eviction plans and continued to exist as 'illegal' squats, until the city finally approved their tenancy in 1992.

14 East Eighth Street eventually fell under concerted attack by the city (see Abu-Lughod, chapter 11. See also Sarah Ferguson's series of articles in the *Village Voice*: 'Squatters Victory?' 9 May 1989, pp. 15–16; 'How to Unify a Neighborhood,' 16 May 1989, pp. 10, 13; and 'Occupied Territories: Inside the Squatters Movement,' 18 July 1989, pp. 22–32. Their homes eventually leveled (the area is now a strip of vacant lots), refugees from Eighth Street would spread out to join squats throughout the neighborhood. Their past experiences on that block inform much of their current participation in the movement.

15 Ferguson, 'How to Unify a Neighborhood.'

16 Adam Purple, a 'metaphysical free-thinker,' also squatted in a vacant building near his garden. He was one of the first people on the Lower East Side to

distribute literature about the 'state' strategy of 'spatial deconcentration.' His eviction was deeply felt by the squatters' movement. 'La Plaza' was a park and garden that for a time became a squatter encampment and a makeshift soup kitchen. Neighborhood residents who tended 'La Plaza' fought off the drug dealing which arose on the site thereafter, and they have so far successfully prevented its destruction by the city through legal appeals at the local, state, and federal levels.

17 The *Shadow* (October–November 1990) listed the addresses of eight squats included in the proposal, but I know of at least one other that later discovered it was also included in the plan.

18 See also Ferguson, 'Occupied Territories,' and Donna Ladd, 'Not Just Young White Males: The Silent Squatters Speak,' *Village Beat* (winter 1991), pp. 6–7.

19 The opaqueness of the 'anarchist' label is compounded by the distinct groups of people who so identify themselves. 'Anarchy' is a common motif in much of punk music and culture, and on that basis alone many punkers of the Lower East Side call themselves 'anarchists.' Alternatively, there are fewer local people who are theoretically conscious participants in the political 'anarchist' movement.

20 For example, here is the demographic breakdown of one 14-unit squat: a single Columbian man, 2 Columbian families, 4 single African-American men and women, 1 single Puerto Rican man, 1 apartment being held for a local Puerto Rican family, 3 white families, and 2 single white women.

21 In some ways a subcommunity unto themselves, punks have played an important (if somewhat controversial) role in the squat movement. They have been very visible in much of the street activism sponsored by squats and others in the neighborhood. And they have given back to the movement as well, through the series of 'Squat or Rot' concerts at the Tompkins Square bandshell organized by punks in local squats or at hardcore clubs like ABC No Rio or CBGB's.

22 Much the same argument has been lodged by housing advocates (including some of those associated with the JPC) against HPD's same income categorizations for other subsidized housing developments. See Bonnie Brower, *Missing the Mark: Subsidizing Housing for the Privileged, Displacing the Poor. An Analysis of the City's 10-Year Plan* (New York: Association for Neighborhood and Housing Development, Inc., 1989), pp. 47–53.

23 Eric, along with other squatters, a local priest, and some of the people living in Tompkins Square Park, had presented just such a plan to soon-to-be Deputy Mayor Bill Lynch in December 1989. The plan proposed that several vacant buildings be opened to people from the park, and in return, the homeless would agree to draw back their reduced encampments to two isolated areas of the park. A week after the proposal was made, the city responded with its first eviction of the park's homeless (see Greshof and Dale, chapter 12).

24 Such 'buy-outs' already threaten Section 8 and Mitchell-Lama housing on the Lower East Side, and yet they are being written into the mortgage stipulations for the proposed LISC/Enterprise projects.

25 How the squatters propose to accomplish this is unclear. There have been discussions about establishing a squat 'land trust,' which would bar any resale of a squat unit for profit and serve as a lower-income alternative to other land trusts on the Lower East Side. But without such a legal instrument, some in the JPC question if squat units will stay affordable on the basis of moral commitment alone. There have even been allegations about older squat units which, now completed, have been advertised in the *Village Voice* as sublets at significant rents.

26 For a fuller treatment of the squatter position on spatial deconcentration, see their 12-page summary, entitled 'Spatial Deconcentration.' This is drawn primarily from Yulanda Ward, 'Spatial Deconcentration: Freedom of Housing Choice or Minority Removal?' (a paper presented to Grassroots Unity Conference, Washington DC, 1980). See also Paul DeRienzo and Bill Weinberg, 'Military Camps for Urban Poor?' *Shadow* (March 1991), p. 14; and A. Bertoli, 'Democracy under Siege: Tompkins Square Police State [and] the Spatial Deconcentration Connection,' *Shadow* (June–July 1991), p. 19.

27 Critics cite what they believe was a preponderance of military and corporate interests on the Commission's panel and research staff. Of special significance is the alleged military connection of the Federal Emergency Management Agency (FEMA). This agency, which has devised plans for creating security encampments to contain Latin American peasants during times of political insurrection, also coordinates federal funding and policy for this country's homeless shelter system – including its use of military bases outside of New York City and elsewhere to shelter large numbers of homeless people allegedly displaced by the government's deconcentration strategy. Squatters also point out the presence of the FEMA-sponsored 'communications center' – a mobile high-tech 'anti-terrorist' command post – at recent squat evictions in the South Bronx and at the June 1991 closure of Tompkins Square Park.

28 National Advisory Commission on Civil Disorders, *The Kerner Report* (originally 1968, reissued New York: Pantheon Books, 1988).

29 Ira Katznelson, *City Trenches: Urban Politics and the Patterning of Class in the United States* (Chicago: University of Chicago Press, 1981).

30 Anthony Downs, *Opening Up the Suburbs: An Urban Strategy for America* (New Haven: Yale University Press, 1973). Yulanda Ward, 'Spatial Deconcentration,' claims that many of these recommendations would reappear in later HUD policy statements, including its 'Regional Housing Mobility Program.' For a related presentation of federal urban policy, see Wilbur Thompson, 'Land Management Strategies for Central City Depopulation,' in *How Cities Can Grow Old Gracefully* (December 1977, Subcommitee on the City, Committee on Banking, Finance and Urban Affairs, US House of Representatives, 95th Congress, Washington DC).

31 Downs, 'Opening Up the Suburbs,' p. 135.

32 Downs, 'Opening Up the Suburbs,' p. 149.

33 See 'Planned Shrinkage,' *Real Estate Weekly*, 4 February 1976; and Roger Starr, 'Making New York Smaller,' *New York Times Magazine*, 14 November 1976, pp. 32–3, 99–106. For an example of African-American and Latino

reaction to Starr's proposal, made when he was head of HDA, see 'Minority Caucus Bids Starr Quit,' *The New York Times*, 5 March 1976.

34 Recent events like the militaristic closure of Tompkins Square Park, the 'shrinkage' of local fire services, and the illogical partitioning of the Lower East Side into two white-majority electoral districts only confirm squatter suspicions about the state's continuing efforts to destroy Loisaida and marginalize its people of color.

35 See also Katznelson, *City Trenches*, and Steven Katz and Margit Mayer, 'Gimme Shelter: Self-help Housing Struggles Within and Against the State in New York City and West Berlin,' *International Journal of Urban and Regional Research* 9 (1985), pp. 15–47.

36 'Tent City' was the loose organization of homeless people living in Tompkins Square Park. It proved to be the main vehicle of connection between the park's residents and the squatters during the early years of the post-1985 movement. In addition to founding its own squat, Tent City won national notoriety after 200 of its 'members' returned from the 'Housing Now!' march to Washington DC in October 1989 and set up a symbolic homeless encampment across from the United Nations on New York's elegant east side.

37 That first eviction occurred late in October 1989, involving violent clashes between over 100 police officers and ABC supporters from the squat community. A second occupation and eviction from the building took place later that winter. As designated by CB3, the site has now been rehabbed by a federally funded senior citizens' foundation.

38 Not all squats have placed this priority on developing ties with the local community. For instance, this can be seen around a few of the newer punk/anarchist squats, where a vastly different (and often defiant) lifestyle and the relative temporariness of the young squatters' tenures have limited the opportunity for positive interaction between them and their immediate neighbors.

39 One squatter has referred to this as the 'pile of rubble' praxis of squatting: i.e., that dealing collectively with an overwhelming pile of rubble in a vacant building provides an inescapable lesson in self-organization which should inform the creation of any larger political movement.

40 That is, episodic (e.g., squat defense, the park curfew, etc.) versus long-term strategizing, aversion to any authoritative body asserting control over any squat or group of squatters, and a commitment not to censure formally any individual political tendency within the movement.

41 The disingenuousness of this message is especially apparent, since the DAC publicly called for the eviction of the 'American' homeless people from the park and their forced removal from nearby vacant lots.

42 Pagan defeated Friedlander by less than 100 votes in the September 1991 Democratic primary for the newly redistricted seat on the recently expanded City Council. During the redistricting battles of the preceding spring, Pagan had been one of the chief proponents for dividing the Lower East Side into two separate voting districts. (JPC liberals and squatter activists had called for the maintenance of a multi-racial, white minority district which would

have kept the Lower East Side electorally intact.) Pagan's two-district lobby won, resulting in the inclusion of Loisaida and Tompkins Square in the same electoral district as the white and wealthy neighborhood of Gramercy Park. It is alleged that Pagan's prodevelopment campaign was heavily bankrolled by construction and real estate interests, as well as by upper-income condo owners in the Christodora House. See Ed Morales, 'East Side Story,' *Village Voice*, 20 August 1991, pp. 11–12; and also Nashua, 'Who is Antonio Pagan?' *Shadow* (August–September 1991), pp. 6, 18. During his campaign, Pagan's resort to divisive labeling did not stop with the squatters. Even Mayor David Dinkins publicly criticized Pagan for disseminating racially inflammatory pamphlets which mischaracterized Friedlander as 'no friend' of local Soviet and east European Jews, a significant voting block in the district. Pagan's campaign was also allegedly marked by reactionary violence, including the beating and hospitalization of one of his opponents on the eve of the election, reported in *New York Newsday* on 12 September 1991 and 13 September 1991, and a baseball bat attack on Friedlander leafletters on Election Day.

43 There are those in the international urban planning community who have made similar recommendations for the rebuilding of first world inner cities such as New York. See Colin Ward, *Anarchy in Action* (London: Freedom Press, 1988), chapters 6–7; and John F. C. Turner, *Housing by People: Towards Autonomy in Building Environments* (Boston: Marion Boyars, 1976).

14

Defending the Cross-Subsidy Plan: the Tortoise Wins Again

Janet Abu-Lughod

As 1991 drew to a close, the situation on the Lower East Side appeared relatively dormant. The neighborhood, like the city of which it was a part, seemed to be entering a phase of hibernation and it was difficult to predict what the future would hold for either. On the surface, the prognosis was not favorable, although as we shall see, behind shells of abandoned buildings and on scattered vacant lots there were signs of activity. Despite the doldrums, or perhaps because of them, new subsidized housing was beginning to be added to the neighborhood's stock of affordable housing.

By year's end, Tompkins Square Park, still impenetrably fenced and gone to seed, no longer needed its police guards, since rat poison had been sprinkled liberally within the wild terrain and conspiciously posted warnings of potential disaster were sufficient to keep trespassers out. The homeless, who had sworn that they would remain together and, by encamping on nearby vacant lots, would thus keep their refugee status alive and visible, had been unceremoniously evicted,[1] as homeless persons were similarly being removed from public spaces throughout the city.[2] Scattered, those without shelter were reduced to huddling under any available roofings in derelict city spaces or sleeping in doorways and over steam vents. Only a relatively mild winter afforded them the protection the city was still failing to provide.

The economy of the city also appeared to be going to seed. Recently released data on jobs and unemployment revealed that in 1991 the city had lost jobs at an even faster rate than in the 1975 recession. And these were jobs not only in manufacturing, which had long been deserting Manhattan, but in the services as well. Service job losses, while they began at the high end of the scale when the stock market first tumbled in 1987, were now being translated, through a negative multiplier effect, into losses within demand sectors that 'yuppies' had formerly supported. Vacancy rates in hotels were rising. It was easier to get a cab, even in bad weather. Reservations were no longer needed at many good restaurants and tickets to concerts and the theater were once again more available. Employees of commercial firms, both high on the ladder and now, in back offices as well, were being let go, and in the interests of reducing municipal and state costs – as New York City and State struggled with mounting budget deficits – the number of public employees was also being reduced. The 1991 Christmas buying season was one of the most disappointing on record.

The bottom was also falling out of the housing market. Real estate agents, never ones to suggest at any time that housing might be a poor investment, were estimating that sale prices on luxury flats in the city had dropped a fourth to a fifth from their peak values in the late 1980s and that there were 'real bargains' to be had in rental units, co-ops, and condominia. But sellers, even those offering 'bargains,' reported months without a single buyer nibble. Advertisements in the Sunday real estate section of *The New York Times* for auctioned residential and commercial units expanded from half a page to several pages, and the lower auction prices established a ceiling beyond which other prospective buyers refused to bid. The commercial firms in Lower Manhattan, whose job holders were the 'white-collar workers' that a walk-to-work gentrifying zone of the East Village was intended to attract, were especially hard hit. Vacancy rates in privately-owned office buildings soared from under 3 percent in 1981 to over 20 per cent in 1991.[3]

In the East Village, although properties were too downscale to warrant private auctions and many residents were already so marginal to the economy that its collapse left them relatively unaffected, the wind was definitely out of gentrifiers' sails.[4] Flipper investors no longer saw any point in speculating on future gains; they were primarily motivated to avoid the risk of being stuck with properties. Owners who had been warehousing units preparatory to converting their buildings to co-ops and condominia were in a quandary. It might be wiser, they reconsidered, to derive some rents from the vacant units than hold them empty in the hope of future, but now uncertain, gains. Developers who had already begun to fix up places abandoned their efforts and some, like Peter

Kalikow, bailed out by declaring bancruptcy.[5] Buyers who had formerly pressured the administration to be allowed to construct 'market-rate' housing on city-owned vacant lots suddenly showed no interest in the properties.

With pressures of gentrification thus reduced, the wind also went out of the sails of protesters. While squatters and 'anarchists' continued to try to organize actions in support of tenant rights, squatter rights, and the rights to housing for the homeless, turnouts for such events reached a low ebb.[6] Rhetoric may have escalated, but the proposals suggested became increasingly fanciful and extreme, as there appeared to be less to lose.[7] Few realistic alternatives seemed open to participants, especially since the city had simultaneously begun to intensify its actions to evict unauthorized residents from city-owned buildings.[8]

Viewed from one side, the picture looked dim indeed. But if one turned it over, one could interpret it as a 'reprieve' for the less affluent.[9] The space left by a collapse of the ambitious plans for the neighborhood suddenly offered an opportunity which few of the housing activists could have anticipated when ten years earlier they had organized to block gentrification. Their efforts are now beginning to pay off. Even five years earlier it appeared that their struggles were doomed to defeat, in the face of development pressures on the neighborhood. However, in retrospect, one could say that their efforts did manage to buy precious time during the most threatening (to them) boom years of the 1980s. And now, their dogged opposition and steady perserverance literally left them the most effective, if not the only, actors on the scene, as the Lower East Side entered the depressed decade of the 1990s.

They are a remarkable group, these (mostly middle-class) women activists with deep and long roots in the neighborhood and with an abiding faith that working 'with the system' – or rather '*pushing* the system,' as one informant put it[10] – is *not* selling out, as the squatters have accused them of doing, but the only realistic way of preserving the special qualities of the Lower East Side. This chapter will recount the origins and activities of these community organizers, based largely on observations, community organization records, and longish interviews with some of its most influential members, and will attempt to evaluate what they have achieved. But first, a brief introduction.

When I first began to study the community organizations of the Lower East Side in 1987, I took L. T., whom I had just met, out to lunch and asked her to give me her picture of the 'power structure' of the neighborhood. She did not hesitate. She singled out the Joint Planning Council, an umbrella group of local organizations, as the key institution to study and identified three women as absolutely central to its operation: Carol Watkins of LESAC,[11] a Catholic charity organization; Frances Goldin of the Cooper Square Organization;[12] and Lisa Kaplan,[13] a former planner and 'housing' person working for a progressive foundation. She described the three, not very sympathetically, as sitting at the center of a dense 'spider web' of interrelated activists, a web that had been built up over decades.[14] Later, one of the three was to tell me in passing that 'their enemies' sometimes refer to them as the 'three witches of Eastwick' (a play on the term 'East Side').

But witches they are not. Picture a typical monthly meeting of the Housing Committee of Community Board 3, held in a drab common room of a local housing project.[15] By about 6 p.m. perhaps ten members of the committee are already seated at a row of formica tables pushed together on one side of the room, while clusters of supplicants seeking board support for their buildings, other interested persons (including researchers like myself), and a few other unidentifiable isolates hug the benches reserved for observers. The low-keyed chairperson, a soft-spoken man with a Caribbean accent, is waiting for a quorum. Next to him is a round-faced woman with a sweet smile, Carol Watson. They are chatting together, possibly about the meeting agenda. A tall silver-haired woman (Fran Goldin) enters, carrying a large bunch of bananas which she proceeds to detach one by one and place next to each participant.[16] The intimacy in the group is palpable, even though members are by no means in agreement on all issues[17] and, once the meeting is over, cliques divide up to leave. What is clear is that they have been working together for a long time and each has an intimate, building-by-building knowledge of the neighborhood.[18]

After a few persons from the floor have been heard from, there is a quiet matter-of-fact announcement that the first seven buildings (one on Clinton Street, one on Avenue C, two on Avenue B, two on Tenth Street and one on Eleventh Street) rehabilitated by the Mutual Housing Association under the cross-subsidy plan will be finished and ready for occupancy by April 1992. Seventy-seven units will soon be available. Although formal applications will not be accepted until 1 January 1992, people can apply earlier to receive an application when the forms are ready, and a waiting list for applications is being compiled. The buildings already carry signs in Spanish and English giving some information, and eventually there will be bilingual ads placed in newspapers. Occupants will be selected by lottery from among the qualified applicants. The Mutual Housing Association is now starting on phase two.

The announcement, while scarcely accompanied by trumpets and drums, is dramatic for those who had followed developments over the past decade. For these apartments are the first tangible results of a process that began many years ago when a moratorium on the disposition of city-owned properties was first achieved and the Joint Planning Council began to develop the cross-subsidy plan that is now in force, albeit somewhat modified from its original uncompromising position. And yet, after the announcement, other business is taken up in the same studied manner, the discussion turning to the perennial question of what to do with the Seward Park Urban Renewal site (an issue dating back to the 1960s) and what should be done with its few remaining derelict buildings on Delancey Street. The participants are in for the long haul, it is clear.

In this chapter we focus on the cross-subsidy 'plan' that is finally adding some limited number of affordable housing units through the rehabilitation of city-owned tenement structures. While it is primarily the achievement of these women who led the Joint Planning Council's ten-year struggle to prevent the city from selling off its *in rem* properties to private developers and who, working through Community Board 3, negotiated with the city's Department of Housing Preservation and Development (HPD) to obtain the Memorandum of Understanding signed between the board and HPD in October 1987, it should be acknowledged that not all of the units for low- and moderate-income occupants they fought for are actually being executed by organizations with which they are associated, or even with whom they share philosophies.

As we shall see, many of the rehabilitation projects in the East Village that are being 'counted against' the cross-subsidy 'quota' have been undertaken by organizations whose approaches diverge drastically from those the original JPC leaders advocated. While these other housing organizations claim that their activities will not lead to gentrification, many residents are not convinced. Although the squatters have tended not to make distinctions among housing 'reformers,' rejecting all of them as interfering with their own extra-market conversions through use and sweat equity,[19] these alternatives are by no means identical. They range from programs that would place ownership in non-profit associations and thus remove land and buildings from the market place indefinitely (such as the ones being undertaken through mutual housing associations) to those that would subsidize a temporary period of controlled profit taking in order to achieve a 'turnaround' in value, after which the units can be recycled to the market place for real profits. And, in terms of initial financing, they range from programs that receive full city subsidies, such as those announced by the housing committee, to those that utilize a public/private partnership. In this latter scheme, corporations agree to contribute to the costs of renovation, in return for certain immediate tax credits and administration costs, but they retain the eventual right to sell off the renovated units for a profit.

While all of these schemes are intended to keep properties out of the hands of pure speculators and quick-turnover developers and can thus be grouped broadly as 'anti-gentrification' programs, they differ considerably in their long-range consequences for the Lower East Side. The protagonists tend to emphasize these differences as they compete for buildings, not only with the squatters, but with each other. They also differ in terms of their sponsorship, their scope and range of activities, and their philosophies of housing. It is still too early to measure or evaluate comparatively the results obtained by these various actors in the East Village. It has really only been in the last year or two that actual results can be seen on the ground, and the number of involved buildings is still small; few projects have been completed and occupied. The jury must remain out, if we are to evaluate the actual outcomes of these competing programs.

This chapter focuses primarily on the local housing reformers who have worked through the Joint Planning Council, an umbrella organization that around 1965 integrated many smaller local associations into a loose confederation. Their leaders, working through member representatives on Community Board 3, developed the cross-subsidy plan and negotiated its details with the city. The chapter presents their reasoning and their commitments and is thus written mostly from their 'perspective.' However, before presenting that perspective, we must acknowledge some of the alternatives because, as we shall see, almost 100 of the 1,000 dwelling units for low- and moderate-income residents the city agreed to in the cross-subsidy plan are already being executed, and not necessarily by groups the reformers support.

The major alternatives to mutual housing associations are offered through the Local Initiatives Support Coalition (LISC) and the Enterprise Foundation. The former was created in 1980 by the Ford Foundation, the latter by developer James Rouse in 1982. While both were established nationally and were designed to help fill the gap created by the discontinuance of other urban development and housing programs in the Reagan administration, the two have somewhat different goals. However, as we shall see, their programs are more interlocked than might at first appear.[20]

> The Ford Foundation helped establish the nation's first community development corporation (CDC) and LISC's principal goal is to strengthen the CDCs that have sprung up across the country over the past quarter century. 'We start with the CDC, not low-income housing or economic development,' says LISC's Marc Jahr.

In New York, LISC provides money and technical assistance to CDC's, some of which (for example, St Nicholas Neighborhood Preservation Corporation, Los Sures, and Banana Kelley in the Bronx) are involved in providing low-income housing. In contrast:

> 'The mission of Enterprise is to assist in providing decent and affordable housing for the poor of this country and assist people out of the cycle of

> poverty,' says Bill Frey, who head's [*sic*] the foundation's New York office. They work with lots of nonprofit groups (not just CDCs). In 1986 the creation of the federal low-income housing tax credit attracted corporate investments. The corporate investments targeted for the city are pooled into a finance entity called the New York Equity Fund. A corporation makes an investment in the fund, generally between $1 million and $5 million, which is paid over a period of seven years. Such sums are invested for more than good works – investors earn federal tax credits with a rate of return equaling about 15 to 20 percent.

The Equity Fund, although theoretically a unit separate from LISC and Enterprise, 'borrows money from banks, which in turn it lends to LISC and Enterprise projects,' after taking its cut for operating expenses. The members of the fund's board of directors are drawn from the two intermediaries.

According to Doug Turetsky, the two intermediary programs have already facilitated the renovation of several thousand dwelling units throughout the city and have another thousand units in the 'pipeline.' Using the carrot of tax incentives that is provided by federal legislation, they have 'lured' some $110 million from local banks and corporations, money they claim 'filters into the hands of neighborhood-based groups.' Both are nation-wide programs, as contrasted with the locally organized mutual housing associations that operate only within the Lower East Side. In this sense, they might be viewed as 'top-down' programs, albeit those that work through locally-organized agents. Furthermore, both depend upon a public/private partnership to attract corporate investments which, since the creation in 1986 of the federal low-income housing tax credit, have been drawn to neighborhood redevelopment.

Local squatters and housing activists are not impressed. They criticize both LISC and Enterprise projects on three grounds. First, critics complain about the 'extra layer of bureaucracy that controls funding and focuses attention on housing development and management – at the expense of grassroots community organizing.' The Equity Fund does seem to constitute a 'holding company' layer that distances investors from projects, with the two major organizations and the local groups they finance intervening still again. Critics question the proportion of investment that is thus siphoned off before projects are actually commenced. According to the head of one of the local groups charged with actually renovating six buildings on West 125th Street:

> [J]ust 55 cents of every dollar invested in the New York Equity Fund actually winds up in the projects . . . [and although] LISC and Enterprise generally get the credit . . . [i]n fact, public funds make up the bulk of the money. In the West 125th Street project, nearly two-thirds of the funds

> for the $3 million renovation comes from the city's capital budget – loaned to the project at just one percent interest. Federal funds are also part of the financial package. In general, the New York Equity Fund provides about a third of a project's funding.

Critics also are concerned that local entrepreneurs, tempted by the funds available, may end up 'trading their community roots – and activist politics – for the promise of corporate cash.' There is potential competition between older grassroots organizations and some newly established ones funded through LISC/Enterprise. On the Lower East Side this competition has already altered the local political scene. One of the groups into whose hands such loans and grants in the public/private partnership plan have filtered is the Lower East Side Coalition for Housing Development, formerly headed by Antonio Pagan. Perhaps more significant for the area's future than the limited number of dwelling units his organization has actually made available is the fact that the funds provided served to catapult its conservative director into New York City politics, a situation deplored by both squatters and housing activists in the Joint Planning Council. (As soon as he defeated Miriam Friedlander for city council, he resigned his housing position.)

The third criticism is the most serious and attacks the basic philosophy of the LISC and Enterprise Foundation programs. Opponents point to the fact that the rehabilitated structures are being made available to 'low-income' tenants on a rental basis only, and that after 15 years such units can be sold off and converted to market-rate apartments.[21] This contrasts markedly with the mutual housing associations that have been set up in the Lower East Side under the cross-subsidy program to handle renovated buildings. The latter depend upon combining city earmarked funds with the labor and material investments of potential residents and are designed to keep the units permanently within the stock of affordable housing. The non-profit housing associations will retain ownership of the land while selling the individual apartments to occupants. Buyers, however, will have to agree to restrictions on their rights to sell or reassign their units and can only recoup the value of their direct expenditures on improvements. No windfall profits from privatization will be possible, either in the short or long runs.

THE EVOLUTION OF THE CROSS-SUBSIDY PLAN

The present cross-subsidy plan, designed to balance off the goals of profit and non-profit housing, is not the first on the Lower East Side. Precedents were established much earlier when middle-income cooperatives were first proposed for a site that had been cleared under Urban Renewal legislation. The middle-income co-ops were eventually built, but in return the neighborhood was promised that displaced persons would be rehoused in cross-subsidized units. 'This procedure was first fought for in Cooper Square,' according to Fran Goldin, and now, 'some 33 years later (!),' many of the remaining units promised so long ago are beginning to be built.[22] The mobilization that was organized back in the 1950s gave experience in community organizing that has been used in later battles.

When I asked Fran Goldin how the Joint Planning Council had prevented the city from selling off the neighborhood's *in rem* properties when the market began to recover in the early 1980s, she replied:

> We worked all the routes, as we did . . . in 1959 and we're doing in 1991. We used the streets, we had parades, we had petitions, we had rallies, we had town meetings so that the people would be educated to what was happening.

She said it wasn't hard to mobilize the community then, because residents were already 'seething' and the city feared riots.

> And the city has had its share of riots! And there were riots on the Lower East Side. Much earlier than the 1980s, much earlier. [In the depression] there were massive rent strikes. [This time] we had torch parades with torches which were soaked rags with fire, you know, which was an expression of our outrage . . . [The people] were close to riots. I mean, there was great pressure from the people who were being pushed out of their homes already by gentrification. Because that's when the market was rising . . . There was banging in their apartments . . . from next door. [Where] they lived, they paid $100; the person moving in next door was paying $500. They could see the handwriting on the wall. They knew that they were being squeezed out. Many [displaced] people were moving into the [nearby public housing] projects with their parents. It wasn't anything you had to explain to them. It's something they could see.

But in addition to 'working the streets,' the Joint Planning Council activists were doing two other equally important things: they were drawing up their own plan to use the city-owned properties to gain affordable housing in the neighborhood and they were politicking at City Hall. As Fran Goldin recounted:

> At the same time that we were working in the streets, which we always have – because if we didn't have th[at] backing we never would have gotten anywhere – we had the big mouths, we knew lawyers, we knew architects, we knew planners. [But none of those skills] . . . mean a thing if you don't have the backing. So from my point of view as an organizer, and if I'm

> nothing, I'm an organizer, we knew that the roots were the most important thing. The tree will die without the roots. The roots was the people.

Once they had their plan, Goldin continued:

> We hit our own legislators. Fortunately, we had Miriam Friedlander, so she was a great advocate. We had Tommy Logan, Manfred Ohrenstein, who agreed with us, so he was a great advocate. [Congressman] Green never took a plunge then. He helped us when he could but he was very careful never to offend the Jewish community which was, by then, no longer poor and downtrodden but more comfortable economically . . . In addition to all that pressure, we met with every member of the City Council. We met with all of our legislators. We met with the Housing Authority. We met with the HPD. And we didn't just go in and say 'blah blah blah.' We presented them with official-looking documents that said 'This is our plan.' . . . And we gave them a three-part plan which included no luxury housing. And we struggled and struggled and struggled and [did] all we could do to to keep them from auctioning [off their properties], because things were being co-oped. We kept them from auctioning! [It was our greatest accomplishment.][23]

The development of the community's (really JPC's) alternative plan was described to me by Lisa Kaplan.[24] She explained that by the early 1980s the 500 properties on the Lower East Side that the city had come to own in the wake of the 1970–80 disinvestments were becoming more valuable. The JPC tried to figure out a plan to use the 'newly found value of [city] land to produce housing for low income people.'

In 1983, the same year that they organized the community, held demonstrations, fought the city-initiated program of AHOP, and staged a multi-thousand person parade to City Hall, the JPC hired staff and consultants (mostly planners from Pratt Institute) to study the changing demographic, ethnic, class, and housing characteristics of the neighborhood and to explore ways that inclusionary zoning could preserve the present income mix of the area. They also explored ways to use potential receipts from the sale of some city-owned properties to generate funds for low-income housing. The plan they came up with, announced in June 1984, included three main provisions:

1 inclusionary zoning for the area that would require developers to provide a certain proportion of low-rent units in any new market-rate construction;
2 an enforcement unit paid for by the city that would make sure housing agreements were honored; and
3 the sale of some city-owned land to entirely subsidize the provision of low-income housing in the neighborhood.

Lisa Kaplan expressed some of the urgency they felt:

> We had to develop our own plan for redeveloping the neighborhood, and to use the 'hook' that the city now had an income generating potential [from its ownership of land]. We attempted to develop a plan under the encouragement of then-Borough President Andrew Stein to set up a kind of land banking proposal that would use the value of the land to subsidize low and moderate income housing.

But the study's conclusions were disappointing: 'We found out that [the money that could be raised from] the sale of the land was not going to be sufficient to generate enough low income housing.' Since the scheme would not be entirely self-supporting and subsidies would be required, the JPC turned to Community Board 3 for further support ('clout,' Fran Goldin called it in her November interview[25]). In the process, it was forced into a compromise about which the originators feel extremely ambivalent.

Lisa Kaplan reported that by June of 1984 the community board had accepted the barest outline of the JPC plan, as presented to it by Val Orseli and Harriet Cohen. But by then the original plan had been significantly modified. Instead of asking the city to subsidize 100 percent of the units for low- and moderate-income housing, the compromise plan asked, in return for an end to the moratorium, that half of the housing units to be built or renovated on city-owned land be subsidized for low- and moderate-income housing (mostly through renovation of tenement buildings); in return for this subsidy, the Community Board Plan agreed that each subsidized unit could be matched by a unit of market-rate housing to be constructed largely on the vacant lots the city would be allowed to sell off.

Fran Goldin couldn't tell me exactly how this compromise had come about. However, she did have a strong response. She recounted that she saw the compromise as a 'bitter pill to swallow. We felt that if we didn't reluctantly accept the compromise, we would lose the entire Lower East Side.' When I asked the same question of Lisa Kaplan, her answer was a bit defensive:

> The JPC plan was written as 100 percent. By the time it was presented to the Community Board, it was presented as 50 percent, because it was recognized that the Community Board would not pass a 100 percent . . . We were familiar with the Community Board; we had attended the meetings for years, and everyone, the political people, were telling us that it was outrageous, that there was a risk, that the idea behind the JPC plan had been a kind of self-subsidization and that we had failed in showing that that could happen, and we could not backtrack and say 100 percent. And that there would have to be a compromise, so 50 percent was considered the best we could do.

She admitted that even after JPC discovered that the low- and moderate-income housing could not be built without significant subsidies, they continued to push for a 100 percent with full subsidies, but 'we never, in our heart of hearts, ever thought we were going to get it. That would be our starting point and that we'd then see how much we could get.' So they were already prepared to compromise by the time they approached the community board. As she remarked:

> Well, we were not in the best position, we were not in a position of power. We were maybe strongly recognized as a Community Board, more than many other community boards, and maybe they could have done it . . . But what power did we have? We organized, I think, but we didn't have any real power . . . So I don't know. *I'll never know to the day I die whether we were right or wrong in compromising.* (interview 9 December 1991, with her emphasis)

Despite this compromise and the backing of Community Board 3, the mayor essentially ignored the request. Instead, in July 1984 Mayor Koch announced his own 'cross-subsidy plan' which, according to Lisa Kaplan, was simply a way of undercutting growing support for the local initiative. His plan included no city subsidy nor did it offer any guarantee of the number of low-income units to be provided. Furthermore, there was no community consultation and, beyond the press release, no substance or action.

There then ensued a two and a half year period during which the city refused to deal seriously with the community's plan.[26] Not until January 1987 did then-new Commissioner Paul Crotty set up a working group with the community board to see whether the CB3 community-initiated plan was feasible. Planners were hired by CB3, paid for by city funds, to inventory the housing and vacant land stock, to analyze the current market values of *in rem* properties, and to determine how at least half of them could be 'reused for low and moderate income people.' During this time, the JPC was pushing to radicalize discussion.

Throughout the first half of 1987, negotiations proceeded slowly to reach a 'Memorandum of Understanding' between Community Board 3 and the city's Department of Housing Preservation and Development on how the 50–50 cross-subsidy plan would actually work. This agreement was approved by CB3 in June 1987 and finally signed by Commissioner Crotty by October 1987. (There have been subsequent amendments.)

SUMMARY OF THE MEMORANDUM OF UNDERSTANDING

The agreement covered all residential city-owned property in an L-shaped zone from Fourteenth Street to Delancey, Forsyth to Avenue A, and Pitt

Street to Avenue D. Within that zone, no city property could be sold for market-rate housing outside of the agreement; there were to be no unrestricted auctions of city-owned properties. The agreed-upon target for the cross-subsidy program was to produce 1,000 units of low- to moderate-income housing and 1,000 units of 'market-rate' housing in the area. Half of the low- to moderate-income units were to be for families earning no more than $15,000 per year and the other half for families earning between $15,000 and $23,000 per year. The low and moderate units were to be gained mostly through the rehabilitation of city-owned buildings, whereas it was expected that most market-rate units would be in new buildings constructed on vacant land. The agreement specified, however, that the low- to moderate- and the market-rate units should be developed in *all parts* of the area, rather than segregated from one another.

Originally, the agreement specified that the proceeds from the sale of land for market-rate housing would be placed in a special 'cross-subsidy fund' earmarked to be spent on the production of low- and moderate-income housing in the area. However, when sales of vacant land to private developers lagged badly (it turned out that most of the vacant land was in Loisaida near the projects, from which developers, quite logically, stayed away in droves), the agreement had to be revised. The city then agreed not to wait for money raised through the sale of land to developers, but rather to advance all the funds needed to create the first 200 units of subsidized housing, although eventually, and to the extent that income was later generated from the sale of land for market-rate housing, those funds would be used to help offset the advance.[27]

The agreement also specified that 'all affordable units created will be developed, owned and managed by a mutual housing association created by the community expressly for this purpose.'[28] In actual fact, however, there are now four mutual housing associations involved in providing housing under the cross-subsidy program. Community Board 3 was designated as the central local body which would participate fully in the planning and implementation of these projects. The agreement also specified that if HPD and CB3 agreed that low- and moderate-income units were not being produced adequately through the existing program, they would jointly develop new methods of production and sales.

The final proviso (which I consider somewhat ill-advised, in that it opened up an opportunity for the city to 'renegotiate' the target figure by including city projects not related to the original intent of the cross-subsidy plan) is one which needs closer scrutiny. That is the arrangement which gives 'credit units,' charged against the goal of 1,000 affordable dwelling units, for *any* low- or moderate-income housing provided outside the mechanism of the mutual housing associations. HPD was to receive one-half unit credit for each unit of low-moderate housing produced in the area, provided that site control had been given to a community-based organization. Furthermore, if such projects receive more than $15,000 funding from cross-subsidy funds, HPD is granted a full unit credit per dwelling unit.

The Achievements to the End of 1991

As noted above, the Community Board's Mutual Housing Association had completed its first 77 renovated apartments for low- and moderate-income families (in seven buildings) and was about to embark on a second phase to generate perhaps another 100 dwelling units. Theoretically, then, it had a large proportion of its 'quota' to go. However, the arrangement whereby HPD gains unit credits for other low- and moderate-income projects being renovated or built in the area had already 'eaten away' more than 300 of the balance left in the cross-subsidy target of 1,000 units.

Lisa Kaplan provided me with a list, as of 8 June 1990, that itemized the 'unit credits' thus far. The largest number of these are funded under already existing federal, state, and city programs, and it might be argued that, with or without the cross-subsidy plan, these facilities would have been built. Most have little to offer in the way of fulfilling the original goals of the JPC plan to make additional family housing available at affordable rates. Another large proportion are being produced through the Enterprise program which, as we have shown above, will not serve the goal of keeping the properties permanently outside the speculative housing market. An analysis of the unit credits already claimed by HPD for specific properties makes these conclusions painfully evident, and there is no reason to believe that this process will not speed up in the future.

Six projects, yielding HPD a total of 102 'unit credits,' were being funded through HUD's Section 202 and/or HHAP (Homeless Housing Assistance Program). These include 50 unit credits given for a HUD 202 senior-citizen housing development being built on vacant land at 80–92 Ridge Street by the New York Federation for Senior Citizens; another 8 unit credits for a small senior project at 234 East Second Street; 20 unit credits for a HUD 202 group home to be built on a vacant-land site at 174–82 Forsyth Street by the New York Society for the Deaf; and 6 unit credits for another modest project at 323 East Houston, funded by 202/HHAP. In addition, HHAP funding was being used to gain 15 unit credits for a halfway institution at 159–63 Avenue B, sponsored by the Women's Prison Association, and another 3 unit credits are being awarded for a HHAP medical (AIDS) facility of 23 beds in 6 apartments, being renovated at 532 East Fifth Street under GOLES sponsorship.

In addition to these federally funded projects, most of which are for institutional uses and would have been provided in any case, the New York State Turnkey program is funding construction of a new institution for the mentally handicapped at 258–66 East Fourth Street, for which HPD is being granted 25 unit credits. Another 20 unit credits are being granted for two New York State Turnkey-funded projects at 195–99 East Second Street and 8–12 Avenue B, sponsored by the LES Mutual Housing Association. Only the latter projects are properly in line with the goals of the original JPC plan.

A very modest number of units are being produced through other programs, notably those sponsored by Catholic organizations (yielding 31 unit credits) and a settlement house (from which 16 unit credits are gained). HFT/312 is funding some five small projects being renovated at 304–6 East Eighth Street, 635–7 East Eleventh Street, 641 East Eleventh Street, 239 East Second Street, and 191 East Third Street. In addition, the Educational Alliance has had a Memorandum of Understanding since August 1987 to build a small project on vacant land at 25–7 Avenue D with funding from DSAS.

Despite the reservations JPCers may have about the long-term effects of the housing renovations done through the Enterprise program, the largest number of non-institutional additions to the affordable housing stock on the Lower East Side within the cross-subsidy area are actually being made with Enterprise funding. These projects are gaining HPD over 90 unit credits, a number that is likely to increase in the future. Enterprise has worked chiefly through two organizations in the neighborhood: AAFE (Asian Americans for Equality), which is most interested in providing housing for an expanding Chinatown; and the LES Coalition for Housing Development, headed in the late 1980s by Antonio Pagan. AAFE is renovating buildings at various scattered sites, all but one of them outside Alphabet City in the zone south of Houston (at 142, 173 and 177 Stanton Street, 129 Rivington Street, 135 and 137 Norfolk Street and 77 Avenue C). HPD will gain 49 unit credits for these projects. Pagan's Coalition Plaza Enterprise Project, renovating buildings at 67–9 Avenue D and 181–3 East Second Street, will earn HPD another 42 unit credits.

It is hard to avoid the conclusion that thus far, the cross-subsidy plan is not working out as its original framers intended, although they seem reluctant to acknowledge this. The city's 'escape hatch' has been the unit credit system whereby a significant number of projects that various government agencies would have undertaken anyway in connection with other goals – i.e., housing for the aged, for the handicapped, for the ill, for prison populations, etc. – are being counted against the 1,000 d.u.

goal for newly renovated low- and moderate-income housing. As noted above, more than 300 units have already been 'removed' through such credits. These include close to 100 units that are being funded through the Enterprise Foundation and which can eventually revert to private profit ownership. This is not what the housing activists associated with the Joint Planning Council had in mind when they first framed their plan to provide an alternative to gentrification and ordinary market processes, an alternative that would have preserved the existing diverse character of the neighborhood through renovating the tenements and making them permanently affordable. Our evaluation of their achievement must therefore be a mixed one.

First, the housing activists succeeded, with the help of a mobilized and irate community[29] and through exerting pressure judiciously on the political system, in blocking the wholesale sell-off of the 500 buildings and lots the city had fallen heir to in the period of maximum disinvestment and tax arrear forfeiture of the 1970s. Had they not done so, the East Village would probably have been gentrified to unrecognizable levels during the booming market period of the 1980s. This did not happen. The time they bought, therefore, was crucial. Second, through their persistence and long-term vision, they succeeded in gaining from an otherwise unsympathetic city administration a commitment to the goal of expanding the supply of affordable housing on the Lower East Side. A third measure of their success – albeit one for which they can take no credit – is that gentrification of existing privately owned structures for higher-income tenants and massive new developments of highrise luxury apartments for newcomers have effectively been aborted, at least for the time being. For that, however, credit (if that be the term) must be given to the present economic troubles in New York. It is the recession that is keeping developers away from the East Village at the very time when, finally, they are being allowed, indeed encouraged, to buy up large numbers of city-owned vacant lots.

In fact, the city is experiencing grave difficulties in 'unloading' its store of *in rem* empty lots, a development that both Goldin and Kaplan see as very promising. They are counting on the fact that at worst, the market-rate program will revert to moderate- and middle-income housing, and, at best from their point of view, the city will end up subsidizing even more low- to moderate-income housing in the area. Although this appears to be a 'win by default,' it does offer some protection from displacement to current residents. Not only have owners stopped warehousing and gentrifiers stopped gentrifying, but sale prices on already gentrified units have declined and rents have stopped escalating. The conspicuous 'pocket' of cheaper housing in this last remnant of Lower Manhattan has, for the time being, been spared.

Three counter-forces, however, lie in the immediate future. First, the stock of city-owned tenements that are still available for renovation on the Lower East Side is fast being depleted. Future renovations will not be able to add much to the housing stock north of Houston because such gains can increasingly be made only at the expense of existing occupants. The squatters will eventually have to be displaced from the remaining city-owned tenements, a goal supported enthusiastically by Antonio Pagan but only reluctantly by housing activists such as Fran Goldin and Lisa Kaplan. Second, and perhaps more significantly, there are new forces that are pressing northward from Chinatown. Thus far, they have operated largely south of Houston Street, but it seems only a matter of time before they begin to affect the future of the East Village as well. And finally, given the economic difficulties New York City is now experiencing, the city may have to withdraw even the modest financial commitment it made to the cross-subsidy program itself, leaving the goals of its program substantially unfulfilled. We explore these future prospects in the next chapter.

NOTES

1 On 15 October 1991, bulldozers crushed the makeshift dwellings that had been reconstructed on empty lots east of Avenue B after their September eviction, destroying the homes of some 200 residents who 'simply packed their belongings in boxes and shopping carts and wandered off in the rain.' (See field notes.) Quotation is from Thomas Morgan, 'New York City Bulldozes Squatters' Shantytowns,' *The New York Times*, 16 October 1991, p. 1. Note the equation drawn between the homeless and squatters, the first time such a congruence appeared in the press.

2 In early September, Nancy Wackstein, the city's adviser on homeless policy, resigned, saying 'It is a reasonable thing to say that I have been very frustrated.' See, *inter alia*, Thomas Morgan, 'Dinkins's Chief Homeless Policy Adviser Resigns,' *The New York Times*, 4 September 1991, p. B2.

3 See Thomas J. Lueck, 'Decline Follows a 2-Decade Boom in Lower Manhattan,' *The New York Times*, 12 September 1991, pp. B1 and B7.

4 See Thomas J. Lueck, 'Prices Decline as Gentrification Ebbs,' in *The New York Times*, Real Estate Section, 29 September 1991. The writer focuses on a woman who bought her 400-square-foot studio in the Christodora House in 1986 for $125,000 and has been trying, so far in vain, to sell it 'even at a loss.'

5 'With the sharp decline in New York real estate values, however, the banks [Peter Kalikow's creditors] believe that Mr Kalikow owes about $242 million more than his buildings are worth.' Quoted from Richard D. Hylton, 'Developer Fights Lenders on Control of his Assets,' *The New York Times*, 20 June 1991.

6 The headline for Evelyn Nieves' article in *The New York Times* on 13 October 1991 captured it all: 'Squatters and Friends March, But Tompkins Sq. is Weary.' A rally in Union Square Park on 22 December 1991 drew one of the smallest and most desultory crowds in memory (field notes).

7 At a meeting jointly organized by squatters and some New School students, held at the New School in December 1991, old hand agitator Flo Kennedy seriously suggested that people should squat in Macy's Department Store where there are beds, blankets, food, and bathrooms. Attendance was only half what a similar meeting had drawn several years earlier, despite the fact that (as we later learned) the homeless, who helped fill a quarter of the empty seats, had been promised a food distribution if they attended (field notes).

8 See Evelyn Nieves, 'Squatters in City Buildings Face Eviction by the Landlord,' *The New York Times*, 20 October 1991, p. E16.

9 One of my informants, a housing activist, described the present period as one of 'remission,' by which she meant a healthy respite from 'cancerous' gentrification. That her premises were the exact opposite of economists is clear from the metaphor.

10 Interview with Lisa Kaplan, 9 December 1991.

11 About 40 years of age, Ms Watkins had worked for LESAC for a number of years. Although we talked informally at two dinners after housing committee meetings, I did not conduct a formal interview because she told me she was 'burned out' and wanted to abandon the unrewarding struggle.

12 Frances Goldin is a handsome gray-haired woman who does not look her age. She claims to have lived in and worked for housing and preservation of the working-class character of the Lower East Side for some 47 years. One of the founders in 1959 of Cooper Square Organization (Cooper Square is a subdistrict of the Lower East Side), she has pursued those interests in addition to her 'real' occupation as a literary agent representing a number of progressive scholars and writers who have since become long-term friends. Among her long-time associates have been Walter Thabet, one of America's first advocate planners who continues to be involved, Staughnton Lynd (son of Robert and Helen Lynd, the authors of *Middletown*) of the anti-war movement who in the early 1960s worked in housing outreach for University Settlement (House), and Frances Fox Piven and Richard Cloward who, in the mid-1960s, worked for Mobilization for Youth on the Lower East Side.

13 Lisa Kaplan came to New York City from upper New York state in 1973 to do graduate work in planning at Hunter College. In the course of her training she was first given a 'field placement' with the Twelfth Street office of the Human Resources Administration and moved to the Lower East Side when in 1973 she was reassigned to Pueblo Nuevo. After finishing school in 1975, she became executive director of Pueblo Nuevo, a post she held until 1980. She joined the JPC when she was director of Pueblo Nuevo. She then worked at Pratt Institute, in Clinton, and finally joined Consumer-Farmer Foundation about five years ago. She has continued to live and work on the Lower East Side (in 1979 she became a homesteader on First Street), and served as a member of Community Board 3 between 1977 and 1991. She was a chief negotiator with HPD on the cross-subsidy plan.

14 This was later confirmed by our research into the 'interlocking directorates' of a significant number of local community organizations. I am grateful to Jan Lin for his analysis of this network.

15 Based loosely on field notes of 10 October 1991.

16 Fran Goldin modestly explained to me later that she routinely brings something to eat, because members go right to meetings after work. That evening, Lisa Kaplan was absent, since she had temporarily withdrawn from the community board to take advantage of a year-long Revson Foundation fellowship.

17 Indeed, Krystyna P., the landlady much hated by squatters and often a minority dissenting voter on Community Board 3 when issues about police, riots, the homeless, and low-cost housing come up, is on the housing committee, although she sits at the margins and participates little.

18 During the meetings, specific buildings are casually referred to by their street addresses and everyone seems to know what they are used for and what their problems are.

19 At the squatters' meeting held at the New School in December 1991, the chant was 'Not *low-cost* housing! *No-cost* housing!'

20 The following account is based on Doug Turetsky, 'The Go-Betweens: The Local Initiatives Corporation and the Enterprise Foundation are Attracting Private Investors to the Poorest Communities – But the New Partnerships Have Their Costs,' *City Limits* (June–July 1991), pp. 8–10, from which the next quotations have been taken.

21 Critics point to the parallels in New York to the middle-income subsidized Mitchell-Lama projects which are now being sold off at great private profit.

22 Interview with Frances Goldin on 18 November 1991.

23 Lisa Kaplan, in her interview, pointed out that there already had been an unspoken moratorium on the sale of city properties. 'By 1974 we had a moratorium on the sale of city-owned properties. It was part of a city wide thing but the Lower East Side was leading it [the battle]. We were saying it [sales and resales] was a revolving door, the property was being sold and then sold again. So we had to [stop them].' In response to my question of whether the moratorium was ever in writing, she said: 'I don't know that they ever issued a statement, but they stopped doing it. They couldn't sell, or some other scum bag bought it, so they weren't generating any money, so why do it? I think our fight brought about certain results, but there was a certain rationality about it.' Note, however, that speculators were making good money flipping apartments during the period she is discussing (see Smith *et al.* and Mele, chapters 7 and 8).

24 In the following section I depend upon a transcript of my interview with her on 9 December 1991, as well as a copy of her notes which she left with me.

25 'Then we realized that we needed more clout in order to go the next step which was to get our plan accepted. So we met with the Community Board – [which was not so hard since] many of us, some of us, were on the Community Board.' Fran Goldin, interview of 18 November 1991.

26 This is the opinion expressed by Lisa Kaplan in her interview.

27 In the course of an informal dinner with Fran Goldin and Carol Watson after a housing committee meeting in June 1991, I was told that the city had already guaranteed (actually deposited) $5 million to pay for the first phase of their low and moderate income renovation projects. For information about the negotiations for this funding, see William Sites, 'Market, Community, and Local State' (New York: City University of New York, doctoral dissertation, 1993), chapters 8 and 9.

28 From Lisa Kaplan's notes.

29 I do not mean to imply here that the developers of the cross-subsidy plan deserve full credit for this result. The squatters and homeless played their roles in discouraging further gentrification, as did a host of tenant-rights organizations such as GOLES, the Anti-Displacement Project, etc., which countered the efforts of landlords to evict low-income tenants throughout the 1980s.

Plate 15.1 What next for the vacant lots between Avenues C and D?
Source: Courtesy of Marlis Momber

Conclusions and Implications

Janet Abu-Lughod

In the face of the remarkable transformations that have taken place in the form of American cities over the last century and a half, the persistence of a multicultural proletarian quarter near the current governmental and financial core of the country's largest metropolitan center is a stunning anomaly. This book has concentrated on the changing character of this particular neighborhood and on the local *dramatis personae* who have accumulated there, layer by layer, in the course of its long history. It has examined a few local conflicts and controversies in considerable detail, giving the impression – shared by so many of its residents – that the fate of the area has been largely determined by their ability to sustain such contests and struggles in the face of powerful outside forces of politics and economics.

To some extent, that is true. Local actions *do* affect what happens in local areas; we would not want to deny this nor to discourage participants in local struggles. But to say that human actions affect outcomes is not to argue that they are all powerful. To paraphrase Marx, humans make their own histories, but not as they choose. They operate always within circumstances given to them from outside and by others. This is especially true of relatively powerless social groups, classes, and neighborhoods.

The purpose of this chapter is therefore three-fold. First, it will synthesize the local community's recent 'ecology of games'[1] by analyzing how the issues and agents came together in the East Village to yield the complex specific outcomes that have materialized over the past few decades. In this analysis we totally reject the concept of the singular, embattled defensive 'community' where empowerment can be defined as a simple matter of 'giving the people what they want.' Determining what 'they' want (and what each player can get) is indeed the essential problematique of agency and local politics.

But we also recognize that this 'local community of games' is never played out in a vacuum; the relative strengths of the groups contending and negotiating in the local arena are determined in large measure by forces that lie beyond the locale. Secondly, therefore, as we have emphasized throughout this volume, sometimes explicitly but more often implicitly, the ultimate causes of the neighborhood's characteristics and the intended and unintended outcomes of local controversies must be sought in the larger forces that extend far beyond the neighborhood: the relevant economic investment climates; city, state, and national politics and policies; and even global economic and political events. This chapter will consider these elements more systematically by situating the Lower East Side within these larger contexts, in order to identify the range of effective actions open to neighborhoods with low economic and social power. In recent years, theoretical discussions of urban political economy have tended to become highly abstract, giving the false impression that macro-causes exercise mechanical and inexorable force upon local outcomes. Our contention is that these *influence but do not entirely determine* what happens in specific locales. One of the questions we want to explore is just *how* local agency and abstract forces tend to interact in poor neighborhoods in the centers of our largest cities.

Which brings us to the third issue to be discussed in this concluding chapter, namely, the 'generalizability' of any findings that can be generated out of a single small-scale 'case study,' especially one that has focused on an admittedly extreme and, in the last analysis, unique area. Throughout, we have emphasized the individuality of our case, contending that its special characteristics are linked (1) to the *specific location* of the neighborhood within the larger physical and social ecology of New York; (2) to the *specific characteristics of its housing stock* and the limitations to gentrification these have imposed; (3) to the *long and complex economic and demographic history* of the zone and its peculiar functions as a port of entry for immigrants and a refuge for marginal and even counter-cultural groups; and (4) to the *particular moment in historical time* when economic restructuring is altering the nature of capitalism and the class structure in major 'world' cities. How, then, could such a case be of relevance elsewhere? And if it is relevant, in what ways?

The Local Community as an Ecology of Games

One of the points this volume has stressed is the large number of 'players' in the East Village 'game,' each with its own interests, ideologies, and goals. While it is possible to 'classify' these players by the usual categories of analysis, such as class, ethnicity, relation to housing tenure and the investment process, subcultures and lifestyles, etc., a second point that has been emphasized is the wide range of variation *within* each group of players. In such a situation, coalitions, realignments, and the waxing and waning of specific powers are bound to occur. This makes the outcome of any particular community controversy somewhat indeterminate and unstable. Paradoxically, it also makes the study of local controversies the best method for uncovering community dynamics.

If we re-examine the case studied in this book, we find that the core of controversy has ever been over different definitions of the neighborhood's function in the city's ecology and over different visions of its future. In this struggle, the park itself always plays a crucial role. The park is a central 'externality' through which these different visions can be achieved, and each faction recognizes that whoever controls the park controls the future. In a very real sense, the contested terrain of the park *is* the battle site where various interests are played out.

At one extreme are the diverse players who view the land and buildings of the Lower East Side simply as 'property' – as commodities with exchange value only. Flippers are perhaps the purest example. Their short-term interests are best served by a degraded environment which generates more and more distressed sellers; the state of the park is of little interest to them. Near to them in the spectrum are small absentee owners saddled with rent-controlled tenements that no longer yield what landlords consider adequate returns. While upset by the degradation of surrounding buildings and the inhospitable or dangerous environment, some owners hang on, hoping some day to pull their chestnuts out of the fire. Deteriorating local conditions just might drive out their rent-protected tenants, thereby opening the way for future 'better,' i.e., more profitable, uses. In the short run, the park holds little interest for them, although in the long run they will want a renewed park. The non-resident developers, while still viewing the area in purely economic terms, have a greater vested interest in improved environmental externalities. For them, what happens in the park is of central importance, because a well policed community and a 'middle-class' park are what they require to attract the higher class of renters and buyers upon which their profits depend. They have close relations to 'the state,' since they count on government to defend their private property rights and to enhance the externalities upon which their success ultimately depends. And the 'state' itself has a strong vested interest in their success, since upgraded properties will eventually yield higher tax returns. Purchasers and renters of rehabilitated apartments share some of the views of developers; they differ only in terms of their relative stakes in a gentrified neighborhood, with owners more concerned than renters.

At the opposite extreme are those players who view the land and buildings of the Lower East Side exclusively in terms of their use value, since they are outside of, or very marginal to, the system of property. The homeless are perhaps the purest example, seeing occupation of public open space in particular as no infringement on the rights of others. The squatters, public performers, and 'hippies' share with them a sense of entitlement to public space focused primarily on the free use of the park, but the squatters extend this ideology to abandoned structures and especially to derelict city-owned properties. For these actors, the 'state' is viewed as a threat to communal use rights, either to be placated (as the homeless tried to do) or to be fought (as the squatters have consistently done).

The various other residents of the area fall somewhere between these extremes and, since they are the majority in the neighborhood, it is they who are 'mobilizable' in support of specific policies sought by either extreme. They have, however, their own complex sets of interests. 'Ethnic' renters are of two major types: older eastern European residents occupying rent-controlled apartments primarily in the tenements of the western part of the East Village; and the younger larger Latino families (formerly almost exclusively Puerto Rican but now heavily intermixed with Dominicans) more concentrated in the eastern half. Both share a strong commitment to preventing gentrification *in their own buildings*, because that would displace them from affordable housing, but they have different views of neighborhood change and toward the other groups in the area. The older whites fear the counter-culture types most, whom they judge as immoral and threatening; they also fear blacks and Latinos, associating them with drugs and crime. They avoid going near the 'projects' and welcome the influx of middle-class whites that gentrification promises to bring, so long as their own apartments and rents are protected from their competitive bidding. This attitude is even more marked among the few owner-occupants who hope that rising values will yield a richer legacy for their children. The Latino population is large enough to constitute a protective community and to offer recognition and sociability in shops and along sidewalks, where life often spills over to the street, and in the precious gardens and *casitas* where they can congregate. While more likely to be victims in their own spaces, they seem to have less fear of their neighbors than of landlords seeking to evict them and of rising rents. The social distance between the tenement and project populations is minimal.

Many middle-class renters with deep commitments to the neighborhood strongly identify with the diversity of the area and are proud of its reputation for tolerance and affordable rents. Ideologically, they too stress 'use value' over 'exchange value.' While this puts them closer to members of the counter-culture (and indeed, many of them participated in the progressive movements of the 1960s), they differ drastically from them in terms of their respect for property rights and in their choice of strategies and tactics. They seek to keep within the letter of the law, while using street and backroom pressure on the state to attain their antigentrification goals. While 'antisystemic,' they try to use the system for their own ends. This puts them into an ambiguous position *vis à vis* the other forces in the neighborhood and in city government. In their cyclical relationship to government, they form broad coalitions with dissidents when events call for putting pressure on the system, but must ultimately disengage from them when they enter a phase of negotiation and execution of programs that depend upon municipal and banking support. Often, their ideological ends create conflicts for them in specific issues. This ambivalence was well illustrated in the positions they took over the homeless. They consistently supported small shelters in the area and indeed were very proud of having rehabilitated the 'Cube Building' to house formerly homeless persons. They strongly sympathized with the plight of the homeless and opposed their eviction from the park until decent alternatives could be provided, and after the homeless were evicted, they took individual and even collective actions to assist them.[2] While they deplored the degradation of this valuable community resource through its usurpation by homeless persons, at the same time they castigated the city for its peremptory park closing which they saw as a complete violation of their 'pact' with city government over self-determination.

The remaining renters in the area have tended to be more passive players in the game – briefly invigorated at moments of crisis, but for the most part viewing the zone as merely one place, among many alternatives, in which to live. This is particularly true of 'transients' such as students, newcomers to the city, and persons whose 'real life' lies elsewhere – at their jobs or with friends scattered throughout the city.

What can be learned from the battles which have recently occurred in the East Village? Here we can only advance a few hypotheses. The first proposition is that poor local neighborhoods do better at obstructing the plans and designs of outsiders than in carrying out their own plans. The force required to stop something from happening is always less than the force needed to initiate or execute a constructive program, which requires economic and institutional resources.[3] Whether that force is sufficient, however, depends on how much a local area is the 'object of desire' of others. To some extent, one could say that the location of the East Village, away from the major north–south lines of mass transport in the city, continues to protect the district from excessive 'desire.' A second quality of the neighborhood's mini-ecology that has offered it some protection from desire is the solid phalanx of public housing projects that pre-empts the most attractive location within it, namely, the waterfront with its spectacular view of river, bridges, and city lights. The projects also exercise a strong inhibition on 'desire' by ensuring the permanent presence in the neighborhood of social groups that repel and to some extent frighten higher-income consumers.

If one defines gentrification as an 'attack' on relatively less powerful holders of city space, then the neighborhood has partially succeeded in repelling that attack. It did so in part by its ability to mobilize in its own defense, but it succeeded finally not only because of its own efforts but because the strength of its opponents was eventually weakened by larger economic forces. The collapse of an investment climate favorable to the expansion of upscale housing in New York City was probably a more significant factor in 'preserving' the neighborhood than all the demonstrations, riots, and solid work of community activists. But as we have demonstrated in the preceding chapter, without such efforts, the time needed to ride out the storm could not have been gained.

While the East Village thus 'succeeded,' by this combination of positive effort and negative climate, in protecting itself from total transformation and in this sense might be held up as a model for other disadvantaged neighborhoods, the story is not an unadulterated triumph. Not every defense of a neighborhood succeeds and, we must admit, not every successful defense succeeds in all ways. A community may succeed in protecting its physical existence and, to some extent, its very acts of defense can strengthen the human bonds and self-identifications of the residents. But if the attacks against it are too powerful, the community can eventually lose its vitality and verve.

This bring us to a second, and perhaps ironic proposition, which is that it is also easier for government to destroy community than to nurture this intangible element of the human spirit. To some extent, while the developers and most particularly, the long arm of the law of the City of New York that aided and abetted them, failed to convert this portion of an old quarter into a paradise for yuppies, they succeeded, at least for the time being, in killing much of the precious spirit of the neighborhood. The funereal pall that in 1991 hung over the community is the legacy of their efforts, although it must be noted that the visible activities of mutual housing associations and other organizations in rehabilitating structures have also rekindled new hopes.

The near-fatal blow the city struck by closing the park in 1991 went directly to the neighborhood's heart, Tompkins Square Park. At an angry and desperate evening meeting of Community Board 3's Park Committee on 3 June when a representative from the city government was trying lamely to defend the abrupt closing of the park that very morning as a necessary step to 'improve the neighborhood,' one irate heckler cried out, paraphrasing the Vietnam war rationalization, 'We had to destroy the village to save it.'[4] His comment put its finger on a deep tragedy from which it will be difficult for the neighborhood to recover. The loss of a central open space in which the diverse groups of the East Village could mingle and be exposed to one another, in which communal events – both collective rites to strengthen a sense of community and collective protests to galvanize its unity of purpose – could take place with spontaneity and verve, a space that served as a magnet to the neighborhood of outsiders seeking a bit of freedom and diversity in an urbanscape that was in marked contrast to the controlled malls or heartless and hurried canyons of Manhattan, is a serious one for the community.

Whereas a few years ago, the vitality of the area was most palpable in the park and its vicinity, during the more than one year when the park was closed it exerted a dead hand on the area, devitalizing a radius of many blocks, not just for the residents but for the flow of visitors and part-time participants in 'the scene.' Clubs, art galleries, restaurants, and boutiques that depended upon the East Village's 'draw' of outsiders and that thought their best interests would be served by further gentrification, were largely devoid of patrons. In the fickle tastes of excitement seekers, the East Village was no longer the place to be. Such tourists turned their sights back to the West Village and to its increasingly upscale southern neighbor, SoHo. Thus, in the interests of achieving more 'law and order' in the East Village, the city managed, at least temporarily, to destroy the one element that probably contributed more to that law and order and safety than the deserted landscape that now prevails: Jane Jacobs' eyes on the street[5] and the mini-scale of multiple street activities that enlivened the zone. It became more frightening to walk through the relatively deserted streets of the neighborhood than it ever was when what the city defined as 'threats to public safety' prevailed. By killing off the life of the neighborhood's center, the city added its destructive blows to ones the neighborhood earlier sustained when its architectural heritage was ravaged by disinvestment, abandonment, and arson.

The cycle has now begun the next turn of the wheel. In August of 1992, an elegantly restored park was reopened to the public. Conspicuously absent was the bandshell which had served as its social and political focus.[6] New interior fences, bordered by a solid phalanx of benches, block access to the grassy areas, confining users to the repaved pathways. The sedateness of the setting has inhibited many of its former users from gravitating to the park, and the absence of a focused assembly space has left it somewhat amorphous. A strict curfew accompanied the opening of the park, enforced by the closing of access gates at night and a heavy police guard. The few attempts to challenge this ruling have thus far ended in scuffles and arrests.

The repercussions in the surroundings streets are already visible. Work has recommenced in the rehabilitation of a number of large derelict buildings near the Square, and the commercial spaces along Avenue A and its side-street outcroppings are newly rented to shops and restaurants catering to tourists. Despite these changes, it is hard to predict the future. All we know is that the future, as the past, will be strongly affected by the larger context of the neighborhood. That context has shaped a series of cycles of renewal in the area and is likely to create a new one in the future. For our starting point must be the idea that change is a constant element in any city and its constituent subareas. Nostalgia and a romantic yearning for the past constitute unrealistic bases for any such analysis.

THE EXTERNAL CAUSES OF NEIGHBORHOOD CHANGE

We have already seen that during the original cycle, the neighborhood's existence was focused on the East River docks and the small-scale industries associated with them. By the time of the Civil War, residents were primarily members of ethnic groups recently immigrated from Ireland and Germany; for both groups, the events that precipitated their emigration were economic (the potato blight for the Irish) or political (the failed revolution of 1848 in Germany). At that time, housing in the area consisted largely of crude wooden shacks built on swampland that had not yet been fully drained. In retrospect, to yearn after that 'character of the neighborhood' would be foolish in the extreme.

The neighborhood entered a second cycle toward the end of the nineteenth century with the massive immigration of peasants from southern and eastern Europe (the latter including large numbers of Jews) and the reconstruction of the zone as a tenement house district whose residents were engaged primarily in decentralized garment production, supplemented by petty commerce and the informal services immigrants provided to each other. There again, the forces that brought these immigrants to the American shore were 'external' to the community, having been set into motion by economic difficulties in the mezzogiorno agricultural areas of southern Italy and the oppressive political actions of eastern European regimes. While considerable nostalgia persists for this quintessential period of the Lower East Side, it is difficult to sustain the belief that the end of this cycle was not a blessing. One has only to consider the harsh conditions of residents' lives, the startling rates of disease and overcrowding, the insalubrious housing conditions exposed by Jacob Riis and the early tenement studies, and the exploitative and miserable working conditions associated with the sweatshops and piecework of garment production before unionization, to be disabused of this tendency.

A third cycle began with the 'decline' of the neighborhood in the 1920s, when prosperity and fuller development in the outer boroughs and suburbs drew off large numbers of the immigrant settlers to better housing and the restrictions on new immigration suddenly shut off the tap of their replacements. This decline intensified during the Great Depression which visited new hardships on the remaining population and began the process of further decay and abandonment in the zone. Hard times, however, gave the neighborhood a reprieve from the first attempts at gentrification and displacement. While it is true that this was a period of intense community mobilization, during which the techniques of community organizing and rent strikes were honed and in which progressive (some say subversive) political and social movements found a fertile soil to develop, it is hard to muster enthusiasm to recreate the real suffering associated with the numerous evictions, deprivation of heat and utilities, not to mention lost jobs that the Depression entailed.

The postwar period introduced a fourth cycle in the neighborhood's history, a cycle of slum clearance, of the replacement of tenements by large-scale housing projects (some constructed for the poor, some constructed for the middle class), and a new cycle of migration, this time from Puerto Rico. The changes during the 1950s and 1960s were perhaps as extreme as any that had previously transformed the zone. And it is this period that is the immediate progenitor of the present conditions in the neighborhood. The old immigrant communities that had formed at the turn of the century were dramatically denuded of their younger generation, which flocked instead to the burgeoning zones of the new suburbia. The by-now superannuated remnants from the heydays of Jewish hegemony in the garment trade barricaded themselves within the confines of the various middle-income union-sponsored cooperatives that replaced the slums around Grand Street, becoming an eventual conservative political force in the Lower East Side. Other middle-class renters barricaded themselves within the confines of Stuyvesant Town which replaced the tenements of the old gas-house district just north of Fourteenth Street. And the slums intervening between these two developments were cleared and replaced by massive, albeit attractive, public housing projects for low-income residents – all around 1950.

It was at this point that migration from Puerto Rico, precipitated by economic difficulties on that island and facilitated by the introduction of cheaper and easier air travel to the mainland, began to step up, bringing hundreds of thousands of newcomers to a New York whose economy was still booming and whose manufacturing sector was still vital. Although Puerto Ricans did not make the Lower East Side their prime area of enclave settlement, they did take advantage of the vacuum that earlier population declines had created within remaining pockets of the Lower East Side. In the process of their settlement, they created the vibrant 'ethnic culture zone' of Loisaida, with its festivals, its efflorescence of wall art, its boisterous and welcoming street life, its creative burst in music and poetry, giving to the East Village a certain exuberance that attracted others fleeing the sterility of more mundane quarters. Their presence also inhibited the degree to which landlords of the tenements that remained in the zone could extract higher rents from their properties.

Such conditions made the East Village attractive to the counter-culture participants of the 1960s, who brought their own lifestyles, music, art, and political concerns to the area. To the radical political forces that were nurturing ambitions for Puerto Rican independence (and which founded their headquarters in the area, just as radical union organizers and political dissidents had in earlier generations) was added the strong anti-war sentiment of so-called hippies, yippies, and others who merely wished to turn their backs on the materialism they accused postwar America as fostering and on the aggressiveness and destruction occurring in Vietnam. In this mix of population, new music, writing, and art movements flourished for a while.

But external events were soon to impinge, ones that propelled the area into its next cycle of change – each cycle increasingly foreshortened, as if the movie camera were speeding up. The 1970s brought a disastrous fifth cycle to the neighborhood's history, one in which there was massive disinvestment in the zone, as property owners sought to 'bail out' from a no longer attractive or profitable environment. The tax forfeitures that reached epidemic proportions by the late 1970s, caused to some extent by a general recession and the city's special economic difficulties, but ironically intensified by the administrative decision to raise cash in a hurry by reducing the grace period of tax arrears from three years to one, led directly to the massive destruction of the area's housing stock, particularly in the zone closest to the public housing projects at the eastern edge. The population that suffered most from this was the Puerto Rican community which at the same time was being battered by the disappearance of jobs it had formerly held in the manufacturing sector of the city's economy. In fairly short order, the projects, which had formerly contained few Puerto Ricans, became overwhelmingly Latino. Loisaida was thus 'displaced' into the projects, but its street life and its informal exuberance disappeared in that new setting. In place of the old community stood vacant shells of burnt-out buildings and, increasingly, weed- and trash-covered vacant lots where the drug trade was the chief 'crop.' Only the few community gardens scattered throughout the zone, some with small *casitas* reproducing the gathering places of the island, the fading murals on the sides of residual buildings, and the Loisaida street sign on Avenue C remained as ghosts of that once-thriving community.

Into this desolate landscape the flippers and then the developers began to move slowly, west to east, buying up ravaged properties made newly attractive by a decay created by the economic desertion of others. During the 1980s they made considerable inroads and some spectacular profits, thanks to the boom psychology that heated up the luxury housing market in New York when conditions in the world economy seemed to promise an economic revival for the city. Some of the heat of that market diffused, albeit at declining temperatures, even to areas as objectively unpromising as the East Village. But investors' way into the zone was partially blocked by the stubborn rent-control and rent-stabilization regulations that prevented wholesale evictions of current tenants except by the most brutal methods, by the large number of properties already in municipal ownership through the prior *in rem* proceedings, and by the steadfast resistance of the neighborhood to the changes developers sought. Had the community not gained an embargo on the sale of those properties, the outcome would have been substantially different.

The pitched battles of the 1980s between the neighborhood and the city administration (in particular, the Parks Department and the police) were an important element in protecting the neighborhood, because they escalated the price of 'capture.' Each time the neighborhood erupted into challenged violence, it cooled the ardor of those who 'desired' it – not only of those who sought to gentrify the area but of those who constituted the potential buyers and renters for whom the gentrifying environment was being prepared. What had been a zone initially made more attractive by its ethnic vitality, its diversity, and its ambience of slight danger and '*outre*-ness' was, when the city was done with it, an area to which such consumers were no longer drawn.

The sixth cycle has now begun. But the cross-subsidy scheme which was to have reconstructed the district physically while retaining its enviable mix of incomes, lifestyles, ethnicities and subcultures seems unlikely to do so. A number of factors mediate against such a scenario. Some are economic, some are social, and some are political. Combined, these factors promise to change the ecology of the zone and its future uses in ways more drastic than ever before. Two mutually exclusive forces are pushing toward the center of the East Village, one from the west, the other from the east. Their convergence will transform the former heart, core, and unifier of the neighborhood, Tompkins Square Park (even in its reconstructed state), into a border zone between two disparate territories.

The gentrification process that began on the western edge of Community District 3's boundaries is likely to continue but at a slower pace. The length of Third Avenue between Fourteenth Street and Houston already demonstrates how far this process has already proceeded. Dormitory 'row' has displaced the small mom and pop stores that once lined the wide street, admittedly in fairly dilapidated fashion. In their places are the multiplex cinema palaces, the coolly decorated restaurants, and the more glittering bars and fast-food chains. Such developments have leap-frogged to Second Avenue, the Gap store that opened a few years ago at the corner of St Marks Place being one of the first signs foreshadowing this change. On the east–west cross streets between Third Avenue and Avenue A, particularly south of East Twelfth Street, are buildings in various stages of rehabilitation and restoration, and it is from these cross streets that minority populations are increasingly being displaced by whites and, most recently, by Asians who may be moving there as vanguards from Chinatown. The single remaining exception is a two-block stretch along East Tenth Street, notorious for its thriving drug trade, but there have been recent hints that the city plans a crackdown (no pun intended) on the economic base of this island of untouched tenements. Whatever mild interest has been exhibited by potential developers of market-rate housing, now being invited to invest by the cross-subsidy agreement, has focused almost exclusively on the few vacant lots in the blocks between First Avenue and Avenue A, that is, the westernmost edge of Alphabet City.

Encroaching from the east, on the other hand, are the public housing projects. A goodly number of low-rise jerry-built developments have recently been constructed on emptied lots, particularly between Avenues C and D, and more are likely to follow. Although these projects were in the pipeline before the cross-subsidy agreement was finalized, it is hard to see how the future of these blocks could have been significantly different. Ironically, most of the vacant land now being made available for new market-rate construction is to be found in this zone least likely to be seen as a promising investment by private builders. No private sales have in fact taken place on these lots. On the other hand, because the 'affordable' housing units designated for low- and moderate-income occupants in the cross-subsidy plan were to have been generated out of the stock of existing tenements, not many of these will be produced along the easternmost edge of Alphabet City, since this is the subarea that was most ravaged by abandonment, arson, and eventual clearance. There are few tenements left there which could be restored. And yet, no funds have been made available to community organizations for new construction. This leaves only the government, and possibly the Enterprise Foundation, the only possible redevelopers of this zone. Since the latter may be interested in the potential profits to be made in future resales, it is drawn more to streets farther west. The government is then the most likely actor. By continuing to construct subsidized public housing on the remaining vacant lots, it can accumulate 'unit credits' against the quota of 1,000 dwelling units of affordable housing it promised in the Memorandum of Understanding. This should push the public housing segregated district almost to the eastern edge of Tompkins Square Park, which may then become a 'no man's land' insulating social groups from one another.

The ability of the community board to resist this transformation in the northern portion of the Lower East Side has recently been undercut by the gerrymandering of city council electoral districts. While the boundaries of Community District 3 and of the Second City Council Electoral District were never exactly congruent, they included large overlapping areas of the Lower East Side, making cooperation between the elected council representative and the community board both easy and essential. Since the local council representative also has a considerable say in who shall be appointed to membership on the community board, the greater separation that now obtains between the constituency of the relevant elected council member and the area over which Community Board 3 exercises ULURP (urban land use review procedures) powers, should make accountability harder to achieve.

The gerrymandering that was done in fall of 1991 resulted in the defeat in the Democratic primary[7] of encumbent Miriam Friedlander, an old-time progressive who had been council woman for decades. While groups in the neighborhood did not always agree with the stands she took and sometimes complained because she did not give her full support to projects they were fighting for, in the last analysis she was respected as a person whose loyalties to the neighborhood were unquestioned.[8] The same does not seem to be true of the person who has replaced her. According to some analysts,[9] Antonio Pagan was elected by an unlikely coalition of disciplined voters – Puerto Ricans from the public housing projects operating out of ethnic loyalty[10] and middle-class Jews from the Grand Street cooperatives who would like to see gentrification go ahead on the Lower East Side[11] – in a race that drew a small turnout and was further muddied by the entrance into the primary of an unknown middle-class professional from the silk-stocking Gramercy Park neighborhood that had just been appended to the electoral district, which split the non-Puerto Rican vote.

This election may presage a major shift in community politics. The housing activists have certainly lost a loyal supporter on the City Council and they are especially hostile to Pagan, whom they view as an unprincipled opportunist who is likely to use his ethnic status to advance himself, rather than the interests either of the neighborhood in general or of 'his' people in particular. If he remains in power, the composition of Community Board 3 can be expected to change in the long run. It was not until about 1985 that representatives of organizations associated with the JPC gained a plurality on Community Board 3 and were thus able to garner its firm backing for their plans and goals. Their control is now threatened. Membership on the board rotates gradually and the local council member has only partial imput into the selection of replacements. Therefore, their displacement from the board will not occur immediately. However, with an unsympathetic council representative, they are bound to lose out in any future appointments and this will undoubtedly have an effect on the power structure, such as it is, of the community board.

Looking at the wider picture, one sees other forces operating that may have even more drastic effects on the Lower East Side, wiping out in one fell swoop the interests of most current players in the struggle for the area and ushering in a seventh cycle of change. Some of the more important of these are generating in a neighboring district which hitherto has played little role in determining events. This is Chinatown, which lies primarily in the southern portion of the Lower East Side around Canal Street. Since the change in US immigration laws in 1965, there has been a major influx of Chinese immigrants to the United States, primarily from Taiwan and Hong Kong, but also from the Chinese overseas communities of southeast Asia. In the process, the number of Chinese in New York City has more than trebled. Despite the formation of a number of satellite communities in the outer boroughs, notably in portions of Brooklyn and Queens, Lower Manhattan's Chinatown has grown to be the largest such quarter in any American city and is now greatly overcrowded and expanding into adjacent zones at a rapid rate. Some goodly proportion of those immigrants have entered the old 'businesses' that predominated when the Lower East Side absorbed the massive waves of immigrants from southern and eastern Europe at the turn of the century – namely petty commerce and garment production, both of which still pay poorly. Residential overcrowding, sweatshops, home work, and the like have made their reappearance after such problems had been prematurely declared solved. This new set of housing consumers is creating a sudden and large demand for low-rent housing.[12]

What is different this time, however, is that capital is also flowing into the area from overseas sources, capital generated in the so-called miracle economies of the 'NICs';[13] at least some of it is flight capital, being removed from politically endangered places such as Hong Kong whose 99-year British lease will run out in a few years, after which the city-state will revert to the People's Republic. At least some of the immigrants, then, are bringing funds with them which they can invest in housing, and other real estate investors are seeing opportunities to make profits by expanding the housing available to Chinatown's burgeoning population. Some of this infusion of capital and population has already begun to change the face of the Lower East Side south of Houston Street, as the remaining zones of Latino residence are increasingly intermingled with Chinese-occupied buildings.[14] One 'sign of the times' appears on a local church whose bilingual billboard reads in Spanish and Chinese; there is no English.

If I were forced to 'read' some message in the clouded crystal ball of the future, I would wager that the Lower East Side may once again become a port of entry for yet another wave of foreign immigration whose roots lie in political and economic forces far outside the purview and control of the neighborhood's residents. Just as earlier controllers of the neighborhood's turf deplored the influx of newcomers that would change forever the environment they knew and were trying to protect, so the present residents mourn the end of their era and try to retain those elements they cherish.

But one thing only is certain. The Lower East Side will change, as it has in the past. And, as in the past, this tenement zone is unlikely to be made into a silk purse. Gentrifiers tried twice but failed each time. The new forces for change may not be defeated so easily, nor should they. New York City still needs the Lower East Side.

Significance of Studying a Single Neighborhood: Can We Generalize?

For readers who have patiently read thus far, perhaps feeling that they now know more about the East Village than they ever cared to ask, several logical questions follow. Does this study have anything to say to students of other areas in other cities? Does it advance our understanding of cities in general? How can it contribute to the theoretical underpinnings of and the methodology for doing urban sociology?

In defense, we contend that the value of our case study lies in two important directions. First, our methodology can serve as a model for a new way to study complex urban subareas. Hopefully, this methodology will be able to overcome the difficulties that led to a decline in the great urban sociological tradition of the 'neighborhood' or community study. And second, although every single subarea in every city is, in an ultimate sense, unique, and therefore one can scarcely hope to find a 'typical' case whose results can easily or mechanically be transferred to many other cases, we strongly argue that the *processes* of colonization, resistance, conflict, and negotiation we have unmasked in our case study are also operative in many other diverse and changing inner-city areas.

Neighborhood studies have been critiqued for their tendency to be abstracted from both time and space. Most studies have concentrated on the (anthropologists') ethnographic present, even when they have presumably taken change as their chief problematic.[15] This has yielded a strangely ahistoric image – if not of a stationary 'traditional' society, then a truncated historical version whose plot line is that of a 'traditional' neighborhood being attacked and destroyed by outside forces.[16] By placing our case study in as deep a time frame as possible, we illustrate three important facts: first, that change is a normal and inevitable part of urbanism; second, that change does not occur capriciously; and third, that change is hardly ever written on a *tabula rasa*. The existing social, physical, and even symbolic landscape limits and shapes future outcomes. An inevitable corollary is, of course, that a neighborhood at any one point in time often contains diverse subgroups that represent its 'archaeological levels' of settlement.

This last fact has important ramifications for methodology. Since most urban subareas do not constitute homogeneous 'communities' with a common set of social characteristics and shared community goals, their study is beyond the capacity of a single ethnographer. Just as the community does not exist *only* at the ethnographic moment, so the researcher does not exist *only* in abstract intellectual space, detached from the bubbling cauldron of interpersonal and intergroup relations *within the neighborhood*. Inevitably, the individual researcher – whether he/she intends it or not – becomes *located* within the matrix of neighbors. This is valuable, because rapport is possible only after establishing one's location, which in turn shapes the social network of those with whom one is likely to interact. The researcher is also a human being and is to some extent 'co-opted' into the world view of significant others, with whom such trust is established in a two-way direction. The team methodology we followed was intentionally selected to allow us to 'triangulate' to a more objective view of the neighborhood than could have been achieved from a single perspective.

Most neighborhood studies have also tended to abstract their unit from its larger spatial context, thus contributing to an inaccurate appraisal of the forces that determine a neighborhood's fate. Certainly, this was not true in the early days of urban sociology, when 'ecological position' was seen as driving change. The theory of ecological determinism, developed when American cities were expanding rapidly and rebuilding at their centers, seemed to put too heavy a stress on the 'location' of a subarea; areas in the path of the juggernaut of urban expansion were thought to be virtually powerless to resist. To some extent, the more recent theories of empowerment, agency, and resistance err in the opposite direction, overemphasizing the potential ability of neighborhoods to resist invasions and colonization and thereby inadvertently blaming residents when they fail to defend themselves. Our study demonstrates the importance of viewing the agency of local actors in a dialectical relationship with powerful and 'external' pressures generated by city, regional, national, and even international forces – some of which are directed toward the local area but most of which have other ends in mind. A neighborhood's future is thus as much the product of unintended consequences as of intended ones.

This assumption also has its methodological implications. To understand the dynamics of change in any small area, one must comprehend *how* larger factors intervene, not just abstractly (as posited in the grand theorizing about urban restructuring and international political economy), but in very concrete ways that strengthen some actors and weaken others. That is why this book has covered many trends that go beyond those usually discussed in a conventional neighborhood case study.

And finally, one comes to the basic issue of generalizability, an issue central to scientific epistemology. Generalizations, particularly in the historical and social sciences, are to be sought in *processes*, not *classes* of phenomena. That is why it is an illicit requirement that a given case be 'typical.' It is enough to ask that it demonstrate the operation of processes common to other cases – even those with markedly different outcomes – and that it deepen our understanding of the way things work in this world. We hope that our efforts have advanced this goal.

NOTES

1 This trenchant phrase was coined by Norton Long in his article, 'The Local Community as an Ecology of Games,' *American Journal of Sociology* 64 (1958). By local, however, he meant municipal. Unfortunately, his approach has seldom been applied in studies of 'street' politics in neighborhood communities, despite its potential power. We acknowledge our indebtedness to this underrated scholar, while dissociating ourselves from his more conservative politics.

2 It was they who funded the rental of the portosans (portable toilets) for the lots to which the homeless moved just after they were evicted from the park.

3 Some of this ambivalence is wrenching. The majority of the individuals who have been most active in actually translating their ideological beliefs in community empowerment and affordable housing would prefer to have independent resources with which to work. However, they recognize that, in practical terms, the *only* resources available for actual rehabilitation must come either from HPD or other city sources or from institutions such as the Enterprise Foundation. They are therefore always in a delicate position of negotiating small degrees of freedom within parameters set by those who control the resources.

4 Field notes, evening of 3 June 1991.

5 Jane Jacobs, *The Death and Life of Great American Cities* (New York: Random House, 1961).

6 Despite an angry protest, held at bay by a large police force, the bandshell was unceremoniously bulldozed on 27 August 1991. A new entrance to the park in the middle of the Seventh Street block was later constructed on its site.

7 The only election that really matters in this solidly democratic district. Miriam Friedlander re-entered the 1993 election, but failed to defeat Pagan.

8 I have watched her stand up to heckling when she took an unpopular position, as she did when working to entice the homeless out of the park by what turned out to be futile efforts to help them receive decent alternative housing and needed social services, but I have also seen her cheered when she expressed solidarity with residents in their search for autonomy and self-determination on the future of the neighborhood. Because of a vague similarity in appearance, I was sometimes mistaken for Miriam Friedlander when I was a participant observer at various demonstrations. In those cases, no one expressed surprise to find 'her' there, and people struck up friendly conversations with me, suggesting a certain amount of affection they felt for 'their' representative.

9 Fran Goldin and Lisa Kaplan were particularly articulate on this question, but they were scarcely the only sources who expressed similar worries about the new leadership. Anti-Pagan graffiti slogans have become increasingly common on East Village walls, in part because Pagan has continued his vocal opposition to squatters, the homeless, and the location of any more social service facilities (AIDS treatment centers, shelters, drug clinics, etc.) in the area.

10 Mobilized, according to informants, by old-time democratic political 'hack' Roberto Napoleon, Pagan's *éminence grise*.

11 Perhaps ironic, since these same co-op residents had been earlier sued by Puerto Ricans for discriminating against minorities and non-Jews. The court ruled in favor of the Puerto Ricans, and required the co-ops to admit an equal number of Jews and 'minorities' in filling any subsequent vacancies. However, given the very low rates of turnover, it will be a very long time before minorities achieve much of a foothold in the Grand Street co-ops.

12 One unintended consequence of certain 'housing reforms' now underway in the East Village has been to intensify the trend that is expanding Chinatown into the area. In order to maximize the fairness of the process of selecting income-eligible residents to occupy the city-subsidized apartments renovated and managed by mutual housing associations, the availability of apartments was widely advertised in English, Spanish, and Chinese language newspapers, and applications were invited. According to one informant I interviewed on 17 February 1993, some 7,000 applications were received by the deadline. A lottery was used to select the first tenants (and subsequent lotteries will be held from the remaining pool as more units are ready). Because of the great overcrowding in Chinatown and the desperate need for lower cost housing (without payment of key money, which has become routine in Chinatown), between 40 and 50 percent of all applicants were Chinese, and the proportion

was particularly high in the subset with large families. Therefore, a disproportionate number of the units renovated by mutual housing associations may go not to the Latinos displaced by neighborhood 'burn-out,' but to meet the needs of the most recent newcomers to the Lower East Side, Asians.

13 The 'newly industrializing countries' of the Pacific Rim.

14 Recall that virtually all of the AAFE-Enterprise rehabilitation sites credited against the cross-subsidy quota are located in the narrow band of the agreement zone that forms the south L extension south of Houston Street. AAFE is the community organization engaged in providing more housing for Chinese.

15 This is certainly not true of the best of the older community studies, among which I would rank the Yankee City series and the Young and Willmott study of East London families.

16 The examples of this plot line are numerous. Perhaps the best known is Herbert Gans' *The Urban Villagers* (originally published Glencoe IL: The Free Press, 1962; reissued by Macmillan several times since).

Bibliography

Abeles, Schwartz, Haeckel and Silverblatt, Inc. *The Chinatown Garment Industry Study* (New York: Local 23–25, International Ladies' Garment Workers Union and New York Skirt and Sportswear Association, 1983).

Abeles, Schwartz and Associates: See Schwartz and Abeles.

Abu-Lughod, Janet. 'Tompkins Square.' *Realm Working Paper No. 1* (New York: New School For Social Research, December 1988).

Abu-Lughod, Janet. *Changing Cities* (New York: HarperCollins, 1991).

Albin, Glenn. 'Swoon over Miami,' *Outweek* 88 (6 March 1991).

Albion, Robert Greenhalgh. *The Rise of New York Port, 1815–1860* (New York: Charles Scribner's Sons, 1939).

Algarín, Miguel and Miguel Piñero, eds. *Nuyorican Poetry: An Anthology of Puerto Rican Words and Feelings* (New York: William Morrow & Co., 1975).

Alson, P. 'The Building That Ate Tompkins Square Park,' *Village Voice*, 18 July 1989.

Anderson, Elijah. *Streetwise: Race, Class, and Change in an Urban Community* (Chicago: University of Chicago Press, 1990).

Anon. 'Tompkins Square,' *Harpers Weekly*, 13 September 1873.

Anon. 'Gotham Court,' *Frank Leslie's Sunday Magazine* (June 1879).

Anon. 'What Happened to 306 Families Who Were Compelled to Vacate Their Slum Dwellings to Make Way for a Large Housing Project,' conducted by the Lavanburg Foundation and Hamilton House, 1933. East Side files, Apartments, Knickerbocker Village, Seward Park Library.

Anon. 'A Study of Low-Rental Vacant Dwelling Units in the Borough of Manhattan, '*Vacancy and Re-Housing Bureau Survey*, 13 October 1938 to 11 November 1938, conducted by WPA. No. 665-97-3-20, New York Public Library.

Anon. 'Planned Shrinkage,' *Real Estate Weekly*, 4 February 1976.

Anon. 'HPD's "Child"' Matures: Rehabs Set to Start,' *City Limits* (November 1978).

Anon. 'The Homesteading Pitch,' *City Limits* (March 1981).

Anon. 'Furor Over City's Lower East Side Scheme,' *City Limits* (August–September 1984).

Anon. 'This Land is Ours,' *City Limits* (June–July 1984).

Anon. 'Lower East Side Real Estate Profile,' *Real Estate Newsletter*, Manhattan Edition, 4 November 1985.

Anon. 'Developers and Rehab Specialists Vie for Lower East Side Properties Not Controlled By City,' *Real Estate Newsletter*, Manhattan Edition, 24 November 1986.

Anon. 'LeFrak Wins Development Right,' *The New York Times*, 26 May 1988.

Appelbaum, Richard and John Gilderbloom. *Private Interferences and Public Intervention in the Rental Housing Market* (Santa Barbara, CA: Foundation for National Progress, 1984).

Asbury, Herbert. *The Gangs of New York* (New York: Dorset Press; reprint of 1927 edition).

Ausubel, N. 'Hold Up The Sun! A Kaleidoscope of Jewish Life in New York,' unpublished manuscript, 1939, in Federal Writers' Project Papers, New York City Municipal Archives.

Axelrad, Sidney. *Tenements and Tenants: A Study of 1104 Tenement Families* (New York: League of Mothers' Clubs, 1932).

Badcock, B. 'Smith's Rent Gap Hypothesis: An Australian View,' *Annals of the Association of American Geographers* 79 (1989).

Badilla-Vega, America, Josh Dewind and Julia Preston. *Undocumented Immigrant Workers in New York City* (New York: NACLA, 1979).

Baker, Russell W. 'Bye Bye Bodega,' *Village Voice*, 17 October 1989.

Barron, James. 'Tompkins Square Protest is Marked by Restraint,' *The New York Times*, 15 August 1988.

Barron, James. 'Removal of Tompkins Square Homeless is Set,' *The New York Times*, 16 November 1989.

Bartelt, David. 'Redlining in Philadelphia: An Analysis of Home Mortgages in the Philadelphia Area' (Philadelphia: Institute for the Study of Civic Values, Temple University, 1979).

Bartelt, David and Ronald Lawson. 'Rent Control and Abandonment in New York City: A Look at the Evidence,' in *Critical Perspectives on Housing*, ed. by Rachael Bratt et al. (Philadelphia: Temple University Press, 1986).

Bartholemew, Harland. 'Toward the Reconstruction of New York's Lower East Side,' *Architectural Forum* (1932).

Belkin, Lisa. 'The Gentrification of the East Village,' *The New York Times*, 2 September 1984.

Bennetts, Leslie. '16 Tenements to Become Artist Units in City Plan,' *The New York Times*, 4 May 1982.

Bennetts, Leslie. 'Lower East Siders Assail Proposal to Destroy Drug Trade Buildings,' *The New York Times*, 22 July 1982.

Berman, Marshall. *All That's Solid Melts into Air: The Experience of Modernity* (New York: Simon & Schuster, 1982).

Berman, Marshall. 'A Struggle to the Death in Which Both Sides Are Right,' *Village Voice*, 12 July 1983.

Bernstein, Iver. *The New York City Draft Riots* (New York: Oxford University Press, 1990).

Bertoli, A. 'Democracy under Siege: Tompkins Square Police State [and] the Spatial Deconcentration Connection,' *Shadow* (June–July 1991).

Biddle, Geoffrey. *Alphabet City* (Berkeley and Los Angeles: University of California Press, 1992).

Blackmar, Elizabeth. *Manhattan for Rent, 1785–1850* (Ithaca: Cornell University Press, 1989).

Bloor, Alfred J. 'Suggestions for a Better Method of Building Tenant-Houses in New York,' *American Architect and Building News*, 12 February 1881.

Boddy, M. *The Building Societies* (Basingstoke, UK: Macmillan, 1980).

Bogen, Elizabeth. *Immigration in New York* (New York: Praeger, 1987).

Boggs, Vernon, Gerald Handel, and Sylvia Fava, eds. *The Apple Sliced: Sociological Studies of New York City* (New York: Praeger, 1984).

Borgos, Seth. 'Low-Income Homeownership and the ACORN Squatters Campaign,' in *Critical Perspectives on Housing*, ed. by R. G. Bratt et al. (Philadelphia: Temple University Press, 1986).

Boulay, Harvey and Alan DiGaetano. 'Why Did Political Machines Disappear?' *Journal of Urban History* 12 (November 1985): 25–50.

Bowler, Anne and Blaine McBurney. 'Gentrification and the Avant-garde in New York's East Village.' *Realm Working Paper No. 4* (New York: New School for Social Research, August 1989).

Boyarin, Jonathan. 'Waiting for a Jew: Marginal Redemption at Eighth Street Shul,' in *Between Two Worlds: Ethnographic Essays on American Jews*, ed. by Jack Kugelmass (Ithaca: Cornell University Press, 1988).

Bradford, Calvin P. and Leonard S. Rubinowitz. 'The Urban-Suburban Investment-Disinvestment Process: Consequences for Older Neighborhoods,' *Annals of the American Academy of Political and Social Science* 422 (1975): 77–86.

Bratt, Rachel, Chester Hartman, and Ann Meyerson, eds. *Critical Perspectives on Housing* (Philadelphia: Temple University Press, 1986).

Brenson, M. 'City's Position Secure as Focus of Art World,' *The New York Times*, 28 February 1983.

Brower, Bonnie. *Missing the Mark: Subsidizing Housing for the Privileged, Displacing the Poor. An Analysis of the City's 10-Year Plan* (New York: Association for Neighborhood and Housing Development, Inc., August 1989).

Brumberg, Esther and Sy Rubin. *The Lower East Side: A Contemporary Portrait in Photographs* (New York: Persea Books, 1984).

Buckley, Peter G. 'To the Opera House: Culture and Society in New York City, 1820–1860' (New York: State University of New York, doctoral dissertation, 1984).

Buckley, Peter G. *The Astor Place Riot* (New York: Oxford University Press, 1988).

Buttenwieser, Ann L. 'Shelter for Whom? On the Route towards Vladeck Houses, 1930–1940,' *Journal of Urban History* 12 (August 1986).

Buttenwieser, Ann L. *Manhattan Water-Bound: Planning and Developing Manhattan's Waterfront from the Seventeenth Century to the Present* (New York: New York University Press, 1987).

Capeci, Jr., Dominic J. 'Fiorello H. LaGuardia and the Stuyvesant Town Controversy of 1943,' *New York Historical Quarterly* 62 (1978): 289–310.

Carey, George W. 'Hippie Neighborhoods and Urban Spatial Systems,' in *The City in the Seventies*, ed. by Robert K. Yin (Itasca, IL: F. E. Peacock Publishers, 1972).

Caro, Robert A. *The Power Broker: Robert Moses and the Fall of New York* (New York: Vintage Books, 1974).

Carr, C. 'Night Clubbing,' *Village Voice*, 16 August 1988.

Carr, C. 'When the Rainbow is Not Enough: People's Park: Round Two,' *Village Voice*, 23 August 1988.

Carr, Ethan. *Three Hundred Years of Parks: A Timeline of New York City Park History* (City of New York, Department of Parks and Recreation, 1988).

Castells, M. *The City and the Grassroots: A Cross-Cultural Theory of Urban Social Movements* (Berkeley and Los Angeles: University of California Press, 1983).

Cavallo, Diana. *The Lower East Side: A Portrait in Time* (New York: Crowell-Collier Press, 1971).

Chan, Elaine. 'Seward Park Battles: Court Dismisses Suit Against LeFrak,' *People's Press*, March 1990.

Chapin, Robert Coit. *The Standard of Living Among Workingmen's Families in New York City* (New York: New York State Conference of Charities and Corrections, 1909).

Chenault, Lawrence R. *The Puerto Rican Migrant in New York City* (New York: Columbia University Press, 1938).

Citizens' Association of New York, Council of Hygiene and Public Health. *Report Upon the Sanitary Condition of the City* (New York: D. Appleton, 1865).

City of New York. 'New York City: An Economic Renaissance,' advertising supplement to *Forbes*, 5 July 1982.

City of New York, Department of City Planning. *The Puerto Rican New Yorkers: A Recent History of their Distribution and Population and Household Characteristics* (1982).

City of New York, Department of City Planning. *Private Reinvestment and Neighborhood Change* (New York, March 1984).

City of New York, Department of City Planning. *Housing Database: Public and Publicly Aided Housing in New York City: 1985 Update Volume.*

City of New York, Department of General Services, Division of Real Property. IPIS Database, (February 1991).

City of New York, Department of Housing Preservation and Development. *HPD Handbook of Programs* (October 1984).

City of New York, Planning Commission. *Forging a Future for the Lower East Side: A Plan for Action.* Prepared by Abeles, Schwartz and Associates (New York: City Planning Commission, 1970).

Clapp, John M. 'The Determinants of Housing Abandonment in New York City' (New York: Columbia University, doctoral dissertation, 1974).

Clark, E. *The Rent Gap and Urban Change: Case Studies in Malmo 1860–1985* (Lund, Sweden: Lund University Press, 1987).

Cohen, R. *Indicators of Gentrification in the Lower East Side* (New York: Community Service Society, 1984 mimeo.).

Colon, Jesus. *A Puerto Rican in New York and Other Sketches* (New York: International Publishers, 1982).

Commission on the Year 2000. *New York Ascendant* (New York: Harper & Row, 1987).

Daly, Stephen. 'The Shape of its Future Splits East Village,' *The New York Times*, 20 March 1983.

DeForest, Robert and Lawrence Veiller, eds. *The Tenement House Problem.* In 2 volumes (New York: Macmillan, 1903; reprinted New York: Arno Press and the New York Times, 1970).

DeGiovanni, Frank. 'Patterns of Change in Housing Market Activity in Revitalizing Neighborhoods,' *Journal of the American Planning Association* 49 (1983): 22–39.

DeGiovanni, Frank. *Displacement Pressures in the Lower East Side* (New York: Community Service Society, 1987).

Delaney, Chuck. 'Lofts for Whose Living?' *City Limits* (October 1981).

DeRienzo, Harry. 'The Public Housing New York City Didn't Want,' *City Limits* (August–September 1985).

DeRienzo, Harry and Joan B. Allen. *The New York City In Rem Housing Program: A Report* (New York: New York Urban Coalition, January 1985).

DeRienzo, Paul and Bill Weinberg. 'Military Camps for Urban Poor?' *The Shadow* (March 1991).

DeRocker, Rob. 'Housing Agency Plans to Auction In Rem Holdings,' *The Villager*, 27 May 1982.

Deutsche, R. and C. Ryan. 'The Fine Art of Gentrification,' *October 31* (winter 1984): 91–111.

Domurad, Frank. 'Where Tax Dollars Went,' *City Limits* (August–September 1985).

Downs, Anthony. *Opening Up the Suburbs: An Urban Strategy for America* (New Haven: Yale University Press, 1973).

Downs, Anthony. 'The Necessity of Neighborhood Deterioration,' *New York Affairs* 7 (1982).

Dreier, Peter and W. Dennis Keating. 'The Limits of Localism: Progressive Housing Policies in Boston, 1984–1989,' *Urban Affairs Quarterly* 26 (December 1990): 191–216.

Dunshee, Kenneth Holcomb. *As You Pass By* (New York: Hastings House, 1952).

Eagle, Morris. 'The Puerto Ricans in New York City,' in *Studies in Housing and Minority Groups*, ed. by N. Glazer and D. McEntire (Berkeley, CA: University of California Press, 1960).

Earley, Brian Francis. 'Puerto Ricans in the New York City Labor Market, 1970: A Structural Analysis' (New York: Fordham University, doctoral dissertation, 1980).

Ellis, Edward Robb. *The Epic of New York City* (New York: Old Town Books, 1966).

Epstein, Amy Kallman. 'Multifamily Dwellings and the Search for Respectability: Origins of the New York Apartment House,' *Urbanism Past and Present* (summer 1980): 29–39.

Ernst, Robert. *Immigrant Life in New York City, 1825–1863* (Port Washington, NY: Ira J. Friedman, Inc., 1949).

Ervin, Wilma. *On the Edge: The East Village* (New York: Times Books, 1985).

Ewen, Elizabeth. *Immigrant Women in the Land of Dollars: Life and Culture on the Lower East Side, 1890–1925* (New York: Monthly Review Press, 1985).

Fainstein, Norman I. and Susan S. Fainstein. 'Economic Restructuring and the Politics of Land Use Planning in New York City,' *Journal of the American Planning Association* 53 (spring 1987): 237–48.

Fainstein, Susan S. and Norman I. Fainstein. 'The Politics of Urban Development,' *City Almanac* 17 (April 1984).

Fainstein, Susan S., Norman I. Fainstein, Richard Child Hill, Dennis R. Judd, and Michael Peter Smith, with P. Jefferson Armistead and Marlene Keller. *Restructuring the City: The Political Economy of Urban Redevelopment* (New York: Longman, 1983).

Fainstein, Susan S., Norman I. Fainstein, and Alex Schwartz. 'How New York Remained a Global City,' in *Atop the Urban Hierarchy*, ed. by Robert Beauregard (New York: Rowan-Littlefield, 1992).

Falcon, Angelo. *Black and Latino Politics in New York City: Race and Ethnicity in a Changing Urban Context* (New York: Institute for Puerto Rican Policy Studies, Inc., 1985).

Ferguson, Sarah. 'Squatters Victory?' *Village Voice*, 9 May 1989.

Ferguson, Sarah. 'How to Unify a Neighborhood,' *Village Voice*, 16 May 1989.

Ferguson, Sarah. 'Occupied Territories: Inside the Squatters Movement,' *Village Voice*, 18 July 1989.

Ferguson, Sarah. 'Tompkins Squares Everywhere,' *Village Voice*, 24 September 1991.

Ferguson, Sarah and Dean Kuipers. 'An Eye for an Eye: Squatters Attack Christodora After Loisaida Demolition,' *Village Voice*, 11 April 1989.

Finder, Alan. 'Koch and LeFrak Agree on Plan for 1,200 Middle-Income Units,' *The New York Times*, 29 February 1988.

Finder, Alan. 'LeFrak's Offer Allows Chance for Conversions,' *The New York Times*, 2 April 1988.

Finder, Alan. 'Lower East Side Housing: Plans and Conflict,' *The New York Times*, 14 May 1988.

Fine, Jo Renee. *The Synagogues of New York's Lower East Side* (New York: New York University Press, 1978).

First Report of the Tenement House Department of the City of New York, 1902–1903 (New York: Martin B. Brown Press, n.d. but probably 1903).

Fitzpatrick, Joseph P. *Puerto Rican Americans: The Meaning of Migration to the Mainland* (Englewood Cliffs, NJ: Prentice Hall, 1971).

Flash, Chris. 'Community Board 3 vs Tompkins Square Park,' *The Shadow* (October 1989).

Foderaro, Lisa. '9 Held in Protest Near Tompkins Square Park,' *The New York Times*, 2 April 1989.

Foner, Nancy, ed. *New Immigrants in New York* (New York: Columbia University Press, 1987).

Ford, James. *Slums and Housing*. In 2 volumes (Cambridge: Harvard University Press, 1936).

Fox, Robert. 'Cross-Subsidy: An Overview and Update,' *Lower East Side News* 1 (February 1990).

Friedmann, John and Goetz Wolff. 'World City Formation: An Agenda for Research and Action,' *International Journal of Urban and Regional Research* 6 (1982): 309–43.

Gale, D. E. *Neighborhood Revitalization and the Postindustrial City: A Multinational Perspective* (Lexington, MA: Lexington Books, 1984).

Gans, Herbert. *The Urban Villagers: Group and Class in the Life of Italian-Americans* (originally Glencoe, IL: The Free Press, 1962, revised New York: Macmillan, 1983).

Gaster, G. and S. Peacock. 'Urban Gentrification: Evaluating Alternative Indicators,' *Social Indicators Research* 18 (March 1986): 321–37.

Gendrot, Sophie and Joan Turner. 'Ethnicity and Class: Politics on Manhattan's Lower East Side,' *Ethnic Groups* 5 (1983): 79–108.

Girouard, Mark. *Cities and People* (New Haven: Yale University Press, 1983).

Glaser, Nathan and Daniel P. Moynihan. *Beyond the Melting Pot: Negroes, Puerto Ricans, Jews, Italians, and Irish of New York City* (Cambridge: Harvard University Press and MIT Press, 1963).

Glueck, Grace. 'The Mayor's Lower East Side Story: Tenements into Co-ops for Artists,' *The New York Times*, 11 August 1981.

Goetz, Edward G. 'Type II Policy and Its Mandated Benefits in Economic Development,' *Urban Affairs Quarterly* 26 (December 1990): 170–90.

Gold, Michael. *Jews Without Money* (New York: Avon Books, 1965, reprint of the 1930 version).

Goldsen, Rose. 'Puerto Rican Migration to New York City' (New Haven: Yale University, doctoral dissertation, 1953).

Goldstein, Richard. 'The Gentry Comes to the East Village,' *Village Voice*, 19 May 1980.

Goldstein, Richard. 'Why Artists' Housing Went Down,' *Village Voice*, 22 February 1983.

Goodman, Cary. *Choosing Sides: Playground and Street Life on the Lower East Side* (New York: Schocken Books, 1979).

Goodwin, Michael. 'Koch Is Expecting City Tax Windfall,' *The New York Times*, 5 October 1984.

Goodwin, Stephen. 'Jewish Communities,' in *Jews of New York*, 7 January 1942. Box 3633, Jewish Communities – Goodwin, FWP, Municipal Archives.

Gordon, David. 'Capitalist Development and the History of American Cities,' in *Marxism and the Metropolis*, ed. by William K. Tabb and Larry Sawers (New York: Oxford University Press, 1978).

Gordon, Diana R. 'The Sixteen-Story Misunderstanding,' in her *City Limits: Barriers to Change in Urban Government* (New York: Charterhouse, 1973).

Gottlieb, M. 'Space Invaders: Land Grab on the Lower East Side,' *Village Voice*, 14 December 1982.

Gould, Elgin R. L. *The Housing of the Working People: Eighth Special Report of the Commissioner of Labor* (Washington, DC: Government Printing Office, 1895).

Gould, Elgin R. L. 'Financial Aspects of Recent Tenement House Operations in New York,' in *The Tenement House Problem*, ed. by Robert DeForest and Lawrence Veiller, Vol. 1: 355–66 (New York: Macmillan, 1903).

Gove, George. 'Reconstruction of Congested Areas of Manhattan's Lower East Side Begins,' *American City* (1930).

Grant, Peter. 'The Lower East Side: "It's All Going to Come Up One Day",' *New York Observer*, 14 March 1988.

Grava, Sigurd. 'Is the Second Avenue Subway Dead in its Tracks?' *New York Affairs* (1980).

Grebler, Leo. *Housing Market Behavior in a Declining Area* (New York: Columbia University Press, 1952).

Griscom, John H. *The Sanitary Condition of the Labouring Population of New York; Annual Report of 1842* (New York: James van Norden, 1843).

Guterbock, Thomas M. 'The Political Economy of Urban Revitalization,' *Urban Affairs Quarterly* (June 1980): 429–38.

Gutman, Herbert. 'The Tompkins Square Riot in New York City on January 13, 1874: A Re-examination of Its Causes and Its Aftermath,' *Labor History* 6 (winter 1965): 45–70.

Hager, Steven. *Art After Midnight: The East Village Scene* (New York: St. Martins Press, 1986).

Haig, Robert M. *Major Economic Factors in Metropolitan Growth and Arrangement* (New York: Regional Plan of New York, 1927).

Hall, Helen, *Unfinished Business: A Firsthand Account by the Former Director of the Henry Street Settlement* (New York: Macmillan, 1971).

Hall, Max. *Made in New York City: Case Studies in Metropolitan Manufacturing* (Cambridge: Harvard University Press, 1959).

Hall, S. and T. Bennet, eds. *Resistance Through Rituals* (London: Hutchinson, 1976).

Harrison, Bennett and Barry Bluestone. *The Great U-Turn: Corporate Restructuring and the Polarizing of America* (New York: Basic Books, 1988).

Hartog, Hendrik. *Public Property and Private Power: The Corporation of the City of New York in American Law, 1730–1870* (Chapel Hill: University of North Carolina Press, 1983).

Harvey, David and L. Chaterjee. 'Absolute Rent and the Structuring of Space by Governmental and Financial Institutions,' *Antipode* 6 (1974): 22–36.

Haswell, Charles H. *Reminiscences of an Octogenarian of the City of New York: 1816–1860* (New York: Harper, 1896).

Hayes, Robert. 'The Mayor and the Homeless Poor,' *City Limits* (August–September 1985).

Helfgott, Roy B. 'Puerto Rican Integration in the Skirt Industry in New York City,' in *The Report of the New York State Commission Against Discrimination and Low Incomes*, January 1958.

Helfgott, Roy B. 'Women's and Children's Apparel,' in *Made in New York: Case Studies in Metropolitan Manufacturing*, ed. by Max Hall (Cambridge: Harvard University Press, 1959).

Henry, John Robertson. *Fifty Years on the Lower East Side of New York* (New York: publisher unknown, 1966).

Hevesi, Dennis. 'Rally in Tompkins Park to Protest Police Action,' *The New York Times*, 12 August 1988.

Hirsch, James. 'Complaints Accuse Police of Wild, Random Brutality,' *The New York Times*, 12 August 1988.

Holmes, Steven A. 'A Neighborhood Battle: Apartments or a Park,' *The New York Times*, 18 December 1989.

Hone, Philip. *The Diary of Philip Hone, 1828–1851*, ed. by Allan Nevins (New York: Dodd, Mead, 1927).

Hoover, Edgar M. and Raymond Vernon. *Anatomy of a Metropolis* (Cambridge: Harvard University Press, 1959).

Hopper, Kim. *Never Again: A Report on Homelessness in New York* (Washington, DC: National Governors' Association Task Force on the Homeless, 1983).

Hourwich, Isaac A. *Immigration and Labor* (New York: G. P. Putnam's Sons, 1912).

Howe, Irving. *World of Our Fathers* (New York: Harcourt Brace Jovanovich, 1976).

Hoyt, Homer, and L. D. Badgley. 'The Housing Demand of Workers in Manhattan: An Income Analysis of the Workers in Manhattan to Determine Rent Levels for New Apartments in the Lower East Side and Other New York Areas' (New York: Corlears Hook Group, 1939). Confidential Report.

Hudson, James, R. *The Unanticipated City: Loft Conversions in Lower Manhattan* (Amherst, MA: University of Massachusetts Press, 1987).

Hulbert, F. *New York: City of Cities* (New York: J. B. Lippincott Co., 1937).

Iglesias, Cesar Andreu, ed. *Memoirs of Bernardo Vega. A Contribution to the History of the Puerto Rican Community in New York* (New York: The Monthly Review Press, 1984).

Interfaith Adopt-A-Building. 'A Portrait of the Lower East Side.' Report dated June, 1978.

Interfaith Adopt-A-Building. 'Loisaida: Strategies for Neighborhood Revitalization and Self-Determination.' Report dated 1979.

Jackson, Anthony. *A Place Called Home, A History of Low Cost Housing in Manhattan* (Cambridge: MIT Press, 1976).

Jackson, Kenneth T. 'The Capital of Capitalism: The New York Metropolitan Region, 1890–1940,' in *Metropolis, 1890–1940*, ed. by Anthony Sutcliffe (Chicago: University of Chicago, 1984).

Jacobs, Jane. *The Death and Life of Great American Cities* (New York: Random House, 1961).

Jaffe, A. J. 'Demographic and Labor Force Characteristics of the New York City Population,' in *The Puerto Rican Population of New York City*, ed. by A. J. Jaffe (New York: Columbia University Institute of Applied Social Research, 1953).

Jensen, Joan M. and Sue Davidson, eds. *A Needle, A Bobbin, A Strike* (Philadelphia: Temple University Press, 1984).

Johnston, Alva. 'French Plans $50,000,000 "White Collar" East Side City,' *New York Herald Tribune*, 20 December 1931.

Johnston, Alva and Gustave Zizmer. 'How Big Buying Was Concealed,' *New York Sun*, 19 December 1931.

Jones, Thomas Jesse. *The Sociology of a New York City Block* (New York: Columbia University Press, 1904).

Jorgenson, Lisa. 'New York's Squatters: Vanguard of Community Control?' *City* (fall 1971): 35–8.

Joselit, Jenna Weissman. 'The Landlord as Czar,' in *The Tenant Movement in New York City, 1904–1984*, ed. by Ronald Lawson and Mark Naison (New Brunswick: Rutgers University Press, 1986).

Kahn, Joseph. 'The Squatters of New York,' *New York Post*, 8 August 1970.

Kaplan, Lisa. 'Seward Park Court Fight to Stop LeFrak Land-Grab,' *People's Press*, June 1989.

Katz, Steven and Margit Mayer. 'Gimme Shelter: Self-help Housing Struggles Within and Against the State in New York City and West Berlin,' *International Journal of Urban and Regional Research* 9 (1985): 15–47.

Katznelson, Ira. *City Trenches: Urban Politics and the Patterning of Class in the United States* (Chicago: University of Chicago Press, 1981).

Keating, Dennis W. 'Linking Downtown Development to Broader Community Goals: An Analysis of Linkage Policy in Three Cities,' *Journal of the American Planning Association* 52 (spring 1986).

Keats, John. *The Crack in the Picture Window* (Boston: Houghton Mifflin, 1957).

Kessner, Thomas. *The Golden Door: Italian and Jewish Immigrant Mobility in New York City, 1880–1915* (New York: Oxford University Press, 1977).

Kessner, Thomas. *Fiorello H. LaGuardia and the Making of Modern New York* (New York: Viking Penguin 1991).

Kifner, John. 'Worlds Collide in Tompkins Sq. Park,' *The New York Times*, 31 July 1989.

Kifner, John. 'Tent City in Tompkins Square Park is Dismantled by Police,' *The New York Times*, 15 December 1989.

Kouwenhoven, John A. *The Columbia Historical Portrait of New York: An Essay in Graphic History* (New York: Harper & Row, 1972).

Kwong, Peter. *The New Chinatown* (New York: The Noonday Press, 1987).

Ladd, Donna. 'Not Just Young White Males: The Silent Squatters Speak,' *Village Beat* (winter 1991).

Ladd, Scott and T. J. Collins. 'Demolition Project Starts, Stops,' *New York Newsday*, 3 May 1989.

Lake, Robert W. *Real Estate Tax Delinquency: Private Disinvestment and Public Response* (Piscataway, NJ: Center for Urban Policy Research, Rutgers University, 1979).

Lampard, Eric E. 'The New York Metropolis in Transformation: History and Prospect. A Study in Historical Particularity,' in *The Future of the Metropolis*, ed. by Hans-Jurgen Ewers, John P. Goddard, and Horst Matzerath (Berlin: Walter de Gruyter & Co., 1986).

Laska, Shirley and Daphne Spain. 'Urban Policy and Planning in the Wake of "Gentrification": Anticipating Renovators' Demands,' *Journal of the American Planning Association* 45 (October 1979): 523–31.

Laska, Shirley and Daphne Spain, eds. *Back to the City: Issues in Neighborhood Renovation* (Elmsford, NY: Pergamon Press, 1980).

Lasker, Loula D. 'Putting a White Collar on the East Side,' *Survey Graphic* 65 (1 March 1931).

Laurentz, Robert. 'Racial and Ethnic Conflict in the New York City Garment Industry, 1933–1980' (Binghamton, NY: State University of New York, doctoral dissertation, 1980).

Laurino, Maria. 'It's a Great Big Room, That's the Way We Live,' *Village Voice*, 6 September 1988.

Laviera, Tato. *AmeRícan* (Houston: Arte Público Press, 1985).

Lawson, Ronald. 'The Political Face of New York's Real Estate Industry,' *New York Affairs* 6 (1980): 88–109.

Lawson, Ronald. 'Origins and Evolution of a Social Movement Strategy: The Rent Strike in New York City, 1904–1980,' *Urban Affairs Quarterly* 18 (March 1983): 371–95.

Lawson, Ronald. 'Tenant Responses to the Urban Housing Crisis, 1970–1984,' in *The Tenant Movement in New York City, 1904–1984*, ed. by Ronald Lawson and Mark Naison (New Brunswick, NJ: Rutgers University Press, 1986).

Lawson, Ronald and Mark Naison, eds. *The Tenant Movement in New York City, 1904–1984* (New Brunswick, NJ: Rutgers University Press, 1986).

Ledwith, Tim. 'Lower East Side Tenants: Squatters or Homesteaders?' *City Limits* (November 1981).

Lee, B. A. and S. G. Lipton. 'Determinants of Gentrification in the United States – A City Level Analysis,' *Urban Affairs Quarterly* 21 (March 1986): 369–87.

Leichter, Franz. *The Return of the Sweatshop: An Investigation of the Garment Sweatshop Problem in Northern Manhattan* (New York: New York State Department of Labor, 1981).

Levine, Louis. *The Women's Garment Workers* (New York: B. W. Huebsch, 1924).

Lieberman, Richard. 'Social Change and Political Behavior: The East Village of New York City' (New York: New York University, doctoral dissertation, 1976).

Lilienthal, Meta. *Dear Remembered World: Childhood Memories of an Old New Yorker* (New York: R. R. Smith, 1947).

Lin, Jan Chien. 'Polarized Development in the "World City": The Chinese Enclave of New York City.' Unpublished paper, 1990.

Lin, Jan Chien. 'Capital and Community in Urban Change: Chinatown, New York City' (New York: New School for Social Research, doctoral dissertation, 1992).

Lindblom, Charles. *The Policy-Making Process* (Englewood Cliffs, NJ: Prentice Hall, 1980).

Lockwood, Charles. *Manhattan Moves Uptown* (Boston: Houghton Mifflin, 1976).

Logan, John and Harvey Molotch. *Urban Fortunes: The Political Economy of Place* (Berkeley: University of California Press, 1987).

Loisaida: Continent of Seven Colors (New York: Taller Latinamericano, 1990).

London, Bruce, Donald Bradley, and James Hudson. 'Approaches to Inner-City Revitalization,' *Urban Affairs Quarterly* 15 (June 1980): 373–87.

London, Bruce, Barratt Lee, and S. Gregory Lipton. 'The Determinants of Gentrification in the United States: A City-Level Analysis,' *Urban Affairs Quarterly* 21 (March 1986): 369–87.

Long, Norton. 'The Local Community as an Ecology of Games,' *American Journal of Sociology* 64 (1958).

López, Adalberto and James Petras, eds. *Puerto Rico and Puerto Ricans: Studies in History and Society* (New York: John Wiley & Sons, 1974).

Lower East Side Joint Planning Council. 'This Land is Ours: A Strategy for the Preservation and Development of Affordable Housing on the Lower East Side' (March 1984).

Lubitz, Edward. 'The Tenement Problem in New York City and the Movement for its Reform' (New York: New York University, doctoral dissertation, 1970).

Lubove, Roy. *The Progressives and the Slums: Tenement House Reform in New York City 1890–1917* (Pittsburgh: University of Pittsburgh Press, 1962).

Lyman, Susan E. *The Story of New York: An Informal History of the City* (New York: Crown Publishers, Inc., n.d.).

Lynn, Frank. 'Dinkins Team: Old Hands Join a Few Newcomers,' *The New York Times*, 4 November 1989.

Lyon, Danny. *The Destruction of Lower Manhattan* (photographs) (New York: Macmillan, 1969).

Maffi, Mario. *Nel mosaico della citta: Differenze etniche e nuove culture in un quartiere di New York* (Milan: Feltrinelli, 1992).

Maffi, Mario. 'Chi Lai, Arriba, Rise Up! Some Remarks on Ethnic Writings in New York City,' in *Multiculturalism and the Canon of American Culture*, ed. by Hans Bak (Amsterdam: VU University Press, 1993).

Maffi, Mario. *Gateway to the Promised Land. Ethnicity and Culture in New York's Lower East Side* (Amsterdam: Rodopi, 1993; New York: New York University Press, 1994).

Maffi, Mario and Franco Minganti. 'City Maps and City Alphabets,' *RSA: Rivista di Studi Anglo-Americani* 6, no. 8 (1990).

Makielski S. J. *The Politics of Zoning: The New York Experience* (New York: Columbia University Press, 1966).

Mallach, Aubrey. 'Knickerbocker Village Tenants' Association,' in Heinz Norden Collection, Box 1, Tamiment Library.

Malon, Patricia E. 'The Growth of Manufacturing in Manhattan, 1860–1900: An Analysis of Factoral Changes and Urban Structure' (New York: Columbia University, doctoral dissertation, 1981).

Mangaliman, Jessie. 'Park Workers Level Tent City,' *New York Newsday*, 15 December 1989.

Marcuse, Peter. *Rental Housing in New York City, 1975–1978* (New York: Department of Housing Preservation and Development, 1979).

Marcuse, Peter. *Housing Abandonment: Does Rent Control Make a Difference* (Washington, DC: Conference on Alternative State and Local Policies, 1981).

Marcuse, Peter. 'Gentrification, Abandonment and Displacement: Connections, Causes, and Policy Responses in New York City,' *Journal of Contemporary Law* 28 (1985). Earlier issued as Report to the Community Service Society, 1984.

Marcuse, Peter. 'The State of the City's Housing,' *City Limits* (August–September 1985).

Marcuse, Peter. 'Abandonment, Gentrification, and Displacement: The Linkages in New York City,' in *Gentrification of the City*, ed. by Neil Smith and Peter Williams (Boston: Allen & Unwin, 1986).

Marcuse, Peter. 'The Beginnings of Public Housing in New York,' *Journal of Urban History* 12 (1986): 353–90.

MARHO. 'Housing for Shelter or Profit?' A Guide to the New York Public History Project Slide Show on the History of Housing, April 1987.

Matias, Bienvenida and Marci Reaven. *The Heart of Loisaida* (video, 1979).

McCabe Jr., James R. *Lights and Shadows of New York Life* (New York: Farrar, Straus and Giroux, 1970, originally published in 1872).

McDarrah, Timothy and Gene Ruffini. 'Park Squatters Swept Up and Out,' *New York Post*, 6 July 1989.

McFadden, Robert. 'Park Curfew Protest Erupts into a Battle and 38 Are Injured,' *The New York Times*, 8 August 1988.

McFadden, Robert. 'One Week After the Clash, Protesters Hold a Quiet Tompkins Square Rally,' *The New York Times*, 14 August 1988.

McGill, Douglas C. 'Art Boom Slows in the East Village,' *The New York Times*, 25 July 1987.

McKay, Richard C. *South Street* (New York: G. P. Putnam's Sons, 1934).

McKinley, Jr., James. 'Melee Site Quiet, But Police Stand Guard,' *The New York Times*, 6 May 1989.

McKinley, Jr., James. 'City Moves to Clean Up Tompkins Square After Raid,' *The New York Times*, 7 July 1989.

McMurry, Terry R. 'Residence, Employment and Mobility of Puerto Ricans in New York City' (Chicago: University of Chicago, doctoral dissertation, 1972).

Mele, Christopher. 'Reinventing the East Village of New York; Capitalist Investment Strategies from 1860 to 1990' (New York: New School for Social Research, doctoral dissertation, 1993).

Mills, C. Wright et al. *The Puerto Rican Journey* (New York: Harper, 1950).

Model, Suzanne. 'Comparative Perspective on the Ethnic Enclave: Blacks, Italians and Jews in New York City,' *International Migration Review* 19 (1985): 64–81.

Mohr, Eugene V. *The Nuyorican Experience: Literature of the Puerto Rican Minority* (Westport, CN: Greenwood Press, 1982).

Mollenkopf, John. *The Contested City* (Princeton: Princeton University Press, 1983).

Mollenkopf, John. 'Economic Development,' in *Setting Municipal Priorities, 1984*, ed. by Charles Brecher and Raymond D. Horton (New York: New York University Press, 1983).

Mollenkopf, John. 'City Planning,' in *Setting Municipal Priorities, 1990*, ed. by Charles Brecher and Raymond D. Horton (New York: New York University, 1989).

Mollenkopf, John, ed. *Power, Culture and Place* (New York: Russell Sage Foundation, 1988).

Mollenkopf, John and Manuel Castells, eds. *Dual City: Restructuring New York* (New York: Russell Sage Foundation, 1991).

Molotch, Harvey. 'The City as a Growth Machine,' *American Journal of Sociology* 82 (September 1976): 309–30.

Moody, Richard. *The Astor Place Riot* (Bloomington, Indiana: Indiana University Press, 1958).

Moore, A. and M. Miller, eds. *ABC No Rio Dinero: The Story of a Lower East Side Art Gallery* (New York: ABC No Rio with Collaborative Projects, 1985).

Morales, Ed. 'East Side Story,' *Village Voice*, 20 August 1991.

Morgan, Thomas. 'Dinkins' Chief Homeless Policy Advisor Resigns,' *The New York Times*, 4 September 1991.

Morgan, Thomas. 'New York Admits Failure of Homeless Family Effort,' *The New York Times*, 18 September 1991.

Morgan, Thomas. 'New York City Bulldozes Squatters' Shantytowns,' *The New York Times*, 16 October 1991.

Morrison, John H. *History of New York Shipyards* (Port Washington, NY: Kennikat Press, 1970, originally published 1909).

Mottel, Syeus. *Charas: The Improbable Dome Builders* (New York: Drake Publishers, 1973).

Moufarrege, N. 'Another Wave, Still More Savagely Than the First: Lower East Side,' *Arts* 57 (1982).

Nadel, Stanley. *Kleindeutschland: New York City's Germans, 1845–1880* (Urbana: University of Illinois Press, 1990).

Naison, Mark. 'From Eviction Resistance to Rent Control: Tenant Activism in the Great Depression,' in *The Tenant Movement in New York City 1904–1984*, ed. by Ronald Lawson and Mark Naison (New Brunswick, NJ: Rutgers University Press, 1986).

Nashua. 'Who is Antonio Pagan?' *The Shadow* (August–September 1991).

National Advisory Commission on Civil Disorders. *The Kerner Report* (New York: Pantheon Books, 1988 reprint).

New York City Department of Welfare. Report Submitted to Mayor William O'Dwyer, 'The Puerto Rican Problem of the New York City Department of Welfare,' 6 September 1949.

New York State Assembly. *Report of the Tenement House Committee of 1894*. Legislative Document No. 37, 17 January 1895.

New York State Department of Labor. *Report on Garment Manufacturing Industry and Industrial Homework* (1982).

New York State Department of Law, Real Estate Financing Bureau. *Report on Conversions*, January 1989.

Ney, William. 'After the Fact,' *The New Common Good* (Sept. 1988).

Ney, William. 'Tompkins Square Police Riot: Before the Deluge,' *The New Common Good* (Sept. 1988).

Oser, Alan S. 'Using Condo Sales to Assist New Rentals,' *The New York Times*, 10 April 1988.

Oser, Alan S. 'Investors Find Value in Lower East Side Walk-ups,' *The New York Times* (n.d., 1984).

Otero, Manuel Ramos. 'The Point Blank Page,' *The Portable Lower East Side* (1991).

Padilla, Elena. *Up From Puerto Rico* (New York: Columbia University Press, 1958).

Palen, John and Bruce London, eds. *Gentrification, Displacement, and Neighborhood Revitalization* (Albany: State University of New York, 1984).

Parmet, Robert D. *Labor and Immigration in Industrial America* (Boston: Twayne Publishers, 1981).

Phillips, H. I. 'Moving New Yorkers Back to New York,' *Literary Digest* 101 (8 June 1929).

Pietri, Pedro. *Puerto Rican Obituary* (New York: Monthly Review Press, 1973).

Pietri, Pedro. *Traffic Violations* (Maplewood, NJ: Waterfront Press, 1983).

Piñero, Miguel. *La Bodega Sold Dreams* (Houston: Arte Público Press, 1980).

Pit, Fenna and Willem van Vliet. 'Public Housing in the United States,' in *Handbook of Housing and the Built Environment in the United States*, ed. by Elizabeth Huttman and Willem van Vliet (New York: Greenwood Press, 1988).

Platzker, J. 'Who Owns the Lower East Side' (New York: 1928). Pamphlet in New York Public Library.

Platzker, J. 'Housing: A Survey of All Structures on the Lower East Side, revealing height of buildings, classification of structures, extent of ownership, percentage wooden and boarded-up houses' (New York: 1931). Pamphlet in New York Public Library.

Platzker, J. 'Changes in Real Estate Conditions on the Lower East Side,' *Real Estate Record* (n.d., 1932).

Platzker, J. 'Taxes: Payments and Arrears on Lower East Side Realty on March 31, 1934 and March 31, 1933' (New York: 1934). Pamphlet in New York Public Library.

Platzker, J. '303 Boarded-up and Vacant Buildings Dot Lower East Side,' *East Side Chamber News* (n.d., 1934).

Platzker, J. 'Corlear's Hook District: A Structural, Financial, Economic, Municipal Service Inventory of the Lower East Side's Giant Slum Area (the old seventh ward) as it approaches its tercentennial' (New York: 1935). Pamphlet in New York Public Library.

Platzker, J. 'Research Studies of Community Problems' (New York: 1935). Pamphlet in New York Public Library.

Platzker, J. '3,029 Tenements on the Lower East Side in Use for Half a Century or Longer' (New York: 1936). Pamphlet in New York Public Library.

Platzker, J. 'Multiple Dwelling Law Changes to Cost $8,000,000,' *East Side Chamber News* (June 1936).

Platzker, J. 'Rear Houses, a Survey of Economic Conditions, Tenancy, Ownership, Rentals, etc. on the Lower East Side,' *East Side Chamber News* (n.d.).

Plunz, Richard. *The History of Housing in New York City* (New York: Columbia University Press, 1990).

Ponte, Robert. 'Manhattan's Real Estate Boom,' *New York Affairs* 8 (1984): 18–31.

Porras, Stephen M. 'Lower East Side Housing Market Dynamics: Policy Implications' (New York: Columbia University, masters thesis, Division of Urban Planning, 1983).

Pratt, Edward E. *Industrial Causes of Congestion in New York City* (New York: Longmans, Green and Co., 1911).

Pred, Allan R. *The Spatial Dynamics of U.S. Urban-Industrial Growth, 1800–1914* (Cambridge, MA: MIT Press, 1966).

Purdum, Todd S. 'Lessons of 60's Forgotten in Park Riot,' *The New York Times*, 11 August 1988.

Purnick, Joyce. 'Freeze on Hiring Imposed by Koch; He Cites Economy,' *The New York Times*, 5 October 1982.

Purnick, Joyce. 'Property Sale is Key to Plan to Renew Lower East Side,' *The New York Times*, 25 July 1984.

Ramsey, Duane V. 'What Some Slum Dwellers Want in Housing: Findings of a Study of One Square Block in the Lower East Side, New York City' (New York: 1935).

Rankin, Rebecca, ed. *New York Advancing 1934–35 Edition* (New York, 1936).

Rapkin, Chester. *The South of Houston Industrial Area* (New York: New York City Planning Commission, 1963).

Ravo, Nick. 'As Homeless Rally, Police Patrol Tompkins Square Park,' *The New York Times*, 9 July 1989.

Ravo, Nick. 'Tensions Ease in Tompkins Park Protest,' *The New York Times*, 10 July 1989.

Reaven, Marci. 'Tompkins Square: Past and Present,' unpublished paper accompanying exhibit sponsored by the Municipal Arts Society, New York City, 1989.

Report of the Select Committee on Tenement Houses in New York and Brooklyn. Assembly Document No. 205, 9 March 1857.

Report by the Small Parks Advisory Committee to Mayor William L. Strong, 28 October 1897. New York Historical Society.

Riis, Jacob A. *How the Other Half Lives.* (New York: Scribners, 1890; reprinted New York: Hill and Wang, 1957).

Riis, Jacob A. *The Battle with the Slum* (New York: Macmillan, 1902).

Riis, Jacob A. *Children of the Tenements* (New York: Macmillan, 1903).

Rischin, Moses. *The Promised Land: New York's Jews, 1870–1914* (Cambridge, MA: Harvard University Press, 1977).

Roberts, Sam. 'Dinkins Gaining Support Among Business Executives,' *The New York Times*, 26 September 1989.

Roberts, Sam. 'Gadflies of Today Parcel the Blame Among Old Allies,' *The New York Times*, 1 July 1991.

Roberts, Sam. 'As Population Grows, Hispanic Power Lags,' *The New York Times*, 18 July 1991.

Robinson, W. and C. McCormick. 'Slouching Toward Avenue D,' *Art in America* 72 (summer 1984): 135–61.

Robison, Maynard T. 'Rebuilding Lower Manhattan 1955–74' (New York: City University of New York, doctoral dissertation, 1976).

Rodrigez, Clara. *The Ethnic Queue in the United States: The Case of the Puerto Ricans* (San Francisco: R and E Associates, 1974).

Rogler, Lloyd Henry. *Puerto Rican Families in New York City: Intergenerational Processes* (Maplewood, NJ: Waterfront Press, 1985).

Rose, Damaris. 'Rethinking Gentrification: Beyond the Uneven Development of Marxist Urban Theory,' *Society and Space* 2 (1984): 47–74.

Rosenberg, Terry J. 'Residence, Employment and Mobility of Puerto Ricans in New York City' (Chicago: University of Chicago Department of Geography, Research Paper No. 151, 1974).

Rosenberg, Terry and Robert Lake. 'Toward a Revised Model of Residential Segregation and Succession: Puerto Ricans in New York, 1960–1970,' *American Journal of Sociology* 81 (March 1976): 1142–50.

Rosenwaike, Ira. *Population History of New York City* (Syracuse, NY: Syracuse University Press, 1972).

Ross, R. and K. Trachte. 'Global Cities and Global Classes: The Peripheralization of Labor in New York City,' *Review* 6 (1983): 393–431.

Roth, Henry. *Call it Sleep* (New York: Noonday Press, 1991; reissued from 1934).

Rowen, William. 'The Big Rent Fix,' *City Limits* (August–September 1985).

Rumsey, Spencer. 'Burn, Baby, Burn,' *East Village Eye* (April 1986).

Safa, Helen, I. 'Runaway Shops and Female Employment: The Search for Cheap Labor,' *Signs* 7 (winter 1981): 418–33.

Salins, P. 'The Creeping Tide of Disinvestment,' *New York Affairs* 6 (1981).

Sanborn Manhattan Land Books. Series.

Sanchez, José. 'Residual Work and Residual Shelter: Housing Puerto Rican Labor in New York City from World War II to 1983,' in *Critical Perspectives on Housing*, ed. by R. Bratt, C. Hartman and A. Meyerson (Philadelphia, PA: Temple University Press, 1986).

Sanchez, José, 'Housing Puerto Ricans in New York City, A Study in Class Powerlessness' (New York: New York University, doctoral dissertation, 1990).

Sanchez Korral, Virginia. *From Colonia to Community: The History of Puerto Ricans in New York City, 1917–1948* (Westport, CT: Greenwood Press, 1983).

Sassen, Saskia. *The Mobility of Labor and Capital: A Study in International Investment and Labor Flow* (New York: Cambridge University Press, 1988).

Sassen, Saskia. *The Global City: New York, London, Tokyo* (Princeton: Princeton University Press, 1991).

Sassen-Koob, Saskia. 'Changing Composition and Labor Market Location of Hispanic Immigrants in New York City, 1960–1980,' in *Hispanics in the U.S. Economy*, ed. by George Borjas and Marta Tienda (New York: Academic Press, 1985).

Sassen-Koob, Saskia. 'Growth and Informalization at the Core: A Preliminary Report on New York City,' in *The Capitalist City*, ed. by Michael Peter Smith and Joe R. Feagin (New York: Basil Blackwell, 1987).

Savitch, H. V. *Post-Industrial Cities: Politics and Planning in New York, Paris and London* (Princeton, NJ: Princeton University Press, 1989).

Scardino, Albert. 'They'll Take Manhattan,' *New York Times Magazine*, Part 2, 7 December 1986.

Schaffer, R. and N. Smith. 'The Gentrification of Harlem?' *Annals of the Association of American Geographers* 76 (1986): 347–65.

Schoener, Allan. *Portal to America: The Lower East Side, 1870–1925* (New York: Holt, Rinehart & Winston, 1967).

Schofield, Ann. 'The Uprising of the 20,000: The Making of a Labor Legend,' in *A Needle, A Bobbin, A Strike*, ed. by Joan M. Jensen and Sue Davidson (Philadelphia: Temple University Press, 1984).

Schur, Robert. 'Holding the Line in the Neighborhood,' *City Limits* (June–July 1981).

Schwartz, Harry and Peter Abeles. *Planning for the Lower East Side* (New York: Praeger, 1973). Same as *Forging a Future for the Lower East Side: A Plan for Action*, listed under City of New York, Planning Commission, 1970.

Schwartz, Joel. 'Tenant Unions in New York City's Low Rent Housing 1933–1949,' *Journal of Urban History* 12 (August 1986).

Seligman, Edwin R. A. *The Tenement Houses of New York City* (New York: Tenement House Bldg. Company, 1891).

Shefter, Martin. *Political Crisis/Fiscal Crisis: The Collapse and Revival of New York City* (New York: Basic Books, 1985).

Shulman, Harry. *Slums of New York* (New York: Albert and Charles Boni, Inc., 1938).

Simmel, Georg. 'Conflict,' in *Conflict and the Web of Group Affiliations*, ed. and trans. by Kurt Wolff and Reinhard Bendix (Glencoe, IL: Free Press, 1955).

Simpson, Charles, *SoHo: The Artist in the City* (Chicago: University of Chicago Press, 1981).

Sites, William. 'Market, Community, and Local State: Neighborhood Revitalization in Manhattan's Lower East Side' (New York: City University of New York Graduate Center, doctoral dissertation, 1993).

Sleeper, Jim. 'This Neighborhood is Not For Sale,' *City Limits* (1984).

Sleeper, Jim. 'Boom and Bust with Ed Koch,' *Dissent* (fall 1987).

Smith, Michael Peter. *City, State, and Market: The Political Economy of Urban Society* (New York: Basil Blackwell, 1988).

Smith, Neil. 'Gentrification and Capital: Theory, Practice and Ideology in Society Hill,' *Antipode* 11 (1979): 24–35.

Smith, Neil. 'Toward a Theory of Gentrification: A Back to the City Movement by Capital, Not People,' *Journal of the American Planning Association* 45 (1979): 538–48.

Smith, Neil, 'Gentrification and the Rent Gap,' *Annals of the Association of American Geographers* 77 (1987): 462–5.

Smith, Neil. 'New York City, New Frontier: The Lower East Side as Wild, Wild, West,' in *Variations on a Theme Park: The New American City and the End of Public Space*, ed. by M. Sorkin (New York: Hill and Wang, 1992).

Smith, Neil and P. Williams, eds. *Gentrification of the City* (Boston: Allen & Unwin, 1986).

Soffer, Jonathan. 'The Story of Mass Arrests of Hippies in Tompkins Square Park, Memorial Day, 1967' (New York: Columbia University, masters thesis, 1986).

Solomon, Arthur. 'Alternative Perspectives on Neighborhood Decline,' *American Planning Association Journal* (1982).

Spain, Daphne. 'Indicators of Urban Revitalization: Racial and Socioeconomic Changes in Central City Housing,' in *Back to the City: Issues in Neighborhood Renovation*, ed. by S. Laska and Daphne Spain (Elmsford, NY: Pergamon, 1980).

Spann, Edward K. *The New Metropolis: New York City, 1840–1857* (New York: Columbia University Press, 1981).

Spann, Edward K. 'The Greatest Grid: The New York Plan of 1811,' in *Two Centuries of American Planning*, ed. by Daniel Schaffer (Baltimore: Johns Hopkins University Press, 1988): 11–39.

Stansell, Christine. *City of Women: Sex and Class in New York, 1789–1860* (New York: Alfred A. Knopf, 1986).

Stark, Sylvia. *Ailing City Areas: An Economic Study of Thirteen Depressed Districts in Manhattan* (New York: Citizens' Housing Council, May 1941).

Starr, Roger. 'Making New York Smaller,' *New York Times Magazine*, 14 November 1976.

State of New York, Office of the State Comptroller, Office of the State Deputy Comptroller for the City of New York. *New York City Planning Commission Granting Special Permits for Bonus Floor Area* (New York: 15 September 1988).

Stegman, Michael. *The Dynamics of Rental Housing in New York City* (New Brunswick, NJ: Center for Urban Policy Research, Rutgers University, 1982).

Stegman, Michael. *Housing and Vacancy Report: New York City, 1987* (City of New York: Department of Housing Preservation and Development, April 1988).

Sternlieb, George. *The Urban Housing Dilemma: The Dynamics of New York City's Rent Controlled Housing* (New York: Housing and Development Administration, 1972).

Sternlieb, George and R. W. Burchell. *Residential Abandonment: The Tenement Landlord Revisited* (New Brunswick, NJ: Center for Urban Policy Research, Rutgers University, 1973).

Sternlieb, George and James W. Hughes. *Housing and Economic Reality* (New Brunswick, NJ: Center for Urban Policy Research, Rutgers University, 1976).

Sternlieb, George and Robert W. Lake. 'The Dynamics of Real Estate Tax Delinquency,' *National Tax Journal* 29 (1976).

Sternlieb, George and David Listokin. 'Housing,' in *Setting Municipal Priorities, 1986*, ed. by Charles Brecher and Raymond D. Horton (New York: New York University Press, 1985).

Stevenson, G. 'The Abandonment of Roosevelt Gardens,' in *Devastation/Reconstruction*, ed. by R. Jensen (New York: Bronx Museum of the Arts, 1980).

Stokes, Isaac Newton Phelps. *The Iconography of Manhattan Island, 1498–1909*, in 6 volumes (New York: R. H. Dodd, 1915–1928).

Stoney, George C. 'Corlears Hook: The Land and the People.' Unpublished manuscript, February 1939. East Side Files, Henry Street Settlement. Surveys, Seward Park Library.

Stoney, George C. and Margaret Knepper. 'Can We Renovate the Slums? A Study of 54 Remodeled Tenements on the Lower East Side.' Unpublished report, June 1939. East Side Files, Settlements, Henry Street Settlement, Surveys, Seward Park Library.

Storper, Michael, ed. *Variations on a Theme Park: The New American City and the End of Public Space* (New York: Hill and Wang, 1992).

Sullivan, Kathleen. 'The Impact of Real Estate Development on Manhattan-Based Apparel Firms: A Study of Locational Needs, Priorities and Proposed Solutions' (New York: Columbia University, masters thesis in Real Estate Development, 1986).

Suttles, Gerald. *The Social Construction of Communities* (Chicago: University of Chicago Press, 1972).

Swanstrom, Todd. *The Crisis of Growth Politics: Cleveland, Kucinich, and the Challenge of Urban Populism* (Philadelphia: Temple University Press, 1985).

Tabb, William K. *The Long Default: New York City and the Urban Fiscal Crisis* (New York: Monthly Review Press, 1982).

Tabb, William K. 'Urban Development and Regional Restructuring, An Overview,' in *Sunbelt/Snowbelt: Urban Development and Regional Restructuring*, ed. by Larry Sawers and William K. Tabb (New York: Oxford University Press, 1984).

Tabb, W. K. and L. Sawers, eds. *Marxism and the Metropolis: New Perspectives in Urban Political Economy* (New York: Oxford University Press, first edition 1978; reprinted 1984).

Tenement House Building Company. *The Tenement Houses of New York City* (New York: Albert B. King Press, n.d.).

Thompson, Wilbur. 'Land Management Strategies for Central City Depopulation,' in *How Cities Can Grow Old Gracefully* (Subcommittee on the City, Committee on Banking, Finance and Urban Affairs, US House of Representatives, 95th Congress, Washington DC, December 1977).

Tobier, Emanuel. 'Manhattan's Business District in the Industrial Age,' in *Power, Culture, and Place*, ed. by John M. Mollenkopf (New York: Russell Sage Foundation, 1988).

Torres, Andres. 'Labor Market Segmentation: African American and Puerto Rican Labor in New York City, 1960–1980,' *The Review of Black Political Economy* 20 (summer 1991).

Turetsky, Doug. 'Industrial Aid,' *City Limits* (April 1986).

Turetsky, Doug. 'Rebels With a Cause?' *City Limits* (April 1990).

Turner, Fayth, ed. *Puerto Rican Writers at Home in the USA* (Seattle: Open Hand Publishing, 1991).

Turner, Joan. 'Building Boundaries: The Politics of Urban Renewal in Manhattan's Lower East Side' (New York: City University of New York, doctoral dissertation, 1984).

Turner, John F. C. *Housing by People: Towards Autonomy in Building Environments* (Boston: Marion Boyars, 1976).

Unger, Craig. 'The Lower East Side: There Goes the Neighborhood,' *New York* (magazine), 28 May 1984.

United States Department of Labor. *A Socioeconomic Profile of Puerto Rican New Yorkers* (Washington, DC: US Department of Labor, 1975).

Vainio, Victor. 'Landlords Meet, Organize Against "Oppression,"' *Tenant* (January 1984).

Varady, David P. *Neighborhood Upgrading: A Realistic Assessment* (Albany: State University of New York Press, 1986).

Vincent, Steven. 'Waiting for Glasnost: Grassroots Democracy on the Lower East Side,' *Lower East Side News* (February 1990).

von Nostitz, Glenn. 'New Tax Program Is the Same Old Giveaway,' *City Limits* (April 1986).

Wacquant, Loic and William Julius Wilson. 'The Cost of Racial and Class Exclusion in the Inner City,' *Annals of the American Academy of Political and Social Science* 50 (January 1989 special issue).

Wade, Richard. 'The End of the Self-sufficient City: New York's Fiscal Crisis in History,' *Urbanism Past and Present* 3 (winter 1976–7).

Waldinger, Roger. 'Immigration and Industrial Change in the New York City Apparel Industry,' in *Hispanics in the U.S. Economy*, ed. by George J. Borjas and Marta Tienda (New York: Academic Press, Inc., 1985).

Waldinger, Roger. *Through the Eye of the Needle* (New York: New York University Press, 1986).

Waldinger, Roger. 'Changing Ladders and Musical Chairs: Ethnicity and Opportunity in Post-industrial New York,' *Politics and Society* 15 (winter 1986–7): 369–402.

Ward, Colin. *Anarchy in Action* (London: Freedom Press, 1988).

Ward, David. 'The Emergence of Central Immigrant Ghettoes in American Cities,' as reprinted in *The Internal Structure of Cities*, ed. by Larry S. Bourne (New York: Oxford University Press, 1971).

Ward, Yulanda. 'Spatial Deconcentration: Freedom of Housing Choice or Minority Removal?' Paper presented to Grassroots Unity Conference, Washington, DC, 1980.

Wasserman, Suzanne. 'The Good Old Days of Poverty: The Battle over the Fate of New York City's Lower East Side during the Depression' (New York: New York University, doctoral dissertation, 1990).

Weichselbaum, L. 'The Real Estate Show,' in *ABC No Rio Dinero*, ed. by A. Moore and M. Miller (New York: ABC No Rio with Collaborative Projects, 1985).

Weidman, Jerome. *Fourth Street East: A Novel of How It Was* (New York: Pinnacle Books, 1970).

Weinberg, Bill. 'Legacy of Rebellion: Tompkins Square and the Lower East Side,' *Downtown*, 14 February 1990.

White, Janet. 'Real Estate Resurgence Continues in East Village as Property Values Soar,' *Real Estate Newsletter*, Manhattan Edition, 23 November 1987.

White, Michelle. 'Housing Abandonment and Taxes: A Report on a Study by Michelle White,' *New York Affairs* (1984).

Williams, Brett. *Upscaling Downtown: Stalled Gentrification in Washington, D.C.* (Ithaca, NY: Cornell University Press, 1988).

Williams, P. 'The Role of Institutions in the Inner London Housing Market: The Case of Islington,' *Transactions of the Institute of British Geographers* 1 (1976).

Williams, P. 'Building Societies and the Inner City,' *Transactions of the Institute of British Geographers* 3 (1978).

Williams, W. 'Rise in Values Spurs Rescue of Buildings,' *The New York Times*, 4 April 1987.

Wines, Michael. 'Behind the Park Melee, A New Generation Gap,' *The New York Times*, 8 August 1988.

Wines, Michael. 'Class Struggle Erupts Along Avenue B,' *The New York Times*, 10 August 1988.

Wolfe, Gerald R. *New York: A Guide to the Metropolis* (New York: McGraw Hill Book Co., 1988).

Wolfe, J. M., G. Drover and I. Skelton. 'Inner City Real Estate Activity in Montreal: Institutional Characteristics of Decline,' *The Canadian Geographer* 24 (1980).

Works Progress Administration (WPA). *WPA Guide to New York City* (New York: Random House, 1982; reprint of 1939 original).

Wypijewski, Joann. 'Tompkins Square Park,' *Zeta Magazine* (November 1988).

Zukin, Sharon. 'Gentrification: Culture and Capital in the Urban Core.' *Annual Review of Sociology* 13 (1987): 129–47.

Zukin, Sharon. *Loft Living: Culture and Capital in Urban Change* (Baltimore: Johns Hopkins University Press, 1982, reissued New Brunswick, NJ: Rutgers University Press, 1989).

Zunz, Olivier and David Ward. *Landscapes of Power* (New York: Russell Sage Foundation, 1992).

Index